The Tanner Lectures on Human Values

THE TANNER LECTURES ON HUMAN VALUES

39

2024

Brown, Fabre, Kolbert, Mills,
Tuck, Wrangham, Zittrain
Mark Matheson, *Editor*

THE UNIVERSITY OF UTAH PRESS
Salt Lake City

Copyright © 2024 by The University of Utah Press. All rights reserved.

All rights reserved

ISBN 978-1-64769-156-1 (cloth)
ISBN 978-1-64769-157-8 (electronic)

ISSN 0-275-7656

♾ This symbol indicates books printed on paper that meets the minimum requirements of American National Standard for Information Services—Permanence of Paper for Printed Library Materials, ANSI A39.38-1984.

Interior printed on recycled paper with 50% post-consumer content.

THE TANNER LECTURES ON HUMAN VALUES

INTRODUCTION

Obert Clark and Grace Adams Tanner endowed the Tanner Lectures on Human Values in 1978. From the first, the Lectures have served as a leading forum for reflection on scientific knowledge and the advancement of philosophical and humanistic thought. They take place annually at nine major universities in the United States and England and occasionally at other centers of learning around the world. Each of the participating universities is given complete autonomy in selecting its Tanner Lecturer for a given year. The list of scholars, writers, artists, and public figures who have delivered Tanner Lectures is especially distinguished, and this high standard continues through the diligent work of the member universities and the Tanner Lectures Board, which comprises the leaders of these institutions.

Obert Tanner and Grace Adams grew up in the early twentieth century in rural Utah, a society that retained much of its pioneer character. Hard work and dedicated service to others were lived values in their families, and education was a profoundly held ideal. A belief in the dignity and transformative power of learning was nurtured in Obert by his mother, Annie Clark Tanner, who encouraged him to study joyfully, to enter the profession of teaching, and to regard the university as the greatest institutional achievement of humankind. Obert was educated at Utah, Harvard, and Stanford, and he went on to teach religious studies and philosophy at Stanford and Utah for more than thirty years. Somehow during this time, he also managed to build the O. C. Tanner Company, the business he began in 1927, into an extraordinary success. Obert's friend Professor Sterling McMurrin, the first director of the Tanner Lectures, once remarked that not since the sixth century BCE, when Thales cornered the wine market in the eastern Mediterranean, had a philosopher been so successful in business. From the early years of this success to his death in 1993, Obert used the wealth produced by his company to endow numerous educational institutions and civic projects. Over the course of this lifetime of giving, he came to regard the Tanner Lectures as his most important educational and cultural legacy.

The Lectures are thus a product of the values and the vision shared by Obert and Grace. They partake of the spirit of Grace's brightness, wit, and sense of humor as well as Obert's passionate devotion to learning as a means of lifting up the human condition. In the context of an unfolding world culture, the continuing role of the Tanner Lectures will be to contribute in constructive and inspiring ways to our collective intellectual and moral life. Reading through a volume of the Tanner Lectures is a remarkable intellectual adventure, and the founders would want the experience to produce both a more abundant life for the reader and a more informed dedication to the well-being of the human community.

Mark Matheson
University of Utah

THE TANNER LECTURES BOARD

CHANCELLOR CAROL CHRIST
University of California, Berkeley

VICE CHANCELLOR DEBORAH PRENTICE AND JEREMY ADELMAN
University of Cambridge

PRESIDENT C. ALAN SHORT AND SLAINE CAMPBELL
Clare Hall, Cambridge

PRESIDENT ALAN GARBER AND ANNE YAHANDA
Harvard University

PRINCIPAL NICK LEIMU-BROWN AND ROOSA LEIMU-BROWN
Linacre College, Oxford

PRESIDENT SANTA ONO AND GWENDOLYN YIP
University of Michigan

VICE CHANCELLOR IRENE TRACEY AND MYLES ALLEN
University of Oxford

PRESIDENT CHRISTOPHER EISGRUBER AND LORI MARTIN
Princeton University

PRESIDENT RICHARD SALLER AND TANYA LUHRMANN
Stanford University

PRESIDENT TAYLOR RANDALL AND JANET RANDALL
University of Utah

PRESIDENT PETER SALOVEY AND MARTA MORET
Yale University

STEPHEN TANNER IRISH
Chair, O. C. Tanner Board of Directors

DAVID AND TERI PETERSEN
CEO, O. C. Tanner Company

MARK MATHESON AND JENNIFER FALK
Director, Tanner Lectures

CONTENTS

The Tanner Lectures on Human Values		v
The Tanner Lectures Board		vii
Preface to Volume 39		xi

Wendy Brown	Knowledge and Politics in Nihilistic Times: Thinking with Max Weber	1
Lecture I.	Politics	3
Lecture II.	Knowledge	21
Cécile Fabre	"To Snatch Something from Death": Value, Justice, and Humankind's Common Cultural Heritage	41
Lecture I.	The Value of Humankind's Cultural Heritage	43
Lecture II.	Justice and Humankind's Common Heritage	68
Elizabeth Kolbert	Welcome to the Anthropocene	103
Lecture I.	What on Earth Have We Done?	105
Lecture II.	What Can We Do about It?	118
Charles W. Mills	Theorizing Racial Justice	131
Richard Tuck	Active and Passive Citizens	183
Lecture I.	Rousseau and Sieyès	185
Lecture II.	Active Democracy	215
Richard W. Wrangham	The Evolution of Institutional Patriarchy	237
Jonathan L. Zittrain	Gaining Power, Losing Control	333
Lecture I.	Between Suffocation and Abdication: Three Eras of Digital Governance	335
Lecture II.	With Great Power Comes Great Ignorance: What's Wrong When Machine Learning Gets It Right	372
The Tanner Lecturers		409

PREFACE TO VOLUME 39

Volume 39 of the *Tanner Lectures on Human Values* includes lectures initially scheduled during the academic year 2019–2020. Owing to the global coronavirus pandemic, some were delivered at a later date.

The Tanner Lectures are published in an annual volume.

In addition to permanent lectures at nine universities, the Tanner Lectures on Human Values funds special one-time lectures at selected higher educational institutions in the United States and around the world.

The Tanner Lectures on Human Values

The Lannel Lectures on Human Values

Knowledge and Politics in Nihilistic Times:
Thinking with Max Weber

WENDY BROWN

THE TANNER LECTURES ON HUMAN VALUES

Delivered at

Yale University
October 22–23, 2019

WENDY BROWN is UPS Professor of Social Science at the Institute for Advanced Study at the University of California, Berkeley. Previously, she was Class of 1936 First Chair in Political Science at the University of California, Berkeley. In addition to appointments at the University of California, Santa Cruz, and Williams College, she has taught at institutions around the world, including the European Graduate School; the London School of Economics; University of Witwatersrand, South Africa; Cornell University; and Columbia University. Drawing from Freudian, Weberian, Marxist, and Foucauldian philosophies, Brown writes about the powers operating beneath the surface of liberalism and generating many of its limits and predicaments, interrogating formations of power, political identity, citizenship, and political subjectivity in contemporary liberal democracies. Among her award-winning books are *States of Injury: Power and Freedom in Late Modernity*; *Regulating Aversion: Tolerance in the Age of Identity and Empire*; *Walled States, Waning Sovereignty*; *Undoing the Demos: Neoliberalism's Stealth Revolution*; and *In the Ruins of Neoliberalism: The Rise of Antidemocratic Politics in the West*. Her work has been translated into more than twenty languages.

LECTURE I.
POLITICS

Weakness it is to be unable to look the fate of the age full in the face.
WEBER, "SCIENCE AS A VOCATION"

We know of no scientifically ascertainable ideals. . . . That makes our efforts more arduous than those of the past, since we are expected to create our ideals from within our breast in the very age of subjectivist culture; but we must not and cannot promise a fool's paradise and an easy street, neither in thought nor in action. It is the stigma of our human dignity that the peace of our souls cannot be as great as the peace of one who dreams of such a paradise.
WEBER, 1909

The honor of these lectures is great; living up to it is difficult. I take it they are meant to be mature reflections on fundamental things, yet such a posture is in some ways inimical to the deeply disorienting features of our times. There is the rise of ferociously antidemocratic forces in settled and relatively newer liberal democracies and their open affirmation of autocrats, supremacies, and violent exclusions. There are the deep corruptions of electoral systems from within and without, above and below—ranging from the capture of politicians by dark money and powers to the capture of electorates by trolling, hate sites, and social and mainstream media. There is the digital revolution continuously revolutionizing work, knowledge, governing, social relations, subjectivity, and bearing, along with its enhancements of human capacities and novel ways of estranging and manipulating them. There is the economic revolution that unleashed finance as a force more powerful and less bound to human and planetary thriving than even capitalist production. There is the chaos of the interregnum between the Westphalian system of nation-states and whatever comes after, a chaos marked by the unprecedented boundary trespass and policing of ideas, peoples, capital, labor, technologies, violence, and goods. And there is the existential emergency posed by climate change, species destruction, and plummeting biodiversity along with the debris of a retrospectively reckless century of production piling up, unmetabolizable, in floating ocean islands and earthly fields of waste. This last includes vast populations themselves cast off as waste: one in eight of our species now lives in makeshift shanty towns, slums, or homeless clusters within and abutting cities across the globe.

How to apprehend and plot possibilities within this novel presently? For me, paradoxically perhaps, apprehending the new has often involved thinking through and against giants of the past struggling for a cartography of their own time. That is what I want to do with Max Weber. Of course, there is a paradox here: Weber is often held responsible for setting twentieth-century social science knowledge on a dangerous course of worshipping faux objectivity and ethical neutrality, intense knowledge specialization, and in the object world, capitalism, and state power. Politically, he is identified with intense German nationalism and early attraction to Ordoliberalism. But there is more to Weber than this, especially in the two lectures he delivered near the end of his life that I will be treating in these sessions, "Politics as a Vocation" and "Science as a Vocation."

Weber was a dark thinker. This was not only a matter of his temperament or times, though each was treacherous. As important was his unrivaled appreciation of certain logics of modernity—its signature rationalities and forms of power, its generation of "human machineries" with unprecedented capacities for domination, its simultaneous proliferation and depreciation of values (and reduction of matters of morality into matters of taste). There was the inadequacy of democracy to resist or transform those and the enormous challenge of cultivating responsible leadership amid them. In a world he viewed as nearly choked by powers destructive of human spirit and freedom as well as forthrightly dangerous, he sought to craft practices by which both scholars and political actors might hold back the dark with their work. This is one reason for turning to him now. We need sober thinkers and leaders who refuse to submit to the lures of fatalism or apocalypticism, pipedreams of total revolution, or redemption by the progress of reason yet aim to be more than Bartlebys or foot soldiers within current orders of knowledge and politics.

A second reason for turning to Weber today pertains to his confrontation, especially in the interwar period, with one of the deepest intellectual and political crises of liberal democracy in the West prior to our own. Intellectually, Weber took Marx and Nietzsche to be the major influences of his time and sought to repel the antiliberal critiques from the left and the right that each inspired. Politically, he took liberalism to be endangered by antidemocratic mass movements; hard nationalists; vain, politically irresponsible demagogues; and the appeal of bureaucratic-legal statism—technocracies fantasized by academics and embraced by leaders.

Weber's response to the crisis was not to rehabilitate the liberal statesman or representative. Rather, it was to cultivate leaders as *rulers*, investing his hopes in those who would honor the rule of law and liberal limits on government while carefully using their power to build a political future that could slip the constraints of bureaucratic administration and also move beyond the imagination of liberal democracy. If we face bowdlerized versions of this on the right in Bolsonaro, Trump, Orban, Erdogan, Farage, Modi, and others today, we may still want to ask about this possibility on the left. Whether we want to rescue or throw in the towel on liberal democracy, the Left has become newly invested in the question of leadership for large-scale transformations that exceed parliamentary tinkering but are short of a revolution. This makes Weber's unblinking confrontation with the crisis of liberal democracy in his time, especially in "Politics as a Vocation," potentially illuminating for the one we experience one hundred years anon.

A third reason for thinking with Weber now, and the main one animating these lectures, pertains to his deep confrontation with the predicaments of a nihilistic age, the problem with which I concluded my most recent book without plotting a way through it. If Weber is better known for his formalizations of methods and ideal types, folding hermeneutics into objective studies of social action, and unique reformulation of materialism to feature the centrality of values, this list of familiars occludes the importance of his reckoning with nihilism in his approach to both knowledge and politics. This feature is signaled by the near-compulsive repetition in his texts of Tolstoy's conclusion that in modernity, death, and hence life have lost meaning and of Dostoyevsky's portrait of the ethical irrationality of the world. Hardly nihilism's most complex theorist—Nietzsche, Heidegger, Adorno, Rorty, Rosen, and Pippin all theorize it more deeply—Weber may be its most political. He establishes nihilism as conditioning contemporary political life and at the same time identifies politics as a vital platform for nihilism's overcoming. As degraded by nihilism as Weber understood contemporary politics to be, he also viewed politics as the domain to articulate and pursue what he calls "ultimate values" or, tellingly, "warring gods"—divine struggles detached from divinity in the aftermath of God's death.

There are many ways to account for the contemporary rise of anti-democratic forces and opportunistic masters of power politics drawing succor from them in the West. Only one of these would feature the political expression of nihilism, a plant Nietzsche predicted would take two hundred years to bloom from the grave of the gods and ideals toppled by science and the Enlightenment. Nihilism is manifest today as ubiquitous moral chaos or disingenuousness but also in assertions of power and desire shorn of concern with accountability to truth, justice, consequences, or futurity. It is revealed in the careless, even festive, breaking of the social contract with others and, with succeeding generations, the witting indifference to a fragile planet and fragile democracies. It manifests as ubiquitous criminality, lying, and dishonesty but also as withdrawal into the trivial, immediate, and personal. It is evident in the purely strategic drape of "traditional morality" over ambitions to resecure historical supremacies of race, gender, and ownership. It is inscribed in the blunt practices of "reputation repair" and shifting-with-the-winds opportunism of even the most self-serious public figures. It resides in an unprecedented popular indifference to consistency, accountability, or even veracity in political leaders. It appears in the shrill epistemological standoff between right and left: the ferocious defense of religion and tradition on the one side, reason and progress on the other, with neither giving quarter *nor* avowing the quicksand in which both flags are planted and on which their battle is played out. And these are only its expressions in political life.

The question for those who want to draw the earth, democracy, and care for justice back from the brink: What prospects are there for a politics that would overcome, dispel, or work through nihilism? And how might knowledge—generating it, curating it, and transmitting it—not only be protected from nihilistic forces but be employed for their overcoming? These are the questions Weber confronted directly, especially in his two famous Vocations lectures, the focus of my own here this week.

By nihilism, I am not suggesting, nor was Weber, that all value has disappeared from the world or that life is widely held to be without purpose or meaning. Rather, understood as a condition rather than an attitude, nihilism generates distinct predicaments for meaning in modernity. On the one hand, it is difficult to find criteria for meaning and value without appealing to discredited sources—religion, tradition, or so-called pure reason—a discrediting that makes such appeals inevitably reactionary, shrill, and defensive. On the other hand, faith in progress is revealed as a secularized version of the Christian millennium and empirically confounded by modernity's failure to deliver generalized peace, prosperity, happiness, or freedom. When appeals to origins and telos thus falter, change itself loses its compass, as if, in Nietzsche's words, "we unchained the earth from its sun." Spinning without tether—dizziness, nausea, yes,

[Brown] *Politics*

but more importantly, this lost ground for knowing what to affirm and negate and this lost temporality for a motion of history—strips both purpose and judgment naked, unbearably so.

There is more. For Weber, science (*Wissenschaft*—all transmissible and evidence-based academic knowledge) undercuts the basis of religion but not its continued existence. Rather, in a rational and rationalized world, Weber declares matter-of-factly, to be religious requires a necessary "sacrifice of the intellect"—religion must reject science on the most fundamental question of how we know what we know. As problematic, as science topples religion from the throne of Truth, it does not and cannot replace religion's meaning-making power. Thus does science change the nature, reach, and implications of Truth. Science can reveal the mysteries of the world—the process Weber calls disenchantment—but cannot generate or rank value. Cost-benefit analysis can even reveal what values may be lost as others are pursued, but it cannot decide the question of what matters or why; it cannot answer Tolstoy's "What shall we do and how shall we live?" Moreover, when it pretends it can, as happens with neoliberalism, a new threshold of nihilism has been reached, one Weber anticipated even if he did not know what its precise form would be.

While science unmoors meaning from its religious and moral foundations, values are also eroded by the spread of instrumental reason, itself enabled by freedom from ethical constraint and gaining ground by virtue of its sheer efficiency in relation to other modes of thought and action, which do not separate means from ends. Instrumental reason, in turn, comes to be embodied in giant "human machineries" built from it and encasing us within their power. In Weber's time, these were bureaucratic states and capitalism; today, we would add digital technologies and finance. Darker still, more than merely independent of value, instrumental reason bears an innate tendency to destroy value, overtaking ends it was designed to serve or converting ends themselves into means, ultimately destroying what Weber calls substantive with instrumental rationality. Again, financialization and digitalization may signify a new threshold for transforming instruments into apparatuses of domination beyond human control, now so powerful that they could crash the entire planet into catastrophe overnight.

In sum, for Weber, in modernity, on the one hand, all meaning is revealed as made, not discovered, and values are undecidable; on the other hand, established meanings are relentlessly unmade by the forces of disenchantment and rationalization, the usurpation of myth by science, and the cannibalization of ends by means in a world governed by instrumental rationality. This much is familiar. The problem of nihilism for Weber, however, exceeds the value-depleting powers of disenchantment and rationalization. Rather, *it rests in the consequential intervals opened up between knowledge, politics, and religion in modernity* and especially the oppositions developed between science and religion, politics and religion, and knowledge and politics. Knowledge requires the value neutrality generative of objectivity; politics features value struggle combined with steely-eyed appreciation that this struggle comprises human rather than divine powers and purposes; and religion rebuffs both sets of assumptions to affirm values derived from otherworldly powers. These partings produce novel political effects, seen at once in the way that Weber shapes the vocations for science and politics. Drawing the notion of *Beruf* from the Protestant imperative to serve God through earthly practices, he iterates vocations for politics and science that are bound not to god but to godheads—religious remainders after the divinity is gone—to avoid descending into raw self-gratification and the will to power. *Beruf* as he will craft it entails near-superhuman attainments of postnihilist dispositions of selflessness, maturity, and responsibility. At the same time, isolating religion from *Wissenschaft* and politics in modernity strips religion itself of accountability to truth *or* power. Thus, when the religious minded do not stay in their quarter but attempt to exercise epistemological or practical power in the political or knowledge domain, the effect is a special kind of corruption, one Weber understands as nihilistic. To put the matter the other way around, paradoxically, the only responsible actor in a nihilistic age, and the only one able to carry us beyond it, is one who fully confronts the predicaments posed for meaning-making now. If modernity is structured by unbridgeable chasms between knowledge and purpose, knowledge and belief, only those who can face these chasms, and craft their passions and endeavors in an ethical relationship to them, are capable of being responsible scholars and political actors.

For Weber, the absence of foundations for values simultaneously reveals them as inherently imbricated with power, contestable, *and* available to critical analysis even if they do not spring from reason or refer to it for legitimacy. These same features are what make values essentially political and also make politics *the* domain for struggling over them. More than only infected by nihilism, which it is, politics is the distinctive venue for countering nihilism's dangerous potential inversion into indifference or worse—fatalism, cynicism, narcissism, or unaccountable deployments of

[BROWN] *Politics* 9

power and violence. In a secular, rationalized, and nihilistic age, when religious and cultural authority has disintegrated, politics acquires unprecedented importance for the articulation, justification, contestation, and pursuit of values. Put another way, when nihilism is full-blown, ultimate values are at once politicized in a trivial way and enlarged as the ultimate stakes of politics. On the one hand, ubiquitous politicization (of taste, consumption, diet, appearance, family form and parenting practices, lifestyle, even body type) is a symptom of nihilism. On the other hand, this makes actual politics a theater of nihilism: it is where nihilism is played out in raw form but is also a site for its potential overcoming.

This paradox—the political sphere as ravaged by nihilism and as a venue for overcoming it—arises because for Weber, the political is quintessentially partisan, by nature interested rather than objective, though not therefore purely subjective or reducible to interest. The relentlessly partisan nature of political life binds it to value struggle, and the inherently nonfoundational character of value in modernity binds it to politics. Thus, Sheldon Wolin comments, for Weber, "values came to be the symbolic equivalent of politics," which is why he banished them from science. But the reverse is also true: values are irreducible in politics and cannot be extinguished without extinguishing political life as such, the threat Weber saw in reducing politics to administration, technocracy, raw interest, or power play. Thus, again, while politics is itself saturated with the dangers of nihilism in modernity, it has the unique potential for enunciating, mobilizing, and fighting over ultimate human purposes after their moral-religious foundations are shattered by disenchantment and rationalization. At the same time, since the currency of politics is power (and its ultimate instrument is violence), and since its essence is partisanship, there can be no neutrality, objectivity, or peace *ever*; these value struggles are eternal—cold comfort for those still invested in narratives of progress.

This is the capsule version of my argument, and why I think Weber's antinihilistic orientation to politics and knowledge may be useful today. Now let me open it up more slowly.

Weber's account of nihilism's effects is informed by Nietzsche's while varying from it. For Nietzsche, nihilism *devalues* values, including the value of Truth itself, while keeping them around. Their foundation eroded, values do not vanish but become malleable, fungible, trivial, and instrumentalizable. They are easily trafficked, traded, and used for purposes beyond themselves. Contemporary examples abound in commerce, politics, religion, and the branding of everything. Indeed, when values are openly treated as capital enhancing—as they are today by individuals, corporations, nonprofits, and states—their trivialization and instrumentalization are complete.

For Nietzsche, the devaluation of values also entails a radical reduction in the force of conscience; the instincts or desires (both primal and socially shaped—Nietzsche's genius) that conscience yokes or reroutes are decontained and desublimated and erupt in antisocial form. Again, examples are abundant: disinhibition (including aggressive and violent forms) is increasingly routine and accompanies cynicism and contractualism in the domain of values. The "conscience" that is liberal democracy is also thrown off: obligations to fairness, inclusion, the rule of law, and future generations. For Nietzsche, hyperindividualism is a related effect. The social contract with others and with the past and future broken, we fall into a world of one and a world of now. Again, this is a formation that dovetailed exquisitely with neoliberal encomiums of the past half century; nihilism may be understood as both facilitating neoliberalism's acceptability and as intensified by neoliberal reason.

Truth, Nietzsche argues, is devalued along with every other value in a nihilistic age. More than strategically overwhelmed by propaganda, fused with commerce, and manipulated by opportunistic demagogues and Russian trolls, Truth—like its cousins honesty, integrity, and accountability—cannot survive the degrounding and diminution of value. So also does the sharp opposition between science and religion abet truth's slide; if religion does not have it, then it doesn't want, need, admire, or burnish it.

This condition generates several possible formations. What Nietzsche calls the "pale atheists" dwell instead in irony, skepticism, and above all, themselves—narcissism is a booming industry in a nihilistic age. With all value diminished, only immediate gratifications and security remain compelling, sentiments that comport well with the governing rationality of both neoliberalism and securitarian authoritarianism. Religionists, on the other hand, clutch their crosses and refuse intellection, making them easily available for mobilization by a Bolsonaro or Trump. Both tendencies—narcissism and self-indulgence and religion without depth or theology—express what Robert Pippin terms the "failure of desire" that is nihilism.

For Nietzsche, the sign of working through nihilism is conviction cultured at a deep and nonreactive level—Pippin identifies this spirit with Eros—and trying to *legislate* or will values for the world. Importantly for Nietzsche, such conviction does not arise from deliberation or choice but

[BROWN]   *Politics*   11

shares the nonrational, nonstrategic character of Eros. As Pippin puts it, "Something grips us, something we cannot help caring about; it would not be love if it were in the service of some instrumental strategy and ... far more than simply a felt desire ... it involves a wholehearted passionate commitment to and identification with a desired end." Overcoming nihilism for Nietzsche does not mean rationally *deciding* what to value across a diverse order of objects and possibilities (which would in any case hoist the fiction of that "little changeling, the subject ... the doer behind the deed, the neutral substratum before willing") but means arriving at this value from a wellspring of passionate attachment. Of course, this attachment can be formed and informed by education, influence, or experience, and we will want to come back to this. Still, that passion is now at the root of value, which means its postnihilist version is divorced from not only authority but cultural reproduction *and* saturation, from foundations securing its Truth and a homogenous culture everywhere generating and reflecting it. Even if widely accepted and successfully legislated (and "legislating new values" is how Nietzsche phrases the "beyond" of nihilism), this inversion remains. This reversal of the origin of value in late- or postmodernity, from inculcation by the world to overt legislation by power, is one reason Weber will locate postnihilist political regeneration of value at the site of charismatic leadership.

Yet Weber's account also diverges from Nietzsche's. For him, disintegrated foundations for authoritative values entail less of the direct weakening and trivialization of values than their proliferation and diversification. The authority that would secure a single and common truth gone, we live now, he says, as the ancients did when they "would bring a sacrifice at one time to Aphrodite and at another to Apollo.... Only now the gods have been deprived of the magical and mythical but inwardly true qualities that gave them such vivid immediacy." His invocation of the Greeks is laden with meaning: if ultimate values are undecidable, we are returned to a certain premodern, pre-Christian condition and suffer an inversion of the Enlightenment promise—its dethroning rather than crowning of Truth in the domain of value. Having lost its ground in truth, and supported neither by science nor capitalism, this makes liberalism and the values it subtends deeply vulnerable. Nothing guarantees liberalism's survival when, as Weber puts it, "each individual has to decide for himself which ... is the devil and which the God *for him*." Indeed, as values proliferate and diversify, peoples and nations will inevitably be splintered and riven and not only face the kinds of external "clashes of civilization" wrought by globalization. Our nomenclatures for this condition—"culture wars" and extreme political polarization—inadequately capture the historical condition Weber charts. For him, the lost foundation for value is primary in fracturing values; neoliberal deracinations, religious-secular, and rural-urban divides only fertilize the plant.

If deep divisions generated by proliferating values are one political expression of nihilism for Weber, destructive hyperpoliticization is another. Everything becomes iconic of the struggle over values—today, these include consumption practices, family forms, décor, gun ownership, curriculums, sports, ecological practices, fashion, sexuality, diet, and exercise regimes. At the same time, hyperpoliticization means that "force and fraud" contaminate principle everywhere. More than merely deployed for branding, moral values and knowledge itself are relentlessly instrumentalized for power purposes. Law and religion, too, shed even the pretense of nonpolitical or suprapolitical status, hence the now quotidian politicization of judicial appointments, interpretations and decisions, and bids by megachurches to throw off constraints on political engagement. This politicization in turn deepens skepticism about truth and politics (let alone truth in politics), about the integrity of faith, and about the worth of constitutionalism and law as neutral arbiters and protectors.

How, then, for Weber, does politics as a struggle over ultimate values emerge as a crucial site for countering nihilism? How, as religious and moral authority wane, and politics itself is saturated with nihilistic effects, might political life be a stage for renewing value and human integrity? Weber's genius is to drive straight into the predicaments of nihilism, to insist that political leadership takes its bearings and develops its ethics from the loss of moral foundations *and* the permanent imbrication of all political purposes with what he calls "diabolical powers." Let us turn to this work.

POLITICS AS A VOCATION

In the dismal, intentionally tedious first two-thirds of "Politics as a Vocation," Weber details the effects of rationalization in modern politics, its generation of bureaucratic and administrative mentalities on the one hand, and party machines, with their hacks and spoils, on the other. There are also the stupid masses, thirsty for demagoguery, who cannot appreciate the complex internal and external relations of modern states and thus cannot be represented, only led. Weber's figure of the ideal political leader is crafted in relation to these conditions but also as a mode of rising above them and redeeming grander possibilities of political life. This figure has a love of power but is without vanity, is committed to realizing a political vision but in a responsible, nonobsessional manner, and is charismatic yet careful, restrained, and capable of withstanding endless setbacks and disappointments without quitting. Each of these is a retort to the depredations of rationalization and nihilism; each responds—perhaps even retorts—to them by centering value and decentering ego and cheap spectacle. This also means there is nothing organic about Weber's ideal politician; it is not immanent to the historical conditions but called from sources external to them even as it must be consummately savvy about them. Nor is this figure "called" by God in a disenchanted age. Rather, Weber gives us *Beruf* secularized *and* constructed, a constructivism so obvious that he does not bother underlining it. Arising neither from dialectics nor immanence, informed neither by social science nor religion, political possibility against the darkness emerges from a leader bearing the spirit, force, and stamina to resist all the features of a nihilistic age with a distinctive purpose. This is Weber's wager: not a revolutionary overthrow of the forces of the present (from which he feared only a different machinery of domination) but the singular promise of political leadership that could recenter the human capacity to instantiate values and a common life forged on their basis within those forces.

But what is the part of charisma in Weber's project of overcoming nihilism in politics? Here, Weber is not just capitulating to contemporary demands for demagoguery. Rather, of the three kinds of authority Weber famously charts, charisma alone compels through the promise of emancipation from the routine and givenness of the present. Charisma attracts its followers by leading somewhere, aspiring to something new, and thus counters the nihilistic depression of value. It is revolutionary in a non-Marxist sense in its moves against the existing state of things and against the value-depleting characteristics of rational-legal authority. It promises to reenchant as it reforms the world yet is distinguished from other revolutionary modalities by balancing "inner determination" with "inner restraint." Much of its power, and of course its ethics, arises from this vital tension: raw determination by itself easily becomes reckless ambition; restraint alone veers toward reluctance or compromise. Thus, the charismatic Weber depicts in this essay combines "heated passion and a cool sense of proportion" to achieve what he calls a "trained ruthlessness" toward one's own cause (what some have called political Kantianism) and a "distance to things and men." All of this—passion for an impersonal cause, restraint, and determination; a sense of proportion; and the pathos of distance—challenges the desublimated aggressions, petty preoccupations, rancorousness, self-absorption, and the desire for immediate satisfactions that nihilism generates. These qualities also oppose what Weber takes to be other political motifs of the day—administrative, legalistic, or technocratic orientations along with sensibilities he disparages as "sterile excitement" (revolutionaries), "naïve idealism" (purists and utopians of any kind), and "frivolous intellectual [or power] play."

Yet the challenge of achieving this ethos is not only due to its being at odds with the times. Sober, dogged, responsible pursuit of an impersonal cause is not passion's natural form, especially but not only in a nihilistic age. The ethos requires routing passion away from its natural course, deferring or altogether denying its gratifications, and coloring it with "habituation to detachment in every sense of the word." Weber has thus drawn a nearly impossible figure: a charismatic personality with a strong instinct for power yet animated exclusively by a cause, whose daily work is "slow boring through hard boards" and struggling against established machineries of power and whose bearing is restrained, sober, detached, and consummately responsible.

Before we pursue this problem further, we need to ask, Why does Weber draw on responsibility rather than reason as political passion's restraining or balancing force? In an age dominated by instrumental rationality, Weber fears that reason alone would only add calculation to decisions. Combined with passion, this leads to the most dangerous of political tendencies, a rationality in which the end justifies the means, and everything—from laws to constitutions, to other causes, and to individuals—may be instrumentalized for other purposes. Not calculative reason, then, but a distinctive ethic of responsibility for *all* effects of an action, including collateral and unintended ones, is required to guide without choking political passion. In addition to avoiding instrumentalism, this ethic is aimed at curtailing vanity, which Weber takes to be among the deadliest forces of contemporary political life.

Vanity for Weber stands for the moment when the political power instinct, essential to political actors, overrides the cause to become what he terms "self-intoxication." It signals identification with rather than distance from the course of history one is trying to alter and the power one wields for that aim. When one *becomes* the cause rather than a vessel for it, detachment, restraint, responsibility, and reflection fall away, and the thrill of power takes center stage. Weber dwells at length on this problem because he understands that vanity is not merely an attribute of certain personalities but an endemic in politics, all the more so when nihilism is in full bloom. When "the demagogue is forced to play for 'effect' . . . he always runs the risk both of turning into an actor and of taking too lightly his responsibility for his own actions." Weber's judgment here is ferocious: "Although, or rather because, power is an unavoidable tool of all politics, and the striving for power, therefore, is one of its driving forces, there is no more destructive distortion of political energy than when the parvenu swaggers around, boasting of his power, conceitedly reveling in its reflected glory." He damns the "impoverished and superficial indifference toward the *meaning* of human activity" embodied in this pose. A pure expression of nihilism, its lack of commitment to anything other than itself and corresponding lack of responsibility, comprise "two kinds of mortal sin in the field of politics."

Apart from the problem of vanity, Weber's argument for a distinctive political ethic of responsibility is conventionally read as a response to the unpredictable effects of action (what he sometimes terms "the tragedy of action") in a dynamic sphere suffused with "diabolical powers," including violence. But it is also aimed at contesting both rationalization and nihilism, the former's swallowing of freedom and greatness, and the latter's reduction of politics to exercising power without right, violence without responsibility, and instrumentalizing hence erasing value. Bound to leadership, the ethic of responsibility aims to recenter values, and politics as their province, after secularism destroyed their foundation, rationalization destroyed their place, and nihilism destroyed their depth and dignity. It aims to recover politics as *the* domain of "struggle over ultimate values" while avoiding turning them into either religious truths or pure weaponry. It seeks to embed values in a project of overcoming nihilism, both in individuals and in culture. And it seeks to reestablish responsibility in the context of an ethically irrational order, one shaped entirely by humans but never fully in their control. Each of these is a postnihilist strategy.

Discussion of the ethic of responsibility comes near the end of "Politics as a Vocation" but is set up early. Weber opens the lecture by defining politics narrowly as leadership of a political organization ("in other words, a state") and then declares, curiously, that the modern state can only be stipulated sociologically by its peculiar means—namely, its monopoly of physical violence. Weber knows that there is more to states—much of his lecture is dedicated to their emergence and consolidation, their apparatuses and institutions, and their distinctive organization of political life.

Why, then, define states in terms of violence—that is, in terms of their distinctive means rather than in terms of their modern characteristics of large administrative machineries and sprawling legal codes?

In part, Weber is setting up a critique of socialism, revolution, and Christian pacifism, doctrines he believes disingenuously and dangerously isolate their virtues from their inevitable imbrication with state violence. Weber, consummate theorist of the power of means separated from ends in capitalism and bureaucracy, is also finely attuned to the wreckage unleashed by political causes when the ends are said to justify means. Hence he conceptually resutures the ultimate political means—state violence—to all political ends. He underscores the use of violence and accidental unleashing of violence as a persistent feature of politics. This potential for violence hovers over every political act and event, whether the aim is to lead, seize, or smash the state; prevent, start, join, or stop a war; initiate, reform, or overturn a law. Again, Weber centers violence in politics not to affirm it as the essence of politics—it is only an instrument. Yet instruments are never "only" for Weber, the master theorist of how instruments swallow ends. Thus, he aims to throw on their feet and take the chair away from those who clutch their principles or defend their actions without reference to this instrument. His strategy is to burden actors with responsibility for *both* means and ends while treating them as distinctive. The same action or actor is responsible for both, and politics always comprises both. Hence neither abstract principle nor raw calculation nor realpolitik have a place in postnihilist politics.

In formulating his ethic of responsibility, Weber famously contrasts it with two others. One he calls an absolute ethic—bound solely to a moral code such as Christian virtue or pacifism. This ethic refuses the delinking of motive, aim, and effect that, for Weber, comprises the ethical irrationality of the political realm. Responsibility is required because of this delinking. The absolute ethic, or what he sometimes terms "an ethic of conviction," disavows this dimension of politics and often ends up, Weber says, decrying a world "too stupid or too base" for one's principles to govern. Thus does an absolute ethic reveal itself as a form of *ressentiment* against politics.

What Weber calls an ethic of ultimate ends refuses the ethical irrationality of politics differently. This ethic is contoured by its commitment to a rational end state, one imagined devoid of distortions by power and partisanship, and justifies any means to achieve that end. Weber's main target here is Bolshevism, but it is noteworthy that the classical neoliberals are also vulnerable to this charge; they imagine the power problem in politics conquered by spontaneous order and justify a good measure of state violence and other collateral damage for that order.

Absolute ethic politicians reduce politics to principles, and ultimate ends politicians reduce it to a teleology of reason; both dangerously divide means from ends and eschew the specific powers, partisanship, and "tragedy of action" that are permanent features of politics. They shirk responsibility for what becomes of the principle they stand for, even if that principle is turned upside down in the course of political events and outcomes. Moreover, if each hyperpersonalizes the ethical dimension of action, referring everything back to their personal motive or aim, they also radically depersonalize action's worldly effects, treating principle or reason as if it governs the meaning of action. This, too, avoids responsibility in politics, where intentions and effects often lay worlds apart.

And yet, Weber famously concludes, only one who marries an ethic of conviction to an ethic of responsibility has a true vocation for politics. So how are they twinned in a single being and set of practices? Weber's vocabulary here is telling: maturity, sobriety, manly fortitude, restraint, ability to withstand disappointment and setbacks without whining, cynicism, or retreat. Converting Nietzsche's complex "pathos of distance" from a class-based sensibility to "distance from self and things," Weber also invokes Luther's resolute "here I stand, I can do no other" to express the moment when conviction reigns supreme. Weightiness, knowingness, tolerance for suffering in place of Nietzsche's gaiety and laughter for overcoming nihilism. Building, not breaking things. Avoidance of resentment, vengeance, even ordinary face-saving—all the reactive and vain temptations. Above all, the postnihilist political actor is willing to sacrifice self but not others to a political cause, contesting the nihilistic reduction of everything to individual interest, power, or security.

This ethic of responsibility also represents a path through nihilism in its representation of "ultimate value" in political life and by inhabiting a set of difficult political epistemological commitments that renew human freedom. Let us consider each briefly.

To take one's own values as True and demonize all others is already to inhabit something of the absolute ethic Weber criticizes; conversely, recognizing political "godheads" as beliefs rather than truths fosters the objectivism and sense of proportion Weber is seeking for political actors. In a sphere that is partisan all the way down, this recognition builds a sense of proportion that in turn builds responsibility at the site of conviction.

Weber here adapts one of Nietzsche's signature moves, in which rejecting the disembodied conceits of science and the absolutism of religion alone approaches the ideal of objectivity. For Nietzsche, only perspectivism permits the possibility of interpretation beyond the interpreter. For Weber, only reckoning with the foundationless and irreconcilable quality of ultimate values retrieves them from nihilistic devaluation—instrumentalization, trivialization, and hyperpoliticization.

Put the other way around, the ethic of responsibility entails acting without the conceit that history and humanity have a natural or necessary ethical shape or teleology or develop from pure intention, reason, God, or science. It entails affirming politics as the domain where value is both imposed *and* transformed by the context within which it is enacted, not a domain in which immanent or divine value is realized. This is refused by both an ethic of conviction and of ends and is why each is irresponsible. That said, Weber's ethic makes an incredible demand on the vanishing human soul—at once to have an unblinking consciousness of the contingent nature of our passions and dedicate ourselves to them. This has nothing to do with relativism, subjectivism, or climbing "empathy walls": rather, it is an unprecedented epistemological political consciousness in which one knows one's values to be situated, temporally and geographically, rather than universal yet is no less committed to them by virtue of that knowingness.

Appreciation of the ethical irrationality of political life formed by the tragedy of action, the unemancipatory rationalities organizing the present, *and* the permanent contest of values in a secular order also facilitates discernment of political predicaments and possibilities, dangers and openings. These become more legible to actors when they are not measured by moral or behavioral logics abstracted from these conditions and contingencies. The ethic also aims to retrieve political life from its overtaking by personality cults and a spirit of *ressentiment* on one side and bureaucratization and rationalization on the other. This in turn makes possible bids for the future that are not rooted in grievances against the past or present or the nihilistic absorption with the personal and the immediate.

Finally, this approach to political renewal aims to recuperate *freedom* from its destruction by rationalization and its nihilistic diminution into irresponsible license. In his social science, Weber defines freedom formally and mechanically as the absence of constraints; thus, he identifies instrumentally rational action as the "freest form of action" because it is unfettered by tradition or ends. However, it is with the soul, Weber says, that human freedom is made—that is, by which we choose values and ends, enacting a life we have chosen. This is why he places *Beruf*—vocation, finding purpose and crafting a life in accord with it—at the heart of freedom. Nihilism, generated by the expansion of freedom's mechanical form, extinguishes the soulful form of freedom. Just as rationalization usurps this kind of freedom with freedom as a power independent of constraints, building economic and administrative systems invert freedom into its opposite.

More than just different, the two forms of freedom have thus turned out to be mutually canceling. Freedom as unconstrained power built an order in which we are, subjectively and practically, nearly bereft of the freedom to craft ourselves and the world according to values we have chosen. Weber's bold bid in *Politics as a Vocation* is to try to reverse this in politics. In foregrounding the pursuit of value as the essence of the political vocation, he aims to retrieve freedom from the dual threat of domination by the machineries of capitalism and administration on one side and the cheapness, frivolity, and indifference to truth, justice, or futurity of a nihilistic age on the other. If politics is saturated with both, indeed, if Weber's greatest dread was giant apparatuses of domination wielded by vain demagogues, it is also where both could be countered.

"Politics as a Vocation" offers a vision for working through nihilism by restoring politics to its ancient function—placing the fight for an ideal of "who we are" and "what we should do" at its heart. It aims to make politics redemptive after the death of God, not by purifying it of diabolical powers or attempting to enshrine values in institutions but by casting it as the essential domain in which we decide and assert value against the predicaments for value that modernity has produced. It is where humans could also become responsible again, not only for their own actions but for the world when this capacity is so imperiled by powers that we generated but have slipped our control. If Weber was alert to the faint prospects for this project, his antidote to despair was not hope but grit—emotional, spiritual, and political. As Weber concludes the essay, "Only those with 'the staunchness of heart that refuses to be daunted by the collapse of all their hopes,'" only those whose "spirit will not be broken if the world . . . proves too stupid or base to accept what he wishes to offer it, and who, when faced with all that obduracy, can still say 'Nevertheless!' despite everything"—only such a person has the vocation for politics. "Nevertheless" or "in spite of it all" does not leap over the nihilistic predicament but resists its world-eviscerating force with all the doggedness and dignity it can muster. We could not be further from Nietzsche now.

One last point before we leave this for today. Weber's certainty that a politics of principle, procedure, or institutions cannot rescue us from the depredations of nihilism or modern machineries of unfreedom led him toward charismatic leadership and away from democracy. While some have a kindred worry about democracy's suitability to global powers, we might reframe the matter this way: if values emanate at least in part from complex regimes of attachment and desire, but nihilism represents a crisis of desire, indeed, a failure to be able to love life and world, this becomes an argument for focusing on political culture. Especially in uneducated democracies, we cannot cling to the hope that reason or interests will force the awakening of those compelled and soothed by authoritarian plutocrats. We cannot expect to recruit through rational argumentation or presentation of evidence that Brexit, Trump, or Bolsonaro are damaging their own life conditions or burning their children's future. Rather, our task is to kindle the desire for a just, livable, and sustainable order, to make this viscerally compelling. In the past four decades, the Right has worked assiduously at developing the cultural attractiveness of its program; it has worked relentlessly at the cultural level. The Left—notwithstanding Gramsci, Stuart Hall, or the program of the early Frankfurt School—has largely ignored this project. Cultivating the desire for a different order of things—against the nihilistic, commercial, and technological forces that pull desire in another direction—is surely as important as rebuilding public education or teaching digital literacy to take us through nihilistic times.

LECTURE II.
KNOWLEDGE

Yesterday, we pondered Weber's efforts to counter nihilism at the site of politics, especially through political action animated by a responsible, selfless pursuit of a collective cause. Today, we turn to Weber's efforts, especially in "Science as a Vocation," to overcome nihilistic effects on knowledge and in the academy, a project that depends on the most severe depoliticization of both that he can imagine and a project that ultimately fails. The failure is important for our own thinking about responsible postnihilist knowledge politics and world making. This afternoon, I will examine at some length his account of nihilism and knowledge before considering its implications for our time.

One prefatory note: the term, *Wissenschaft*, routinely translated into English as science, refers to all systematic academic study, not just the hard sciences. At the core of the Humboldtian model of education in which Weber was formed, the term carried the implications of knowledge pursuit that was both unbiased and independent of influence (especially by church, state, and market), hence capable of discovering truth. This complex meaning bundle is at stake each time we hear "science" in Weber's lecture.

Weber opens "Science as a Vocation" with a dark view of contemporary German academic life. There is its feudal organization, poor conditions for advancement, and frequent failure to reward excellence; there are the confines of specialization and the inevitable eclipse of every achievement by scientific progress. Above all, there is science's own disenchanting effect. With its promise that we can, in principle, understand everything, science depletes whatever it touches of mystery and intrinsic value; it bleeds spirit with explanation. In its way, it is as violent as politics and as desacralizing as capitalist commodification. In its way, it violates and desacralizes not peoples, nations, vocations, and relations but meaning and value. It topples faith and puts nothing in its place. It dispirits as it rationalizes whatever it touches. It divorces progress from its millenarian promise of improvement, emancipation, or happiness and reduces it to an accumulation of knowledge and technique. It leaves the world more suffused with power but empty of value than it finds it.

Such is the deep nihilism Weber believes we face consequent to the dethronement of religious authority and mystery of nature with scientific knowledge. As science topples religious and theological perspectives on origins, order, and meaning, it cannot replace what it has destroyed. The

[21]

inclination to do so, more than merely misguided, is itself a dangerous nihilistic effect: the voids opened in a radically desacralized world create a demand, Weber says, for prophets and demagogues everywhere. At the same time, performances in the realm of knowledge that properly belong in the church and public life are themselves part of nihilism's destructive force in which, as Weber formulates it, "the ultimate and most sublime values have withdrawn from public life," and theology, with its inescapable "assumption that the world must have a meaning," is finished.

From another angle, in "Science as a Vocation" and the essays on method from which he draws much of the argument, Weber is at war. He is at war with Marx and Nietzsche for the soul of the social sciences, contesting what he regards as the norm-laden faux science of Marx and the antiscience of Nietzsche. He is at war with colleagues who preach German nationalism, scholars who are value positivists, and scholars who are syndicalists. The nationalists make the university "into a theological seminary—except that it [lacks] the latter's religious dignity." The positivists make a category error, refusing the Kantian dictum to submit everything to critical scrutiny, eschewing the interpretive dimension of understanding action and values, and overvaluing the coordinates and norms of the present. The syndicalists both spurn objectivity and exploit the power of the academic podium in what is a manifestly inegalitarian setting. Weber is at war with those who believe truth rests in balancing or achieving a compromise between contesting views, which is a technique of politics, not science, and expressive of a nihilistic relativism and trivialization of facts *and* ultimate worldviews. He is at war with those who would submit diverse views to competition, which is a technique of markets, not science, and expressive of the invasion of the university by market values. He is at war with those who pretend "the facts speak for themselves" when facts do not speak at all, when this likely means that both matters of interpretation and "inconvenient facts" have been strategically ignored, moves that also bring the rhetorical sleights of hand appropriate to parliament into the classroom. He is at war with those who believe they have achieved neutrality by structuring their historical or sociological accounts with *realpolitik*, with Darwinian adaptation, or with metanarratives of progress—each is an ungrounded theological remainder. He is at war with economists who believe their science establishes the normative supremacy of capitalism when it only describes its mechanisms. He is at war with philosophers and social theorists who believe they can assess let alone certify the validity of norms rather than merely

[BROWN] *Knowledge*

analyze their predicates, logics, entailments, and implications. And he is at war with those who believe in pure reason, who acknowledge neither hermeneutics nor differing modes of rationality within which there are also always irrationalities.

Weber is at war, but his enemies are not timeless stalwarts. Rather, he takes much of what he is fighting to symptomatize the political, epistemological, and existential crisis of his time. He understands his moral-political age to be one simultaneously drained of value, proliferating value and cheapening value, one in which value judgments themselves are reduced to judgments of taste, one that fosters personality in place of integrity and honesty and fosters license within unprecedented orders of domination. It is an age he famously depicted in *The Protestant Ethic and the Spirit of Capitalism* as featuring "sensualists without heart" and "specialists without spirit," where neither feeling nor intellect is preserved from the rationalization that simultaneously renders us cogs in economic machineries and superficial individualists. Truth has come apart from Meaning and Value, residing only in facts, themselves infinite in number, a reality hard to bear and hence generating reaction in the form of polemics, positivism, and millenarianism. Progress no longer comprises growing happiness, peace, or truth but is reduced to advancements of knowledge that turn perverse, building the basis for growing organizational, technological, economic, and political powers that escape human control and become world-blistering forces of power without right.

Boundary breakdown is also a key symptom of the age. Nothing stays in its place because, absent a moral lodestar as well as traditional organizing principles, place itself loses its coordinates and its value. In the domain of knowledge, the ramifications exceed the problem of impurity or bowdlerization: the incessant mixing of what Weber refers to repeatedly as "absolutely heterogeneous" practices—most notably analysis of facts and value judgments about them—degrades both and thus intensifies disregard for facts, truth, accountability, responsibility, *and* values. Nihilism ramifies as it corrodes the boundaries between preaching and teaching, entertainment and information, culture and politics, and as depth, sobriety, historical consciousness, and care for both the soul and the world give way to superficiality, excitability, gratification, and presentism.

Weber responds to this crisis and the spiraling miscegenation of elements it foments with his infamous stipulation of arch opposites and epistemological and ontological hygiene aimed at isolating these opposites from each other. The familiar binaries are politics and science, the classroom and the public square, fact and value, empirical and theoretical claims, normative judgments and the truth of empirical propositions. For Weber, not mere conceptual tidiness but the world is at stake in drawing and enforcing these separations. If the relative organicism of earlier epochs has given way to fragmentation and specialization in the age of capitalism, bureaucracy and secularism, this means order once maintained by hierarchy and authority has given way to capitalist and bureaucratic machineries cleaved by the disorder of value concatenation. With both organicism and authority receding, tightly enforced organization alone keeps things in place. Notwithstanding Weber's sensitivity to the complexity of what he calls the "chaos of infinitely differentiated and contradictory complexes of ideas and feelings" in any epoch or ideational regime, and notwithstanding his admonition to scholars to avoid conflating concepts and typologies with reality, Weber's way through nihilism in the intellectual sphere depends on epistemological-ontological distinctions that, more than descriptive, are sent into the field as police.

But why formulate these "absolutely heterogeneous" spheres of endeavor and practice—knowledge/politics, empirics/values—not as simply different but as opposites that destroy each other if they touch or mix? Weber's adamance on this front aims to quarantine nihilistic effects, ranging from the final destruction of Truth (prevailing everywhere except in empirical knowledge), to the final destruction of meaning (prevailing everywhere except in value), to the destruction of greatness (prevailing everywhere except *Beruf*, dedication to a cause larger than oneself for which one sacrifices the self). Thus, for example, only by insulating the certainty of facticity from the undecidability of values can the nihilistic condition assaulting and degrading both be repelled. Only by securing knowledge from charisma can the classroom "unlock the world by means of the intellect" when students crave value in a world of moral chaos. And paradoxically, only by imposing moats between church, politics, and knowledge can the elements they once harbored together be secured in the wake of their fragmentation.

Weber's protocols, then, do not simply shed the fetters of a less scientific era but address the world-destroying desublimations and boundary breakdowns of nihilism with a program of hygiene. They aim at challenging value warriors and politicians of every stripe, bending facticity to their cause to the point of breaking it. They challenge journalists and teachers who practice open partisanship via faux objectivity, selections,

[BROWN] *Knowledge*

and arrangements of facts said to speak for themselves. They challenge the conceit that neutrality is obtained by balancing or synthesizing views through "competition among ideas" or finding a middle ground. They seek to preserve truth by confining it to facts and preserve value by confining it to politics where its undecidability is on permanent display.

Since he is conventionally understood as mainly codifying protocols of a value-neutral social science for a secular age, it is worth pausing over the specific crisis for knowledge that Weber aims to redress with his category purifications. What has vanished in recent decades, Weber writes in his 1917 essay "The Meaning of Ethical Neutrality," is "the widespread conviction among social science scholars that of the various possible points of view in the domain of practical-political preferences, ultimately only one was the correct one." In its stead, he continues, "a patchwork of cultural values *and personalities*" to advance them have replaced the "relatively impersonal" character of the old ethical imperative. In addition to value proliferation, what is generated by Truth's dethronement in morals and politics is the elevation of the individual and personality as carriers of values. For Weber, this is what creates the demand for demagoguery in all spheres. However, the fusion of values with personality is especially troubling in the domain of knowledge and its transmission: as facticity wobbles along with ethical monoculture, the politico and the preacher invade the classroom dressed in professorial garb. Thus, the very historical conditions necessitating pristine scholarly integrity—respect for facts and consideration of values only as analytic objects—undermine it with the rise of personality. That cult of personality, Weber suggests, is everywhere: students crave it, and teachers feed it. Today, of course, the ubiquitous culture of celebrity combined with metrics for student evaluations of pedagogy positively demands it.

The classroom, Weber insists, is for training, not molding students; developing capacities, not shaping views. This means teaching the importance of "inconvenient facts," distinguishing facts from evaluations and judgments of them and disciplining students to "repress the impulse to exhibit [their own] personal tastes or sentiments" in their studies. They must be taught that intellectual greatness rests in training, hard work, selfless devotion, and restraint—all the familiar Protestant virtues bundled into the scholarly vocation. These demands aim to not merely harness but choke the will to power in intellectual life; though as Nietzsche and Freud understood, that life force would have to go somewhere. Weber also knows that these demands aggrandize the ascetic forces—objectivism, neutrality, dispassion, denial of the subject of knowing—that Nietzsche grasped as turning us relentlessly against ourselves: our senses, bodies, historicity, faculties of interpretation, desires, and will to truth. Such turning, Nietzsche insisted, would reach a crescendo in Western civilization where we would come to will nothingness even as we broke into decadence—two powerful features of political culture today. What is a refusal to stem climate change but also the valorization of human governing by market forces other than the will to nothingness? And what is the festive spurning of facts and truth by power without right other than decadence?

* * * * *

And yet. Notwithstanding Weber's insistence that science dwells exclusively in facts, his fiercest and finest moments in "Science as a Vocation" concern how scholars and teachers ought to analyze values. Why? Yesterday, I argued that Weber identifies values with politics and politics with partisanship, power, force, and at the extreme, violence. In fact, this chain of identifications is a shorthand for the historical process Weber charts that has a significant bearing on our problem. In one of his earlier methodological essays, Weber identifies values not with politics but with culture. To be cultural creatures, Weber says, is to be "endowed with the capacity and the will to take a deliberate attitude towards the world and to lend it *significance*." The very concept of culture, he adds, is a "value concept. . . . Empirical reality becomes 'culture' to us because and insofar as we relate it to value ideas." How then does value shift from the cultural to the political plane in late modernity? Values become political in Weber's terms when they are deracinated and hence detached from a shared worldview, when they become matters of struggle undecidable except (provisionally) by rhetorical, legal, or physical force. As we saw yesterday, this is when they also become at risk for nihilistic hyperpoliticization. Moreover, the politicization of culture—arising from value uprooted from foundations, detached from authority—is part of what makes liberalism crack: multiculturalism in the broadest sense only works when culture remains depoliticized, a depoliticization possible only so long as value is both anchored and common. Identity politics did not change all that but is, rather, its measure.

The chain of distinctly contemporary identifications Weber establishes between values, politics, partisanship, and force does three consequential things: first, it converts all values into practical positions available to beady-eyed analysis, and it situates their worldly enactment in a realm where the disjunction between motives and effects demands responsibility to that disjunction rather than to principles alone. No religious or other moral garb can shield them from this. Second, it makes the political domain a gladiatorial theater for contests of value or "warring godheads." Third, it renders that theater a potential, though noninevitable, stage for a postnihilist recuperation and pursuit of value in the context of historically specific forces, both raging and quiet, that are destructive of value.

This chain of identifications, however, also has implications for scholarship, curriculums, and pedagogy; it animates Weber's argument that developing and teaching knowledge must not be infected or inflected with values. If values are political because they are contingent and partisan, then the slightest normative impulse is poison in scholarly waters. More than bias, it brings undecidability but also force and potentially charisma into a place wrecked by them. Again, these stern demands for objectivity in research and analysis, and for value neutrality in the classroom, are themselves the result of a postfoundational framing of values. No universal norms or transcendental moral commitments for Weber, no tests or thresholds or tissues of justifications to establish validity. It is *because* they are ungrounded, cannot be secured by or as truth, and are irreconcilable with one another that values are in a permanent war with each other in the political realm. Far from lamenting or seeking to solve the irrationality of that domain, Weber dreams only of tethering it to responsibility and limiting its violence.

Values are political, politics is a field of power and violence, and knowledge materializes only where all of this—power, passion, partisanship, violence—is in abeyance. Weber inscribes this opposition in language itself: "[In the political sphere], the words you use are not the tools of academic analysis, but a way of winning others over to your political point of view. They are not plowshares to loosen the solid soil of contemplative thought, but swords to be used against your opponents: weapons, in short. In a lecture room, it would be an outrage to make use of language in this way." Words of seduction versus words of analysis, words as weapons versus words as plowshares, war, and peace—the differences are polar, not matters of degree. "*Whenever an academic introduces his own value judgment,*" Weber thunders, "*a complete understanding of the facts comes to an end.*" The impartiality, neutrality, adherence to facts, and method are absolute opposites to the investments, demeanor, and effect of "the prophet and the demagogue."

One traffics in cool reason, the other in hot passion; one seeks truth, the other power. One stirs curiosity and contemplation, the other attraction and repulsion. Weber's fierce enunciation of this divide is an eruption of that will to power in knowledge that we knew to be irrepressible.

Yet Weber does not simply eject values from objective knowledge fields. This would leave their power intact, a power that must be devitalized to insulate knowledge from it. Rather, he shifts them from the subject to the object of knowledge. Transposing the register of values from the knower to the knowable gives science dominion over them and reveals their inner logics and external implications as it reveals their foundationlessness. The aim is to neutralize if not neuter their magical powers by analyzing them as norms with programmatic and policy entailments. Their "meaning" is reduced to their relation to other values. As Weber puts it, the obligation of the scholar or teacher is to show that "if you choose this particular standpoint, you will be serving this particular god and will *give offense to every other god.*" This is how "we can compel a person, or at least help him, to render an account of the ultimate meaning of his own actions. . . . And if a teacher succeeds in this respect I would be tempted to say that he is acting in the service of 'ethical' forces, that is to say, of the duty to foster clarity and a sense of responsibility."

If the idea of such value neutrality is widely challenged today, this is not what interests us in Weber's wrestle to protect knowledge *and* value in a nihilistic age. Rather, how does this approach to values, in which they are cast as normative positions with analyzable precepts and logical entailments, transform its object? What does it mean to bracket their charismatic, religious, and other nonrational dimensions, and to lift them from historical contexts that give them specific meaning, as their premises and entailments are analyzed? Weber knows that we attach to values for all sorts of historical, visceral, and experiential, even ineffable reasons. And not only attach: values emanate from cultural and political traditions, of course, but also from desires, ambitions, hopes, delusions, resentments, rancor, revenge—all that Nietzsche depicts as "erecting ideals on earth."

To compress the point, notwithstanding his insistence that "*life is about* the incompatibility of ultimate *possible* attitudes and hence the inability ever to resolve conflicts between them," Weber's demand that the scholar and especially the teacher approach the study of value as purely contingent standpoints with inevitable entailments, oppositions, and exclusions both distorts and devitalizes the practice he identifies with our deepest humanity. It accelerates disenchantment as it converts worldviews into dry logical norms drained of their captivating and motivating forces and of their capacity to alter the meaning of history and the present, hence their own meaning in practice. Weber insists that the academy be this drying shed and that faculty be laborers within it. This is a more profound assault on values than even Nietzsche's demand for their revaluation—the latter leaves intact their seductive powers and weaponry, Weber's mandate aims at disarming both. And in direct contrast with Nietzsche's reembedding of postnihilist value in Eros and will, in expression rather than choice, Weber treats value as if it could or should be based on rational consideration of its abstract entailments, even as he knows this is not how values work. Thus do Weber's knowledge protocols simultaneously abet the emptying of the world of value and constrain the reach of human knowing.

Treating values thus requires Weber to refuse Nietzsche's insistence on the absurdity of accounts from nowhere, his eulogy for "the dangerous old conceptual fiction" of a "pure will-less, timeless knowing subject," with its "eye turned in no particular direction" and its attempt at expunging "the active and interpreting forces." More than rejecting Nietzsche's radical interpretivism and exposé of the will to power at work in all knowing, however, Weber *demands* the asceticism in intellectual life that Nietzsche diagnoses as the illness generative of nihilism. Weber *affirms* the "castration of the intellect," the "no to life," but also the "protective instinct of a degenerating life" that Nietzsche identifies with the ascetic ideal, this "program of starving the body and the desires" as the will to power turns against the life instincts themselves in the scholar. "An ascetic life is a self-contradiction," Nietzsche writes, "here rules a *ressentiment* without equal, that of an insatiable power-will that wants to become master not over something in life but over life itself, over its most profound, powerful and basic conditions; here an attempt is made to employ force to block up the wells of force." Weber knowingly insists on this masochistic diversion of the will to power and salts the wound by underscoring the fleeting quality of scientific achievement. The scholar as spiritless vessel of a meaningless cause requiring self-negation and also draining meaning from the world one analyzes—this is the ascetic practice Nietzsche predicted would culminate in willed nothingness.

More than merely proscribing a regime of spiritual-intellectual starvation, Weber builds a torture chamber for the man with a vocation for science. He is condemned to the frenzied accumulation of facts combined with the destruction of value that is at the heart of Weber's own diagnosis of modernity's slide into darkness. "Like the Calvinist [of the Protestant Ethic] [Weber's] scientific man accumulates" even as "what he amasses has no more lasting value than other things of the world," writes Sheldon Wolin. Thus does Weber repeat in a scholarly register both the morphology of capitalism once its spirit settles into what he calls "mechanical foundations" and the morphology of depression that nihilism induces: agitated but aimless, obsessive without purpose, desire choked but repose unavailable. With eyes wide open about the modern machineries killing human freedom, value, and satisfaction, Weber builds his cage of knowledge and scholarship from their blueprint: means separated from ends, the scientist reduced to a means, the ends receding altogether, a wheel whose turns we never get off.

Unlike his crafting of *Beruf* for politics, Weber makes the true scholar immanent to and replicative of these forces, embodying the frenzied accumulation and overtaking of ends with the means to become a slayer of value and complicit with modern apparatuses of domination. Affirming knowledge as contributing to such power while denying its Enlightenment link to human emancipation, Weber would have been unsurprised by an "information age" producing unrivaled capacities for surveillance and manipulation of subjects, an epoch of capital that subjects everything and everyone to the vicissitudes of finance, and academic knowledge so compartmentalized that most disciplines were useless in apprehending the mounting crises of ecology, humanity, and democracy now upon us. Weber saw the dark ahead, but his path to containing nihilistic destructions of knowledge and Truth drove straight into it. This is the tragic force of his stipulations for knowledge and our inheritance of these stipulations in the social sciences.

EMERGENCY TIMES

Against conventional readings of Weber's lecture as codifying scientific protocols for their own sake, I have emphasized his nearly hyperbolic efforts to protect knowledge against its own late modern effects. At the same time, I have been suggesting that his approach to nihilism's boundary breakdowns, trivialization of fact *and* value, evisceration of depth and integrity, and dethronement of Truth was a kind of pharmakon in both senses of the word—a scapegoating to produce order and a cure drawn from the poison. His performative counter to nihilism's ablative force was to stipulate, separate, narrow, and quarantine. Knowledge gets rationality and secularism, politics gets charisma and its religious spirit;

[BROWN] *Knowledge*

knowledge gets mind, politics gets body and soul; knowledge is drained of passion, judgment, or ardor for a different world, politics runs on their fuel; politics traffics in power, knowledge in truth; knowledge is specialized and removed from the world, politics deals with the whole and the visceral. Intended to restore order and place when nihilistic decadence was destroying both, these divisions let the beast in by another door. As Weber submitted what remained of value to the grinding gears of disenchantment in the knowledge realm, he surrendered its prospects for renewal to the magical force of charismatic domination in the political one. He affirmed empirical study of the present while rejecting knowledge as a platform of critique or for the development of alternative futures. Knowledge as he conceived it was pinned to the powers of the present; only charisma in the political realm charts the new and different. To the extent that neo-Weberianism shaped the modus operandi of social science in the last century, it choked scholarly aspirations to criticize and challenge the powers bringing us to our current pass. Instead, disruptions have been left largely to the acquisitive drives of markets and technology and to charismatic leaders devoid of the characteristics Weber assigned to the genre—restraint, selflessness, responsibility.

These divisions also deprived social science of intellectual mediums through which to fathom modern political subjects constituted by complex desires, frustrations, wounds, reactions, fears, and anxieties, indeed animated by abjection, rejection, subjection, and resentment as much or more than by the reflection on norms or even economic interest. At the same time, these divides abandon an informed, active democracy either as an academic mission or an agent of political change—they leave that citizenry to its cultural-psychic stew. In this, too, Weber limits the relevance of academic endeavor to postnihilist world-making, to reinfusing the struggle over values with intelligence and accountability. His protocols for knowledge meant that the academy would perversely withdraw from the world at the moment it was released from the church.

Opposing fact and value as Weber does also ignores how values acquire meanings and valences through the historically specific rationalities that administer them, other discourses they intersect, and the purposes and projects that transform them as they are actualized. Far from self-governing, the meaning of values in politics varies according to context, interpretation, and tactical deployment. This is why genealogies matter, why norms in the political sphere do not have strict logical entailments as they do in philosophy, why "originalism" on both the right and left is always only another political tactic, and why whining about cooptation of principles always misses the point. Abstractly, liberalism promises to protect human dignity and political equality; in fact, it sacrifices these as it intersects with the powers of class, racial, and gender superordination or is transmogrified by the governing form of rationality we call neoliberalism. Liberalism has no pure operation outside the philosopher's study any more than socialism does. Thus, its porous account of liberty has not been cynically "weaponized" by the Right to wave free-speech banners over Klan rallies, by corporations to dominate electoral democracy with their economic might, or by organized Evangelicals to erode sexual and gender equality. Yes, there are calculated, strategic moves here, but they are not outside liberalism's bounds; rather, they nest comfortably within and draw succor from its neoliberalization, which supplants democratic legislation with traditional morality and markets to order social life. Thus, just as we cannot think well about free speech today in abstraction from the powers of contemporary social media or mobilized social hatred, we cannot think well about liberalism in abstraction from its plutocratic, neoliberal, authoritarian, and other antidemocratic instantiations.

This example reminds us that a postnihilist approach to values, in both knowledge and politics, requires more than reckoning with their lack of foundations or disconnect between their aims and effects and more than their affective claims. Rather, it requires grasping their embeddedness in specific forms of governing reason and technologies through which they are interpreted and deployed. It requires addressing their actualization by meanings and powers both humanly made and beyond our control. If this was part of what Weber sought to capture with his ethic of responsibility in political life, we would do well to incorporate it in political theory as well, something for which his own treatment of values as abstract ideas, ideologies, or policy entailments does not provide guidance.

Weber is surely right that we must teach students about facticity, even if this means teaching them about the constitution and interpretation of facts—their inescapable historical, material, and discursive sources of production. He is right to insist that we are bound to explain why no value system is ever True, but that far from bringing analysis and judgment to an end, this heightens their importance. He is right to insist on self-consciousness and restraint in proffering our own political views, even if this cannot be fulfilled in the way he demanded because—from the study of Kant to evolution, to climate change, to the Constitution— there are only ever readings.

Moreover, however vital it is to open out the silos and methodological lockdowns of the current organizations and protocols of knowledge, equally vital is articulating and protecting the interval between politics and knowledge. Discovery, critique, and reflection are fundamentally different from political action, legislation, and dicta—they beckon different subjects and subjectivities and draw on different languages, temporalities, aims, and ethoi. Thus, the demand that a curriculum comport with any political program must always be countered with explanations of how they destroy one another when conflated. As important as keeping political agendas at a distance, however, scholarly knowledge today needs protection from being bought, valued only for its commercial applications or for job training, and from the destruction by those with antidemocratic ambitions to keep the masses stupid.

Thus, even with the world in an emergency state, where every scholarly hand is needed on deck, we need a version of the moat between knowledge and politics that Weber sought to establish. It is essential to the protection of reflection, imagination, and accountability in knowledge and thinking. It is essential to avoid the error of conflating intellectual concepts with what Weber termed the "density and chaos of reality." It is essential to distinguish the place where values are struggled for and where they are probed and queried. Or as Stuart Hall shaded the matter, it is essential to avoid conflating the domain where we deconstruct meaning, or make it slide and wobble, and the political domain where we arrest that slide to make *our* meaning prevail as hegemonic. Health care is a human right, trees have standing, no person is illegal, women's right to choose, science is real, Black lives matter—such slogans cannot be taken apart in the midst of political battle but must be queried and probed in the classroom. Critiques of racial and gender essentialism, consent, autonomy, choice, human rights and examinations of the unstable meaning of capitalism, the changing nature of corporations and personhood, and the problematic elements of quests for sovereignty and statehood by the stateless—all these may inform political projects but can't be performed in the midst of battle. Nothing is more corrosive to thinking and knowledge than domination by a political program, and nothing is more impotent in politics than the unending reflexivity, critique, and self-correction required for serious intellectual inquiry.

Yet the relations are as important as the corridors of separation, especially for democratic life, which cannot survive without an educated public. Put the other way, neither political nor scholarly life can be democratized alone, and we are currently in a downward spiral of their mutual de-democratization. Indeed, erosion of access and quality in public higher education, and denigration of its value apart from job training, remains one of the most underappreciated strategies of the combined neoliberal and right-wing assault on democracy in the past four decades. At the same time, it is vital to contour research and teaching in more worldly directions than academic specialization and professionalization encourage and more to the public good than private support of research incentivizes.

In this regard, perhaps we have lately been too much absorbed by issues of academic freedom and too little by matters of academic responsibility. The former is not trivial, but the stakes of the latter are huge and bear on our collective future. In the context of the multiple perils that I sketched at the beginning of the first lecture, the most urgent question for scholars is not "what have I the right to say and do inside or outside the classroom" but what curriculums, strategies, and classroom conversations might contribute to holding back the dark and limn new possibilities? How do we interrupt the cultures of reactive local, personal politics in which they have been steeped to incite deliberation about large-scale political, economic, and ecological trajectories? How do we break the siloization and professionalization of knowledge turning *us* away from the world? And how do students, faculty, and administrations alike shed absorption with enhancing personal and institutional capital that prevents that break?

Essential to this work is turning hard toward rather than away from values in the classroom today. Classrooms are where values can be studied and developed as more than opinions, viewpoints, ideologies, family, party, or religious loyalties and more than distractions from the empirical, technical, instrumental, or practical. It is where they can be deepened and dignified as worldviews yet elaborated in the contexts of power that mobilize and transmogrify them. It is where they can be examined genealogically, culturally, economically, and psychically— for example, as complex reaction formations—not only analytically or through the prism of morality and religion. Above all, it is where they can be framed as undecidable by pure reason or transcendental morality yet decisive in responding to the multiple crises of our time. This would constitute a vital counter to a nihilistic age in which values are trivialized and instrumentalized; a political age when they are widely perceived as monopolized by religionists on the right and, by identity, political correctness or moral handwringing on the left; an era of consumer capitalism

[BROWN] *Knowledge*   35

in which they are reduced to branding and celebrity; a technocratic era in which they are buried in platforms and apps or consigned to ethics consultants; and a secular age in which they are personalized and privatized. Recentering the study of values in higher education would also counter the steady pressure on universities, especially public ones, to elevate vocational training and STEM fields above all else. This push, which threatens to eliminate the one remaining venue for informed open reflection on the world and one's place in it, could not come at a worse time in history.

If Weber worried about classroom polemics destroying conditions of objective knowledge transmission, these are hardly the main threat to classroom integrity today. Nor, despite the obsessions of the Right and even the mainstream media, is concern with triggering all that widespread or important, especially outside the tiny universe of elite schools. Rather, the quotidian depressant of intellectual seriousness in classrooms today is anxiety about individual futures manifest as preoccupation with grading rubrics and techniques for meeting requirements with minimal investment. Combined with growing reliance on Google for all knowledge, it is little wonder that student expectations for learning in college are at historic lows and that the question "is college worth it" is routinely answered with data about return-on-investment or the tellingly named "college premium"—the metric for measuring the income enhancement generated by a college degree.

And then there are the crushing effects of the unprecedentedly schismatic consciousness borne by sentient young people today. On the one hand, they have internalized the neoliberalized mandate to precisely calculate and titrate their every educational, social, civic, and personal self-investment, relentlessly tending their human capital value to build their individual prospects. On the other hand, they are alert to the global ecological, political, and economic catastrophes ahead that make the world in which they are tending this value likely to crash out of the universe. No generation has ever stared so directly into its own lack of collective future while managing such intense, complex requirements for building its personal one. More than "cruel optimism," this predicament is too much for many young spirits, leading them to put one entrepreneurial foot in front of the other as if they were not walking through and toward catastrophe. If they dwell mostly on one side of this impossible split, the other part periodically shrieks through, and a great deal of medication may be required to manage the suppression. They are in a mode of preapocalyptic survivalism, as are we all in some ways.

Our task, it seems to me, is to address this condition not by telling students what to think but by acknowledging their predicament and breaking it open with deliberately postnihilist questions: "What are you living for?" "What world do you want to live in?" "How should or could humans order our common arrangements at this juncture in world history?" Again, empirical analysis—how things work—and material analyses—what historical forces brought us to this pass, what powers organize it—are critical in framing and answering such questions. Literary, theoretical, philosophical, artistic, and other modes of depicting and interpreting the world are indispensable as well.

To be clear, this is not an argument to place the question "what is to be done?" at the heart of the college curriculum. Nor is it an argument for "tolerating all viewpoints" in the classroom, a liberal shibboleth that diminishes rather than builds the stature of values. Weber identifies the virtue of replacing tolerance with fearless scrutiny and depersonalization of values in the classroom. Here it is worth remembering that relentlessly personalized justice and ethics—where "I'm offended/wounded/excluded" substitutes for value development and interrogation, and values are imagined very nearly written on the body—mark a nihilistic loss of world. This loss and its expression need to be compassionately received and at the same time exposed, directing students toward study of the larger-order values governing the world and their alternatives. Failing to make this central in college curriculums at this moment is as irresponsible as continuing to mine coal, manufacture plastic, or clear-cut rainforests.

Yet this is not how undergraduate curriculums are designed today. Apart from enormous pressure from every quarter to turn all but elite colleges in increasingly vocational directions, or to serve the interest of present and future donors, it is also the case that continued adherence to putatively norm-free methods in mainstream social science, where values are unwelcome, indeed treated as illegal aliens, actively discourages scholarly discussion of this kind in most social science classes. Positivist approaches focused on content that burrows ever deeper into microanalyses and predictions from the present order of things while eclipsing how novel, strange, and crisis-ridden this present is foreclose deep reflection on who we are, what we might be, and how we might live differently. This is compounded by the reduction of values to norms, norms to opinions, and opinions to personal beliefs or attitudes.

For Weber, values simultaneously bear our individual human depth and are at the heart of collective self-making. They are uniquely threatened by the forces of modernity, diminishing our capacity to craft our lives and their condition; this is the essence of nihilism. Culturing value is all that carries the alternative to rule by unchosen forms of rationality and apparatuses of domination, by pure power-mongers, or by technocrats. Indeed, Weber's insistence on warring godheads as the essence of political life is itself an antinihilist counter to Schmitt's infamous identification of that struggle with the friend-enemy distinction, Lenin's reduction of politics to "who-whom," or Morgenthau's insistence that politics is governed by objective laws with their roots in human nature. However, Weber's appreciation of the inherently political nature of value, and politics as the platform for struggles over value, is also what led him to reject, after the death of God, the neo-Kantian effort to ground value in moral universals, the neo-Marxist effort to embed them in materialism and teleology, the neo-Nietzschean effort to invest culture or great individuals with their future redemption, and what would become the neoliberal surrender of values to markets and moral traditionalism. Yet while rejecting rationalist, theological, historical determinist, or naturalist foundations for values, Weber sought to make them accountable to thought and tether their actualization to responsibility. We have spent these evenings with Weber because he understood that rekindling the value of value amid its nihilistic diminution or destruction entails recommitting to our humanness in a double sense. Values carry our distinctly political capacity to craft the world according to chosen purposes when that capacity seems nearly extinguished by forces now governing and threatening our lives and future. This recommitment also entails an embrace of the purely human construction of values and our complexly human, not only rational, attachment to them. Far from nihilism, as some have suggested, this embrace bears the promise of nihilism's overcoming.

REFERENCES

Adorno, Theodore. *Negative Dialectics*. Translated by E. B. Ashton. 1973; New York: Continuum, 1997.

Burawoy, Michael. "Sociology as a Vocation." *American Sociology Association Journal* 45, no. 4 (2016): 379–93.

Dostoyevsky, Fyodor. *The Brothers Karamazov*. Translated by R. Pevear and L. Volokhonsky. New York: Farrar, Straus and Giroux, 2002.

Douglas, Mary. *Purity and Danger: An Analysis of Concepts of Pollution and Taboo*. New York: Routledge and Kegan Paul, 1966.

Eden, Robert. "Political Leadership and Nihilism: A Study of Weber and Nietzsche." *International Journal for Philosophy of Religion* 18, no. 1 (1985): 96–97.

Hall, Stuart. "Culture and Power." Interview by Peter Osborne and Lynne Segal. *Radical Philosophy* 86 (Nov./Dec. 1997): 24–41.

Heidegger, Martin, and Ernst Junger. *Correspondence*. Translated by T. S. Quinn. 1949–75; Lanham, MD: Routledge, 2016.

Hennis, Wilhelm. "The Pitiless 'Sobriety of Judgment': Max Weber between Carl Menger and Gustav von Schmoller—the Academic Politics of Value Freedom." *History of the Human Sciences* 4, no. 1 (1991): 27–59.

Nehamas, Alexander. *Nietzsche: Life as Literature*. Cambridge, MA: Harvard University Press, 1987.

Nietzsche, Friedrich. *Beyond Good and Evil*. Edited and translated by W. Kaufmann. New York: Random House, 1966.

Nietzsche, Friedrich. *On the Genealogy of Morals*. Edited and translated by W. Kaufmann. New York: Random House, 1967.

Nietzsche, Friedrich. *Writings from the Late Notebooks*. Edited R. Bittner. Translated by K. Sturge, Cambridge: Cambridge University Press, 2003.

Owen, David, and Tracy Strong. Introduction to *Max Weber: The Vocation Lectures*. Indianapolis: Hackett, 2004.

Pippin, Robert. Review of *The Affirmation of Life: Nietzsche on Overcoming Nihilism*, by Bernard Reginster. *Philosophy and Phenomenological Research* 77, no. 1 (July 2008): 281–91.

Pippin, Robert. *Nietzsche, Psychology and First Philosophy*. Chicago: University of Chicago Press, 2011.

Rosen, Stanley. *Nihilism: A Philosophical Essay*. South Bend, IN: St. Augustine's, 1999.

Roth, Guenther, and Wolfgang Schluchter. *Max Weber's Vision of History*. Berkeley: University of California Press, 1976.

Satkunanandan, Shalini. "Max Weber and the Ethos of Politics beyond Calculation." *APSR* 108, no. 1 (February 2014): 169–81.

Schluchter, Wolfgang. *Paradoxes of Modernity: Culture and Conduct in the Theory of Max Weber*. Translated by N. Solomon. Stanford, CA: Stanford University Press, 1996.

Stepenberg, Maia. *Against Nihilism: Nietzsche Meets Dostoyevsky*. London: Black Rose Books, 2019.

Vázquez-Arroyo, Antonio. *Political Responsibility: Responding to Predicaments of Power*. New York: Columbia University Press, 2018.

Warren, Mark. "Max Weber's Liberalism for a Nietzschean World." *APSR* 82, no. 1 (March 1988): 31–50.

Weber, Max. *Economy and Society*. Edited by G. Roth and C. Wittich. Berkeley: University of California Press, 1978.

Weber, Max. *Methodology of Social Sciences*. Translated and edited by E. Shils and H. Finch. New York: Routledge, 2011.

Weber, Max. *The Protestant Ethic and the Spirit of Capitalism*. Translated by T. Parsons. New York: Dover, 2003.

Weber, Max. "Religious Rejections of the World and Their Directions." In *From Max Weber: Essays in Sociology*, edited by H. H. Gerth and C. Wright Mills, 323–57. New York: Oxford University Press, 1946.

Weber, Max. *The Vocation Lectures*. Edited and introduced by D. Owen and T. Strong. Translated by R. Livingstone. Indianapolis: Hackett, 2004.

Wolin, Sheldon. "Max Weber: Legitimation, Method, and the Politics of Theory." *Political Theory* 9, no. 3 (August 1981): 401–24.

"To Snatch Something from Death":
Value, Justice, and Humankind's
Common Cultural Heritage

CÉCILE FABRE

The Tanner Lectures on Human Values

Delivered at

Stanford University
May 10–12, 2022

CÉCILE FABRE is a political philosopher and a senior research fellow at All Souls College, Oxford. She is also a professor of political philosophy at the University of Oxford, affiliated with the Faculty of Philosophy, the Department of Politics and International Relations, and Nuffield College, Oxford. She is a fellow of the British Academy. Her research interests are in theories of distributive justice, the philosophy of democracy, just war theory, the ethics of foreign policy with a particular focus on the ethics of economic statecraft, and the ethics of espionage. Her many publications include *Spying through a Glass Darkly: The Ethics of Espionage and Counter-Intelligence*; *Economic Statecraft: Human Rights, Sanctions and Conditionality*; *Cosmopolitan Peace*; *Cosmopolitan War*; *Justice in a Changing World*; and *Whose Body Is It Anyway?*

LECTURE I.
THE VALUE OF HUMANKIND'S CULTURAL HERITAGE

INTRODUCTION

When Notre-Dame Cathedral was engulfed by fire on April 15, 2019, the world (it seemed) watched in horror. On Twitter, Facebook, in newspapers and on TV cables ranging as far afield from Paris as South Africa, China and Chile, people expressed their sorrow at the partial destruction of the church, particularly the collapse of the spire, and anguish at what very nearly happened—the complete destruction of a jewel of Gothic architecture whose value somehow transcends time and space.

The fire that almost destroyed Notre-Dame was an accident. As we know all too well, however, the damage sustained by cultural and natural landmarks is more often than not anthropogenic. Most obviously, it arises as a part or outcome of military conflicts. To give some examples from a long and deplorable litany, in the autumn of 1925, following days of intense aerial bombing, French military forces entered Damascus to crush an incipient revolt against France's mandate. Not content to slaughter civilians, they reduced parts of the city to rubble, at a loss of countless historic buildings, mosques and bazaars. In March 2001, the Taliban destroyed the monumental sixth-century statues of Buddha in the Bamiyan Valley in Afghanistan on the grounds that they were idols and thus condemned by the Taliban's interpretation of Islam. When President Trump threatened to bomb Iran's cultural sites in the closing days of 2019, in defiance of the laws of war, he elicited outrage not just on behalf of Iranians but on behalf of the world at large: the ancient city of Persepolis, for example, is widely regarded as one of the world's most significant archaeological sites. As I am writing this, the conflict between Ukraine and Russia is raging, and there is evidence that Russian troops are targeting Ukrainian cultural sites. On March 3, 2022, the United Nations Educational, Scientific and Cultural Organization (UNESCO) issued a statement unequivocally condemning the Russian regime—first and foremost for its attempt to erase traces of a distinctive Ukrainian identity but also for risking the destruction of World Heritage Sites in L'viv and Kyiv. In the autumn of 2023, following the resumption of war between Israel and Palestine, Blue Shield International—created by the International Council on Archives, the International Council of Museums, the International Federation of Library Associations and Institutions, and the International Council on Monuments and Sites with the aim of protecting endangered cultural

[43]

heritage—issued a statement expressing alarm at reports of serious damage to heritage sites in the area, particularly in Gaza itself. In November of that year, UNESCO adopted a resolution expressing similar concern.[1]

The destruction does not stop there: entire libraries, museums and archival repositories have been burned, bombed and dispersed to religious and political ends. Landscapes—be they 'natural', rural or urban—are destroyed by land mines and troop movements. In many of those cases too, it is hard not to think that the loss suffered by the communities and peoples against which those actions were committed is, in some important sense to be elucidated in those essays, our loss too.

Our destructiveness is not confined to war. We relentlessly exploit the earth. We farm the land, destroy forests, throw the detritus of our industrial and domestic activities into its rivers and oceans, erode coastlines, damage buildings and kill entire species. From the melting of the Greenland ice sheet to the depletion of the Amazonian forest, from the cascading effects of climate change to our seeming inability to do much about it, we may well have reached a tipping point such that whatever we do now will not reverse the impact of our activities on our planet. Not only does this threaten the quality of human life in its most basic dimensions; it threatens our successors' enjoyment of what we have so far taken for granted.

In 1959, faced with this predicament, the governments of Egypt and Sudan asked UNESCO for help. As a result of the construction of the Aswan High Dam, a number of monuments in the Valley of Nubia, some of them three thousand years old, were at risk of destruction from the rising waters of Lake Nasser. In March 1960, UNESCO and its member states launched an international campaign to salvage the monuments. To preserve humankind's common heritage, the then-French culture minister and intellectual André Malraux said in an often-quoted speech, is to 'snatch something from death'.[2]

The campaign was a remarkable technological achievement. It lasted twenty years and heralded the beginning of the World Heritage movement. In 1972, UNESCO's General Assembly adopted the Convention Concerning the Protection of World Cultural and Natural Heritage. Yet admirable as the campaign was in those respects, in others, it proved deeply controversial. In fact, so is the institution of the World Heritage. Claims of universalism, it was then and is still argued now, all too often mask Western-centric value judgements and power relations which are a legacy of colonial expansion and its concomitant acts of cultural appropriation. In a depressingly apt illustration of universalists' egregious moral and epistemic failings, Malraux himself was convicted by the French authorities in 1923 for having stolen bas-reliefs from the Cambodian temple of Banteay Srei. In his defence, he argued (blatantly falsely, as Cambodia was subject to France's territorial jurisdiction at the time) that the temple and its riches were *terra nullius*, for all and any to plunder for the sake of collectors and museums worldwide.[3]

I take those criticisms seriously. Nevertheless, my aim in these essays is to offer a philosophical account of the view that some goods are universally valuable and are part of humankind's common heritage, and that we have stringent moral duties in respect of that heritage. I hope to show that we can embrace that view without committing ourselves to the egregiously wrongful acts which have been committed in its name: I use Malraux's 1960 speech as my main title to indict, not to vindicate, the Malraux of 1923.

In this first essay, I argue that there are cultural goods which are universally valuable and are part of humankind's common cultural heritage. In the second essay, I argue that the protection of our heritage not only is a moral imperative: more strongly put, it is a duty of justice.

I begin in 'A Doomed and Flawed Ideal?' with a brief summary of the main criticisms which have been levelled at UNESCO. In 'The Value of Heritage', I elucidate what it means to say that something has heritage value. In 'Pluralism, Humanity and Heritage', I argue that some of the landmarks, monuments, and tangible objects which we have inherited from our predecessors have universal value and constitute humankind's common heritage. As we shall see throughout, to say that something is valuable is to imply that we have a range of practical reasons in relation to it; typically, those reasons are not construed as moral reasons, let alone moral duties. To prepare the grounds for my argument, in the second essay, that we are under duties of justice in respect of humankind's common heritage, I end this essay, in 'From Reasons to Duties', with a discussion of important differences between reasons, moral reasons and duties.

Before I begin, one final and important point: there is much work to do on the political and moral philosophy of cultural heritage. I am painfully aware of the fact that I have painted my philosophical defence of our common heritage in broader brushstrokes than some readers might wish for. Moreover, I have little to say about the best way to institutionalize the principles of justice I defend here. It is entirely possible that, in the light of the difficulties which beset UNESCO, which after all is the most sustained attempt to protect humankind's heritage, we should, at best, dismantle it; at worst, abandon any hope we may have once entertained for a just world in that respect too. Indeed, at the time of writing this, the fact that UNESCO has still not suspended Russia from its institutions (unlike, for example, FIFA, which expelled it from the 2022 Football World Cup) is cause for despair. Still, in case not all hope is lost, it pays to begin to investigate its philosophical foundations.

A DOOMED AND FLAWED IDEAL?

The notion of humankind's heritage immediately brings to one's mind UNESCO and its World Heritage List on which it inscribes, every year, natural landmarks, sites and buildings which the World Heritage Committee deems to have 'outstanding universal value'. The work of the committee is framed by the 1972 World Heritage Convention and its operational principles.[4]

There are currently (as of January 2024) 1,199 sites on the List. Of those, close to half are located in Europe and North America, while under 10 percent are located in Africa. The overwhelming majority of the sites are cultural (934), although 39 sites are listed as mixed cultural-natural. All but 39 sites are located on the territory of one state. Transboundary sites include the Architectural Works of Le Corbusier (across seven countries, spanning Europe, Latin America and Asia); the W-Arly-Pendjari Complex in Benin, Burkina Faso and Niger; the Stećci Medieval Tombstone Graveyards in Bosnia and Herzegovina, Croatia, Montenegro and Serbia; and the Silk Road in China, Kazakhstan and Kyrgyzstan.

The List is a visual, cultural and educational feat. It is also deeply controversial. As many scholars of heritage argue, it relies on and gives expression to a particular conception of heritage—what Laurajane Smith calls the Authorized Heritage Discourse—which, far from being universal, is now widely thought to be deeply Eurocentric, elitist, statist and 'Pollyannaish'.[5]

It is deemed Eurocentric in four ways. First, sites located in Europe and sites located outside Europe but of demonstrably colonial and thus European origin or inspiration dominate the List. Second, the preponderance of cultural sites and, within that list, of monumental sites, speaks of a distinctly Europeanisation of value. Non-European conceptions of value such as the view articulated by some Aboriginal communities that lived-in landscapes have value—or the view, at the heart of much Chinese cultural history, that monuments matter less than landscapes, paintings and words—are correspondingly marginalized. In a related vein, claims that a particular geographical area is valuable for its wilderness often ride roughshod over the historical fact that it was cultivated and/or used by Non-White, Native populations, long before first contact with European White settlers.[6] Third, the sharp distinction between the cultural and the natural which the Authorized Heritage Discourse has long relied on harks back to familiar Western dichotomous hierarchies between the mind and the body. Fourth, the obligation to preserve humankind's heritage is couched in (again) a distinctly European conception of authenticity as 'preserving as we found it'.

The charge of elitism comes in two guises. On the one hand, the cultural sites it has privileged over time tend to symbolize the culture of rulers and propertied groups to the detriment of that of the ruled. Relatedly, the List's cultural sites tend to be the product of a literate and written culture, which is routinely deemed superior to vernacular and oral modes of communication and transmission.[7] On the other hand, the process by which a site gets onto the List is dominated by experts— archaeologists, historians, conservationists, scientists and civil servants— who are often at best inattentive to, at worst ignorant of, the meaning which the site has for local populations.

The charge of statism flows from those criticisms. Unsurprisingly, the sites which have made it on to the List have more often than not been nominated not so much for their supposed universal value but rather for their importance to the host state's national culture, at the expense of minorities within the nation such as Aborigines in Australia and New Zealand and Native Americans in the United States. Furthermore, states use what they regard as *their* heritage as bargaining chips in the never-ending game of international realpolitik, with sometimes devastating consequences for the sites which they ought to protect and the human beings whose livelihood often depends on those sites.

Moreover, states are tasked with preserving those sites: if a state fails to live up to its commitments, there is very little that UNESCO can do other than place a site on the List of Endangered Heritage, send teams of inspectors (with the state party's consent), withhold funding or take the radical step of delisting a site. And when it does act, it does so with staggering partiality, not to say hypocrisy. Thus, in marked contrast with its Russia-targeted condemnatory rhetoric about the destruction of Ukraine's universally valuable heritage, UNESCO has consistently desisted from explicitly condemning Saudi Arabia and its allies, which have been fighting an attritional war against the Houthi movement in

Yemen since 2014 for the destruction of that country's similarly valuable heritage. This is not particularly surprising: one need not be a conspiracy theorist to note that the United States, the UK and France are backing the Saudi-led coalition in its fight against ISIS in Yemen. In fact, not only has UNESCO failed to rebuke Saudi Arabia and its allies: since 2015, it has listed a number of its landmarks on the World Heritage List.[8]

Finally, the Authorized Heritage Discourse is Pollyannaish. Heritage is almost always construed as something to be proud of. The overwhelming majority of the landmarks on the World Heritage List are described as outstandingly beautiful or as the illustration of human creativity. When a landmark is listed for its negative valence, for example, when it is a commemorative site of atrocities, the description always contains positive elements. Thus, Robben Island, where the South Apartheid regime imprisoned its opponents and where Nelson Mandela spent twenty-seven years in captivity, is described by the World Heritage as a witness to 'the triumph of democracy and freedom over oppression and racism.' The description of Auschwitz-Birkenau stresses the fact that the complex 'is also a monument to the strength of the human spirit which in appalling conditions of adversity resisted the efforts of the German Nazi regime to suppress freedom and free thought and to wipe out whole races.' The description of the Island of Gorée, which served as Africa's largest slave-trading centre from the fifteenth to the nineteenth centuries, states that the island now serves as 'a space for exchange and dialogue between cultures through the confrontation of ideals of reconciliation and forgiveness.'[9]

The World Heritage Committee and those who advise it have attempted to respond to some of those criticisms. The 2005 Convention on the Protection and Promotion of the Diversity of Cultural Expression aims to correct the Eurocentric and elitist biases of the 1972 Convention. Sites of quotidian yet vitally important practices are making their appearance on the List. For example, the Ancient Ferrous Metallurgic Sites of Burkina Faso, which attest to early iron production in Africa, were listed in July 2019. Furthermore, scholars and practitioners of heritage are increasingly calling for states and UNESCO to pay greater attention to negative or 'dissonant' heritage. In that vein, UNESCO launched a project on the Slave Route Project in 1994, with the aim of fostering research on and promoting the remembrance of what is now widely regarded as a crime against humanity.

Those attempts have not been met with uncritical acclaim. Too little, too late, it is sometimes said: it is still the case (the criticism goes) that the official discourse values as universal that which, on the List, is in fact particularistic, and at the same time fails to value as universal, for prejudiced reasons, much of what is not on the List.[10]

My aim is not to provide a verdictive assessment of UNESCO's successes and failures.[11] Rather, I seek to provide a philosophical account of the universal value of some of our heritage goods which does not fall foul of those criticisms—or at least, which is less vulnerable to them than their institutional expression, in the form of the Authorized Heritage Discourse, has been. With that in mind, I do not seek to defend the List as it stands. It may well be that our common heritage in fact has far fewer elements than is often supposed. Conversely, it may also be that it ought to have cultural goods which have not so far been regarded as candidates for inclusion.

In what follows, I restrict my inquiry to the tangible bases of our cultural heritage, to the exclusion of both purely environmental goods and cultural practices. On the first count, I do not consider what heritage value if any we should confer on and which duties if any we have in respect of Lake Baikal as the oldest and deepest lake in the world, but I do consider which heritage value if any we should confer on and which duties we have in respect of, for example, the Ancient Tea Plantations of Jingmai Mountain in China. On the second count, I do not consider which duties if any we have in respect of, for example, the practice of music playing, but I do consider whether there is a duty to help preserve outstanding exemplars of musical instruments, recordings or scores.

To be clear, I do not deny that environmental goods and cultural practices are part of our heritage. But they raise distinct issues which I lack the space to tackle here properly—hence my focus on tangible cultural heritage. However, I construe that heritage relatively broadly so as to include literary works, artworks, artefacts, buildings and archives; those parts of our natural environment, or landscapes, which are the product of and sustain (or have sustained) cultural practices; and human fossils.

THE VALUE OF HERITAGE

Something is part of our heritage only if (roughly put) it has come to us from our past and we are somehow connected to it. On constructivist accounts of heritage, something counts as part of our heritage only if, in addition, we recognize it as such. On realist accounts, heritage is what we have inherited from our predecessors, irrespective of whether we recognize this to be the case. In neither case does heritage need to be valuable or to be valued by those whose heritage it is. On constructivist accounts, we can accept something as part of our past and yet deny that it is valuable; on realist accounts, our value judgements in respect of that heritage are irrelevant to its having been handed down to us by our predecessors.

Realist accounts are more plausible. They render intelligible claims that a community is failing to see as its heritage that which in fact is part of it. They make sense of the thought that some goods are part of our heritage even if we have not discovered them yet (a point that is particularly relevant with respect to underground and underwater sites). They also accommodate the intuitively plausible claim that a decision to recognize or reject something as part of our heritage is subject to independent moral evaluation. Constructive accounts struggle on those three fronts.[12]

An account of the value of humankind's heritage must show why its constitutive elements, or heritage goods, are valuable *as* heritage goods, as distinct from cultural goods *simpliciter*. It must also articulate what it is about those goods which licenses us to say that they are part of that heritage, as distinct from, or in addition to, being part of a local or national heritage.

In these essays, I rely on the following account of value. Something is *valuable* insofar as it has certain properties which ground reasons to experience and engage in a range of fitting pro-attitudes in relation to it. To value it just is to experience and engage in those pro-attitudes. Something is valuable, then, insofar as there are good reasons to value it. By parity of reasoning, something is *disvaluable* insofar as it has certain properties which ground good reasons to experience and engage in a range of fitting anti-attitudes towards it—in other words, to disvalue it.[13]

What gives value to a heritage good (henceforth, H) depends on its properties and on whether those properties give us reasons to value it. H's temporal properties, such as location in time and duration, are necessary conditions for H to be valued *qua* heritage good. However, they are not enough on their own to confer value on it. The fact that a piece of parchment is 250 years old does not in itself make it valuable. But if it exemplifies a technique for creating parchment which was first developed 250 years ago and if it is the only known exemplar of its kind, the combination of all those properties does make it valuable as a piece of heritage.[14]

As this example shows, we need an account of which properties combine with temporal properties so as to confer *heritage value* on a particular good. H's value typically supervenes one or several of those properties such as (nonexhaustively) beauty, excellence, integrity, uniqueness, originality, authenticity, genuineness, contributing to something else that is itself of value and semiotic value. Some of those properties, such as beauty and integrity, are internal to H—in which case we shall say that H has intrinsic value; others, such as uniqueness, contributing or symbolizing, are external to it—in which case H has extrinsic value. Interestingly, an object's properties can but need not be essential to that object's value. Thus, while a beautiful building would not be valuable *qua* beautiful building were it not for the fact that it is beautiful, its beauty in part supervenes contingent properties such as colour, architectural design, and so on.

Cultural goods can have disvalue. Recall that something is disvaluable insofar as (some of) its properties give us reasons to experience and engage in fitting anti-attitudes toward it. In the context at hand, H can have *dis*value by dint of the opposite of the value-conferring properties we have examined so far: ugliness, in opposition to beauty; lack of physical integrity, in opposition to physical deterioration; being a copy, in opposition to being an original; bringing about a bad state of affairs, blocking the emergence of a good state of affairs or failing to prevent the occurrence of a bad one—in opposition to bringing about a good state of affairs and blocking the emergence of a bad state of affairs.

Value and disvalue can interact in complex and interesting ways. Consider a place of atrocities—say the Central Slave and Ivory Trade Route, which is on the World Heritage's Tentative List. It symbolizes and was part of the causal nexus for one of the worst moral mistakes human beings have ever made and can make—the abject and wilful failure to value others as ends in themselves. It represents and contributed to something of egregious disvalue. At the same time, and *precisely* for that reason, there is a sense in which it has heritage value—as a reminder of the worst of what human beings are capable of. Similarly, a site which is now a ruin and thus no longer has the property of architectural integrity might nevertheless be beautiful and thus have aesthetic value, *precisely* for that reason. It might also acquire symbolic value, again because it is a ruin. The Genbaku Dome at Hiroshima, which is the only structure to have survived the 1945 blast and which has been on the World Heritage List since 1996, illustrates the point well.[15]

PLURALISM, HUMANITY AND HERITAGE

The Universal Value of Humankind's Heritage

At the outset of 'The Value of Heritage', I said that an account of the value of humankind's heritage must explain, first, what confers heritage value on its constitutive elements and, second, what it is about it that makes it *humankind's* heritage.

52   *The Tanner Lectures on Human Values*

Intuitively, it is a necessary condition for a heritage good to belong to humankind's heritage that it should be universally valuable. Yet individuals deem things to be valuable from standpoints which often are very particular to them, such as familial, cultural, social and economic background. What makes Notre-Dame valuable to me are the facts that I was baptized and raised in the Roman Catholic Church, that I am a Parisian by birth and kinship and that I am French. Those facts partly emerge from and continue to be shaped by a range of social practices: the fact that Notre-Dame has been regarded by generations of French people as a part of France's cultural heritage provides me with yet another reason to value it as a *heritage* good. None of those reasons in respect of Notre-Dame apply to, for example, a Buddhist. Conversely, what makes the Bamiyan statues valuable to her does not apply to me. The value judgements which heritage goods typically elicit are so complex, diverse and seemingly particular to valuers as to defy calls for universality.

We might think at first that cultural cosmopolitanism offers us a route between universality and particularism. On the most influential accounts to date, the cultural cosmopolitan denies that, in Jeremy Waldron's words, 'the social world divides up neatly into different cultures—one to every community' and that 'what everyone needs is just one of these entities—a single, coherent culture—to give shape and meaning to his life'.[16] More positively, as Samuel Scheffler puts it, cultural cosmopolitanism 'emphasises the fluidity of individual identity, people's remarkable capacity to forge new identities using material from diverse cultural sources, and to flourish while so doing'.[17] The cultural cosmopolitan need not deny that individuals have a wide range of reasons for valuing heritage goods. What she denies is that those reasons are necessarily shaped by valuers' culture of birth and upbringing.

Someone who takes herself to have reasons to value Notre-Dame Cathedral, the rice fields of China and Japanese ink painting even though she is not French, Chinese or Japanese, has lived in neither of those countries and does not intend to do so is a cultural cosmopolitan. Yet the fact that she takes herself to have reasons to value cultural goods which are not particular to the culture in which she was born and grew up does not tell us why she has reasons to value those goods *as part and parcel of* humankind's common cultural heritage.

What we need, then, is an account of universal value. A standard move, in axiology and heritage studies, consists in drawing a distinction between two different conceptions of universality. On the one hand, to say that a heritage good has universal value is to say that we all have reasons to value it from different socially constructed, practice-dependent standpoints. On the other hand, it is to say that we all have reasons to value it merely by dint of our humanity. As Erich Hatala Matthes puts it, the first conception is pluralist, while the latter is monistic.[18]

The pluralist view relies on too thin a conception of universality for our purposes here. All that it requires, for a good to be universally valuable, is that all of us should have reasons to value it from our particularistic standpoints: some of us may have reasons to value a landmark for the place—good or bad—which it occupies in the history of our country, while others, who are not our compatriots, may have reasons to value it for the fact that it is one of its kind or a landmark of outstanding beauty whose aesthetics somehow 'resonates' with us. So long as we can all agree that this landmark is valuable, we can say that it is valuable universally. However, even if the pluralist view offers a plausible conception of universal value, it does not account for our value judgements about humankind's common heritage *qua* such heritage. For humankind's *common* heritage is not just the set of those heritage goods which we all have reasons separately to value: it is *our* heritage rather than *mine and yours*; it is something which we *together*, and not merely *each of us*, have reasons to value. In order for it to count as ours, thus, it seems that we must have additional reasons to value it—above and beyond our particularistic reasons. What, though, are those reasons?

In separate works, Anthony Appiah, Sheyla Benhabib and Michael Walzer argue that we all have an impersonal reason, irrespective of our particularistic standpoints, to value one another as autonomous and creative beings. To value fellow human beings as autonomous and creative beings is to recognize as valuable (within limits) the practice-dependent paths which they have shaped for themselves. Those value judgements are more robust and grounded for the fact that we are willing and able to engage in a form of intercultural dialogue, thanks to which we may come to understand why our fellow human beings value the particular things that they do. I may not at first see why a given building is seen as valuable by members of another culture. But through a process of dialogical and reciprocal justification, I may come in time to understand better that value judgement and those who make it, even if my own aesthetic sensibilities, my upbringing and the history of my country are such that I will never myself deem that building valuable for those particularistic reasons.[19]

On the pluralist conception, then, a good is universally valuable in a way that justifies its inclusion in humankind's common cultural heritage if all of us have reasons to value it from our particularistic standpoints *and* insofar as that very fact itself is a reason to value it, impersonally, as the culturally and socially mediated instantiation of our fellow human beings' different such standpoints. It is in that sense that we together, and not just each independently of one another, have reasons to value it. From now on, this is what I shall have in mind when I speak of the pluralist conception of universality.

Compare the pluralist conception with the monistic or mere-humanity view of universality as it is standardly framed. On the mere-humanity view, a good is universally valuable just if all human beings have a reason to value it merely by dint of the fact that they are human beings. So stated, note, the view does not differ from the claim that there is an impersonal reason to value what our fellow human beings have reason to value from their own particularistic standpoints, for that impersonal reason is one which we all have, merely by dint of the fact that we are human beings. If it is to be distinguished from the pluralist view, the mere-humanity view must be recast as follows: a good is universally valuable just if all human beings have a nonmediated reason to value it merely by dint of being human.

On its own, however, this claim does not tell us which universal goods are universally valuable such that they belong to *our* heritage. Proponents of the mere-humanity view typically restrict their account of humankind's cultural heritage to prehistoric sites, objects and skeletons which tell us something about the evolution of the planet or about our common predecessors' life and thus our shared past, long before humans 'branched out' into a multitude of cultures. As David Lowenthal observes, being the first or the most ancient in existence is deemed to confer value on an object, practice or site precisely because it is close 'to the dawn of time, to the earliest beginnings', and because contemplating it brings *us* closer to those earliest beginnings. On this view, the Maros-Pangkep Caves in Indonesia, which are on the World Heritage's Tentative List and whose extraordinarily vivid renditions of our predecessors' lives in the Palaeolithic era are the oldest paintings on record, are in; anything that does not exhibit the same properties is out.[20]

The rationale for the small list is that there are things about who we are and what we do as human beings—aspects of our humanity—which have universal value. It provides building blocks for a longer list, along the following lines.

First, heritage goods whose value supervenes on the fact that they symbolize, represent and/or contributed to major events and practices in *global* human history writ large are apt candidates for inclusion. By global history, I mean events which have affected more or less all of us as well as events in which most of our predecessors, via our political communities, have jointly participated. We thus ought to include sites of mass, cross- and transcontinental population displacements, such as the slave trade route and trade routes like the Silk Road, pilgrim routes and transatlantic migration routes from Europe to the Americas. We also ought to include landmarks and sites whose value supervenes on the fact that they represent, symbolize and instantiate cross- and transcontinental cultures. The major sites of all religions are part of humankind's heritage, as are the cultural landscapes whose significance reaches beyond their borders, such as (*inter alia*) the wine-growing areas of Europe, the rice terraces of China, the coffee plantations of Columbia, the tea plantations of the Jingmai Mountain in China and the Darjeeling region in India.[21] Likewise, with cultural artefacts of global significance, such as (nonexhaustively) the tangible bases of Indian classical music, the collective works of Shakespeare, the Bible, the Koran, the works of Confucius and Homer and the *Mahābhārata*. We also ought to include sites and landmarks of global political significance, such as the major battlefields of both World Wars, as well as objects and documentary sources—or archives—which attest to historical events of that kind, along the lines of UNESCO's Memory of the World Programme.

Second, landmarks and sites which attest to what we have shown ourselves capable of doing, as human beings, *to and for* another, as human beings, also belong to our common heritage. It is a serious objection to the austere conception of the mere-humanity view that it does not make space for the claim that heritage goods whose value supervenes on the fact that they symbolize, signal, represent and contribute to crimes *against humanity* have universal value. Yet if one accepts that there are such crimes, one can accept that those goods have such value. Paradigmatic examples of crimes against humanity are acts of genocide as well as enslavement, torture and rape insofar as they are part of a systematic policy. In the language of the preamble to the Universal Declaration of Human Rights, they are 'barbarous acts which have outraged the conscience of [humankind]'. At worst, their perpetrators regard their victims' humanity *as a reason to* kill, murder, destroy and enslave. At the fractionally less bad, they manifest utter disregard for their victims' humanity, as exemplified in the wanton discounting of the lives of millions of soldiers on the battlefields of both World War I and World War II, the systematic targeting of civilian populations culminating in the nuclear obliteration of Hiroshima and Nagasaki in 1945, the labour camps of Stalin's empire, the Killing Fields of Cambodia and Apartheid in South Africa.

Judgements of those crimes as crimes against humanity are issued at the bar of one's humanity; the sites where such crimes took place have universal value and ought to be regarded as part of humankind's heritage, as well as part of their victims' specific heritage. One can easily see why Auschwitz-Birkenau, the Atomic Bomb Dome in Hiroshima's Peace Memorial and Robben Island were added to the World Heritage List and why work has begun to list sites of the Rwandan Genocide and the Central Slave and Ivory Trade Route. One can also see why Senegal was successful in its bid to inscribe the Island of Gorée on the List.

Third, if heritage goods whose value supervenes on the fact that they symbolize, represent or have contributed to the worst of what human beings can do to one another are parts of humankind's common heritage, so are heritage goods whose value supervenes on the fact that they symbolize, represent or have contributed to the best that they can do *for* one another. To the extent that sites of atrocities are also sites which witnessed exceptional courage, resilience and generosity, they can aptly be valued as part of humankind's heritage on this ground too, so long as one does not occlude the main reason why they are part of that heritage in the first instance. By that token, sites, objects and artefacts, where or thanks to which lives have been purposefully saved, are part of that heritage. Think, for example, of the buildings where antibiotics were first invented or of the earliest known example of sanitation systems, at Moenjodaro in the Indus Valley.

Fourth, humankind's common heritage includes goods whose value in part supervenes on the fact that they are the products of, represent or symbolize humankind's achievements *tout court*, be they artistic (writ large), technological, industrial, sporting or agricultural. Although those goods are shaped by the distinct social and cultural practices to which they owe their existence, we have reasons to value them impersonally, irrespective of those social and cultural practices.

Fifth, there are goods whose value in part supervenes on the fact that they are the products of, contribute to, represent or symbolize humankind's failures and achievements in relation to other species—at least insofar as those failures and achievements rest on a particular conception of

[FABRE] *The Value of Humankind's Cultural Heritage* 57

what it is to be human, be it in contrast to or common with those species. The indiscriminate, multimillennia slaughter of animals, for example, has its roots in humans' objectification of the latter and, more fundamentally, in their construal of their superior moral status, as human beings, compared to that of nonhumans. Conversely, the growing acknowledgment, on our part, that we have stringent obligations to nonhumans flows from a deeper acknowledgment of what unites us to, rather than separates us from, nonhumans.[22]

One final point. The claim that some heritage goods are universally valuable on the mere-humanity view is compatible with the thought that different individuals and groups have participated in those events and practices in different ways. This in turn is likely to shape their attitudes towards the tangible bases and remnants of global history in different ways. Put in general terms, the mere-humanity and pluralist views can and often will converge on the same heritage goods.

In summary, there is considerably more to our common cultural heritage than sites which tell us something about our prehistoric shared origin. It is, in fact, an extraordinarily rich heritage, which we all have reasons to value.

The Problem of Proliferation

My account of the value of humankind's heritage seems vulnerable to the charge that it includes too many of such goods.[23] Consider sites of suffering. Granted, the critic might concede that the Hiroshima Dome's universal value in part supervenes on its being and representing the first place on which the atomic bomb was dropped, thereby ushering in the age of the potential wholesale annihilation by human beings of all human civilization. For all those reasons, it is conceivably part of humankind's heritage and valuable as such (as well as from the particularistic standpoints of American and Japanese citizens). But surely, we should not include in our common heritage all the battlefields of World War I, all the battlefields of World War II, all the sites where civilians were deliberately killed and all the sites where they are discriminated against. The objection is not unique to sites and landmarks of suffering: it also arises with sites of outstanding beauty or sites of human excellence. In the critic's eye, the accumulation of examples which I have given throughout proves the anti-universalist point.

In response, some readers might simply deny that proliferation is a problem. On the contrary, they might say, there simply *are* many heritage goods of universal value. Rather than despair at our inability to give them the care and attention they warrant, we should regard their sheer number as an opportunity to engage with the richness of our cultural world.[24]

Perhaps. At the same time, as seen in 'The Value of Heritage', heritage goods are valuable by dint of more than one property. Other things equal, the greater the number of properties on which the value of H supervenes, the greater the value of H. An intact Gutenberg Bible is all the more valuable for being intact *and* for being one of a small set. With that in mind, I am inclined to accept the World Heritage's requirement that candidates for inclusion should have more than one value-making property—or in its language, meet more than one criterion.[25] For example, criterion (vi) stipulates that a heritage good must be 'directly or tangibly associated with events or living traditions, with ideas, or with beliefs, with artistic and literary works of outstanding universal significance.' However, 'the Committee considers that this criterion should preferably be used in conjunction with other criteria.' Of the other nine criteria, those which refer to human-made sites or landmarks (including cultural landscapes) are complex, containing at least two, sometimes three, properties. For example, criterion (iii) stipulates that a heritage good must 'bear a unique or at least exceptional testimony to a cultural tradition or to a civilization which is living or which has disappeared'; according to criterion (iv), it must 'be an outstanding example of a type of building, architectural or technological ensemble or landscape which illustrates (a) significant stage(s) in human history'. Uniqueness and outstandingness are not enough: the good must have testimonial and/or representational value. Requiring that a heritage good be valuable by dint of at least two properties goes some way toward meeting the proliferation objection. Only 'some way', though: we still need to ascertain how to weigh those properties up against each other. Suppose that H_1 is both older and more beautiful than H_2, while H_2 has greater historical significance than H_1 and is the only one of its kind. Should they both be included? If not, why not?[26]

I do not (I confess) have well-developed answers to those enormously complex questions. In any event, I suspect that worries about proliferation do not so much target the aptness of our value judgements about common heritage as the possibly excessive moral demands which those judgements entail and the difficult decisions which we might have to make when deciding which parts of our heritage to protect and which to let go of, all things considered. I shall address the first worry in the next essay (though I will unfortunately have to set aside the second worry, which is about trade-offs). To prepare the grounds for my arguments therein, in the next section, I sketch out some of the things which the properties of our common heritage give us reasons to do and highlight some important differences between reasons, moral reasons and moral duties.

FROM REASONS TO DUTIES

Heritage and Practical Reasons

Something is valuable insofar as it has certain properties which ground reasons to experience and engage in a range of fitting pro-attitudes in relation to it. Some of those attitudes are affective (awe at the beauty of a landmark, sadness at the loss of that heritage, etc.), while others consist of doing, or not, certain things to and with heritage. In the remainder of these essays, essentially for lack of space, I focus on four practical reasons in respect of our common heritage: reasons not to destroy it, reasons to preserve it, reasons to grant access to it and reasons to acquire and impart knowledge about it.

Not Destroying

We have reasons not to destroy humankind's heritage. Our reasons not to destroy are *pro tanto* reasons (as, indeed, are any practical reasons), which may sometimes be outweighed. Indeed, we sometimes have reasons *to* destroy or damage heritage goods which belong to our common heritage, whether deliberately or unintentionally (albeit foreseeably). Suppose that a mass shooter makes his way into the British Museum. Security guards can only shoot him, thereby saving lives, through the Rosetta Stone, thereby irretrievably destroying it. It seems—though I shall not defend this claim here—that they have reasons to do so.

We may also have reasons to destroy what C. M. Lim calls 'tainted' commemorative goods, such as the statues of Confederacy soldiers or of Cecil Rhodes.[27] These are different from the goods which, I argued in 'The Value of Heritage', we have reasons to value precisely because they represent or are the locus of grievous wrongs. The goods I had in mind there, such as Hiroshima's Atomic Dome, were not erected in celebration of grievously wrong acts. The claim that there are reasons not to destroy those goods is compatible with the claim that there are reasons to destroy goods which are 'tainted' in Lim's sense.

Finally, in some cases, the value of a work of art sometimes lies *precisely* in the fact that it will cease to exist. For example, take Banksy's painting,

The Girl with Balloon, which partially self-destroyed via a shredder built into its frame, a mere moment after it was purchased at auction. To the extent that the painting is valuable in part by dint of its in-built shredder, we have a reason to destroy it.[28]

Preserving

We have reasons to preserve humankind's heritage. Preservation takes the form of protecting heritage goods from damage, for example, by storing them under appropriate conditions (to do with temperature, humidity, etc.), as well as repairing or restoring them.

This seemingly simple claim belies a number of difficulties. Restoring cultural goods such as paintings, sculptures or buildings often involves using different materials. So does reconstructing. From a purist view of restoration and reconstruction, anything which involves using numerically different materials is the creation of a new, different object so that we can no longer say that the restored or reconstructed object is the same as the original object. For the purist, given that authenticity—construed as retaining original properties—is a necessary condition for aesthetic appreciation, restoration and reconstruction cannot be a way of preserving the object's value.

The dispute between purists and their opponents, which is rooted in metaphysical debates regarding diachronic numerical identity, is a long-standing one.[29] I do not wish to adjudicate it. Let me simply make two points. First, the purist's argument does not apply to heritage goods whose value supervenes on the aesthetic qualities of what they represent, on their epistemic value or on their contributory value to historical events. The purist need not deny this, but it is worth drawing out the limits of her arguments. Consider, for example, badly damaged archives relating to the slave trade or Gavrilo Princip's gun. Even if one grants the purist the claim that physical continuity is a necessary condition of diachronic identity, such that active conservation or restoration would be issued in a different archival object and a different gun, one would be hard-pressed to affirm that restoration empties those (new) objects of their value.

Second, even if restoration creates a new object whose aesthetic value is not reducible to that of the original object, it does not follow that we have reasons not to restore damaged heritage goods. For a start, not restoring will inevitably, over time, lead to the loss, if not of those objects, at least of some of their aesthetic value. It is odd to suppose that any kind of restoration, at the cost (let us grant) of some aesthetic value

[FABRE] *The Value of Humankind's Cultural Heritage* 61

is always and necessarily worse than the wholesale loss of those goods and the concomitant loss of all its aesthetic value. Furthermore, while a beautiful good would not be valuable *qua* beautiful good but for the fact that it is beautiful, its essential internal property of beauty supervenes on contingent internal properties such as colour, architectural design and so on. Restoration thus need not always lead to the loss of that good's aesthetic value. The point is compatible with the fact that we may have reasons not to restore a damaged heritage good on the grounds that (as we saw in 'The Value of Heritage') its aesthetic or symbolic value supervenes the fact that it is a ruin. Thus, the city of Hiroshima decided not to rebuild the Genbaku Dome as a way to remember the victims of the atomic blast and to remind humankind of the sheer scale of its destructive powers. (Over time, of course, maintaining the dome in its 1945 state of ruin does require a good deal of preservation work.)

So far, I have assumed that enough is left of the original building or object that it makes sense to speak of restoration. But suppose it has been completely destroyed. Does valuing it as part of our common heritage provide us with reasons to rebuild it de novo? The issue arose in 2001 with the Bamiyan statues: following their near obliteration by the Taliban, a number of scholars and, crucially, Afghani politicians, villagers and policymakers called for their reconstruction. At the time of writing this, UNESCO's focus is on stabilizing what is left of the statues' niches and on making the site safe.[30] Even if, *ex hypothesi*, that which conferred the object no longer has the properties which gave it universal value at the bar of our shared humanity, it may still have properties which give it universal value at the bar of pluralism. On the pluralist conception, you recall, a heritage good is universally valuable if we all have reasons to value it each from our own particularistic standpoint and at the same time also to value it impersonally as the culturally and socially mediated instantiation of our fellow human beings' different standpoints. Suppose that Afghanis and Buddhists believe either that it is apt to speak of reconstructing *the* statues (such that we can still speak meaningfully of the Bamiyan statues) or that constructing new statues *in situ* is an apt way of honouring their heritage. We, who are neither Afghanis nor Buddhists, may well have reasons, from our own particularistic standpoints, to value the newly built statues as well as impersonal reasons to value Afghanis and Buddhists' value judgements in respect of the desirability of reconstruction. On either construal of the statues—whether they are construed as *the* Bamiyan statues or as

62 *The Tanner Lectures on Human Values*

their successors—we can still say that they have universal value, which opens the justificatory door for a reason to reconstruct.

Granting Access

Valuing humankind's common cultural heritage gives us reasons to grant access to it. Some of our heritage's landmarks and buildings are universally valuable by dint of their outstanding beauty. While one can look at photos or read descriptions of those landmarks and buildings, nothing replaces contemplating them *in situ*. Other heritage goods are universally valuable by dint of what they tell us about our shared past. We can best learn the lessons they teach us by visiting or consulting them. It would be odd to say, for example, that the Taj Mahal is valuable as part of humankind's common heritage yet at the same time deny that there are reasons to enable people to admire it *in situ*. It would be similarly odd to say that archives relative to the slave trade are valuable yet deny that there are reasons to open those archives up.[31]

Reasons to grant access, thus, include reasons to allow freedom of movement across borders, to open up archives and (where relevant) to display heritage goods. Displaying, in turn, may involve displaying *in situ* or (in the case of moveable heritage goods) allowing other countries to do so. Uncontroversially, there are reasons to organize and sponsor touring exhibitions. Much more controversially, we have distributive reasons in relation to that heritage. First, we have reasons to distribute resources to those who lack them so as to enable them to access heritage goods (for example, by subsidizing entry into heritage sites). Second, we also have reasons to redistribute some of our common heritage's constitutive parts. It is often noted that some museums have millions of artefacts and artworks locked in their vaults, which are unlikely ever to see the light of day. Suppose some of those artefacts have outstanding value. Then it seems that there are reasons for those museums to divest themselves of such goods and transfer them to countries which will be able and willing to display them.

Here, too, reasons to grant access may be overridden by reasons to preserve. Consider the Prehistoric Sites and Decorated Caves of the Vézère Valley in France. They were discovered in 1940, date from the Palaeolithic era, cover roughly 1,200 km², span about 350,000 years, and contain, among other things, the Lascaux caves, whose mural paintings offer extraordinarily detailed and vivid paintings of hunting scenes and animal fauna. They were closed to the public in the 1960s, as exposure to air, visitors' exhalations and natural light threatened to destroy them: they are a textbook example of the tension between the value-conferring properties of age and integrity. Valuing the caves provides reasons to restrict access to all save for a handful of researchers and conversation specialists.

Informing

Finally, we have reasons to act in particular ways in respect of the acquisition, exchange and construction of knowledge about our common heritage. More specifically, we have reasons to ensure that, when appropriate, knowledge about our common heritage is appropriately framed and transmitted. The World Heritage's summary description of the Maritime Mercantile City of Liverpool, which was placed on the World Heritage List in 2004 and delisted in 2021, is a good example of what *not* to do. It holds that the value of the site supervenes on the following extrinsic properties: the fact that the city was at the heart of global trade in the eighteenth and nineteenth centuries, the fact that its merchants and seamen developed modern dock technology and the fact that the port of Liverpool played a major role in the 'mass movement of people, e.g., slaves and emigrants from Northern Europe to America.' The slave trade—one of the most abhorrent *longue durée*, crimes in the history of humankind—is mentioned in the same descriptive breath as mass voluntary migration and the development of dock technologies: there is little sense that the slave trade was instrumental to the latter and that there are salient differences (to put it mildly) between shipping slaves and allowing people to migrate to a new life.

Reasons, Moral Reasons, and Duties

Our practical reasons in respect of our common heritage are normative reasons: they are reasons in favour of or against doing something. Moral reasons are a subset of normative reasons. A moral reason in favour of or against x is a consideration that counts in favour of or against x such that my act or my failure to act is amenable to moral evaluation. Some moral reasons are grounded in duties such that my act or failure to act is aptly characterized as wrong.

The question, then, is whether our practical reasons in respect of humankind's heritage are moral reasons and, if so, whether they are grounded in duties. Matthes thinks not. As he puts it, 'simply being human may be sufficient to ground reasons for valuing the history of our species or natural wonders, without giving us compelling reason to do so—we may have other interests and circumstances that render these things unimportant to us, despite our having reason to value them.'[32]

64 *The Tanner Lectures on Human Values*

I am not persuaded. When faced with the competing claims of our heritage and of our other interests or circumstances, we may well have good reasons to prioritize the latter, but this is entirely compatible with the view that our heritage-related practical reasons are also moral reasons.

That being said, the mere fact that a heritage good belongs to humankind's heritage does not *in itself* give us moral reasons to preserve it, grant access to it and so on, let alone put us under a duty to do so. In that respect, I agree with Matthes's conclusion, albeit not his argument for it. Suppose that the British, U.S. and French governments decided to erase all mentions of the slave trade from those of their monuments and places which were central to it. Intuitively, I suspect that many of us would think that this would be bad, indeed wrong, not merely for their respective citizens but for all of us. But simply appealing to the claim that those goods belong to humankind's common cultural heritage will not get us very far. Pending further argument to the contrary, it is open to each of those governments to say that while the fact that those goods are part of our common heritage provides them with a range of practical reasons, those reasons fall short of moral reasons and *a fortiori* duties. In the next essay, I try to provide such an argument.

CONCLUSION

In this first essay, I have tried to defend the view that some goods are universally valuable and form part of humankind's heritage. In doing so, I appealed to two different conceptions of universality: the pluralist conception, whereby we all have reasons to value those goods from our particularistic standpoints in combination with the fact that we all have nonparticularistic reasons to value those goods for the fact that others also value them, and the mere humanity conception, to the effect that we have reasons merely at the bar of our humanity to value some of those goods. The fact that humankind's common heritage is valuable, I further noted, provides us with *pro tanto* reasons not to destroy it, to preserve it, to grant access to it and to provide the right kind of information about it. As we shall now see, those reasons are not mere practical reasons: they are moral duties—indeed, duties of justice.

NOTES

1   See https://theblueshield.org/current-events-in-israel-and-palestine/ and https://unesdoc.unesco.org/ark:/48223/pf0000387432 (accessed December 30, 2023).

2   Malraux's speech is available at https://en.unesco.org/courier/may-1960/andre-malraux-action-man-who-snatches-something-death.
3   J. Greenfield, *The Return of Cultural Treasures* (Cambridge: Cambridge University Press, 2007), 393–96.
4   In addition to the 1972 Convention, UNESCO has adopted conventions pertaining to the trafficking of cultural property, as well as to the protection of cultural property during armed conflicts, of underwater heritage and of the diversity of cultural expression. For an extensive discussion of this legal framework, see C. Forrest, *International Law and the Protection of Cultural Heritage* (London: Routledge, 2010). At various points in those essays, I will refer to the descriptions of sites which have been placed on various World Heritage Lists. Those descriptions can be found at https://whc.unesco.org/en/list/ (accessed October 25, 2023).
5   L. Smith, *Uses of Heritage* (London: Routledge, 2006). The points made in the remainder of this section are a staple of heritage studies. See, for example, C. Brumann, "Creating Universal Value: The UNESCO World Heritage Convention in Its Fifth Decade", in *The Oxford Handbook of Public Heritage—Theory and Practice*, ed. A. M. Labrador and N. A. Silberman (Oxford: Oxford University Press, 2018); I. Hodder, "Cultural Heritage Rights: From Ownership and Descent to Justice and Well-Being", *Anthropological Quarterly* 83, no. 4 (2010): 861–82; D. Lowenthal, *The Heritage Crusade and the Spoils of History* (Cambridge: Cambridge University Press, 1998); and A. Gonzalez-Ruibal, "Vernacular Cosmopolitanism: An Archeological Critique of Universalistic Reason", in *Cosmopolitan Archeologies*, ed. L. Meskell (Durham, NC: Duke University Press, 2009).
6   See, for example, P. Cafaro, "Valuing Wild Nature", in *The Oxford Handbook of Environmental Ethics*, ed. S. M. Gardiner and A. Thomson (Oxford: Oxford University Press, 2017), 125–36.
7   On this latter point, see esp. S. Labadi, *UNESCO, Cultural Heritage, and Outstanding Universal Value* (Lanham, MD: Rowman & Littlefield, 2013). Labadi's book is a fascinating study of several dozens of nominations files and thus of states' interpretation of the convention.
8   See L. Meskell and B. Isakhan, "UNESCO, World Heritage and the Gridlock over Yemen", *Third World Quarterly* 41, no. 10 (2020): 1776–91. See also L. Khalidi, "The Destruction of Yemen and Its Cultural Heritage", *International Journal of Middle East Studies* 49, no. 4 (2017): 735–38.
    To date, only three sites have been fully delisted: the Arabian Oryx Sanctuary in Oman was delisted in 2007 due to the decision by the Omanian authorities to reduce the area of the site by 90 percent, the cultural landscape of Germany's Dresden Elbe Valley was delisted in 2009 as a result of the decision by the German authorities to build a four-lane motorway through the site and the Maritime Mercantile City of Liverpool was delisted in 2021 as a result of extensive property developments about which the World Heritage had long expressed concerns. For a recent articulation of the charge of statism, see L. Meskell, *A Future in Ruins—UNESCO, World Heritage, and the Dream of Peace* (Oxford: Oxford University Press, 2018).
9   The description is available at https://whc.unesco.org/en/list/26/. For a discussion of Robben Island and Auschwitz along those lines, see, for example, E. H. Matthes, "Who Owns up to the Past? Heritage and Historical Injustice", *Journal of the American Philosophical Association* 4, no. 1 (2018): 87–104.
10 Smith, *Uses of Heritage*, esp. chap. 3; Labadi, *UNESCO, Cultural Heritage*, 144–45.

11   For an unsparing indictment, to which I am wholly sympathetic, see Meskell, *A Future in Ruins*.

12   For a good overview of difficulties inherent in defining cultural heritage, see R. Harrison, *Heritage: Critical Approaches* (London: Routledge, 2013).

13   This account, also known as the fittingness account of value, has generated a huge literature. For an early canonical statement, see F. Brentano, *The Origin of Our Knowledge of Right and Wrong* (London: Routledge & Kegan Paul, 1969), esp. 11, 15. See also A. C. Ewing, *The Definition of Good* (London: Routledge and Kegan Paul, 1948), esp. 152; R. Chisholm, "Defining Intrinsic Value", *Analysis* 41, no. 2 (1981): 99–100; T. M. Scanlon, *What We Owe to Each Other* (Cambridge, MA: Harvard University Press, 1998), chap. 3; and M. J. Zimmerman, *The Nature of Intrinsic Value* (Lanham, MD: Rowman & Littlefield, 2001), esp. chap. 4. On the affective dimension of valuing, see S. Scheffler, "Valuing", in *Reasons and Recognition: Essays on the Philosophy of T. M. Scanlon*, ed. S. Freeman and R. Kumar (Oxford University Press, 2012). As Scheffler and others note, I can without contradiction recognise that an object is valuable, for example, by dint of the place it occupies in the history of Western art yet have no admiration for it, no desire to go and see it in situ, and so on. See also J. Raz, *Value, Respect, and Attachment* (Cambridge: Cambridge University Press, 2001); and E. Anderson, *Value in Ethics and Economics* (Cambridge, MA: Harvard University Press, 1993).

14   On old age as a value-conferring property, see S. P. James, "Why Old Things Matter", *Journal of Moral Philosophy* 12, no. 3 (2015): 313–29. On the value, or not, of surviving the passage of time, see A. Savile, *The Test of Time—an Essay in Philosophical Aesthetics* (Oxford: Clarendon, 1982).

15   For interesting discussions of the aesthetics of ruins, see, for example, C. Desilvey, *Curating Decay—Heritage beyond Saving* (Minneapolis: University of Minnesota Press, 2017); and J. Bicknell, J. Judkins, and C. Korsmeyer, eds., *Philosophical Perspectives on Ruins, Monuments and Memorials* (London: Routledge, 2019).

16   J. Waldron, "Minorities Cultures and the Cosmopolitan Alternative", *University of Michigan Journal of Law Reform* 25 (1991): 751–93, esp. 781–82.

17   S. Scheffler, "Conceptions of Cosmopolitanism", *Utilitas* 11, no. 3 (1999): 255–76, esp. 257.

18   E. H. Matthes, "Impersonal Value, Universal Value, and the Scope of Cultural Heritage", *Ethics* 125, no. 4 (2015): 999–1027, esp. 1016–17. For an articulation of the distinction in heritage studies, see Harrison, *Heritage*, 116. For an interesting application of this line of argument to the World Heritage's practices, see Labadi, *UNESCO, Cultural Heritage*.

19   K. A. Appiah, *Cosmopolitanism* (London: Allen Lane, 2006); S. Benhabib, *Another Cosmopolitanism—Tanner Lectures on Human Values* (Oxford: Oxford University Press, 2006); and M. Walzer, *Nation and Universe—Tanner Lecture on Human Values* (Tanner Lectures on Human Values, 1989), available at https://tannerlectures.utah.edu/_resources/documents/a-to-z/w/walzer90 .pdf. The point on intercultural dialogue draws on Elizabeth Anderson's pragmatic account of justifications for evaluative judgements. See E. Anderson, *Value in Ethics and Economics* (Cambridge, MA: Harvard University Press, 1993), chap. 5. Thanks to Margaret Moore for pressing me on this.

20   Lowenthal, *Heritage Crusade*, 176. On the small list, see Matthes, "Impersonal Value, Universal Value", 1015; H. Cleere, "The Concept of 'Outstanding Universal Value' in the World Heritage Convention", *Conservation and Management of Archaeological Sites* 1, no. 4 (1996): 227–33; and A. Omland, "The

Ethics of the World Heritage Concept", in *The Ethics of Archaeology: Philosophical Perspectives on Archaeological Practice*, ed. Geoffrey Scarre and Chris Scarre (Cambridge University Press, 2006), 242–59.

21 For a similar point, on the universal value of migratory routes and of some cultural landscapes—though he focuses on Europe's wine-making region—see P. Fowler, *Landscapes for the World* (Bollington, UK: Windgather, 2004), 202–3.

22 Thanks to K. Lippert-Rasmussen for the point.

23 See, for example, E. H. Matthes, "History, Value, and Irreplaceability", *Ethics* 124, no. 1 (2013): 35–64, esp. 39; Lowenthal, *Heritage Crusade*, chap. 1.

24 Thanks to C. Korsmeyer for the suggestion.

25 For the World Heritage's policy on inclusion, see its 'The Criteria for Inclusion', available at https://whc.unesco.org/en/criteria/ (accessed October 25, 2023).

26 Thanks to K. A. Appiah for pressing me on this.

27 C. M. Lim, "Vandalizing Tainted Commemorations", *Philosophy & Public Affairs* 48, no. 2 (2020): 185–216. By the same token, and to anticipate, we may have reasons to preserve tainted heritage. See D. Matravers, "The Reconstruction of Damaged or Destroyed Heritage", in *Philosophical Perspectives on Ruins, Monuments and Memorials*, ed. J. Bicknell, J. Judkins, and C. Korsmeyer (London: Routledge, 2019), 189–200.

28 M. Busby, "Woman Who Bought Shredded Banksy Artwork Will Go through with Purchase", *Guardian*, November 10, 2018.

29 For a well-known contemporary defence of the purist position, see M. Sagoff, "On Restoring and Reproducing Art", *Journal of Philosophy* 75, no. 9 (1978): 453–69. For a classic defence, though one which (mistakenly) claims that restoration is necessarily deceitful, see J. Ruskin, "The Lamp of Memory", in *The Seven Lamps of Architecture—the Works of John Ruskin*, vol. 8, ed. E. T. Cook and A. Wedderburn (Cambridge University Press, 2010), 242–45. For critical discussions, see, for example, P. Lamarque, "Reflections on the Ethics and Aesthetics of Restoration and Conservation", *British Journal of Aesthetics* 56, no. 3 (2016): 281–99; R. Wicks, "Architectural Restoration: Resurrection or Replications?", *British Journal of Aesthetics* 34, no. 2 (1994): 163–69; S. J. Wilsmore, "What Justifies Restoration?", *Philosophical Quarterly* 38, no. 150 (1988): 56–67; and C. Korsmeyer, *Things—in Touch with the Past* (Oxford: Oxford University Press, 2019), esp. chaps. 2 and 4.

30 For an interesting philosophical discussion of this case, and an argument against reconstruction, see J. Janowski, "Bringing Back Bamiyan's Buddhas," *Journal of Applied Philosophy* 28, no. 1 (2011): 44–64. For a detailed critique, see W. Bülow and J. L. Thomas, "On the Ethics of Reconstructing Destroyed Cultural Heritage Monuments," *Journal of the American Philosophical Association* 6, no. 4 (2020): 483–501.

31 For a thoughtful discussion of the importance of being 'in the presence of the real thing', see Korsmeyer, *Things*. I shall return to this point in 'Justice, Humankind and Common Cultural Heritage'.

32 Matthes, "Impersonal Value, Universal Value", 1017.

LECTURE II.
JUSTICE AND HUMANKIND'S COMMON HERITAGE

INTRODUCTION

In the first essay, I have tried to provide an account of the universal value of humankind's heritage. I now argue that we are under duties *of justice* to one another (our contemporaries but also our predecessors and successors) as members of humankind not to destroy it but to preserve it, to grant access to it and to supply appropriate information about it.

The claim that we are under a duty not to destroy our common cultural heritage might seem obviously true. Indeed, the wanton destruction of cultural goods is a war crime under article 8 of the Rome Statute of the International Criminal Court—a provision which is rooted in the 1954 Hague Convention for the Protection of Cultural Property in the Event of Armed Conflict. This led to the prosecution, in 2016, of Ahmed Al Faqi Al Mahdi by the International Criminal Court under indictment for the deliberate destruction of several religious buildings in Timbuktu at the height of the conflict in Mali. Al Mahdi pled guilty and received a nine-year sentence. Although the Rome Statute does not draw a distinction between World Heritage Sites and sites which are not afforded that status, the court stated that the fact that all but one of the sites were protected World Heritage Sites added to the gravity of Mahdi's crime. In an earlier case, the International Criminal Tribunal for the former Yugoslavia condemned Admiral Jokic, Yugoslavia's last head of its Navy and commander of its forces at the siege of Dubrovnik, to a seven-year jail sentence, for (*inter alia*) the destruction of Dubrovnik's Old Town. In the eyes of the tribunal, Jokic's crime was worse for the fact that Old Town was a World Heritage Site.[1]

Obvious as the point may be, the duty not to destroy needs defending; so do the other aforementioned duties. I mount my case to that effect in sections 'Justice, Humankind and Common Cultural Heritage' and 'Looking Ahead to the Future, Looking Back to the Past'. In 'Territory, Self-Determination, and the Protection of Humankind's Heritage', I draw out some implications for states' putative right to govern over the territories on which our common heritage is located, lived in, passed on and transformed. In 'Cultural Appropriation', I respond to the objection that my account opens the door to cultural appropriation. In 'Conclusion', I offer concluding remarks and outline avenues for further research.

[68]

Two caveats. First, I focus on those four duties, as these seem to be the most important. There are others—which the lack of space prevents me from addressing here.[2] Second, the duties I defend here are *pro tanto* duties. All things considered, it may well be that faced with conflicts between the demands of justice with respect to our common heritage and the imperative of saving lives, we are under a moral duty to do the latter. Indeed, it may also be that faced with conflicts between the demands of justice with respect to humankind's heritage and the demands of justice with respect to heritage that is only of particular value to a community, we ought to give priority to the latter. For lack of space, I do not address those difficult questions. This is one of the limitations of those essays. At the same time, in order to ascertain what are the right trade-offs, we need to know what our *pro tanto* duties in respect of humankind's common heritage are.

JUSTICE, HUMANKIND AND COMMON CULTURAL HERITAGE

To say that we owe it to one another to act in certain ways in relation to our (by which I mean, ours as humankind's) common heritage as a matter of justice is tantamount to saying that we have rights against one another, wherever we reside, in relation to that heritage.[3] At first sight, this might seem a straightforwardly moral-cosmopolitan claim. According to moral cosmopolitanism, national-cum-political borders are irrelevant to individuals' rights: if X has a right to p at the bar of justice, then so does Y, whether or not Y and X belong to the same political community; moreover, X has no greater duty at the bar of justice to respect and promote his compatriot Z's right to p than to respect Y's same right. Illustratively, the mere fact that Y is from Kenya while Z is from Germany does not license X, who is also from Germany, to save Z's life rather than Y's.

However, in just the same way as cultural cosmopolitanism does not properly account for the value of humankind's heritage *qua* such heritage, moral cosmopolitanism does not properly account for the requirement to protect humankind's common cultural heritage *qua* such heritage. It is coherent on the one hand to affirm that the notion of such heritage is illusory and on the other hand to maintain that we are under as stringent duties of justice to distant strangers in relation to *their* heritage as we are in relation to ours. The question of the scope of justice, to which moral cosmopolitans respond by denying the moral relevance of borders, is orthogonal to that of its content and grounds, about which cosmopolitans *qua* cosmopolitans have little to say.

In order to show that we have duties of justice to fellow human beings—conversely, that they have rights against us—in relation to our common cultural heritage, I rely on the following account of justice.

A just world is one in which all individuals, wherever they reside, are treated with equal concern and respect, and in which (where possible) they securely enjoy, as a matter of rights, equal opportunities for a flourishing life—a life worthy of human beings. In the language of the capabilities approach developed independently of each other and collaboratively by Amartya Sen and Martha Nussbaum, a just world is one in which individuals, as a matter of rights, enjoy the following capabilities, which are constitutive of human flourishing: being able to live for as long as one's life is worth living; bodily health; bodily integrity; being able to use one's senses, imagination and thoughts; being able to form attachments to other people and to things and to experience and express a range of negative and positive emotions; being able to frame and revise a conception of the good life; being able to form a range of meaningful social interactions with others without fear of being discriminated against or humiliated; being able to show concern and to interact with the nonhuman world; being able to engage in recreational activities, laugh and play; being able to have control over one's political and material environment. Furthermore, a just world is one in which individuals are in a position to exercise their capabilities without violating other people's claims to be treated with equal concern and respect.[4]

Moreover, duties of justice are enforceable. Failures to comply with the demands of justice warrant retortive action, ranging (depending on the seriousness of the wrongdoing, and the necessity, likely effectiveness and proportionality of the response) from war to public rebuke: duties of justice are not just any kind of moral reasons: they are particularly stringent kinds of duties. As a matter of justice, individuals whose rights have been violated have remedial rights that are steps to be taken to repair, as far as is feasible, the injustice to which they have been subjected.

Finally, there are limits to the sacrifices that we are under a duty to incur for the sake of ensuring that everyone enjoys their central capabilities. In the language rendered familiar by Samuel Scheffler, we have a personal prerogative (at least up to a point) to confer greater weight on our projects and attachments than on other persons' central interests—and in particular, not to sacrifice our own prospects for a flourishing life for the sake of others' similar prospects.[5]

As a matter of justice, thus, all human beings have rights against one another to the freedoms and resources which are necessary to and/or constitutive of their having those capabilities, compatible with their treating others with equal concern and respect. This includes freedoms and resources that pertain to cultural goods. Those goods provide the context within which we enjoy those capabilities and thus lead a flourishing life, but they also are their constitutive elements. To that extent, we owe it to one another not to impede on one another's access to and enjoyment of those goods and, more strongly still, to provide one another with the means to do so.

Now clearly, we cannot, as a matter of justice, preserve for and provide to one another all and any of the cultural goods which, at any given time, form the background for and/or are the constitutive elements of our flourishing. The stream which runs at the bottom of my garden, a particular symphony by an eighteenth-century composer and a set of archives relating to my hometown may all be important to me here and now. But while this may well provide you with moral reasons not to needlessly destroy them, it is implausible to say that you—via the relevant institutions—are *under duties of justice* to me to ensure that I always have access to them: not only might other people have competing and stronger claims to other such goods; ensuring that I always have such access, failing which you would wrong me, seems overly demanding.

The question, then, is what wrong—what *injustice*—is done to any of us, *qua* human beings, by the destruction, or the unwarranted failure to preserve, to grant us access to and to properly inform us about those goods which have universal value and which form part of our common heritage.

Those destructive acts and failures occasion at least four kinds of injustice to our contemporaries. (I examine duties to future generations and to the dead in 'Looking Ahead to the Future, Looking Back to the Past' below.) First, they would suffer an aesthetic and creative injustice. One of the central capabilities is the ability to use our senses and imagination. We enjoy it when we are able to (*inter alia*) admire goods of great beauty, which often takes our imagination in directions which we might not have anticipated. As we saw in 'The Universal Value of Humankind's Heritage', some cultural goods have universal value by dint of their outstanding beauty: they can be admired by all of us and more strongly still can inspire awe and wonder in all of us, precisely because they are outstandingly beautiful. To deprive fellow human

72 *The Tanner Lectures on Human Values*

beings of the opportunity to enjoy this central capability in this way, without warrant, is unjust.[6]

While the point holds of universally valuable cultural goods in general, it is particularly apt with respect to those goods as *heritage* goods. Consider a recording of traditional Chinese music played on a nine-thousand-year-old flute thought to be the oldest playable instrument in existence. Had I been living in China nine thousand years ago, I might have been awed by that music. But my sense of awe here today flows not merely from the hauntingly beautiful music itself but also from the fact that someone was playing *that very instrument* back in the neolithic era. Or consider the very scratchy 1904 recording of Alessandro Moreschi singing Gounod's *Ave Maria*. It has heritage value which a 2024 recording does not have: Moreschi was the last known *castrato*, and his recordings, of which the 1904 is the best known, are the only audible remnants of this particular kind of voice. I have no doubt that a remastered version would sound better. Yet it feels in the 1904 version, without the adornments of modern technology, that he sings to us, directly, across the century that separates him from us. It is *that which*, in the true sense of the word, is awesome about it.[7]

Second, destroying, failing to preserve, and hiding information about some of those universally valuable heritage goods, as well as their sequestration, is an epistemic injustice.[8] Many of the heritage goods which together constitute humankind's heritage, as I have described them in the first essay, have universal value—on both the pluralist and the mere-humanity conception thereof—by dint of what they tell us about our shared past. Our ability to use our senses and imagination, and to frame and revise a conception of the good life, depends in part on our having some knowledge about what makes us human, how we have evolved, how our distinctive social and cultural practices are shaped as much by what our predecessors have borrowed from other cultures as by what they have discarded, how our supposedly natural environment has in fact been moulded by long-standing population movements and settlements, what feats of creativity and ingenuity our fellow human beings have accomplished but also what unspeakable crimes they have committed.

Third, and relatedly, the destruction of and failure to preserve some of those landmarks and objects, as well as the failure to impart accurate information about them, can give rise to an 'agential injustice'. Many of our decisions impose harms or risks thereof on our fellow human beings,

[FABRE]   *Justice and Humankind's Common Heritage*   73

particularly such decisions that we make, or are made on our behalf and our behest, as political and economic agents. To make or authorize those decisions in ignorance of the relevant facts when one could have informed oneself of those facts is morally wrong—I take it, uncontroversially so. Crucially, to expose moral agents to the risk of imposing wrongful harm on third parties is to inflict on them a moral injury, and one which is severe enough, I believe, to cause them an injustice. This applies to the person who is oblivious to the wrongful harms, or wrongful risks thereof, which she imposes on others. To the extent that we—as well as those who act on our behalf and for our sake—need to know about the most significant phases of our global shared history in order to avoid enjoying our capabilities wrongfully—and to the extent that the preservation of those objects, landmarks and sites help us gain that knowledge—we are victims of a form of injustice if they are allowed to be destroyed or to decay.

Fourth, by unwarrantedly failing in the aforementioned ways to treat a culture's or a social and political community's heritage as part of humankind's common heritage, we in effect deny that culture or community, and thus their members, their rightful place in the narrative of our shared human history. This in fact is one of the distinctive wrongs done by colonizers to those whom they subjugated.[9]

One may perhaps wonder whether we need (a) those goods *themselves* or (b) *all* of those goods. After all, on the first count, we can digitize archives, rebuild destroyed monuments, and build or even print (in 3D) replicas thereof. A sceptic might hold that even if we need to be in the presence of original beautiful things to fully get a sense of their aesthetic value, we do not need to be in the presence of historically significant heritage goods in order for us to grasp their significance. Walking around the 3D replica of the Arch of Palmyra, which the Institute for Digital Archaeology commissioned and exhibited around the world after the Arch was destroyed by ISIS in 2015, seems enough. Exploring the digital replica of the Tomb of Tutankhamun which was installed near the entrance of the Valley of the Kings also seems enough.[10]

In one sense, the sceptic is correct. We need not have visited Auschwitz in order to learn most of what we need to know about the Holocaust; we need not see a human fossil in order to understand the basics of evolution; we need not hold a Gutenberg Bible in our hands in order to know the basics of the history of printing. Nevertheless, there are precautionary reasons for not destroying those goods, indeed for preserving them: technology might one day fail us, and we may not have extracted

74   *The Tanner Lectures on Human Values*

from some objects all the knowledge that there is to extract from them. Moreover, while we can look at photos or read descriptions of those landmarks and buildings, nothing replaces contemplating them *in situ*. Even if replicas and digital versions would tell us everything we need to know, we would still incur a loss—the loss of that which enables us not only to learn about our shared past but, more elusively, to *understand* it better and thus somehow to connect with it and with those of our fellow human beings who inhabited it. Replicas and digital versions cannot do that for us: they do not give us this direct historical link to our predecessors. Indeed, I wager that if we had a choice between visiting, for example, the Tomb of Tutankhamun itself, or touring the exact replica which was installed a few years ago near the entrance to the Valley of the Kings, most of us would opt for the former.[11]

Consider next, on the second count, the suggestion that even if we need opportunities to see and access originals rather than replicas, we do not need opportunities to see and access all of the constitutive parts of humankind's heritage.[12] It surely cannot be the case—the sceptic presses—that burning a Gutenberg Bible, bulldozing archaeological sites containing nine-thousand-year-old musical instruments and letting one cathedral go to ruins does an injustice to everyone in the world, here and now. After all, millions of us throughout the world have never heard of Gutenberg and have no idea what a castrato is; and for all we know, countless artefacts and landmarks of outstanding beauty or universal significance have been destroyed over the centuries by our predecessors, without us being any the wiser: it is hard to believe that we here today, *qua* human beings, would lead a less than flourishing life if, for example, the conquistadors had destroyed the historic Inca site of Machu Picchu—widely regarded as one of the greatest architectural and land-use achievements of all time. Moreover, many of us have plenty of other beautiful and historically significant cathedrals to admire, and we still have access to old Chinese musical instruments such as the guqin. So what injustice, really, would be done to us, to our fellow human beings, so long as there's an adequate range of those goods left?

In reply: the first limb of the objection rests on an experiential account of wrongdoing, such that something wrongs us only if we experience it or its impact, or at any rate are likely to do so. I reject it on the grounds that its premise is problematic. It implies, for example, that the pure voyeur, who obsessively observes another person without her being ever aware of it and without his actions having any impact on her life, does not wrong her. It seems however that the voyeur's target does have a grievance—even if she never finds out. If so, the fact that someone is unaware of the existence of parts of humankind's heritage does not impugn the claim that destroying, failing to preserve, indeed denying her access to it (albeit unbeknown to her) is to do her an injustice.

Second, the claim that the existence of many goods of a particular kind licenses the destruction of, or failure to preserve, one such good is not persuasive. Suppose for the sake of argument that the nine-thousand-year-old Chinese flute belongs to our common heritage, as does a twenty-five-hundred-year-old guqin. It may be of course that allowing the former to fall into disrepair to the point of being unplayable is less of an injustice to humankind for the fact that we still have the latter. But it would be an injustice all the same. For even if it is true of some individuals here and now that they can and will flourish even if they lack the opportunity to, for example, listen to a nine-thousand-year-old Chinese flute, it cannot be known, for every person in the world, what constitutes *an adequate range of universally valuable goods for them.* Here, too, under conditions of uncertainty, we are under *pro tanto* precautionary duties to one another not to subject one another to the risk of being wrongfully denied access to, learning from or enjoyment of any of our heritage's constitutive parts. If some course of action is, or is likely to be, damaging to our common heritage such as to undermine human flourishing, and if we do not have full knowledge of the causal connection between that course of action and such damage or of the probability that the damage will occur, then we must either desist or postpone proceeding until such time as we have better information. The fact that the risk of wrongful damage to our heritage and thus to human flourishing might not materialize does not impugn the claim that we are under a *pro tanto* duty of justice not to impose it.[13]

LOOKING AHEAD TO THE FUTURE, LOOKING BACK TO THE PAST

So far, I have focused on our heritage-related duties to our contemporaries. I now argue that we have such duties to our successors and to our predecessors.

Duties to Our Successors

Heritage studies and heritage discourse, whether authorized or not, are replete with claims to the effect that we are under duty to our successors to preserve our, and indeed their, common heritage. Indeed, to the best of our knowledge, our successors too will have central capabilities similar to ours; they too will need cultural goods in order to enjoy those capabilities. While we do not know what cultural and social practices they will engage in and nurture, and therefore which cultural goods they will need access to, we do know that their central capabilities will include the capability to exercise their senses, imagination and thought; that they too will need to know what makes them human and to understand their shared past as part of the long, unbroken chain of humankind; that they too will need to know both the best and the worst of what human beings are capable. The fact that we are certain about that while uncertain about what exactly they will have reasons to value supports a precautionary duty to preserve as much of our common heritage as we can. It is in that sense that we, here and now, should construe our role in relation to it as that of a steward rather than an owner.

Duties to Our Predecessors

Duties with respect to humankind's cultural heritage are almost always construed as duties to future generations. Yet they hold, *mutatis mutandis*, to the dead. Here are two arguments to that effect.

The first argument rests on the mere-humanity conception of universal value. As I averred in 'The Universal Value of Humankind's Heritage', our judgement of certain crimes as crimes against humanity is issued at the bar of our mere humanity. The sites where such crimes took place have universal value and belong to humankind's heritage, as well as to victims' specific heritage. We do not only have moral reasons to value them: we are under duty to the victims of those crimes to do so. Elsewhere, I mount a defence of postwar commemorative duties which appeals to what valuing fellow human beings, whoever and wherever they are, implies. It implies, in this context, not forgetting those who are victims of the horrors of war and, more broadly, crimes against humanity. Failing publicly to remember those victims is tantamount to a failure to acknowledge the seriousness of the wrongdoings to which they were subject and denotes a fundamental lack of basic respect.[14] Were we, the world at large, to, for example, accede to or fail to condemn and forestall the destruction of the sites of their suffering, we would wrong them.

Consider, second, the pluralist conception of universal value. While we do not know whether our successors will have reasons to value those goods, as we do, from their particularistic standpoints, we know that some of our predecessors did: think of the sheer effort and expense of building the pyramids, the cathedrals, the palaces and temples of pre-Colombian America; think of the commitment involved in engaging with intangible heritage goods such as music, drama, dance and thus with the tangible bases and components of those practices and with hybrid heritage goods such as culturally embedded farming and agricultural practices. To value fellow human beings as creative and autonomous beings is in part to recognize as valuable what materially underpins, and emerges from, their social and cultural practices. Duties to the dead, in general, are grounded in the importance of respecting and promoting those of their (morally justified) plans, projects and attachments which were central to their lives and about which they formed (or, at least, may be presumed to have formed) posthumous preferences. Those two points together provide support for duties to the dead—in particular, a duty not to destroy what they did and replace it with copies.[15]

That said, those duties are subject to three qualifications. First, we cannot assume that every stonemason in medieval Europe and pre-Colombian Latin American, every tea grower in India and China, every forger in the metallurgy sites of Burkina Faso has since time immemorial valued those landmarks as central to their lives. On my account, we have no duties *here and now* to individuals who were indifferent to those goods. This is compatible with the view that, while those individuals were alive, those goods were central to their flourishing regardless, which imposed relevant duties on their contemporaries.

Second, other things equal, whether our predecessors intended to leave and preserve those heritage goods for us makes a difference to the stringency of our duties to them. Granted, the fact that in some cases and to the best of our knowledge, they were building for the long term is not in itself an indication that they were doing it for us: building temples to gods whose existence is assumed to be temporally unbounded is not the same as building them with the intention that one's successors should inherit them, preserve and restore them if necessary and thereby benefit from the protection of the gods. Nevertheless, we sometimes know that they acted for our sake—as the World Heritage movement shows.

Third, we might have to choose between preserving a heritage good of outstanding universal value which was of considerable value to our dead predecessors on the one hand and preserving a heritage good of outstanding universal value which was not of great value to them but which is to us and, we plausibly surmise, will be so to our successors. I am inclined to think that other things equal (and to the extent that we can make such judgements),

78   *The Tanner Lectures on Human Values*

we are at least permitted, and might perhaps be obliged, to give priority to those who will experience the loss over those who will not.

The claim that we are under duties to the dead in respect of humankind's common heritage raises the following difficulty.[16] Suppose that a landmark which is unquestionably part of that heritage was built three hundred years ago over another, more ancient landmark, dated from eight hundred years ago, which is also part of that heritage. In order to access the latter, we would have to destroy the former. To say that we owe it to our predecessors to respect and preserve that which they not only had reasons to value but indeed did value, and *a fortiori* so when theses goods are part of our common heritage, will not help us decide what to do in this particular case if (let us assume) we have every reason to believe that our predecessors three hundred years ago equally valued that which they built compared to our predecessors eight hundred years ago.[17] A good example is the Old City of Acre in Israel, which was inscribed on the List in 2001: much of the old Crusaders' town is underground. It is possible to visit it—but one can easily see the force of the point if one imagines that one would have to destroy the more recent buildings which sit on top of it, such as the eighteenth-century mosque, in order to access it.

Note that the difficulty is specific neither to goods which are parts of humankind's common heritage nor to duties to the dead: a similar problem arises if I have to choose between a heirloom which I inherited from my paternal grandfather and a heirloom which I inherited from my mother; and the problem also arises if I have to choose between two universally valuable goods which are each valued by different cultural groups from their particularistic standpoint. In order to adjudicate those conflicts, then, we will need to advert to (*inter alia*) the number and range of value-conferring properties of those goods, the costs attendant on preserving or accessing one rather than the other and the degree to which current cohorts, on whom those costs will fall, also have particularistic reasons to value those goods. These judgements are too complex to be fully explored here. It seems to me, however, that those things being equal, there is a presumption (rooted in the doctrine of acts and omissions) against destroying part of our common heritage even for the sake of accessing another of its constitutive elements—even if the latter will remain invisible to us as a result.

One final point on our duties to the dead. Unlike reparative duties to the descendants of dead victims of injustice, they are not superseded by changing circumstances the further back one goes in time. Duties to the dead are grounded in duties more generally to treat fellow human beings with concern and respect and thus to respect and promote, posthumously, projects which were central to their lives and about which we have reasons to suppose they had posthumous preferences; they can also be grounded in duties to commemorate the victims of atrocities. Location in time is, *in itself*, irrelevant to the stringency of those duties. This makes for a demanding view, for it implies that we do owe it as a matter of justice to the stonemasons who built Notre-Dame Cathedral, and *a fortiori* to those who built the Mayans and Egyptian pyramids, to preserve those buildings; that we do owe it, as a matter of justice, to those who toiled tirelessly on the Ancient Tea Plantations of Jingmai Mountain in China millennia ago to preserve this agricultural landscape—both by dint of the fact that landmarks have global historical significance and were the sites of (we may readily suppose) enormous suffering. Put even more sharply, they really have *rights* against us that we do so.[18]

My rejection of supersession might invite two objections. First, the further back one goes in time, the less we know about our predecessors' posthumous preferences. In reply: pending information to the contrary, we have little reason to suppose that a stonemason who worked on one of Egypt's pyramids four millennia ago cared less about its life-span than workers who are currently working on its maintenance.

Second, it might also be objected that the more such predecessors there are, the more demanding our duties—so overly demanding as to extinguish them. In reply: the claim that the sheer number of rights-holders renders the task of fulfilling our duties overly demanding does not impugn the view that the passage of time itself is irrelevant to the stringency of those duties. Suppose (extravagantly) that all of our hundreds of millions of dead predecessors had no preference whatsoever with respect to the persistence of our shared heritage but that hundreds of millions of our contemporaries had strong preferences that it should be preserved. If the claim of overdemandingess applies to the dead, it also applies to the living—irrespective of time. In any event, the claim does not apply to our duties and rights with respect to the cultural goods which belong to our common heritage, since there are relatively few such goods (relative—that is, to the number of cultural goods which are not universally valuable).

TERRITORY, SELF-DETERMINATION, AND THE PROTECTION OF HUMANKIND'S HERITAGE

I have argued that we—all of us, members of humankind—have (diachronic) duties of justice to one another in respect of our common cultural heritage. However, those heritage goods are located on the territories of states which make laws regarding the books which can be read, the archives which can be accessed, the objects which can be exported abroad and the buildings which will be repaired. Indeed, without prejudice to the possibility that the World Heritage's List might in some respects be overinclusive, all of its 1,199 sites bar one (the Old City of Jerusalem) are attributed to state parties to the 1972 Convention—fuelling the charge (which we encountered in 'A Doomed and Flawed Ideal?') that the Authorized Heritage Discourse is overly statist. With that inescapable fact in mind, we must investigate the implications of my argument for citizenries' rights over and in respect of the territory on which some parts of that heritage are located (for short, the right to self-determination).

When tackling this question, we must distinguish between two issues: (a) the issue of *discretion*, to wit, which rights of self-determination, if any, citizens have in respect of humankind's common heritage; (b) the issue of *legitimacy*, to wit, whether citizens' right to govern over a particular territory is conditional upon their fulfilling their obligations of justice in relation to that heritage. As we shall see, my account of our heritage-related duties is compatible with two rather different views of the normative status of the territorial state as the institutional vehicle for collective self-determination and thus of citizens' jointly held right of self-determination over a given territory.

The Right to Self-Determination

On one view of the right of self-determination, the state is instrumentally valuable, and the right to self-determination is thus justified as a means to allocate the task of fulfilling and enforcing general duties of justice. The rationale for imposing on country A's citizens a duty to provide their compatriots with the resources they need to enjoy their central capabilities does not lie in the special relationship that unites them *qua* compatriots. Rather, it lies in the fact that they are better placed, by dint of their subjection to the same territorially bounded institutions, to help one another than to help country B's citizens. So construed, special duties to one's compatriots are derivative of general duties of justice, and citizens' right to self-determination serves to fulfil those duties.[19]

On another set of views, the justification for the territorial state and for citizens' right to self-determination over a given territory does not lie in this being the best way to discharge general duties of justice to the world at large. Consider, for example, Anna Stilz's recent and sophisticated defence thereof.[20] All individuals, wherever they are in the world, are under a natural duty of justice to protect one another's autonomy, understood as the capacity to frame, revise and pursue a conception of the good life with which one identifies. More specifically, they are under duties to one another to respect one another's right to occupy a geographical space where they can form such a conception of the good life, as well as rights to subsistence, security and the freedoms necessary for autonomy and to self-determination. The territorial modern state is the institution which best ensures that those who live within its borders enjoy those rights. Or consider the view that territorial rights are held by a group, a people or a nation which enjoys a particular relationship to a particular territory and that the state is justified in so far as it enables them to exercise those rights. On some variants of that view, that relationship takes the form of long-term settlement; on other variants, attachment to that territory has constituted and structured the group's communal identity over time; on other variants still, the group not only has long been settled on that territory but more importantly has engaged in self-reflection about the centrality of that territory to its identity. On those accounts, the fulfilment of duties to outsiders forms no part of the *justification* for the right to self-determination, though it may be a condition for having and exercising it.[21]

On instrumental accounts of the right to self-determination, it makes sense to impose on a citizenry duties in relation to the heritage goods which are located on or are part of its territory. That duty is derivative of a general duty, held by all to all, to preserve our common heritage and is compatible with a duty to help other states meet *their* derivative duties to all of us. It finds expression in articles 4 and 5 of the 1972 World Heritage Convention. On noninstrumental accounts, which do not deny that the right to self-determination is constrained by consideration of outsiders' important interests, one can without inconsistency impose on citizens the set of heritage-related duties which I defended above.[22]

Discretion

Citizens do not enjoy an untrammelled right to self-determination over humankind's common cultural heritage. For if they did, they would not be under duties of justice not to destroy or to preserve and grant access to it (in the latter case, by allowing freedom of movement across borders, opening archives and displaying—when appropriate—heritage goods). Yet not only are citizens, via their states, under the aforementioned duties; they are also under duties, again via their state, to regulate private actors' decisions in relation to those goods by enacting relevant laws and directives. Suppose for the sake of argument that it is not unjust that private actors—collectors, museums, private corporations and so on—should enjoy some rights over those goods, such as rights to transfer them or rights to control access to them. At the bar of justice, however, those rights are highly restricted. If the destruction, neglect, sequestration and misrepresentation of universally valuable heritage goods is an injustice to humankind, it is so whoever is causally and morally responsible for it—be they public or private actors. This implies that states ought to institutionalize private actors' duties in respect of those goods.[23]

If those points are correct, it seems that there is no space, on my account of our heritage-related duties, for citizens' right to make decisions about those elements of our common heritage which are located on or under the territory over which they exercise collective self-determination. Yet insofar as there is some value to self-determination, so to constrain it seems particularly problematic.

On closer inspection, however, both accounts offer some scope for fulfilling some of those duties in a number of ways without falling foul of justice. Indeed, on the pluralist conception of universal value, which relies on acknowledging that some heritage goods are of central value to particular cultures, there are strong reasons for the world at large to respect the local, particularistic views of those cultures. To the extent that those views are expressed via the state, my defence of duties in respect of our common heritage not only is compatible with but in fact requires granting the state the right, on behalf of those individuals, to make the relevant decisions. Let me give two examples, the first involving a decision not to restore, the second a decision to do so. I noted in 'The Value of Heritage' that the city of Hiroshima had taken the decision after World War II to preserve the Genbaku Dome as a ruin, in memory of the victims and as a way to bear witness, for all of our sake, to the destructive power of atomic weapons. Suppose, conversely, that they had decided to rebuild the dome, in deference to their own conception of authenticity, and to commemorate both the victims and the blast itself in different ways. They would not (it seems to me) have committed an injustice in so doing. Likewise, and conversely, suppose that the French authorities had decided *not* to rebuild Notre-Dame's spire to its nineteenth-century design but, instead, had embraced Norman Foster's proposal for a steel-and-glass spire, in deference to centuries-old practices of using contemporaneous materials and building techniques. Again, I doubt that they would have committed an injustice.[24]

Furthermore, institutionalizing our heritage-related duties can take many different forms: it can involve criminalizing the wilful destruction of heritage; banning and/or refusing to confer validity on, for example, the unconditional sale of heritage goods to foreign buyers over whom it will not be possible to exercise oversight; refusing to acknowledge as valid wills stipulating that the testator should be buried with those goods; providing incentives, in the form of tax breaks or grants, for the preservation and display of those goods; making it compulsory for private owners to display those goods via a system of museum loans; ensuring that heritage goods are displayed, catalogued and archived with appropriate information—and so on. It seems plausible that a state of affairs in which it is lawful wilfully to destroy heritage goods whose universal value supervenes at least in part on their continuing survival would be unjust: not much scope, if any, for discretion there. (Given the extensive scope, worldwide, of legal private ownership rights over artworks, artefacts and fossils, including the legal right to destroy those goods, much of the world is rife with heritage injustice.) By contrast, justice does not require providing tax incentives for, rather than imposing fines on, private collectors who would otherwise sequester heritage goods; nor does it mandate the criminalization of certain kinds of speech in relation to heritage rather than public subsidies for relevant educational programmes.

The general point is this: justice imposes stringent duties, yet there is latitude for interpreting what it demands of us. By analogy, an education policy which forbids the teaching of evolution is unjust (insofar as it deprives children of absolutely basic knowledge about the world in general and themselves as human beings and is thus capability impairing); one which gives some priority to the teaching of history over foreign languages or vice versa is not. Likewise, while failing to make any kind of welfare provision for the elderly and condemning many of them to abject poverty is unjust, there is a range of acceptable options (acceptable—that is, at the bar of justice) for such provision. The same considerations apply, mutatis mutandis, to our common heritage.

Legitimacy

Let me now turn to the question of legitimacy. On the most stringent account of the relationship between justice and legitimacy, citizens have the right to collective self-determination over a given territory, such that their and their officials' decisions over that territory are legitimate *only if* they fulfil all their duties of full justice—understood as ensuring that all individuals in the world enjoy all of their central capabilities. The most stringent account seems implausible. Consider the Taj Mahal, widely regarded as an outstanding exemplar of Indo-Islamic architecture. It seems implausible to suppose that Indian citizens would lack the right to collective self-determination over the territory of India were they to fail via the relevant institutions to maintain it (assuming for the sake of argument that maintaining the Taj Mahal for generations to come is a demand of justice)—or indeed, that the citizens of the countries of the Central Slave and Ivory Trade Route would also lack that very same right if they decided, negligently, not to preserve any of the Route's landmarks.

On a less stringent view, citizens have a right to make decisions in relation to humankind's common heritage—put differently, their collective decisions in respect of that heritage are legitimate—only if they do not, in so doing, fail to fulfil their duties, on behalf of humankind, in respect of that heritage. While their dereliction of duty does not undermine their right to collective self-determination in all of its dimensions, it undermines it in its common-heritage-related respect. This view seems more plausible. It also denies that citizens have the right to do wrong in those respects. For even if there is such a thing as a right to do wrong in general, and even if political communities can have such a right (by no means foregone conclusions), there cannot be such a thing as a right to violate one's duties of justice—put differently, to violate other people's rights. Someone has a right to ϕ if her interest in ϕ is important enough to place third parties under a duty to her not to hinder him in respect of ϕ and, in some cases, to support him in relation to ϕ. It is hard to see how one's interest *in violating other parties' rights* could ever be important enough to hold third parties, including his victims themselves, under those duties. To claim otherwise is to claim, in effect, that his victims have no meaningful recourse against him. Yet on such a view, failures to comply with the (rights-based) demands of justice would not warrant retortive action, and rights would be worthless.[25]

The interesting question, then, is what may legitimately be done in response to citizenries' acts of heritage injustice. At one extreme, some might be tempted to argue that the defence of humankind's common heritage warrants military action; at another extreme, others might hold that it only warrants diplomatic remonstrations. Between those extremes lies a range of measures, such as (*inter alia*) economic sanctions, threats to withhold material assistance unless the wrongdoer state and its citizenry comply with their heritage-related duties, offers of assistance conditional upon compliance and expulsions from international organizations. Which retortive measures are morally justified depends on the seriousness of the dereliction of duty and on whether the proposed measures would be proportionate and effective. Full exploration of this complex issue, and of the difficulties inherent in institutionalizing the enforcement of heritage-related duties without further entrenching inequalities between powerful and less-powerful states, must await another occasion.[26]

CULTURAL APPROPRIATION

In 'A Doomed and Flawed Ideal?', I rehearsed the main criticisms of the Authorized Heritage Discourse: that it is Eurocentric, elitist, statist and Pollyannish. Contrastingly, I have attempted to provide an account of the universal value of humankind's heritage and of the moral demands it makes on us which do not rely on European conceptions of value and do not give primacy to cultural goods prized by the elites. Furthermore, my account sets stringent limits on states' rights with respect to those parts of our heritage which happen to be located on or are part of their territory, and it affirms the importance of negative heritage. Nevertheless, there remains a serious concern—namely, that my account is not sufficiently sensitive to the risks of cultural appropriation.

Cultural appropriation, roughly, is a process or act by which some agents regard as their cultural goods (widely construed as cultural physical objects and practices) which belong to some other agents. It takes different forms, such as the actual physical seizure and refusal to relinquish tangible objects, the replication or borrowing, without due acknowledgment, of cultural content, styles or themes and the imposition of one's aesthetic, anthropological and/or historical interpretations of the value and meaning of cultural goods, in particular when those interpretations come with little or no acknowledgment of their origins and embeddedness. Cultural 'appropriators' include artists, museums, scholars, governments and private corporations. Archaeologists, museum curators, heritage institutions and scholars of heritage studies have begun scrutinizing and calling those acts and processes into question: philosophers less so.[27]

Cultural appropriation is usually framed in morally laden terms, such that to appropriate a good which belongs to another culture is by definition wrongful. This is a mistake: whether something belongs to a particular culture does not in itself settle the question of which rights, if any, that culture has over this object.[28] A full exploration of the wrongfulness of cultural appropriation—if and when it is wrongful—is beyond the scope of my inquiry. My focus is on the charge that to say that we, as members of humankind, have rights with respect to certain heritage goods is to ride roughshod over the claims of particular cultures whose goods these are. Thus, I do not address conflicts as may arise between, for example, a culturally dominant majority and culturally endangered minorities within a single political community or between artists from such minorities who claim primary rights over a particular style precisely on grounds of cultural membership and artists who wish to borrow and modify that style.[29]

In the context of these essays, the charge of wrongful cultural appropriation does not seem apt when deployed against very ancient artefacts and artwork such as those found in prehistoric caves of the Palaeolithic era. In all other cases, the charge is levelled at claims of universal value, as well as at claims that humankind as a whole has entitlements in respect of that heritage. The 'value variant' of the charge goes like this: heritage goods which have universal value also have particularistic value; the risk, however, is that the particular will be erased by the universal—or more damningly so, by the *putatively* universal. Here are two examples: consider a heritage good whose universal value supervenes on the fact that it represents, or was the site and instrument of, a genocide—the paradigmatic example of a crime against humanity. Genocide, however, is, by definition, an attack on a particular ethnic group. To say without further ado that the site has universal value by dint of those representational, locational or contributory properties, and thus to deem it a fitting locus of rights and duties whose content is partly determined by this value judgement, risks occluding the fact that this genocide was primarily an attack on that group.

Consider now a heritage good whose universal value lies in the fact that it is valuable, pluralistically, to many different groups and individuals, who also have reasons to value the fact that it is valuable in this way. By focusing as it does on *tangible* heritage, my account occludes the cultural and quotidian practices in which those tangible goods are embedded and which they both reflect and instantiate. It is all very well to say

[FABRE] *Justice and Humankind's Common Heritage*

that the Bamiyan statues have universal value by dint of being particularly valuable to most people; the fact is, however, that they occupy a place in the past of Afghanis and Buddhists which they simply do not have, and which nothing can replace, in the past and lived-in geography of, say, Parisians; and exactly the same can be said, conversely, of Notre-Dame Cathedral.

There is a deeper concern there—namely, that partly as a result of existing power structures, which are the product of centuries of colonial violence, the particularistic value of those goods for the powerless and dispossessed will be erased by the particularistic values of the privileged under the guise of universalism. 'This is ours too', the powerful will say, 'and we understand it as well as you do; what we say about it is as important, as authoritative, as what you have to say. So if we think that all human beings in the world should, for example, have access to it, while you don't, well, tough: we'll just have to battle it out somehow'. Except, of course, that this is a battle which the powerful will likely win.

The charge of wrongful cultural appropriation is also deployed against claims of justice. When we claim as ours—all of us, without distinction—that which 'belongs' primarily, or at least significantly, to a subset of us, we risk allowing the powerful to appropriate that heritage and denying the powerless a voice in the construction and transmission of that heritage. In so doing, we subject the powerless to an epistemic injustice. Moreover, there is a risk that when heritage goods are destroyed or allowed to go to ruins, the wrong putatively done to humankind as a whole eclipses that which is done to those who are more directly harmed by such a loss. Finally, one might worry that my account is unable to accommodate the plausible intuition that physically removing heritage goods from the territory where they were found, or refusing to return them therein, is (at least in some cases) deeply wrong.[30]

As those remarks suggest, the charge of cultural appropriation sometimes relies on the assumption that cultural goods in general and heritage goods in particular are a culture's patrimony, over which that culture has a form of property entitlements. It also presupposes that it makes sense to speak of distinct, individuated cultures. On the first count, I am doubtful that a culture, *qua* culture, can own such goods.[31] On the second count, I am less doubtful that it is possible, at least in broad terms, to speak of distinct cultures while at the same time recognizing their mutual permeability. With both points in mind, the charge of cultural appropriation as deployed against the formation of value judgements about heritage can be answered by careful consideration of the history and location of that heritage's constitutive parts. Moreover, as we saw in 'Discretion', insofar as it is deployed against the institutional operation of those value judgements in heritage institutions, it can be answered by ensuring, as far as possible, that different voices are properly heard, thereby reducing the risk of committing an epistemic injustice. This, in turn, requires of us—not merely epistemically but morally speaking—that we interpret our duties in respect of that heritage somewhat differently than we might have done otherwise.

To illustrate, until fairly recently, international institutions such as UNESCO had a tendency to construe being authentic as that which is real and therefore must be preserved as it is. The 1964 Venice Charter for the Conservation and Restoration of Monuments and Sites is one of the best-known articulations of this view, in which the property of authenticity goes hand in hand with the property of integrity. Thirty years after its adoption, the 1994 Nara Declaration on Authenticity proclaimed that the official heritage discourse embodied in the Venice Charter fossilized the past and occluded the fact that conceptions of authenticity differ widely from one culture to the next. For example, the fact that in Japan some historic buildings are regularly repainted and rebuilt with modern materials does not (on an alternative and no less plausible understanding of authenticity) make them less real, less genuine, by this culture's own lights than if they were left alone—on the contrary. In determining what we owe to one another with respect to the protection of Japan's historic buildings which are part of our common heritage, it behooves us to defer to what the Japanese tell us. Our failure to do so is a failure to fulfil our duties in respect of our common heritage *qua* common heritage.[32]

Let me now turn to the worry that to say that we, all of us, are wronged by, for example, the wilful destruction and neglect of heritage goods mis-identifies the real victims. We should take that worry seriously. However, my account is compatible with the claim that some victims are wronged more grievously than others. By analogy, to kill a child is a grievous wrong to that child, yet it is also a wrong, albeit a lesser one, to her parents, inso-far as it destroys without warrant one of their most valuable, treasured relationships. The important thing is never to lose sight of who the primary victims are: however great my loss at the destruction of the Bamiyan statues, it pales into close to insignificance compared to the loss suffered by Buddhists all over the world. However devastating it would be to all of us were Venice to sink into the Adriatic, this is very little compared to what it would do to Venetians.

Those various replies enable us to tackle another serious concern which one may have about my account, to wit, that it cannot explain why it is unjust to seize cultural goods from, for example, Native Americans, to loot artworks from war zones or to refuse to return items taken in the course of colonial expeditions. It is easy to see why the concern arises. If a heritage good has universal value, its location does not matter. What matters is that it be displayed in encyclopaedic museums, whose aim is to keep them for the sake of posterity.[33]

Assuming that it is appropriate for those objects to be kept and displayed in an *encyclopaedic* museum, the argument cuts both ways: there is no reason why those goods should stay in the encyclopaedic museum where they currently are rather than in any other encyclopaedic museum. If the Egyptian or Greek authorities were to establish one such museum, and so long as they could vouch for the upkeep and preservation of (respectively) the Rosetta Stone and the Elgin Marbles, it is hard to see what objections the British Museum (and for that matter, Parliament, which would have to enact legislation to that end) could raise against return. In fact, as I suggested in 'Heritage and Practical Reasons', in the light of the vastly unequal distribution of artworks across museums, there is a case for *redistributing* those goods from richer to poorer countries.[34]

In any event, it is not clear that heritage goods of universal value should be removed or kept in an encyclopaedic museum—*a fortiori* in the encyclopaedic museums in which they currently are. In fact, justice sometimes mandates otherwise. For a start, as I noted in 'The Value of Heritage', some heritage goods are universally valuable by dint of the fact that they are part of an outstandingly beautiful and/or historically significant whole, such that we can only fully appreciate them, or properly understand, *in situ*. Not only ought they not to be taken from the latter without warrant: when they have been unwarrantedly taken away, there is a particularly strong case for their return.

Furthermore, as we saw in 'The Universal Value of Humankind's Heritage', claims of universality are compatible with claims that some heritage goods are especially significant to particular individuals and groups, by dint of their cultural identity and/or geographical location. This point on its own supports a *pro tanto* duty not to physically appropriate those goods. Moreover, as we also saw in 'Justice, Humankind and Common

Cultural Heritage', as a matter of justice, individuals whose rights have been violated have robust rights that steps be taken to remedy, as far as is feasible, the injustice to which they have been subjected and out of recognition of the fact that they suffered an injustice in the first instance. Those two points together support a *pro tanto* right to have those goods returned. They are particularly salient in respect of heritage that was looted in the course of wars or so-called punitive expeditions of colonial expansion. To the extent that lethally violent appropriation is a betrayal of the universal ideals on which the notion of global heritage rests, so is the unwarranted refusal to return them.[35]

In summary, advocating wholesale appropriation and blocking the return of any and all universally valuable heritage goods is no more a serious proposition than advocating an unqualified ban on taking and an unqualified obligation to return. Considerations of preservation may sometimes support appropriation and constrain return: at the bar of justice, there is a strong case for removing elements of humankind's heritage before they are destroyed. Conversely, considerations of historical significance and of aesthetic and epistemic value both constrain appropriation and support return. True, museums outside the richest countries in the world may not have the wherewithal to preserve and display those goods. The answer, though, does not lie in a refusal to return; rather, it lies in a proper redistribution of the requisite financial resources from (essentially) the Global North to the Global South.

CONCLUSION

In this essay, I built upon the conception of the universal value of some heritage goods deployed in the first essay and developed an account of justice with respect to humankind's common cultural heritage. At the bar of justice, I argued, we are under duties to one another, to our predecessors and to our successors not to destroy but also to preserve, to grant access to and to provide accurate information about that. As I sought to show, the claim that we are under such duties is compatible with some degree of territorial self-determination; it is also sensitive to the charge of undue cultural appropriation.

Every single one of the many claims I have made here needs developing. Furthermore, there are at least three lines of inquiry which I have briefly mentioned without being able to develop them.

First, I have focused on the tangible basis of our cultural heritage. It would pay to investigate whether natural landmarks and intangible cultural goods are part of humankind's common heritage *tout court* and, if so, whether my account applies to those goods too.

Second, my account of our duties in respect of humankind's common heritage remains seriously incomplete. While I have explored duties not to destroy and to preserve that heritage, as well as to grant access to it and to impart knowledge about it, I have not said much at any length, if at all, about other duties we may have. In particular, a full treatment of the value of a common heritage needs to account for our affective reactions to that heritage, such as awe at its beauty or sadness at its possible disappearance. A full treatment of our moral obligations in respect of that heritage would therefore need to ascertain whether they can be such a thing as a moral obligation, in general, and in this particular case, to *feel* awe and sadness, failing which we are guilty of wrongdoing to our fellow human beings. The claim that there is such an obligation is far from straightforward.

Finally, I have not addressed trade-offs between, on the one hand, the protection of humankind's heritage and, on the other hand, the protection of heritage which, though of considerable value to a particular people or community, is not part of humankind's; nor have I tackled tensions between our heritage-related duties and the provision of other goods which is also mandated by justice. I do think, or at any rate, I hope, that it is merely a limitation (albeit an important one), and not an indictment, of those essays—in just the same way as an account of our obligations in respect of health care, of the justice system or of education does not lose merit simply for not adjudicating the conflicts that inevitably arise between them. Nevertheless, a fuller, certainly longer normative study of our duties with respect to our common heritage would need to say something about those trade-offs. On an often-cited view—powerfully articulated by Frederico Veronese, UNESCO's director general at the launch of the Nubia campaign—'True, when the welfare of suffering human beings is at stake, then, if need be, images of granite and porphyry must be sacrificed unhesitatingly. But no one forced to make such a choice could contemplate without anguish the necessity for making it'.[36] Admirable though the commitment to give priority to lives over stones may be, UNESCO has not always been seen to live by it. To be sure, sometimes, saving our heritage goes hand in hand with protecting lives and livelihoods. In war, for example, diverting troops and planes away from densely populated areas may well save heritage sites. Protecting lived-in landscapes of outstanding natural beauty helps secure the livelihood of their inhabitants. Heritage preservation campaigns have sometimes provided impetus for improving basic facilities, such as access to clean water and sanitation.[37] These are relatively easy cases, though. The much harder cases are those in which a choice has to be made between our duties of justice in relation to our common heritage and our nonheritage duties not to destroy but indeed to protect the lives and livelihoods of our fellow human beings. I do not yet have a solution to this dilemma. Indeed, I am not sure that there is one.

There is much more work to be done, in other words. Be that as it may, I hope to have made some progress towards convincing you, if you were initially a sceptic, that the fate of the Bamiyan statues, Notre-Dame Cathedral, the Central Slave and Ivory Trade Route, the few remaining copies of the Gutenberg Bible, India's tea plantations and China's ancient musical instruments is a matter of justice—for all of us.

ACKNOWLEDGMENTS

These essays are based on the Tanner Lectures I delivered at Stanford University on May 10–12, 2022. I am deeply grateful to the Stanford Tanner Committee for their invitation and to my respondents—K. Anthony Appiah, Lynn Meskell, Anna Stilz and Leif Wenar—for their generous engagement and helpful suggestions, on the basis of which I made further revisions. I am aware that, in part due to space constraints, I have not been able to meet their objections in full.

Earlier drafts were presented at various named lectures, seminars and conferences, whose participants I thank for their penetrating insights: the Heritage in War Group, the Centre for the Study of Social Justice at Oxford, the University of Glasgow (2020 Dudley Knowles Memorial Lecture), the University of St Andrews, Queen's University Belfast (2021 Frank Wright Memorial Lecture), King's College London (2021 Annual Peace Lecture), the University of Toronto (2022 Roseman Lecture in Practical Ethics). For incisive written comments on earlier materials, I am grateful to Carla Bagnoli, C. M. Lim, Connor Kianpour, Kasper Lippert-Rasmussen, Mary McCabe, David Miller, Margaret Moore and Zosia Stemplowska. Andrew Cohen, the director of the Jean Beer Blumenfeld Center for Ethics at Georgia State University, organized a workshop on the typescript in March 2022. The commentators on that occasion were Avery Kolers, Carolyn Korsmeyer, Erich Hatala Matthes and Gopal Sreenivasan. Their rigorous responses, together with the audience's generous engagement, were invaluable at a crucial stage of the writing process.

All Souls College is an ideal intellectual community for pursuing a project of that kind, and it gives me great pleasure, once again, to thank its Warden, Sir John Vickers, and its Fellows for their unstinting support. I am particularly grateful to Sir Keith Thomas, one of the world's leading historians and a former Trustee of the British Museum. Keith Thomas is somewhat sceptical of philosophers' love for abstract theorizing. (I sympathise—well, at least sometimes.) Under his rigorous yet gentle probing, I have tried never to lose sight of the culturally specific dimensions of our heritage. Whether I have succeeded is not for me to say.

NOTES

1 Interestingly, Emmerich de Vattel himself, who is best known for his statist account of war, offers a stark condemnation of the wartime destruction of cultural property that is of value to humankind as a whole. See E. De Vattel, *Le Droit Des Gens—Principes De La Loi Naturelle Appliqués À La Conduite Et Aux Affairs Des Nations Et Des Souverains* (Washington, DC: Carnegie Institute, 1916), bk. 3, chap. 9, §168. For discussion, see J. H. Merryman, "Cultural Property Internationalism", *International Journal of Cultural Property* 12, no. 1 (2005): 11–39. On the place of heritage in the history of Western war theory, see D. Brunstetter, "A Tale of Two Cities", *Global Intellectual History* 4, no. 4 (2019): 369–88. The judgement of the ICC in the Mahdi case can be found at https://www.icc-cpi.int/Pages/record.aspx?docNo=ICC-01/12-01/15-171 (see, in particular, para. 80 of the judgement for the claim that the protected status of the sites adds to the gravity of the crime). The ICTY's judgement in the Jokic case is available at https://www.icty.org/x/cases/miodrag_jokic/tjug/en/jok-sj040318e.pdf (see esp. paras. 48–53).
2 For example, we might think that taking selfies at Auschwitz is a dereliction of duties. Thanks to E. H. Matthes for the point and for drawing my attention to relevant literature, for example, C. Bareither, "Difficult Heritage and Digital Media: 'Selfie Culture' and Emotional Practices at the Memorial to the Murdered Jews of Europe", *International Journal of Heritage Studies* 27, no. 1 (2021): 57–72.
3 I assume, without arguing for it, that justice is rights based.
4 Due to space constraints, this is a very rough account. In particular, there are differences between Sen's and Nussbaum's approaches, which I cannot rehearse here. See, for example, M. C. Nussbaum, *Creating Capabilities—the Human Development Approach* (Cambridge, MA: Harvard University Press, 2011), esp. 33–34 for the list; A. Sen, *Development as Freedom* (New York: Oxford University Press, 1999); and A. K. Sen, "Elements of a Theory of Human Rights", *Philosophy & Public Affairs* 32, no. 4 (2004): 315–56. For the view that cultural heritage is central to human flourishing, which in turn imposes on us a range of obligations in respect of it, see also S. Harding, "Value, Obligation, and Cultural Heritage", *Arizona State Law Review* 31, no. 2 (1999): 291–354. For a sceptical take on the relationship between capabilities-based human rights and the ethics of heritage, particularly universal heritage, see L. Meskell, "Human Rights and Heritage Ethics", *Anthropological Quarterly* 83, no. 4 (2010): 839–59.

5 S. Scheffler, *The Rejection of Consequentialism—a Philosophical Investigation of the Considerations Underlying Rival Moral Conceptions*, rev. ed. (Oxford: Clarendon, 2003).

6 On the ability to feel awe as a component of human flourishing, see, for example, K. Kristjánsson, "Awe: An Aristotelian Analysis of a Non-Aristotelian Virtuous Emotion", *Philosophia* 45, no. 1 (2017): 125–42.

7 For a scientific note detailing the discovery of the flute, see J. Zhang et al., "Oldest Playable Instrument Found at Jiahu Neolithic Site in China", *Nature* 401 (September 23, 1999): 366–68. The instrument can be heard on the website Open Culture at https://www.openculture.com/2017/01/hear-a-9000-year-old -flute-the-worlds-oldest-playable-instrument-get-played-again.html. Moreschi's recording can be heard at https://archive.org/details/AlessandroMoreschi.

8 The epistemic injustice under study here differs from the injustice done to agents whose testimonies about the wrongful harms which they incur are not heard or taken seriously, as a result of prejudicial stereotyping. I return to this point in sec. 'Cultural Appropriation'.

9 Thanks to A. Kolers for the point.

10 A. Stilz, "Reply to My Critics", *Journal of Social Philosophy* 52, no. 1 (2021): 40–49. For discussions of the case of Palmyra, see, for example, Z. Kamash, "'Postcard to Palmyra': Bringing the Public into Debates over Post-conflict Reconstruction in the Middle East", *World Archaeology* 49, no. 5 (2017): 608–22; R. Khunti, "The Problem with Printing Palmyra: Exploring the Ethics of Using 3D Printing Technology to Reconstruct Heritage", *Studies in Digital Heritage* 2, no. 1 (2018): 1–12. The replica of the Tomb of Tutankhamun was produced by the foundation Factum Arte (https://www.factum-arte.com/). Thanks to K. A. Appiah for the suggestion.

11 On the importance of being 'in the presence of the real thing', see Korsmeyer, *Things*; and P. Lamarque, *Work and Object—Explorations in the Metaphysics of Art* (Oxford: Oxford University Press, 2010), 59. Thanks to M. McCabe for helping me firm up the connection between connecting with goods and connecting with the people who made them. Note that my point here is compatible with the claim that, in the light of the damage sustained by some landmarks as a result of exposure to air, light and carbon dioxide, our *pro tanto* duties to grant access to them are outweighed by our duties to preserve them for posterity: replicas may well be the best compromise we can hope for between those competing demands.

12 It was put to me by a participant at the Oxford Centre for the Study of Social Justice seminar in February 2020. Thanks, too, to G. Sreenivasan, A. Stilz and L. Wenar for pressing me hard on this.

13 Thanks to C. Kianpour for suggesting I appeal to precautionary duties.

14 C. Fabre, *Cosmopolitan Peace* (Oxford: Oxford University Press, 2016), 296.

15 J. Thompson, "Obligations of Justice and the Interests of the Dead", *International Journal of Applied Philosophy* 30, no. 2 (2016): 289–300; Z. Stemplowska, "Duties to the Dead", in *Oxford Studies in Political Philosophy*, ed. D. Sobel, P. Vallentyne, and S. Wall (Oxford: Oxford University Press, 2020), 32–60. See also James, "Why Old Things Matter", 317–18, in the specific context of old objects. John Ruskin argues in 'The Lamp of Memory' that the built heritage belongs to the dead, and that consequently, 'we have no right whatever to touch it' (Ruskin, "Lamp of Memory", 245). Even if the premise (of ownership) were true, which is doubtful, it would not follow that restoration is morally wrong (see 'Heritage and Practical Reasons'). Note that our

duties to the dead are *pro tanto* duties: like any duty, they may be overridden by weightier considerations.

16   Thanks to Sarah Fine for raising it.

17   Thanks to Sarah Fine for the point.

18   A classic defence of the supersession thesis is J. Waldron, "Superseding Historic Injustice", *Ethics* 103, no. 1 (1992): 4–28.

19   For a seminal defence of that view, see R. E. Goodin, "What Is So Special about Our Fellow Countrymen?", *Ethics* 98, no. 4 (1988): 663–86.

20   A. Stilz, *Territorial Sovereignty—a Philosophical Exploration* (Oxford: Oxford University Press, 2019).

21   A. Kolers, *Land, Conflict, and Justice—a Political Theory of Territory* (Cambridge: Cambridge University Press, 2009); T. Meisels, *Territorial Rights* (Dordrecht, Netherlands: Springer, 2005); D. Miller, "Territorial Rights: Concept and Justification", *Political Studies* 60, no. 2 (2012): 252–68; M. Moore, *A Political Theory of Territory* (Oxford: Oxford University Press, 2015).

22   Proponents of noninstrumental accounts do not address the implications of their views for humankind's common heritage (although they accept that the state does not have exclusive jurisdiction over the natural resources which happen to be located on or under its territory). I extract those implications, in Stilz's case, in C. Fabre, "Territorial Sovereignty and Humankind's Common Heritage", *Journal of Social Philosophy* 52, no. 1 (2021): 17–23.

23   Two points. First, I do not intend that claim to apply to the case of artists destroying their own works of art. For an interesting discussion, see J. Young, "Destroying Works of Art", *Journal of Aesthetics and Art Criticism* 47, no. 4 (1989): 367–73. Young thinks that Bach would have acted wrongly had he burned the one and only score of *St Matthew's Passion*. I am tentatively inclined to agree though cannot develop the thought further without a full-blown philosophical account of intellectual property rights.

Second, my argument relies on the assumption that individuals themselves are under duties of justice, whether or not those duties are enforced in the law. This is not an uncontroversial position. (See, for example, G. A. Cohen, *Rescuing Justice and Equality* [Cambridge, MA: Harvard University Press, 2008]). Yet I do think that a private collector who would elect to 'play darts with a Rembrandt' would commit an injustice even if the law allowed him to do so. I borrow that phrase from Joseph Sax's wonderful book on the interplay and conflict between private and public rights of ownership over cultural goods (J. L. Sax, *Playing Darts with a Rembrandt—Public and Private Rights in Cultural Treasures* [Ann Arbor: University of Michigan Press, 1999]).

24   J. Hilburg, "Foster + Partners Pitches New Notre-Dame Spire as Competition Heats Up", *Architect's Digest*, April 22, 2019. In her response to the lectures, A. Stilz raised the following example: suppose that Russian democrats manage to overthrow President Putin's administration and to transform Russia into a functioning liberal democracy. They decide to raze the Kremlin— that symbol of their country's autocratic past—and to build in its place a new building, whose aesthetic, they think, will embody their aspirations for openness and freedom. On Stilz's view, they would commit no wrong. My intuition is that they would. The difference between this case and the hypothetical destruction of the Genbaku Dome is that the latter remains (in the example as I construe it) commemorative and is of a piece with Japanese conceptions of authenticity. Not so in the Kremlin example. I am aware I am on shaky grounds here, though, and hope to revisit those cases in future work.

25 I take Stilz to endorse, by implication, the view that a state that acts wrongly in respect of our common heritage nevertheless has the right to do so (Stilz, *Territorial Sovereignty*, 237 and 240–41). Against Stilz's defence, see C. H. Wellman, "Do Legitimate States Have a Right to Do Wrong?", *Ethics & International Affairs* 35, no. 4 (2021): 515–25.

26 On the protection of heritage in war, see H. Frowe and D. Matravers, *Stones and Lives: The Ethics of Protecting Heritage in War* (Oxford: Oxford University Press, forthcoming). To illustrate the challenge of enforcing heritage-related duties impartially, recall that at the time of writing this, Russia is still a member of UNESCO, despite mounting evidence that its forces are deliberately targeting Ukraine's cultural heritage. The challenge is not specific to those duties, of course.

27 Useful works with interesting case studies include Greenfield, *Return of Cultural Treasures*; C. Renfrew, *Loot, Legitimacy and Ownership* (London: Duckworth, 2000); and J. O. Young, ed., *The Ethics of Cultural Appropriation* (Oxford: Wiley-Blackwell, 2009).

28 J. L. Thomas, "When Does Something 'Belong' to a Culture?", *British Journal of Aesthetics* 61, no. 3 (2021): 275–90.

29 For a book-length treatment of those conflicts, whose central thesis is that cultural appropriation is not always morally wrong, see J. O. Young, *Cultural Appropriation and the Arts* (Oxford: Wiley-Blackwell, 2010). For criticism, E. H. Matthes, "Cultural Appropriation and Oppression", *Philosophical Studies* 176, no. 4 (2019): 1003–13.

30 For the worry about epistemic injustice, see A. Pantazatos, "The Ethics of Trusteeship and the Biography of Objects", *Royal Institute of Philosophy Supplement* 79 (2016): 179–97; A. Pantazatos, "Epistemic Injustice and Cultural Heritage", in *The Routledge Handbook of Epistemic Injustice*, ed. J. M. Kidd, J. Medina, and G. Pohlhaus (London: Routledge, 2017), 370–85. Pantazatos's concern is with epistemic injustice and heritage in general and not specifically with ascriptions of universal value to heritage goods, but it is highly relevant to it. For the worry about who the real victims are, see L. Meskell, *A Future in Ruins—UNESCO, World Heritage, and the Dream of Peace* (Oxford: Oxford University Press, 2018), chap. 8. For a general discussion of return, see Greenfield, *Return of Cultural Treasures*, chap. 13.

31 See also K. A. Appiah, "Whose Culture Is It?", in *Whose Culture? The Promise of Museums and the Debate over Antiquities*, ed. J. Cuno (Princeton, NJ: Princeton University Press, 2009), 71–86.

32 Smith, *Uses of Heritage*, 54. On shifting understandings of authenticity within UNESCO, see, for example, Labadi, *UNESCO, Cultural Heritage*, 117.

33 See N. MacGregor, "To Shape the Citizens of 'That Great City, the World'", in *Whose Culture? The Promise of Museums and the Debate over Antiquities*, ed. J. Cuno (Princeton, NJ: Princeton University Press, 2009), 37–54; J. Cuno, *Who Owns Antiquity? Museums and the Battle over Our Ancient Heritage* (Princeton, NJ: Princeton University Press, 2008). For contrasting positions, see, for example, Greenfield, *Return of Cultural Treasures*, esp. chap. 2 on the Elgin Marbles; and D. Hicks, *The Brutish Museums: The Benin Bronzes, Colonial Violence and Cultural Restitution* (London: Pluto, 2020), on the Benin Bronzes.

34 I also moot this possibility in C. Fabre, "Looted Artworks: A Portrait of Justice", in *Philosophers Take on the World*, ed. D. Edmonds (Oxford: Oxford University Press, 2016), 34–36. For a longer argument, see E. H. Matthes, "Repatriation and the Radical Redistribution of Art", *Ergo* 4, no. 32 (2017): 931–53.

35 For a particularly trenchant articulation of this point, see Hicks, *Brutish Museums*, chaps. 16 and 18.
36 F. Veronese's speech can be accessed at https://en.unesco.org/courier/june-1960/egypt-gift-nile (accessed October 10, 2023).
37 For a recent discussion of the ways in which authorities in India have grappled with this issue, see L. Meskell, "Toilets First, Temples Second: Adopting Heritage in Neoliberal India", *International Journal of Heritage Studies* 27, no. 2 (2021): 151–69. As Meskell notes, India's record in that record is far from blemish free.

REFERENCES

Anderson, E. *Value in Ethics and Economics*. Cambridge, MA: Harvard University Press, 1993.

Appiah, K. A. *Cosmopolitanism*. London: Allen Lane, 2006.

Appiah, K. A. "Whose Culture Is It?" In *Whose Culture? The Promise of Museums and the Debate over Antiquities*, edited by J. Cuno, 71–86. Princeton, NJ: Princeton University Press, 2009.

Bareither, C. "Difficult Heritage and Digital Media: 'Selfie Culture' and Emotional Practices at the Memorial to the Murdered Jews of Europe." *International Journal of Heritage Studies* 27, no. 1 (2021): 57–72.

Benhabib, S. *Another Cosmopolitanism—Tanner Lectures on Human Values*. Oxford: Oxford University Press, 2006.

Bicknell, J., J. Judkins, and C. Korsmeyer, eds. *Philosophical Perspectives on Ruins, Monuments and Memorials*. London: Routledge, 2019.

Brentano, F. *The Origin of Our Knowledge of Right and Wrong*. London: Routledge & Kegan Paul, 1969.

Brumann, C. "Creating Universal Value: The UNESCO World Heritage Convention in Its Fifth Decade." In *The Oxford Handbook of Public Heritage—Theory and Practice*, edited by A. M. Labrador and N. A. Silberman. Oxford: Oxford University Press, 2018.

Brunstetter, D. "A Tale of Two Cities." *Global Intellectual History* 4, no. 4 (2019): 369–88.

Bülow, W., and J. L. Thomas. "On the Ethics of Reconstructing Destroyed Cultural Heritage Monuments." *Journal of the American Philosophical Association* 6, no. 4 (2020): 483–501.

Busby, M. "Woman Who Bought Shredded Banksy Artwork Will Go through with Purchase." *Guardian*, November 10, 2018.

Cafaro, P. "Valuing Wild Nature." In *The Oxford Handbook of Environmental Ethics*, edited by S. M. Gardiner and A. Thomson, 125–36. Oxford: Oxford University Press, 2017.

Chisholm, R. "Defining Intrinsic Value." *Analysis* 41, no. 2 (1981): 99–100.

Cleere, H. "The Concept of 'Outstanding Universal Value' in the World Heritage Convention." *Conservation and Management of Archaeological Sites* 1, no. 4 (1996): 227–33.

Cohen, G. A. *Rescuing Justice and Equality*. Cambridge, MA: Harvard University Press, 2008.

Cuno, J. *Who Owns Antiquity? Museums and the Battle over Our Ancient Heritage*. Princeton, NJ: Princeton University Press, 2008.

Desilvey, C. *Curating Decay—Heritage beyond Saving*. Minneapolis: University of Minnesota Press, 2017.

De Vattel, E. *Le Droit Des Gens—Principes De La Loi Naturelle Appliqués À La Conduite Et Aux Affairs Des Nations Et Des Souverains*. Washington, DC: Carnegie Institute, 1916.

Ewing, A. C. *The Definition of Good*. London: Routledge and Kegan Paul, 1948.

Fabre, C. *Cosmopolitan Peace*. Oxford: Oxford University Press, 2016.

Fabre, C. "Looted Artworks: A Portrait of Justice." In *Philosophers Take on the World*, edited by D. Edmonds, 34–36. Oxford: Oxford University Press, 2016.

Fabre, C. "Territorial Sovereignty and Humankind's Common Heritage." *Journal of Social Philosophy* 52, no. 1 (2021): 17–23.

Forrest, C. *International Law and the Protection of Cultural Heritage*. London: Routledge, 2010.

Fowler, P. *Landscapes for the World*. Bollington: Windgather, 2004.

Frowe, H., and D. Matravers. *Stones and Lives: The Ethics of Protecting Heritage in War*. Oxford: Oxford University Press, forthcoming.

Gonzalez-Ruibal, A. "Vernacular Cosmopolitanism: An Archeological Critique of Universalistic Reason." In *Cosmopolitan Archeologies*, edited by L. Meskell, 113–39. Durham, NC: Duke University Press, 2009.

Goodin, R. E. "What Is So Special about Our Fellow Countrymen?" *Ethics* 98, no. 4 (1988): 663–86.

Greenfield, J. *The Return of Cultural Treasures*. Cambridge: Cambridge University Press, 2007.

Harding, S. "Value, Obligation, and Cultural Heritage." *Arizona State Law Review* 31, no. 2 (1999): 291–354.

Harrison, R. *Heritage: Critical Approaches*. London: Routledge, 2013.

Hicks, D. *The Brutish Museums: The Benin Bronzes, Colonial Violence and Cultural Restitution*. London: Pluto, 2020.

Hilburg, J. "Foster + Partners Pitches New Notre-Dame Spire as Competition Heats Up." *Architect's Digest*, April 22, 2019.

Hodder, I. "Cultural Heritage Rights: From Ownership and Descent to Justice and Well-Being." *Anthropological Quarterly* 83, no. 4 (2010): 861–82.

James, S. P. "Why Old Things Matter." *Journal of Moral Philosophy* 12, no. 3 (2015): 313–29.

Janowski, J. "Bringing Back Bamiyan's Buddhas." *Journal of Applied Philosophy* 28, no. 1 (2011): 44–64.

Kamash, Z. "'Postcard to Palmyra': Bringing the Public into Debates over Post-conflict Reconstruction in the Middle East." *World Archaeology* 49, no. 5 (2017): 608–22.

Khalidi, L. "The Destruction of Yemen and Its Cultural Heritage." *International Journal of Middle East Studies* 49, no. 4 (2017): 735–38.

Khunti, R. "The Problem with Printing Palmyra: Exploring the Ethics of Using 3D Printing Technology to Reconstruct Heritage." *Studies in Digital Heritage* 2, no. 1 (2018): 1–12.

Kolers, A. *Land, Conflict, and Justice—a Political Theory of Territory.* Cambridge: Cambridge University Press, 2009.

Korsmeyer, C. *Things—in Touch with the Past.* Oxford: Oxford University Press, 2019.

Kristjánsson, K. "Awe: An Aristotelian Analysis of a Non-Aristotelian Virtuous Emotion." *Philosophia* 45, no. 1 (2017): 125–42.

Labadi, S. *UNESCO, Cultural Heritage, and Outstanding Universal Value.* Lanham, MD: Rowman & Littlefield, 2013.

Lamarque, P. "Reflections on the Ethics and Aesthetics of Restoration and Conservation." *British Journal of Aesthetics* 56, no. 3 (2016): 281–99.

Lamarque, P. *Work and Object—Explorations in the Metaphysics of Art.* Oxford: Oxford University Press, 2010.

Lim, C. M. "Vandalizing Tainted Commemorations." *Philosophy & Public Affairs* 48, no. 4 (2020): 185–216.

Lowenthal, D. *The Heritage Crusade and the Spoils of History.* Cambridge: Cambridge University Press, 1998.

MacGregor, N. "To Shape the Citizens of 'That Great City, the World.'" In *Whose Culture? The Promise of Museums and the Debate over Antiquities*, edited by J. Cuno, 33–54. Princeton, NJ: Princeton University Press, 2009.

Matravers, D. "The Reconstruction of Damaged or Destroyed Heritage." In *Philosophical Perspectives on Ruins, Monuments and Memorials,* edited by J. Bicknell, J. Judkins, and C. Korsmeyer, 189–200. London: Routledge, 2019.

Matthes, E. H. "Cultural Appropriation and Oppression." *Philosophical Studies* 176, no. 4 (2019): 1003–13.

Matthes, E. H. "History, Value, and Irreplaceability." *Ethics* 124, no. 1 (2013): 35–64.

Matthes, E. H. "Impersonal Value, Universal Value, and the Scope of Cultural Heritage." *Ethics* 125, no. 4 (2015): 999–1027.

Matthes, E. H. "Repatriation and the Radical Redistribution of Art." *Ergo* 4, no. 32 (2017): 931–53.

Matthes, E. H. "Who Owns up to the Past? Heritage and Historical Injustice." *Journal of the American Philosophical Association* 4, no. 1 (2018): 87–104.

Meisels, T. *Territorial Rights*. Dordrecht, Netherlands: Springer, 2005.

Merryman, J. H. "Cultural Property Internationalism." *International Journal of Cultural Property* 12, no. 1 (2005): 11–39.

Meskell, L. *A Future in Ruins—UNESCO, World Heritage, and the Dream of Peace*. Oxford: Oxford University Press, 2018.

Meskell, L. "Human Rights and Heritage Ethics." *Anthropological Quarterly* 83, no. 4 (2010): 839–59.

Meskell, L. "Toilets First, Temples Second: Adopting Heritage in Neoliberal India." *International Journal of Heritage Studies* 27, no. 2 (2021): 151–69.

Meskell, L., and B. Isakhan. "UNESCO, World Heritage and the Gridlock over Yemen." *Third World Quarterly* 41, no. 10 (2020): 1776–91.

Miller, D. "Territorial Rights: Concept and Justification." *Political Studies* 60, no. 2 (2012): 252–68.

Moore, M. *A Political Theory of Territory*. Oxford: Oxford University Press, 2015.

Nussbaum, M. C. *Creating Capabilities—the Human Development Approach*. Cambridge, MA: Harvard University Press, 2011.

Omland, A. "The Ethics of the World Heritage Concept." In *The Ethics of Archaeology: Philosophical Perspectives on Archaeological Practice*, edited by Chris Scarre and Geoffrey Scarre, 242–59. Cambridge: Cambridge University Press, 2006.

Pantazatos, A. "Epistemic Injustice and Cultural Heritage." In *The Routledge Handbook of Epistemic Injustice*, edited by J. M. Kidd, J. Medina, and G. Pohlhaus, 370–85. London: Routledge, 2017.

Pantazatos, A. "The Ethics of Trusteeship and the Biography of Objects." *Royal Institute of Philosophy Supplement* 79 (2016): 179–97.

Raz, J. *Value, Respect, and Attachment.* Cambridge: Cambridge University Press, 2001.

Renfrew, C. *Loot, Legitimacy and Ownership.* London: Duckworth, 2000.

Ruskin, J. "The Lamp of Memory." In *The Seven Lamps of Architecture—the Works of John Ruskin,* vol. 8, edited by E. T. Cook and A. Wedderburn, 221–47. Cambridge: Cambridge University Press, 2010.

Sagoff, M. "On Restoring and Reproducing Art." *Journal of Philosophy* 75, no. 3 (1978): 453–69.

Savile, A. *The Test of Time—an Essay in Philosophical Aesthetics.* Oxford: Clarendon, 1982.

Sax, J. L. *Playing Darts with a Rembrandt—Public and Private Rights in Cultural Treasures.* Ann Arbor: University of Michigan Press, 1999.

Scanlon, T. M. *What We Owe to Each Other.* Cambridge, MA: Harvard University Press, 1998.

Scheffler, S. "Conceptions of Cosmopolitanism." *Utilitas* 11, no. 3 (1999): 255–76.

Scheffler, S. *The Rejection of Consequentialism—a Philosophical Investigation of the Considerations Underlying Rival Moral Conceptions.* Rev. ed. Oxford: Clarendon, 2003.

Scheffler, S. "Valuing." In *Reasons and Recognition: Essays on the Philosophy of T. M. Scanlon,* edited by S. Freeman and R. Kumar, 23–48. Oxford: Oxford University Press, 2012.

Sen, A. K. *Development as Freedom.* New York: Oxford University Press, 1999.

Sen, A. K. "Elements of a Theory of Human Rights." *Philosophy & Public Affairs* 32, no. 4 (2004): 315–56.

Smith, L. *Uses of Heritage.* London: Routledge, 2006.

Stemplowska, Z. "Duties to the Dead." In *Oxford Studies in Political Philosophy,* edited by D. Sobel, P. Vallentyne, and S. Wall, 32–60. Oxford: Oxford University Press, 2020.

Stilz, A. "Reply to My Critics." *Journal of Social Philosophy* 52, no. 1 (2021): 40–49.

Stilz, A. *Territorial Sovereignty—a Philosophical Exploration.* Oxford: Oxford University Press, 2019.

Thomas, J. L. "When Does Something 'Belong' to a Culture?" *British Journal of Aesthetics* 61, no. 3 (2021): 275–90.

Thompson, J. "Obligations of Justice and the Interests of the Dead." *International Journal of Applied Philosophy* 30, no. 2 (2016): 289–300.

Waldron, J. "Minorities Cultures and the Cosmopolitan Alternative." *University of Michigan Journal of Law Reform* 25, nos. 3–4 (1991): 751–93.

Waldron, J. "Superseding Historic Injustice." *Ethics* 103, no. 1 (1992): 4–28.

Walzer, M. *Nation and Universe—Tanner Lecture on Human Values*. Tanner Lectures on Human Values, 1989.

Wellman, C. H. "Do Legitimate States Have a Right to Do Wrong?" *Ethics & International Affairs* 35, no. 4 (2021): 515–25.

Wicks, R. "Architectural Restoration: Resurrection or Replications?" *British Journal of Aesthetics* 34, no. 2 (1994): 163–69.

Wilsmore, S. J. "What Justifies Restoration?" *Philosophical Quarterly* 38, no. 150 (1988): 56–67.

Young, J. O. *Cultural Appropriation and the Arts*. Oxford: Wiley-Blackwell, 2010.

Young, J. O. "Destroying Works of Art." *Journal of Aesthetics and Art Criticism* 47, no. 4 (1989): 367–73.

Young, J. O., ed. *The Ethics of Cultural Appropriation*. Oxford: Wiley-Blackwell, 2009.

Zhang, J., G. Harbottle, Z. Kong, and C. Wang. "Oldest Playable Instrument Found at Jiahu Neolithic Site in China." *Nature* 401 (September 23, 1999): 366–68.

Zimmerman, M. J. *The Nature of Intrinsic Value*. Lanham, MD: Rowman & Littlefield, 2001.

Welcome to the Anthropocene

ELIZABETH KOLBERT

The Tanner Lectures on Human Values

Delivered at

Princeton University
April 28–29, 2022

ELIZABETH KOLBERT is a journalist and author best known for her work on climate change and the environment. She has been a staff writer at the *New Yorker* since 1999. Her work has received numerous honors, including two National Magazine Awards, a National Academies Communications Award, a Heinz Award, a Guggenheim Fellowship, the Blake Dodd Prize from the American Academy of Arts and Letters, and the Pell Center Prize for Story in the Public Square. Her books include *Field Notes from a Catastrophe: Man, Nature, and Climate Change*; the Pulitzer Prize–winning *The Sixth Extinction: An Unnatural History*; and most recently, *Under a White Sky: The Nature of the Future*, which was shortlisted for a Wainwright Prize in the Global Conservation Writing category and was selected as a top ten book of 2021 by the *Washington Post*.

LECTURE I.
WHAT ON EARTH HAVE WE DONE?

It's a tremendous honor to be here today. It's also disconcerting. As a journalist, I spend a lot of my time hanging out on university campuses, conducting interviews, touring labs, and viewing specimens stored in drawers or vats of liquid nitrogen. I've spent time doing just that here at Princeton. I also often go out with academic researchers in the field. Most of the material in the articles I've written has come from traveling with and interviewing people very much like you. For a journalist to address an academic audience upsets the natural order of things—hence the disorientation. It feels strange to be up here talking instead of listening to you and taking notes.

Since I am here as a journalist, I am going to do what journalists do, which is to tell stories. The stories I've been telling recently are about the natural world and the vast unsupervised experiments we are performing on it. Today, I'm going to relate three stories on that theme, set in three different places, each involving an experiment. And here I mean a deliberate experiment, a controlled experiment, the sort of experiment scientists undertake in an effort to understand the world rather than the crazy, whole-earth experiment we have collectively embarked on. My first story begins with a book.

A lot of books are sent to the *New Yorker*'s offices by publishers in the hopes that someone will take an interest in them. Way more books are sent than can be reviewed in the pages of the magazine, and most of them end up on what is called the bench, which is just what it sounds like—a bench. Books on the bench are free for anyone in the office to take home with them. And one day, I was wandering by the bench and saw a book called the *Two-Mile Time Machine*. As it happens, it was published by Princeton University Press. It's by Richard Alley, who's a geologist at Penn State. I'm guessing some of you know him. And the book looked interesting, so I grabbed it.

The *Two-Mile Time Machine* is about ice coring projects. When I picked up the book, I had never heard of an ice core. At that point, in 2000, I thought of myself as a political reporter, the kind of person who hung out in Albany and City Hall. But I was fascinated by Alley's account of his work. So when I finished the book, I called him up and asked if I could go with him on his next expedition, to the Greenland ice sheet. It

[105]

turned out the project he had been working on—which was known as GISP 2—was completed. But he recommended that I get in touch with a Danish team that was drilling a new core at a site called North GRIP. Which I did. And that summer, I flew to Greenland with the New York Air National Guard, which operates these special ski-equipped C130s that provide support for the scientific operations on the ice sheet. When you fly with the Air National Guard, you fly in the cargo hold. We flew from Schenectady to Kangerlussuaq, on Greenland's west coast, where we picked up some Danish dignitaries, including a cabinet minister. And then we flew up to North GRIP, which was at the very center of the ice sheet, and had a runway made out of snow.

NorthGRIP, itself, wasn't much of a place. A geodesic dome had been ordered, prefab, from Minnesota. It was where everyone ate and also where you could use the camp's sole toilet, a very high-tech device from Sweden. The drilling chamber, where the work actually got done, was under the ice.

The reason Alley's book was called the *Two-Mile Time Machine* is because at its center, the Greenland Ice Sheet is two miles thick. Drilling straight down through two miles of ice is no easy feat. What you do is you take what's basically a long steel tube, with some sharp teeth at one end, and set that spinning. And that cuts through the ice. And if you are lucky, when you pull up the tube, inside is a cylinder of ice that's several feet long and about six inches in diameter. And you do that over and over again. Meanwhile, as you are drilling, the ice is moving. Ice, like water, flows, just a lot more slowly. Over several drilling seasons, the movement of the ice makes the borehole start to bend. The movement of the ice also affects the drilling chamber, which is really just a room that has been hollowed out of the ice sheet to contain the equipment. When I got to NorthGRIP, several years into the endeavor, the drilling chamber was starting to collapse. They'd installed these big wooden beams to prop up the ceiling, but these had shattered under the weight of the snow that was building up on top.

That season, the team at NorthGRIP was getting close to the bottom of the ice sheet. Just to lower the drill down the borehole took an hour. Then it took another hour to raise it back up. And in that interval, there was nothing for the drilling team to do but stand around, trying to keep warm, and listen to music. In those days, they liked to listen to ABBA.

To the naked eye, a section of an ice core looks pretty unremarkable. It just looks like a cylinder of ice. If you know how to read it, however, it is loaded with information.

[KOLBERT]   *What on Earth Have We Done?*

An ice sheet is basically just a big pile of snow. Every year in Greenland, a new layer is added, and this presses down on the older layers, which are compressed and ooze out toward the sea. The reason cores are drilled at the very center of the ice sheet is because that's where you find the greatest number of layers. Within the layers are bubbles of air that were trapped at the time the snow originally fell. These bubbles are actual samples of ancient air, and they provide an archive of the atmosphere. The ice contains a record of anything that was in the air at the time; this includes volcanic ash from Krakatau, lead pollution from ancient Roman smelters, and dust blown in on ice age winds. The layers also contain information about what the temperature over Greenland was going back in time. The temperature data can be extracted by analyzing the isotopic composition of the ice.

And this is what the second part of Alley's title, the time machine part, referred to. An ice core in essence allows us to look back in history, so far back that we push beyond recorded history. Way beyond recorded history. The Greenland record takes us back to a time before agriculture, and then it keeps going, to a time when modern humans were just beginning to migrate beyond Africa. In Greenland, the layers at the bottom of the ice sheet date back about 130,000 years, so the record extends all through the last ice age and also through the last interglacial period. On Antarctica, the layers are not as thick, so the information contained in them is not as detailed, but the record goes much, much farther back in time, all the way to eight hundred thousand years ago. At eight hundred thousand years, we haven't just drilled beyond prehistory, we've drilled beyond anatomically modern humans altogether.

And to me, in 2001, this all seemed quite marvelous and exciting. And it still seems that way to me today. That you can drill into the ice and bring history out of cold storage, as it were, is quite extraordinary. It's an indication of how extraordinary the world is and also of how extraordinary humans are, that they should figure out how to get at this information and go to such amazing lengths to gather it. The experience of being on top of the Greenland ice sheet I found thrilling, and I think every day was thrilling for the drilling team, even though the work they were doing was often cold and frustrating. They were a cheerful bunch. And their cheerfulness stood in stark contrast to what they were learning, which was actually quite disturbing. What ice core data reveal makes one's hair stand on end.

There are several key revelations. One is the correlation between CO_2 levels and temperature. This is shown very clearly in the data from what's known as the EPICA core, from Antarctica. This is the longest ice record we have, though there are currently efforts underway to drill back even farther in time, again in Antarctica, to extract more than a million years of data. This eight-hundred-thousand-year record shows how temperature and CO_2 levels move in synchrony. When CO_2 levels go up, temperatures go up. When they go down, temperatures drop. And those up-and-down cycles, those are the ice ages. It's been understood since the mid-nineteenth century that CO_2 is a greenhouse gas, and theory would have predicted—and did—that changes in CO_2 levels in the atmosphere would produce changes in average global temperatures. The ice cores verified that theory and went a step further. It was now possible to quantify that relationship.

The second key revelation concerns current CO_2 levels, which are, quite literally, off the charts. CO_2 levels have not been as high as they are now for at least eight hundred thousand years. So since long before our species evolved.

A third revelation, which is a bit less well known outside glaciological circles but every bit as fascinating, concerns the stability of the climate system or, really, the lack thereof. Here we have to go back to Greenland because the Greenland data are more detailed. And what these data show is that during the last ice age, average annual temperatures bounced around wildly. During the last ice age, the Wisconsin, there were temperature swings over Greenland that were almost unimaginably extreme. In one fifty-year period, temperatures shot up by 8 degrees Celsius—more than 14 degrees Fahrenheit. Then they dropped again, nearly as abruptly. Something similar happened two dozen more times. To get a sense of what this means, imagine New York City suddenly acquiring the climate of Houston and Houston exchanging its climate for Riyadh's. That's the magnitude. The temperature swings in the tropics or the temperate latitudes were probably not as dramatic as they were in the Arctic; still, they must have been intense. These swings have become known as Dansgaard-Oeschger events, after a Danish scientist named Willi Dansgaard and a Swiss researcher named Hans Oeschger.

And then, at the end of the ice age, the climate warmed, and just as strikingly, it settled down. This relatively stable period is the Holocene, or wholly recent epoch, in which, technically at least, we still live. In this period of roughly ten thousand years, there are no D-O events.

One night at NorthGRIP, I was sitting in the geodesic dome, having a beer with some of the researchers. And one of them, a Danish glaciologist named J. P. Steffensen, pointed out something about the graph that I've never been able to get out of my head. By the middle of the last ice age, anatomically modern humans were pretty widespread. They were obviously in Africa, and they were also in the Middle East, South Asia, and even Australia. But nowhere were there permanent settlements, at least as far as we know, and there was no agriculture.

Steffensen asked me,

Why did human beings not make civilization fifty thousand years ago? You know that they had just as big brains as we have today. When you put it in a climatic framework, you can say, well, it was the ice age. And also this ice age was so climatically unstable that each time you had the beginnings of a culture, they had to move. Then comes the present interglacial—ten thousand years of very stable climate. The perfect conditions for agriculture. If you look at it, it's amazing. Civilizations in Persia, in China, and in India start at the same time, maybe six thousand years ago. They all developed writing and they all developed religion and they all built cities, all at the same time, because the climate was stable. I think that if the climate would have been stable fifty thousand years ago, it would have started then. But they had no chance.

If you accept Steffensen's premise, that human civilization is a product of climate stability, then it puts us in, let's just say, an awkward position. The climate stability that gave rise to civilization is the climate stability that we are bringing to an end. Already, we are seeing very dramatic impacts from climate change, as I'm sure this audience is all too aware: fiercer droughts, fiercer heat waves, longer wildfire seasons, more intense rainfall, a loss of mountain glaciers all around the world, the loss of Arctic sea ice, and increasing ice loss from Greenland and Antarctica, which is accelerating sea-level rise. And we know more warming is in the pipeline. Even if we were to dramatically reduce greenhouse gases starting tomorrow, the climate would keep on warming for decades and perhaps longer. And some of the effects of warming—for instance, to use the example of Greenland once again, speeding up the rate at which big outlet glaciers are flowing and dumping ice into the ocean—could take centuries, even millennia to play out. And of course, we are not stopping emitting greenhouse gases tomorrow. That is not at all the trajectory we are on.

The second experiment I want to talk about today is known as the Biological Dynamics of Forest Fragments Project (BDFFP). It has been running now for more than forty years. It's one of the world's longest-running experiments as well as one of the largest.

The experiment was set up owing to an argument that grew out of a book. That book was *The Theory of Island Biogeography*, coauthored by Ed Wilson, who just passed away a few months ago, and a Princeton professor named Robert MacArthur. The book took up two well-established patterns in island ecology: big islands host more species than small islands, and near-shore islands hold more species than remote islands. And the question Wilson and MacArthur wanted to answer was, Why? Why is this the case? And the theory they came up with concerned the rate at which new species migrate to an island (or evolve there) and the rate at which established species wink out. And over time, these two, they concluded, would even out, and there would be a constant number of species on the island, even as the species themselves changed.

The Theory of Island Biogeography, published in 1967, is a very dense book, full of mathematical equations. And it's doubtful that many people outside of academia have ever read it. But it is considered a key text in ecology, and it had a very large impact. And one of the reasons for its impact was that people—both inside and outside the academy—soon realized that its implications extended way beyond actual islands. Isolate a piece of terrestrial habitat and the same processes that Wilson and MacArthur had analyzed come into play, only in reverse. Just as a new island, rising out of the sea, would gain new species until it reached an equilibrium, an island torn out of the forest would shed them. And from that theoretical insight stemmed predictions—once again, based on theory—about how best to preserve species. And some very heated arguments ensued because living systems tend to confound theories. For obvious reasons, these arguments could not be settled by theory; they had to be tested in the field.

In the late 1970s, a biologist named Tom Lovejoy figured out a way to do this. Tom passed away at the end of last year. He was truly an exceptional person, as anyone who was fortunate enough to know him can attest. Tom and Ed Wilson were friends, both part of what Wilson jokingly referred to as the "rainforest mafia." And rather eerily, they died within a day of each other, in December.

Tom's idea was a variation on the old line attributed to Churchill: never let a good crisis go to waste. In the late 1970s, the Brazilian government was promoting deforestation. It was essentially paying ranchers to settle north of Manaus, in what was called the Manaus Free Zone, which at that time was sparsely inhabited. Most of the free zone was rainforest,

[KOLBERT] *What on Earth Have We Done?* 111

and to graze cattle, the ranchers were going to cut down the forest and burn it. At the same time, though, Brazilian law required landowners to maintain 50 percent of the forest on their property intact. Tom's thought was that if he could work with the landowners to create fragments of different sizes, these could be studied, and some of the theoretical questions about "islands" of habitat could be settled. He went to talk to officials in Manaus, and somewhat to his surprise, they agreed to his idea. And that was how the BDFFP was born. There are twelve fragments that make up the project: some are a few acres in size; some are much bigger—up to 100 hectares, or 250 acres.

I went to see the project about ten years ago. I visited most of the fragments and also a spot called Camp 41, which was the control plot, where a piece of intact rainforest was connected to a very large stretch of intact forest. Tom liked to bring to Camp 41 anyone who he thought might help preserve the Amazon. He took Al Gore there; he took Tom Cruise there. Camp 41 is pretty rustic, and everyone who visits, including senators and movie stars, sleeps in a hammock that's slung in a shed that's just solid enough to keep the rain out. When I visited, it was mating season for a rather loud frog called the Manaus slender-legged tree frog. Apparently, some of the frogs had figured out that if they parked themselves in the drainpipes of this shed, their mating calls would be amplified. So that's what they had done. And the din, all night, was incredible.

In the forty years that it's been running, the BDFFP has yielded mountains of information. And while some of the debates about the best way to save species continue, the data from the project clearly show that it is key to preserve as large an area as possible. The smaller the habitat fragment, the fewer species that persist on it. On an intuitive level, you would expect small fragments to lose their large species, like primates and peccaries, and they do. But there are many effects that are less intuitive. For instance, the Amazon has lots of species of antbirds. Some of these are obligate antbirds, meaning they are birds that feed only on ants, and more specifically on army ants, which march around the forest in long columns, foraging for prey—they're really voracious—and then hunker down for a while to raise a new generation. At the BDFFP, even fragments that retain several colonies of army ants ended up losing their antbirds. That seems kind of hard to explain, but it's believed that the reason for this is that obligate antbirds need to follow actively foraging ants. And even if you have several colonies, there are going to be times when they're all hunkered down, and then the antbirds will have nothing to eat. This is an example of the peculiar danger of fragmentation, which is also the peculiar danger of living on a small island: when the numbers are low—this could be the number of ant colonies you have to feed off, or the number of potential mates you have to reproduce with, or whatever—bad luck can pretty easily turn fatal. And over many generations, bad luck is hard to avoid. So you get local extinctions and then, potentially, global ones.

And of course, the reason this is so significant is that habitat all over the planet is being fragmented. It is estimated that humans have already directly transformed more than half of the ice-free land on the earth—some twenty-seven million square miles. We've done this by cutting down forests, plowing up grasslands, and building cities. Indirectly, we've probably transformed half of what's left by pulling in roads and laying pipelines. The result is that we live in a world of artificial islands—islands on dry land.

Interestingly, or perhaps ironically, since the BDFFP was started, many of the ranches in the area have been abandoned. They just weren't profitable. To keep the fragments as fragments, researchers with the project have had to keep cutting back the encroaching scrub and second-growth forest. But across the Amazon, the cutting of primary forest continues. The rate had been declining for a while but recently has gone way up again; last year, some 5,100 square miles were lost. In the Amazon, people talk about the "fishbone," which begins with the construction of one road—the spine—and leads to the construction, often illegal, of many smaller, riblike roads. The net result is a forest cut up into long, skinny fragments. Meanwhile, these days, even reserves are not immune to fragmentation. According to a recent book on Central African forests, thirty-three so-called development corridors are either planned or already under construction in sub-Saharan Africa; these would bisect four hundred existing nature reserves. So the conversion of the continents into islands is very much continuing; indeed by some measures, it's accelerating.

And so, like a Greenland ice core, the BDFFP is a kind of time machine. Only this time machine opens toward the future. It shows us what is going to happen to species diversity thanks to our carving up of the world. And it's a very profoundly sad picture; it's a world where we've lost practically all of our large animals, at least outside of zoos, and a great many of our smaller ones as well. If Ed Wilson's calculations are correct,

[KOLBERT] *What on Earth Have We Done?* 113

then through fragmentation, we've already consigned something like 20 percent of the world's terrestrial species to oblivion.

Before I move on to the next experiment, I just want to take a quick detour to discuss another trend that might be thought of as fragmentation's mirror image. Even as we are cutting the world up into smaller and smaller pieces, we are also eliminating the barriers that once divided the world into discrete ecosystems.

It is estimated that on any given day, as many as five thousand different species are being transported around the world in ballast water. Countless other species are hitching rides in cargo. Then there are the pet and garden trades and global tourism.

Plants and animals obviously made their way around the world in the past as well. It is exactly this natural process of migration and colonization that Wilson and MacArthur were interested in. But new arrivals were few and far between. Consider, for example, the case of Hawaii. Before people settled there, a new species succeeded in establishing itself on the archipelago around once every ten thousand years. Nowadays, this happens around once a month. And the results are, for many native Hawaiian species, devastating.

Hawaii, for example, used to have some 750 species of land snails. These are small, unassuming creatures. In the 1950s, a snail from the continental United States, the rosy wolfsnail, was introduced to the islands. The wolfsnail gobbled up the local snail species, more than half of which are now extinct. And what goes for Hawaii's land snails goes for a host of other creatures. Frogs and toads around the world are being killed off by an introduced fungus, known as Bd, that people have spread around the world. Native mollusks in the United States are being wiped out by quagga mussels, which were imported from Ukraine. In Guam, native birds are being devasted by the brown tree snake, which was probably imported to the island from Papua New Guinea by the U.S. military. Ash trees in the Northeastern United States, and I'm sure here in Princeton, are being killed off by the emerald ash borer, which is from Asia. Our reshuffling of the biosphere is unprecedented in the history of life, and it will determine the future of life.

It may seem paradoxical to claim that humans are driving extinction by fragmenting the world and also by unifying it, but that's what's happening. Around 250 million years ago, all the world's land masses were squished together in one giant supercontinent, Pangaea. And then they

114   *The Tanner Lectures on Human Values*

broke up into the world we know today. And by bringing together all of these lineages that evolved separately, biologists say we are, in effect, creating a New Pangaea.

Castello Aragonese is a tiny island in the Bay of Naples, not far from the larger island of Ischia. At the top of the island, there's a medieval fortress that's now a museum. Nearby, there's also a venerable marine biological station. And just offshore, there's a geological oddity. The waters around Castello Aragonese stream with tiny bubbles. This is a very volcanically active area, and the bubbles rise out of vents in the seafloor. If you are in the water, the effect is a bit like being immersed in a glass of champagne.

In the early 2000s, a British scientist named Jason Hall-Spencer was on board an Italian research vessel when the group decided to anchor off Castello Aragonese and take a swim. His colleagues just wanted to cool off, but the champagne experience got Hall-Spencer thinking. He decided to have the water analyzed and found that the bubbles contained almost pure carbon dioxide.

When CO_2 dissolves in water, it forms an acid, carbonic acid. Carbonic acid is, to be sure, a weak acid; we drink it all the time in Coke and other carbonated beverages. But add enough of it and you can change the chemistry of even a well-buffered solution. Hall-Spencer reasoned that the CO_2 released by the vents was acidifying the water around Castello Aragonese. This would have been an interesting situation to investigate under any circumstances. Thanks to our transformation of the atmosphere, it was more than merely interesting. The oceans and the air have to be in equilibrium, so by burning fossil fuels, we are, effectively, pumping CO_2 into the seas, which are, as a result, acidifying. Already, the surface waters of the oceans are about 30 percent more acidic than they were in preindustrial times. The surface waters used to have an average pH of around 8.2; now it's down to 8.1. If we continue to emit CO_2 at current rates, then by the end of this century, pH will be down to 7.8, which represents a 150 percent increase in acidity.

At Castello Aragonese, versions of this acidified future already exist. In the waters around the island, there are regions where the pH is 8.1, regions where it's 7.8, and regions where it is still lower. This gradient makes it possible to study what the progressive impact of acidification on marine life will be. At Castello Aragonese, you can, in effect, swim into the oceans of the future. This was Hall-Spencer's key insight. The island's waters represented a kind of time machine.

[KOLBERT] *What on Earth Have We Done?* 115

In 2009, I went to Castello Aragonese with Hall-Spencer and also an Italian researcher named Maria Buia. It was January, and tourist season was long over, and the waters were bitterly cold. Even in a wet suit, I felt a whole lot colder than I ever did on the Greenland ice sheet. Pretty much every adventure I have gone on in my career as a journalist I would cheerfully repeat except for that one. We started our swim in a region far from the vents where sea life was pretty much normal—or what counts as normal nowadays in the Bay of Naples. In this area, there were fish and seagrass, sea-urchins and corals. As we swam into the future, there was less and less to see.

The pH of the seas is crucial to basic processes ranging from metabolism to protein function. Declining pH can affect the dispersion of sound, which many sea creatures depend on to navigate. It alters the availability of nutrients. And it interferes with calcification. At Castello Aragonese, this last effect is far and away the most visible. Hall-Spencer and Buia showed me creatures that had made the mistake of wandering into the vent area whose shells had holes in them. They looked like they had been dropped in acid, and in a manner of speaking, they had been.

There are many calcifiers that are missing entirely from around the vents. The list includes the perforated barnacle, which is a tough little creature that resembles a volcano as well as the Mediterranean mussel. The Mediterranean mussel, too, is very tough—it's invasive in many parts of the world, but it can't make a go of it near the vents. Also on the list is the keelworm, a tube worm that secretes a white calcareous tube that it never leaves, and Noah's ark, a mollusk whose shell looks a bit like a boat. Ditto for the spiny fileclam, and the grooved top shell, a species of sea snail.

The oceans of the world are full of calcifiers. And calcifiers play a key role in most major marine ecosystems. In some cases, there's no ecosystem at all without them. Consider, for example, the Great Barrier Reef. The Great Barrier Reef is not a single reef but a whole string of reefs running along the Western Coast of Australia. It is an immense structure; compared to it, the Great Wall of China is just a kid's sandcastle. The Great Barrier Reef is entirely built by calcifiers, corals working in conjunction with coralline algae.

Corals are finicky; they build reefs only under very specific conditions. And one of those conditions has to do with what's known as the aragonite saturation state; corals need a very high saturation state. Owing to acidification, the saturation state is falling. It's falling more or less in tandem with the pH. That's happening everywhere in the world's oceans, all at once, and it's putting a lot of stress on corals. It's getting harder for them to just keep up with forces that are constantly wearing reefs down, which include all these creatures that are munching on and boring into them. "It's like a tree with bugs" is how Chris Langdon, a marine biologist at the University of Miami, once put it to me. "A reef needs to grow pretty quickly just to stay even."

Scientists who have gone looking for analogs for what's happening to the oceans today have been unable to find them. A study led by Bärbel Hönisch, at Lamont, found that although there have been several severe episodes of ocean acidification in the record, "no past event perfectly parallels future projections in terms of disrupting the balance of ocean carbonate chemistry—a consequence of the unprecedented rapidity of CO_2 release currently taking place." So what we are doing to the oceans is once again unprecedented.

Journalists are often accused of being hype artists—of exaggerating the importance of the issues or developments they're writing about or, worse still, of cherry-picking the data to lend these developments more significance than they actually have. I would say that the reverse is true when it comes to the subject that I've been talking about today—what is often blandly referred to as "global change." Stories about human impacts on the planet tend, I think, not to be overplayed in the media but underplayed. This happens for reasons that I think many of you will be able to relate to. About a decade ago, Michael Oppenheimer, who's a professor here at Princeton, coauthored a paper about the charge of alarmism, which, as you know, is often leveled against mainstream climate scientists by think tank denialists. Oppenheimer and his colleagues looked at how the climate scientists' predictions had measured up against events—actual measurements taken in the field. They found that pretty much across the board, the predictions were either on target or erred in the direction of being too conservative. Sea-level rise, the loss of Arctic sea ice, and the frequency of extreme rainfall events were among the phenomena that were happening faster than scientists had predicted. Scientists, they concluded, were not biased toward alarmism "but rather the reverse: toward cautious estimates." They gave a name to this tendency: "erring on the side of least drama," or ESLD. I do not want to argue that journalists suffer from ESLD, but I do want to argue that when it comes to conveying the magnitude of human impacts on the planet, we are constrained in some of the same ways that scientists are.

[KOLBERT] *What on Earth Have We Done?* 117

Our situation is just too dire and too weird to narrate convincingly. Here we are this, incredibly imaginative, incredibly resourceful species—a species capable of dreaming up an ice coring expedition at the center of the Greenland ice sheet and executing it. And yet we are also the kind of heedless creatures that can lay waste to entire ecosystems and do so knowingly. All of which raises the question of what comes next: What can we do, what should we do, what will we do about the situation we find ourselves in—in truth, the situation we've invented for ourselves? This will be the subject of my next lecture.

LECTURE II.
WHAT CAN WE DO ABOUT IT?

Yesterday, I organized my talk around three experiments set in different parts of the world, each of which represented, I suggested, a different kind of time machine. Today's talk will mirror that structure. Today, as well, I'm going to take you to see three experiments related to the vast, unsupervised experiment that has become known as the Anthropocene.

The first experiment involves coral reefs, whose troubles I discussed yesterday. Reefs are threatened by ocean acidification. They're also threatened by global warming. The creatures that build reefs are known, unflatteringly, as polyps. Coral polyps live together in vast colonies and are tiny gelatinous animals. Individual polyps are usually just a couple millimeters across—and yet even smaller plants live inside them. These tiny, tiny plants are photosynthetic algae, and they play a key role in reef building. The algae provide their hosts with energy, and in return, they get protection.

Climate change threatens the world's reefs because it disrupts this symbiotic relationship. When water temperatures spike, the algae produce dangerous levels of oxygen radicals, and the polyps expel them. Then the corals go hungry. This is what is known as coral bleaching. Since polyps are transparent, it's the algae that give the corals their color. During a bleaching, a reef turns white because all the algae are missing.

If a bleaching episode doesn't last too long, corals can reclaim their symbionts and recover. But if it persists, they can starve to death. Coral bleaching episodes are becoming more frequent and longer lasting. There was a global bleaching event in 1998, and then another in 2010, and a third that stretched from 2015 to 2017.

It is estimated that the Great Barrier Reef has lost half its coral cover over the last thirty years, and one of the main reasons for this is bleaching. In 2016, in the midst of that brutal, three-year bleaching event, Terry Hughes, a marine biologist at Australia's James Cook University, chartered a plane and, over several days, flew the length of the reef taking photographs. When he was done, he showed the results to his students. "And then we wept," he tweeted. This past winter, which was summer in Australia, once again, there was widespread bleaching on the Great Barrier Reef.

In 2019, I flew to Townsville, Australia, which is situated inshore from the central part of the Great Barrier Reef. I went there to visit Australia's

[118]

[KOLBERT] *What Can We Do about It?* 119

National Sea Simulator, which is situated on a spit of land that juts out into the Coral Sea. It's a huge structure with more than 30,000 square feet of floor space and, perhaps more importantly, 25 miles' worth of pipes. It's a very state-of-the-art facility that, by its own description at least, is the world's most advanced research aquarium. And I went there to watch a group of marine biologists who are trying to engineer tougher corals. Corals that can withstand warmer and more acidified water. They call their approach assisted evolution.

The project is the brainchild of two scientists, Ruth Gates, who was British but worked in Hawaii, and Madeleine van Oppen, who is Dutch but works in Australia. And tragically, Ruth died a few years into the project. I was fortunate enough to meet her when she was still in good health. She was such a dynamic person, someone who really knew how to get things done against long odds. And the fact that this project continues, and it is still ongoing, is a tribute to that.

So the idea behind assisted evolution is that ordinary evolution—unassisted evolution—is just too slow. It can't keep up with the rate at which the oceans are changing. And this is why reefs are doing badly. If corals could adapt quickly enough to the warmer temperatures and lower pH that we are subjecting them to, then we wouldn't be seeing all this damage. But Gates and van Oppen decided that perhaps there is a way to speed the process along—to "assist" evolution. And the particular assisted evolution experiment I went to watch was timed to take place during a mass spawning.

Corals reproduce in all sorts of ways, mostly asexually, by budding. But once a year, after a full moon, there's an orgy. A lot of corals are hermaphrodites, and on the night of a mass spawning, they release little bead-like bundles containing both eggs and sperm into the water. The bundles then split apart, spilling their contents. A certain number of the gametes meet and create embryos, some of which will grow into coral larvae that eventually settle out of the water column and start new colonies with new genetics. And scientists have discovered that if you collect corals and keep them under the right conditions, they will spawn on the same night as the corals out on the reef. And that night can usually be predicted to within a couple of days.

In the weeks leading up to the spawning, researchers at the SeaSim had collected corals from distant parts of the reef, which they were keeping in tanks. They'd collected corals from the central part of the reef and from the southern tip of the reef. Such is the size of the Great

Barrier Reef that these corals lived hundreds of miles apart. During a spawning event, these corals would never naturally mate. Their little bundles couldn't travel far enough. But the point of assisted evolution is not to leave things to nature. And so on the night of the spawning, researchers and an army of students collected the gamete bundles as they were released, separated the eggs from the sperm, and then performed all these crosses that would not have naturally occurred. So as not to disturb the corals, everyone wore red headlamps.

After these crosses were completed, the plan was to raise up the offspring and subject them to stress. And the hope was that some of the offspring of these unnatural unions would prove to be more resilient than their parents, more heat tolerant, and more tolerant of ocean acidification. This is a phenomenon that's seen in plant breeding: it's known as hybrid vigor. And if more vigorous offspring could be produced in this way, then perhaps these hybrids could be used to seed the reefs of the future. And there were several other parts to this experiment as well. For instance, researchers were also trying to raise more heat-resistant algae in the hopes that these could help corals withstand higher temperatures.

The Great Barrier Reef is not easy to get to, and even many Australians have never seen it for themselves. Nevertheless, Australians are attached to the reef. It's part of the national identity, the way Yellowstone is for Americans. And the reef, like Yellowstone, is a big national park.

Australia is also very attached to coal. According to the Australian government, the country is currently the world's fifth-largest coal producer and the second-largest coal exporter, after Indonesia. A few years ago, the Australian government approved a huge new mine, the Carmichael mine, about two hundred miles southwest of Townsville. That mine is now completed and is shipping from the port of Bowen, just south of Townsville, so that coal is being shipped basically right over the Great Barrier Reef. Most of it is destined for India.

These two attachments are very difficult to reconcile. It's very difficult to preserve the Great Barrier Reef, or what's left of the Great Barrier Reef, while the world continues to mine and burn coal. But the official position of the Great Barrier Reef Marine Park Authority, which goes by the awkward acronym "gabrumpa," is that this is possible. This is why projects like the one I visited in Townsville are being funded. The Australian government has committed one hundred million dollars toward research into possible interventions. The possibilities include developing thermally tolerant corals—that's assisted evolution. There's also shading

[KOLBERT]   *What Can We Do about It?*   121

and cooling reefs—so for example, pumping deeper, cooler water onto reefs; developing reef probiotics; and creating robots that could outplant corals that had been raised on land. When I was at the SeaSim, a lot of people were gathered there, waiting for the spawning, which is a big event for a lot of research teams. And one of those people was the head of the Australian Institute of Marine Science, a man named Paul Hardisty.

"We're not talking about coral gardening here," Hardisty told me. "We're talking about major, industrial-scale—all-of-reef scale—interventions." The Great Barrier Reef has an area the size of Italy. So "all-of-reef interventions" means interventions on the scale of Italy. First, you warm the oceans; then you try to engineer new breeds of coral that can survive in those warmer oceans.

And if this way of proceeding seems to you kind of crazy, I share your misgivings. But I have come to believe that it is an exemplary kind of craziness. As I mentioned yesterday, I have been on the "global change" beat for more than twenty years now. And during that time, I have come across this pattern over and over again. The defining feature of the Anthropocene is that we are changing the world on a geological scale, that we have overtaken the great natural forces like vulcanism and orbital cycles. Not surprisingly, there are side effects, many of them deeply problematic. And so we go back to the drawing board. We try to change the world yet again, this time to correct for the changes introduced earlier.

Cane toads are the main actors in another Anthropocene experiment. Up until the nineteenth century, cane toads were creatures of the Americas. Initially, they could be found in South America and Central America and the very southernmost tip of Texas. Then roughly a century and a half ago, people changed that. Sugarcane, which is native to New Guinea, had been imported to the Caribbean, and while the plant was succeeding there, yields were reduced by pests, especially beetle grubs. Someone decided that a good way to control the beetle grubs would be to bring over cane toads to eat them. Cane toads are very large; some are the size of dinner plates. And they'll eat almost anything.

Early in the twentieth century, the toads were taken on yet another voyage, this time to sugar plantations in Hawaii. From there, they were shipped to Australia. In 1935, 102 cane toads were loaded onto a steamer in Honolulu, bound for Sydney. One hundred and one of them survived the journey and were delivered to a sugarcane research station on Australia's northeast coast, outside of Cairns. Within a year, they'd produced more than 1.5 million eggs, which were released into the region's rivers and ponds.

As the years went by, the cane toads continued to multiply like crazy. And as they multiplied, they spread, far beyond sugarcane country. Nowadays, they are almost as far south as Sydney. They're as far north as the Cape York peninsula, and they've made it all the way to Darwin. And they're still expanding their range.

Cane toads probably never did anything to protect Australia's sugarcane crop. But they have wreaked ecological havoc. Cane toads have two glands, one behind each eye, where they store a milky-colored goo that is toxic. In its raw form, the goo is toxic enough to make an animal, or a person, sick. But when cane toads are attacked or agitated, they produce an enzyme that bumps up the potency of the toxin a hundredfold. Australia has no native poison toads. In fact, it has no native toads at all. So a lot of animals try to eat the toads, an experience that they generally do not survive. The list of native species whose decline has been attributed—at least in part, to cane toad consumption—is long and varied: it includes several species of snake, several species of lizards, and perhaps most notably, a very cute but actually quite ferocious marsupial, the northern quoll.

Having unleashed this ecological disaster, Australians have tried to rein it back in by going after cane toads. They run them over with their cars, they smash them with golf clubs, and they form squads to collect toads, which they euthanize by sticking them in the freezer. The toad-busting hasn't done much to arrest the toads' spread. And so a new, super high-tech effort was launched, one that was interesting enough that I went to take a look at it.

The Australian Centre for Disease Preparedness is a fortresslike building situated south of Melbourne, in the city of Geelong. If you've ever seen the movie *Contagion*, there's a shout-out to the center in the film; one of the panicked doctors says they're sending a sample to Geelong. It's one of the world's most advanced high-containment labs. It has 520 air lock doors, and its concrete walls are thick enough to withstand a plane crash, or at least so I was told.

At the Geelong facility, two researchers, Caitlin Cooper and Mark Tizard, are attempting to control the cane toad by gene editing it. When I got there, the first gene-edited toads had already been produced. These toads represented a sort of proof of concept. Since no one had ever gene edited a cane toad before, Cooper had to invent a method. And the first thing she did, which is a fairly typical thing to do in gene editing, was

[KOLBERT]   *What Can We Do about It?*

fiddle around with the toads' pigment genes. When you mess around with an animal's pigment, you see at a glance whether or not you've succeeded. And Cooper did in fact succeed, or at least partially succeed in this first attempt. She created a toad she named Blondie. Blondie has light-colored legs, proving that a pigment gene was knocked out or disabled. The next task that Cooper undertook was to try to knock out the gene that codes for the enzyme that pumps up the potency of the toads' toxin. The enzyme is called bufotoxin hydrolase. And that effort also succeeded: she produced toadlets that can't produce bufotoxin hydrolase. These toadlets look perfectly normal, but if you were a quoll, and you bit into one, you'd be OK. You might be disgusted and feel sick, but you wouldn't die.

Cooper has other ideas for how cane toads might be gene edited, and these have to do with reproduction. Female cane toads produce a lot of eggs—up to thirty thousand at a go—and these have a gel coating. And Cooper thought it might be possible to knock out genes involved in producing the coating so the eggs could not be fertilized. She was just toying with that idea when I visited, but anything that reduced the toads' fertility could be quite powerful. Now in terms of spreading that trait, you obviously have a problem, because toads that don't reproduce don't pass on their genes. But there is, potentially, a way around that too.

In high school, most of us were taught that the odds of any particular gene, or really, gene variant, getting passed down from a parent to a child is 50–50. But that's not always the case. There are genes—known as driving genes—that regularly beat the odds. Driving genes get handed down more than 50 percent of the time, sometimes 100 percent of the time. And there are all sorts of genes out there that do this, that have evolved this ability to beat the odds. So that's already happening in nature. But now, we have the ability to produce a synthetic version of gene drive. This is thanks to a gene-editing technology known as CRISPR, which itself is actually borrowed from bacteria. With CRISPR, *we* can decide which genes will get passed down more than 50 percent of the time. I'm not going to go into the mechanics right now, but it has to do with the fact that the CRISPR gene-editing system is itself encoded in genes. By adding these genes, along with the instructions for genes you want to edit, you can get the process to repeat itself through the generations. And you can target an existing gene variant or one that humans have created. Researchers have already produced gene-drive mosquitos that pass down a variant of a gene called *doublesex*, which makes it impossible for the mosquito's offspring to reproduce. And if you release just a few of these gene-drive mosquitos into a population, in several generations, you can drive the population down to zero. This has been demonstrated in captive populations. And these mosquitos are now kept in secure cages. But the hope is one day to release them in parts of the world where malaria is a big danger and eliminate populations of malaria-carrying mosquitoes.

The South Australian Health and Medical Research Institute, in Adelaide, is housed in a cool-looking building that's been nicknamed the Cheese Grater. During the same trip I went to Geelong, I also visited the institute, where I met up with a researcher named Paul Thomas. Thomas is working to develop a gene-drive mouse. Thomas's idea—the idea he was working on at the time—is a gene-drive mouse equipped with what's called an X-shredder. As with humans, male mice produce two kinds of sperm—X chromosome sperm and Y chromosome sperm. And X-shredder mouse would produce normal Y sperm and defective X sperm. When those X-shredder mice mated, they would produce only XY, which is to say male, offspring. Supercharge this with gene drive, and the trait would be passed on through the generations until you had only males, and the whole population crashed. Thomas had not yet succeeded in producing a gene-drive mouse, but he was quite confident that one would soon be developed. You may have recently read that researchers in the UK have gene-edited mice that produce either all-male or all-female mouse litters. This was announced in December. These researchers were not working on gene-drive mice, but it shows you how fast this sort of research is moving.

Thomas was working on a gene-drive mouse in collaboration with a group called GBird, which is a consortium of research institutions in the United States, Australia, and New Zealand. These include government institutions like the USDA and the Commonwealth Scientific and Industrial Research Organisation, which is sort of Australia's version of the NSF. GBird stands for Genetic Biocontrol of Invasive Rodents. Yesterday, I talked about the threat posed by invasive species, especially to island ecosystems. On islands, mice and rats are some of the deadliest invasives. Islands often lack any native rodents, and so the native species haven't evolved defenses against them. But virtually, wherever people have settled, and even on many islands where they've just visited, mice and rats have hitched a ride. Ground-nesting birds, like the albatross, are very vulnerable to rodents. And some rat species can climb trees, so tree-nesting birds also often suffer. Rats also eat a

[KOLBERT] *What Can We Do about It?* 125

lot of invertebrates, like crustaceans, and they consume a lot of seeds, so they can really change the vegetation. So finding a way to rid islands of rodents would be a huge win for island ecosystems and biodiversity. The X-shredder mouse would do that for you. It's a very powerful technology. That's the attraction of it and the danger of it. If one of these gene-drive mice, say, got to the mainland United States, the trait could spread from New York to California, wiping out a continent's worth of mice. Gene-drive technology has been compared to Kurt Vonnegut's ice-nine, a single speck of which was sufficient to freeze all of the water in the world. A gene-drive mouse outfitted with an X-shredder could, in theory at least, eliminate all of the mice of a given species in the world. Call it mice-nine.

And if it seems to you crazy that people—very serious people, very knowledgeable people, people who care deeply about biodiversity—would be contemplating taking such a risk, once again, I share your concerns. But it follows the same logic as the coral story. When we transported cane toads and mice and rats around the world, we wittingly and unwittingly remixed the biosphere. We may not have thought of it as such, but this remixing was a radical and unprecedented intervention in the history of life. As I mentioned yesterday, by bringing species together, we are creating what some biologists have called the New Pangaea. We are, in effect, running geological history backward and at warp speed.

In the context of this planet-wide reshuffling, in the context of what we've already done, an X-shredder mouse or a gene-edited toad doesn't, you could argue, really stand out. Mark Tizard, the molecular biologist who's supervising the cane toad experiment, put it to me this way: "What we're doing is potentially adding maybe ten more genes onto the twenty thousand toad genes that shouldn't be there in the first place, and those ten will sabotage the rest and take them out of the system. The classic thing people say with molecular biology is: Are you playing God? Well, no. We are using our understanding of biological process to see if we can benefit a system that is in trauma."

Tizard's point was also Ruth Gates and Madeleine van Oppen's point about assisted evolution. When we think about what we are doing, we have to be honest about what we've already done. It doesn't make sense to judge the impact of our actions against some idealized version of nature. Because that's gone. It has already been transformed. That glass is already broken. We need to judge the risks of any intervention against the risks of *not* intervening. "Really, what I am is a futurist," Ruth Gates told me

126 *The Tanner Lectures on Human Values*

when I visited her in Hawaii in 2016. "Our project is acknowledging that a future is coming where nature is no longer fully natural."

Yesterday, I began by talking about climate change, and I am going to end today by talking about climate change. Climate change has all sorts of impacts that are problematic not just for the species we share the planet with but for ourselves. If sea levels rise—and as I mentioned yesterday, they are rising, faster and faster—this threatens cities all around the world. And so we really care. We care enough that, of course, we want to control it.

The U.S. Army Corps of Engineers, for example, has proposed a series of dikes and gates around Galveston, Texas. The idea is when there's a storm surge expected, giant gates, each of which is 82 feet high and 650 feet wide, would close, and they would shut off Galveston Bay from the Gulf of Mexico. A similar but even more massive storm surge barrier has been proposed for New York. The barrier would stretch for six miles, across New York Harbor. People have, to be sure, been putting up sea walls for a long time. What's new in this case is the motivation for these projects: these are second-order engineering projects. They are efforts to intervene in the world to correct for a previous round of intervention— the massive human intervention that is climate change.

Second-order projects are also planned for countering sea-level rise at the source, as it were. Antarctic glaciers typically terminate in an ice shelf. As the oceans warm, seawater is increasingly seeping in under the ice. So these ice shelves are melting from above and from below. When an ice shelf melts, it's not a big deal for sea levels, because that ice is floating. But ice shelves act a bit like corks, constraining the glaciers behind them. And if you get rid of the shelves—if you pop that cork—then the worry is the glaciers' flow will speed up, and a lot of land-based ice will rapidly get dumped into the sea. And when that happens, it has massive sea-level implications. So some very serious scientists are proposing schemes that would artificially prop up the ice shelves that we ourselves are undermining. One of the proposals involves constructing a one-hundred-meter-high berm, which would block warm water from infiltrating under the ice shelf. I don't know how long that berm is supposed to be, but the Thwaites Glacier, which has been nicknamed the Doomsday Glacier, is eighty miles wide. So that's the sort of scale we're talking about. Another proposal is to create three-hundred-meter-high artificial islands to jam the ice shelf and buttress the glacier behind it. Once again, the details of how many you'd need, and so on, are a little

[KOLBERT] *What Can We Do about It?*

vague. I'm not sure how seriously anyone takes this sort of proposal, but when the alternative is drowning New York and Shanghai and Osaka and Miami, some pretty far-out ideas, I think, are going to be entertained.

Other smaller experiments are already up and running. In 2020, I went to visit one of these experiments in Iceland that focused on a process known as direct air capture. A company, called Climeworks, had built a series of direct air-capture units that could pull CO_2 directly out of the air. First, a fan sucks ordinary air into the unit. The air flows over chemicals that bind with CO_2, effectively captured. When the chemicals are saturated with CO_2, they are heated, and the CO_2 is forced off. Then it is piped deep underground. Two kilometers underground. Deep underground, the CO_2 reacts with the volcanic rock to form calcium carbonate. This experiment has been a success; currently, Climeworks Iceland units are capable of removing from the atmosphere four thousand tons of CO_2 a year. And if you are interested, you can pay Climeworks to remove some of your own emissions from the air, which I did. When I went to visit the first unit in 2020, I was, to use Climeworks' term, a carbon pioneer. I still pay Climeworks to remove twelve hundred pounds of carbon per year from the atmosphere, and it costs me about $600. And to put this in perspective, just flying to Iceland to visit the capture units that were capturing my carbon, I used up my entire annual allotment.

Another figure that puts things in perspective is the world's annual output of CO_2, which is around forty billion tons. So roughly speaking, Climeworks is each year extracting one ten-millionth of the CO_2 we are all putting up. Or to put this differently, to remove what we add each year would mean building ten million versions of the Climeworks setup. And I should make another point here. The operation of capture units requires energy. Most of this energy goes to heating the chemicals to drive off the CO_2 so that the process can be repeated over and over again. The Climeworks machines get around this bind by relying on geothermal heat from a nearby volcanic zone. So again, to deal with our global problem, we would need to erect ten million operations as big as Climeworks' that could operate on some form of carbon-free energy, and all of them would have to be located near some geological formation that could hold CO_2. It doesn't do any good to capture CO_2 if there's no place to put it.

So you can look at the Climeworks setup two ways. You can say that it proves what's possible, or just as reasonably, you can say it proves what's not possible. But regardless of your views, or my views, the world is already banking on carbon removal. In the aftermath of Paris, the

128   *The Tanner Lectures on Human Values*

Intergovernmental Panel on Climate Change (IPCC) put together a series of scenarios for holding average global temperature increase to 1.5°C. And all of the scenarios the IPCC came up with rely on some form of carbon removal, on the order of billions of tons a year. And the same holds true for most of the scenarios aimed at limiting warming to 2°C; they rely on massive amounts of clean energy deployment *and* massive amounts of carbon removal. So when we talk about holding warming to 2°C, we are, implicitly, saying that both of these massive projects are doable, and not just doable in the abstract, but will, in fact, get done. This is true even though we are not deploying clean-energy technologies anywhere near as fast as we need to and even though no one has figured out yet how to scale up carbon removal. Climeworks' four-thousand-ton project in Iceland is, as far as I know, the largest direct air-capture operation out there.

So what happens if one or both of these projects don't get done or don't get done in time? Are there any other alternatives?

One possibility that is widely invoked and widely feared is solar geoengineering. The idea behind solar geoengineering is based on volcanoes. A major volcanic eruption blasts a lot of sulfur dioxide into the stratosphere. As the sulfur dioxide drifts around, it forms these tiny droplets that are very reflective. These droplets, or aerosols, reflect sunlight back toward space. The result is that less direct sunlight hits the earth, and global temperatures fall for a year or two until the droplets fall out of the stratosphere. And if you could mimic that—if you could spray reflective particles in the stratosphere—you could, potentially, offset the warming effect of dumping CO_2 into the troposphere.

Solar geoengineering has been described as "unimaginably drastic," "dangerous beyond belief," and a "broad highway to hell." Just recently, several dozen scientists from around the world published an open letter calling for a ban not just on the use of solar geoengineering but on any experiments relating to it. There are certainly many reasons to be concerned about the prospect of solar geoengineering—with the possibility that humanity might consciously attempt to dim the sun. Shooting a lot of reflective particles in the stratosphere would not return us to a preindustrial climate, even though it might return us to preindustrial temperatures. It would produce a different world, potentially with very different regional weather patterns. And billions of people depend on the regional weather patterns we have now, for example on the South Asian monsoon. Some regions might benefit from solar geoengineering while others suffer, and that could lead to global conflict. Meanwhile, whatever reflective particles we might put up in the stratosphere are going to fall out in a few years, meaning they would have to constantly be replenished. And if, for whatever reason, they weren't, then temperatures would suddenly and dramatically shoot up. This phenomenon has become known as "termination shock."

But just to denounce geoengineering as too dangerous even to be researched, as many have done, is, I think, unfair. Here, again, we have to be honest about the situation that we're in. We are already running a vast unsupervised experiment on the climate. By now, scientists have been warning us about the potential for catastrophic climate change for more than half a century. In that half a century, there have been dozens of major international meetings and a series of climate accords, including Kyoto, Copenhagen, and Paris. But even as we keep agreeing to reduce greenhouse gas emissions, we keep pumping them out.

The people who say we need to study geoengineering say, "Look at that contradiction." In terms of cutting emissions, we have made, to a first approximation, zero progress. And yet climate change *must* be dealt with. As Frank Keutsch, a chemist who directs Harvard's Solar Geoengineering Research Program, put it when he said to me, "When I started this, I was perhaps, oddly, not as worried about it. Because the idea that geoengineering would actually happen seemed quite remote. But over the years, as I see our lack of action on climate, I sometimes get quite anxious that this may actually happen. And I feel quite a lot of pressure from that." Dan Schrag, a Harvard geologist and an adviser to the geoengineering project, told me that when you account for the inertia of the climate system, "we are already at 2 degrees C. We are going to be lucky to stop at 4 degrees C. That's not optimistic or pessimistic. I think that's objective reality."

This is the context for geoengineering. The glass is already broken. And this is what links geoengineering, assisted evolution, and gene-edited toads. Such technological interventions make no sense in a world under control. But that, sadly, is not the world we live in. These efforts arise less out of faith in the power of technology than out of almost the opposite impulse, a kind of technological fatalism. The fear is our social structures are weak and our technologies are strong. You could say seductively strong.

So what is it that, in the end, I am advocating? I hope no one who has been kind enough to come to these lectures will infer that I am urging us down the path of second-order control. As the techno-fatalists themselves will tell you, techno-fatalism can end badly, potentially very

130 *The Tanner Lectures on Human Values*

badly. When you find yourself looking to the source of your problems for an answer to your problems, this is a bad sign. Just ask the old lady who swallowed a fly.

So I would like to be able to recommend a different way forward. I would love to end by saying that instead of reengineering the world, we should rethink our ethics and our politics. Clearly, we *do* need a fundamental rethinking of our ethics and our politics. But how do we get there except through the very same political structures that have already proved so ineffective? It is far easier to assert that we need something totally new than it is to actually lay hold of it. I'm reminded of the old joke about the academics who find themselves marooned on a desert island. They have nothing except a crate of canned beans. How to get at the food? Let's assume we have a can opener, one of them helpfully suggests.

When I speak to impressionable young people, I try to end on a more upbeat note. But I think this is an audience that doesn't require careful handling. So in conclusion, I will say that just because there is a problem—a world-threatening problem—it doesn't follow that there's a solution.

Theorizing Racial Justice

CHARLES W. MILLS

THE TANNER LECTURES ON HUMAN VALUES

Delivered at

The University of Michigan
February 12, 2020

CHARLES W. MILLS was a Distinguished Professor of Philosophy at the Graduate Center, CUNY (City University of New York). He worked in the general area of social and political philosophy, particularly in oppositional political theory as centered on class, gender, and race. He was the author of over one hundred journal articles, book chapters, comments and replies, and six books. His first book, *The Racial Contract* (Cornell University Press, 1997), won a Myers Outstanding Book Award for the study of bigotry and human rights in America. His second book, *Blackness Visible: Essays on Philosophy and Race* (Cornell University Press, 1998), was a finalist for the award for the most important North American work in social philosophy of that year. Other books are *From Class to Race: Essays in White Marxism and Black Radicalism*, *Contract and Domination* (coauthored with Carole Pateman), and *Radical Theory, Caribbean Reality: Race, Class and Social Domination*. His most recent book is *Black Rights/White Wrongs: The Critique of Racial Liberalism*.

Mills received his PhD from the University of Toronto and previously taught at the University of Oklahoma, the University of Illinois at Chicago, and Northwestern University. He was the president of the American Philosophical Association Central Division for 2017–18. In 2017, he was elected to the American Academy of Arts and Sciences.

THEORIZING RACIAL JUSTICE

This lecture seeks to address the issue of racial justice and, in the process, to look also at the question of why the subject has been so *little* addressed in Western and, more specifically, American political philosophy.[1] For it is not as if the demand for racial justice is a new one. The protests of recent years, above all "Black Lives Matter," have brought the topic solidly back on to the national agenda, effectively shattering the widespread "postracial society" illusions that Barack Obama's 2008 election had encouraged in some quarters. But of course, the demand is much older. One could go back to the earlier civil rights movements of the 1950s–70s, both mainstream and radical. Or before that, to the debates around postbellum Reconstruction, and the later Black disappointment and anger over the betrayal of Reconstruction. Or before that, during the epoch of slavery, to the long history of antebellum abolitionism. And this list just focuses on Blacks. I have not even said anything about Japanese internment, Chinese exclusion, anti-Latinx discrimination, or—returning to the founding colonial encounters—Native American expropriation and genocide. So the outcry against the inequitable treatment of people of color by whites—if not always under the explicit banner of "racial justice"—has in a sense always constituted the discordant counterpoint, the dissonantly off-key chorus, to what could be thought of as the self-congratulatory soundtrack, the approved theme music and national anthems, official and unofficial, of the republic, a republic that was, after all, effectively founded as "a white man's country."

And yet despite—or should that be "because of"?—this history, and the larger history of modern Western imperialism and conquest in which it is embedded, (white) American political philosophers in particular, and (white) Western political philosophers more generally, have almost completely ignored this subject. But philosophers, at least in their own minds, are supposed to be the professional experts, the go-to guys, on questions of justice, stretching back twenty-five hundred years to ancient Athens and the book often seen as the foundational text of the tradition, Plato's *Republic*.[2] Moreover, the Western philosopher widely credited with reviving Anglo-American political philosophy, which had been judged at the time to be moribund, was himself an American citizen, John Rawls. His famous 1971 book, *A Theory of Justice*, is standardly regarded not merely as reorienting the normative focus of the field from the issue of our political obligation to the state to the issue of the justice

[133]

of society's "basic structure," but as making "grand theory" in the field possible again (as against boring logic-chopping and linguistic analysis).[3] Surely, then, the ideal conceptual and theoretical environment had now been created to talk about issues of racial justice, especially in the wake of 1960s protests and global postwar decolonization. Yet as emphasized, the topic is marginalized not just in Rawls but in the vast secondary literature his work would generate over the next half century, both Rawlsian and non-Rawlsian, and including theorists on the right of the liberal spectrum and the nonliberal communitarian tradition as well.[4] So, though I will be focusing on liberalism in general and Rawls in particular, it needs to be appreciated that the pattern of neglect in the field is much broader.

The lecture will be in three sections. In part 1, "Illiberal Liberalism," I will begin by locating this seemingly puzzling failure within a much longer history of liberal political philosophy's betrayal of its ostensible ideals. In part 2, "Doing Injustice to 'Justice': How Rawls Went Wrong," I will then turn specifically to Rawls and the ways in which his particular version of the liberal social justice project was flawed from the start. Finally, in part 3, "Liberal Racial Justice," I will indicate, if only sketchily, one possible strategy for deriving liberal principles of racial justice via a modified version of the famous Rawlsian thought experiment.

ILLIBERAL LIBERALISM

Liberalism, Ideal and Actual

Our starting point is the political philosophy of liberalism. I should quickly clarify that I am using the word as a term of art, the way political philosophers and political theorists do. Liberalism in this broad sense does not refer just to the left wing of the Democratic Party. Rather, its reference is to the political ideology that developed over the seventeenth through nineteenth centuries in Western Europe in opposition to the doctrines of monarchical absolutism, natural social "estates," ascriptive social hierarchy, and inherited status. Associated with John Locke, David Hume, Adam Smith, Immanuel Kant, Thomas Paine, Thomas Jefferson, Jeremy Bentham, John Stuart Mill, and others, liberalism becomes the philosophy of the new social order, indeed of modernity itself. The rule of law, limited government, democratic consent, individual equality, and equal rights all became the slogans of the revolt against the *ancien régime.* Hence the American Revolution's famous opening statement of the Declaration of Independence, penned by Jefferson, "We hold these truths to be self-evident, that all men are created equal," and the "Liberty,

[MILLS]   *Theorizing Racial Justice*   135

equality, fraternity" of the French Revolution. Being a liberal commits you to belief in these broad principles. (As has been pointed out, this designation is to a significant extent anachronistic, being applied now to political theorists who would not have been thought of as "liberals" in their own time.[5] But in retroactively constructing the tradition, this is the usage that has come to be accepted.)

So, from this perspective, we have liberals on the right who insist on market solutions to social problems and liberals on the left who argue for a state that intervenes on behalf of the disadvantaged. But by these minimal criteria, both groups count as liberals. (Hence conservatives' characterization of themselves as "classical liberals.") Liberalism can then be seen as the most important political ideology of the last few hundred years, the ideology that—especially after the 1989–91 collapse of the East Bloc—had seemingly emerged triumphant over all its challengers. As I don't have to tell you, this celebratory moment was pretty brief. We are now in a period when liberalism is under assault by right-wing populism and authoritarian ethno-nationalism, and there are no guarantees about who will be the eventual victor. But certainly, we have to hope that liberalism will survive and eventually prevail, given the attractiveness of its ideals and the contrasting ugliness of those of its main current opponents.

In the official story, then, liberalism has historically maintained a principled opposition to reactionary premodern political ideologies, ideologies that denied people "individual" status and equal rights and entitlement to government by consent. It's a great story, an inspiring story . . . but the problem is that it happens to be untrue. Or at least, the extent to which it is true is severely qualified. Far from being in principled combat from the start against antiegalitarian beliefs and systems of ascriptive hierarchy of all kinds, liberalism has been *complicit* with many of them until comparatively recently. (And some critics would say, it is in effect, if no longer overtly, still thus complicit today.) Liberalism as an ideal turns out to be illiberalism in actuality.[6]

Consider, for example, gender. From the "first wave" of feminism onward (e.g., the British Mary Wollstonecraft's *A Vindication of the Rights of Woman*, the French Olympe de Gouges's *Rights of Women*, and the United States' own Abigail Adams),[7] feminist theorists have pointed out that the promise of liberalism was not extended to women, a challenge that would of course be greatly deepened and expanded in the "second" and later waves. Denied equal rights, unable to own property or run for political office or even vote, their legal identities subsumed into their husbands' under the doctrine of coverture, women are clearly not ranked among the "free and equal" individuals liberated by this new political philosophy of government by consent. Rather, their status seems to be a kind of gender "estate" analogous to those subordinated in the feudal hierarchy.[8] But women of all races constitute half the population to begin with; this is not a minor exclusion but a huge one. Then think of race. Though this history is now marginalized in the official liberal story, we need to remember that most of the Western European states now uncontroversially considered part of the "liberal" West had, at one time or another, empires (British, French, Dutch, Spanish, Portuguese, Belgian . . .) in which non-Europeans—Indigenous peoples and in some cases African slaves—were systemically subordinated. Together, these Western countries ruled undemocratically over the vast majority of humanity.[9] Indeed, this global racial inequality was so firmly entrenched as a norm, so taken for granted, that at the 1919 post–World War I Versailles Conference to set up the League of Nations, the Japanese delegation's proposal to include a racial equality clause in the Covenant was emphatically rejected by the six "Anglo-Saxon nations" (as they were then called): Britain, the United States, Canada, South Africa, Australia, and New Zealand.[10] Or think of class. Though modernity is surely supposed, at the very least, to equalize status hierarchies among white males, even here the process is very uneven. The birth of liberalism may date to the seventeenth century, but property restrictions on the franchise in many European countries remained in place till the late nineteenth and even early twentieth centuries. (In the United States, it is really only with nineteenth-century "Jacksonian Democracy" that you get "universal" suffrage even among white men.)[11]

The point is, then, that once we put together all the exclusions of actual historical liberalism, we should be able to see that a conceptualization that represents them as "anomalies" and "deviations" is fundamentally wrong. *The dominant varieties of historical liberalism excluded the majority of the world's population from equal normative consideration.* But if exclusion is modal—if propertied white males are the major beneficiaries of modernity's liberalization—then how can the conventional narrative of a clear transition from the world of hierarchical "estates" to a world of equal "individuals" be sustained?

Otherwise put, "liberalism" has historically been "illiberalism" for all but a minority. But then shouldn't our periodization be changed to reflect this reality? Shouldn't we be working with a different temporal and conceptual map, as in the contrast between figures 1a and 1b?[12]

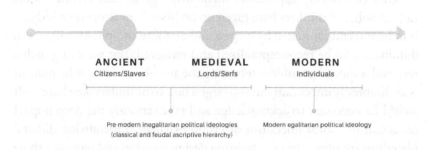

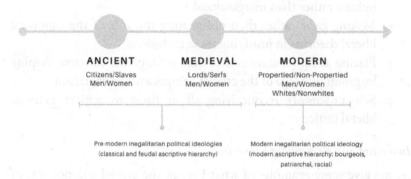

So, we would reconceptualize/retheorize liberalism to emphasize its *continuity* with the past rather than its putative sharp break with it. And on this basis, we would then start to look at liberalism very differently, with, shall we say, a far more suspicious and critical eye. Rather than automatically presuming that liberalism as a political philosophy is going to be adequate for dealing with the particular social problem facing us, we would begin by asking ourselves the question, If liberalism has been illiberalism along so many central axes of social subordination, how has this pernicious shaping by group domination affected its crucial concepts, norms, frameworks, and assumptions? What silences, what opacities, what inadequacies, might we expect to find in liberalism, given this history? Indeed, isn't it *likely* to be the case that where class, gender, and race are involved, the inclusion of groups previously formally excluded is going to be merely nominal unless the deep structuring of the theory *by* its previous history is acknowledged and self-consciously addressed?

One can readily appreciate, then, why—given this record—some radical political thinkers have given up on liberalism altogether, judging it to be too contaminated by its past and ongoing complicity with social domination to be reconceptualized and retrieved. But assuming such a retrieval is indeed possible—rebutting the antiliberal critique by radicals is undoubtedly important but too large a task to be undertaken here[13]—it would be necessary to acknowledge and take seriously the deep impact on actual historical liberalism of group privilege. Liberalizing illiberal liberalism (to offer a tongue-twisting designation) would require a thorough and radical rethinking. For example:

1. Rewriting the history of liberalism so its exclusions are highlighted rather than marginalized
2. Making clear rather than obfuscating the role of the canonical liberal theorists in justifying these exclusions
3. Placing at center stage rather than offstage the concrete shaping by group privilege of the crucial components of liberalism
4. Self-consciously reconceiving all of these to achieve genuine liberal justice

Analyzing and Rethinking Liberalism

Let me give some examples of what I see as the crucial components of liberalism, as mentioned in number 3, and then illustrate in sequence both how they are likely to be negatively affected by an unfair group advantage and how they would therefore need to be reconceived to correct for this unfair group advantage.

I would suggest the following list. Liberalism can be thought of as having the following: (a) a characteristic set of value-commitments, (b) a certain social ontology, (c) a conceptual cartography of the sociopolitical, (d) an account of the history that has led up to the present (varying—obviously—from society to society), and (e) a schedule of rights, protections, and freedoms for individuals.

The first, (a), is seemingly the most straightforward: liberalism is classically represented as committed to the moral equality, freedom, and self-realization of individuals. But as we just saw, the reality is that only some people were deemed worthy of attaining "individual" status, and for others, institutional moral inequality and unfreedom were the actual norms. This fundamental division of the deserving/undeserving population inevitably affects (b). Again, the traditional claim is that liberalism presupposes an ontology of atomic individuals, ruling out an ontology of social groups. But this claim is multiply mistaken.

To begin with, noncontractarian utilitarian and Hegelian liberalisms can also be found in the tradition, for which societal belonging and group membership are crucial. So, we need to demarcate *moral* individualism (the individual as the locus of moral value) from *descriptive* individualism (the individual as abstracted out of society and history). Liberalism only requires the former, not the latter. Secondly, historical (actual non-sanitized) liberalism did indeed have a group ontology (class, gender, and racial "estates"), though today, in keeping with the official story, it is denied or glossed over. But thirdly, the crucial additional point liberal progressives today would want to make is that if liberal society has indeed historically been divided as in (a), then the appropriate revisionist replacement group ontology needs to register this fact and, rejecting naturalism, center social group *domination* (e.g., men over women, whites over people of color) as fundamental. Given the actual record (anticipating [d]) of polities depicting themselves as "liberal," a social ontology appropriate for real-life liberal societies cannot, or at least cannot automatically, be predicated on symmetry. Rather, it must acknowledge the deep asymmetries (with implications both for people and institutions) of social privilege and social subordination.[14] Glossing over this reality, as is standardly done in official liberal ontologies, whether "atomic" or "social," will only consolidate an illicit group advantage by effectively generalizing the unrepresentative status of these dominant groups to the society as a whole. (Indeed, the failure of liberalism historically to develop an ontology critically tracking group domination and subordination in supposedly liberal states is itself one of the clearest indications of its "illiberalism.")

Likewise, the conceptual cartography, (c)—the mapping of the polity—must be drawn so as to be genuinely inclusive rather than complicit with boundaries entrenching group domination. Think, for example, of the feminist liberal challenge to the standard delineation of the public-private demarcation and its removal of women and gender equity from the realm of the public sphere. Or consider an imperial topography that legitimizes the relegation of "natives" to an inferior conceptual space that justifies the "mother country's" undemocratic rule over them. Moreover, if the map is supposed to be true to the territory, as maps are definitionally supposed to be, then it should not represent the polity

140   *The Tanner Lectures on Human Values*

as something that it is not. An ostensibly liberal democratic society that is in actuality (whatever its aspirations) a white-supremacist state needs to be categorized as such in the map's overall picture. The history, (d), is thus essential, not in the sense of the Whig progressivism sometimes ascribed to liberalism, but as an account that tracks the actual—not mythical—genealogy of the polity, the possible injustices marring that history, and the structures of group domination it has created, with corresponding implications for (b) and (c). So you can appreciate how they are all interconnected.

The overall goal, then, would be to develop an alternative liberalism predicated on the full inclusion of the human beings that are its ostensible subjects. Rather than taking existing hegemonic liberalism's structure for granted, we would then be better theoretically positioned to examine it critically from the "external" perspective (though quite immanent in another sense) of *counterfactual* liberalism not shaped by group domination. We could then ask—given these alternative social ontologies, redrawn conceptual cartographies, and revisionist histories (all designed to be revelatory rather than, as at present, obfuscatory)—what would the familiar value-commitments of liberalism require in the way of rights, protections, and freedoms for the divergently positioned individuals of the liberal polity? In other words, what would social justice demand?

Far from being *inconsistent* with liberalism, therefore (at least an ideal liberal liberalism, as against actual illiberal liberalism), such a normative enterprise should be seen not merely as *permissible* within a liberal framework but as indeed *mandated* by any serious commitment to liberal social justice. For we would now be trying to guarantee, (a), the institutionally recognized moral equality, freedom, and possibilities for self-realization of individuals by taking into account, (b), the group memberships of those individuals, how they are unfairly privileged or subordinated by them, and developing accordingly mappings of society and the polity, (c), that accurately track political and economic power and social status in the light (d) of the actual history of these groups and the legacy of that history in the present, thereby, (e), providing an informed basis upon which to prescribe rights, protections, and freedoms. Insofar as "transparency" is also a liberal value, though usually applied to institutions, it could be argued that liberalism's typical *lack* of transparency on (b), (c), and (d) is, at the metalevel, itself a violation of liberal norms. It would, ironically, turn out that the revisionists, far from being the subversives, are the real liberals!

Racial Liberalism

Let us now turn specifically to race and the distinctive strategy of revision it would require. Class and gender rethinkings of liberalism are both completely familiar and well established in the literature of political theory and political philosophy, as well as in social activism guided by these political orientations. The social-democratic critique targets what could be called "bourgeois" liberalism, a liberalism shaped by capitalist power, while the feminist critique targets "patriarchal" liberalism, a liberalism shaped by male power. The aim in each case is to develop an emancipatory liberalism sensitized to, and restructured to overcome, the exclusions of these dominant forms of liberalism. But as can be confirmed by consulting any introduction, guide, handbook, or companion to political theory or political philosophy, the antiracist critique of what could be thought of as "racial" liberalism, shaped by white power, is far less extensively developed and represented in these circles.[15] Yet racial injustice in liberal states in modernity has been at least as flagrant as, or indeed far more flagrant than, class and gender injustice, involving great atrocities (Indigenous conquest and expropriation, genocide, racial slavery, colonial forced labor, Jim Crow, and apartheid) in the very time period when human moral equality as a general norm was supposed to have been established by the new liberal order. On a global scale, a case can easily be made that racial injustice has significantly affected the fate of the *majority* of the world's population, both in terms of discrete events and their legacy and in terms of the establishment of enduring racialized structures of sociopolitical domination. Why, then, has it not received more discussion in political philosophy?

I suggest that a major—perhaps the major—contributory factor is demographic. Philosophy is one of the very "whitest" of the humanities. In the United States, for example, Blacks make up only about 1 percent of professional philosophers, a figure that has not changed in decades. In Europe, it's even lower. (At a January 2019 international critical race theory conference in Paris, I met the single Black Frenchwoman with a PhD in the field teaching in a philosophy department. There was a second, but she chose to leave philosophy.) In theory, of course, anybody can work on anything, and there's nothing to stop white philosophers from working on racial justice (and a few have).[16] But in practice, even in a subject so self-conceivably removed from the material body as philosophy, identity makes a difference. Over the twenty-five-hundred-year (Western) history of the profession, there was nothing to stop male philosophers from

142   *The Tanner Lectures on Human Values*

working on gender and gender justice either. But it does not surprise us that only with the relative influx of women into the field from the 1970s onward do we begin to get a systematic critical examination of the issue. And what these pioneering feminists find, of course, is a pattern of discriminatory theoretical treatment dating from premodernity to modernity, taking the form, in modernity, of liberalism in which (white) men as equal individuals rule over women as inferiors: patriarchal liberalism.

Against this background, then, it should not really be controversial to claim that the (far greater) demographic whiteness of the profession will likewise foster a "conceptual" whiteness. Narratives, frameworks, assumptions, scenarios, and thought experiments are presented as colorless and universal when all too often they are really based on the European and Euro-American experience. In political philosophy in particular, our focus here, the nonwhite political subject is almost always assimilated to the white political subject, without any attention being paid to the distinctive political history of people of color in modernity, a history that—as just pointed out above—has involved being subject to colonialism, imperialism, expropriation, genocide, chattel slavery, and ongoing post-Emancipation/postcolonial racial subordination. Correspondingly, the role of liberalism in justifying and rationalizing these practices will not be part of the official philosophical story. Yet the supposed political ideology of individualism, egalitarianism, and universal rights and freedoms was far more often complicit with than in principled opposition to these practices. Locke, Hume, Kant, Jefferson, Mill, et al. all had racist views that arguably shaped the way their liberal principles applied (or not) across the color line. Capacities for self-ownership, civilization, autonomy, full personhood, and cultural development were all seen as influenced by race.[17]

Thus we get a racialized liberalism, a racial liberalism, in which all five of the components earlier cited are affected: who is entitled, (a), to "individual" status and the enjoyment of equality, freedom, and self-realization; how the social ontology, (b), is conceived of; what is the mapping, (c), of the sociopolitical; what historical account, (d), is presupposed; and finally, (e), what racialized schedule of rights, protections, and freedoms will actually be drawn up. And it then means, I would claim, that in order to *correct* this history of systemic exclusion and structurally differentiated treatment, we need to begin by acknowledging it and asking ourselves what conceptual and theoretical moves will be necessary to redress it. For if racial liberalism in the past took an overtly racist form, denigrating people of color as natural inferiors (whether because of biology or culture), racial liberalism in the present epoch (postcolonial, post-civil rights) will look quite different. It will present itself as *facially* raceless while continuing to be conceptually shaped and ethically oriented by the interests, perspectives, and priorities of the racially privileged white population. The failure to make racial justice central to the renascent Anglo-American political philosophy of the past half century is thus, I will now suggest to you—especially given the myriad historical racial injustices of the "Anglosphere," the combined Anglo-American empires[18]—*itself* the clearest manifestation of the continuing racial "whiteness" of liberalism.

DOING INJUSTICE TO "JUSTICE": HOW RAWLS WENT WRONG

Consider now John Rawls, as a paradigm case, I will argue, of racial liberalism.

Rawls and Social Contract Theory

Rawls is generally viewed as the most important American political philosopher of the twentieth century. Indeed, some would go further and declare him the most important political philosopher, period, of the twentieth century.[19] And his central theme, as emphasized, was social justice. His influence on discussions of justice over the past half century has, accordingly, been huge, certainly in the Western world but elsewhere also. So, if I can demonstrate the deeply problematic nature of Rawls's framing of this issue, I will have gone a long way, given his significance, to establishing my indictment of what I am claiming is (whatever the denials) still a racial liberalism. And here I should mention, for anyone who knows my previous work, that my line of argument today actually represents a change of position on my part. I have recently come to the conclusion that I have been misinterpreting Rawls all along, so many of my criticisms of him over the years have been unjustified. But I also believe that my new position, if it can be successfully defended, actually represents a *superior* line of critique. Rawlsian liberalism and the secondary literature it has generated would, if I am correct, turn out to be even *more* deeply racialized than I had earlier thought. (However, if I am wrong, I would claim that my original position—now my fallback position—though admittedly weaker, still constitutes a challenge strong enough that it deserves to be, but has yet to be, answered by Rawlsians.)

Before I continue, though, I should give at least a brief gloss of Rawls's theory. In addition to being credited with the revival of

Anglo-American political philosophy, Rawls is also seen as resurrecting Western social contract theory. The "golden age" of contractarianism was the century and a half from 1650 to 1800, the four most important contract theorists and texts being Thomas Hobbes, *Leviathan* (1651), John Locke, *Two Treatises of Government* (1689), Jean-Jacques Rousseau, *The Social Contract* (1762), and Immanuel Kant, *The Metaphysics of Morals* (1797).[20] Social contract theory directs us to think of the creation of society and government through the metaphor, the iconography, of a "contract" among presocial (somewhat qualified in Locke) and prepolitical human beings in the "state of nature." So it is not actually meant as a literal account but a hypothetical one, an "as if" story. On this basis, the different contract theorists offered varying analyses of what they thought a good society and a fair political system would look like and what our resulting civic rights and obligations to the state would be. But as noted earlier, critics—utilitarian and more historically oriented philosophers—argued that even as a hypothetical, nonliteral account contract theory was deeply flawed and suggested that there were better ways to conceptualize both. So, by the early 1800s, contract theory fell by the philosophical wayside, seemingly becoming a mere historical curiosity in the development of the field.[21]

However, Rawls's 1971 *A Theory of Justice* rethought the "contract" to make it a thought experiment not directed now at justifying political obligation but deriving principles of justice for what he called the "basic structure" of society (the Constitution, the legal system, the economy, the family).[22] You choose principles of justice on prudential rather than moral grounds, motivated by how you judge you will fare comparatively in alternative societies respectively structured by these different principles. But because crucial aspects of society and your own identity are hidden from you by a "veil of ignorance," the combination of self-interest and stipulated ignorance produces the equivalent of a moral choice. For example, you will not choose a racist or sexist or plutocratic society because you don't know whether or not you will be a member of the privileged race or gender or socioeconomic class. To use language from the Continental tradition, you will be concerned about the oppressed "Other" because—once the veil lifts—you could turn out to *be* the "Other"! So, in this new incarnation, contract theory would experience a remarkable rebirth. Not only would it revive interest in the original versions of the "contract" (1650–1800), but it would

[MILLS] *Theorizing Racial Justice* 145

also give rise to competing contemporary "contract" models of social justice by theorists opposed to Rawls's left-liberal/social-democratic picture of the ideal society, whether from the right or from positions further left.

So contract theory is once again alive and well. But why then, given that racial membership will be one of the facets of our identity concealed from us in Rawls's version, can't the thought experiment handle issues of racial injustice, contrary to my claims above? The problem is that the choice situation as designed by Rawls is limited to principles of justice within "ideal theory"—that is, principles for an ideal, perfectly just society, what Rawls calls a "well-ordered society."[23] Everybody, regardless of race, will thus be guaranteed equal rights, but though this will justify preemptive principles of antidiscrimination in hypothetical ideal societies, it will not address the correction of historical racial injustices in actual nonideal societies, such as our own. Such matters are covered by *nonideal* theory, and the problem is that neither Rawls nor subsequent Rawlsians would go on to explain what such principles ("compensatory justice") might be.[24] In addition, I pointed out in various critical essays over the years that Rawls's idealizations seemed not to be limited to normative theory but to be extended to *factual* matters as well, including the features of actual societies, in a way that ignored the racist record both of the United States in particular and the West more generally. (For example, nowhere in his work does he mention the expropriation and genocide of Native Americans, postbellum Jim Crow segregation, and the historically white-supremacist nature of the United States nor the Atlantic slave trade or European colonialism and imperialism in the non-European world.)[25] So, this seemed to me to be evidence of the "whiteness" of Rawls (and Rawlsianism also).

Yet in the opening pages of *Theory*, Rawls himself had explicitly conceded that the problems of nonideal theory, including "compensatory justice," were the "pressing and urgent" ones.[26] My frustration with Rawls and Rawlsianism, then, was that there seemed to be no real interest on their part—almost fifty years after the book had first appeared—in making the transition to nonideal theory and the obviously pressing and urgent matter of the theorization of racial justice in the United States and elsewhere. To the extent that in recent years, a body of work in nonideal theory has begun to develop, but it is not really concerned with corrective justice and certainly not with race.

146   *The Tanner Lectures on Human Values*

A New Reading of Rawls

However, as emphasized, I now believe (as a result of a recent theoretical epiphany) that I have been operating with a mistaken interpretation of Rawls all along. Here is my new position, bolded for the sake of dramatic emphasis:

Rawls's theory of justice does not apply to the United States.

Now obviously, this is a very startling and counterintuitive claim. Why would Rawls, an American citizen, have devised a theory of justice not applicable to his own country? And considering that we are approaching the fiftieth anniversary of *A Theory of Justice*, one of the most celebrated and widely read philosophical texts of the twentieth century, wouldn't some of his innumerable readers and commentators have noticed such a strange exclusion by now?

I'll get back to the second question later, but for now, let us just focus on the first. Note that I did not say that Rawls *intended* his theory of justice not to be applicable to the United States. What I said, or implied, is that as a matter of *fact* (taking "facts" broadly enough to include structural states of affairs), it does not so apply. Why? Because of what Rawls takes himself to be doing. Here are two interpretations of Rawls's project, my original one and my new one:

MY ORIGINAL INTERPRETATION (at least the first three premises of which are, I think, widely shared, if not the rest):

> It is important to ϕ.
>
> We should be trying to ϕ.
>
> Rawls is trying to ϕ.
>
> Rawls is doing a bad job of ϕ-ing.
>
> So, Rawls should be criticized for doing a bad job of ϕ-ing.

MY NEW REVISED INTERPRETATION:

> Rawls is not trying to ϕ in the first place.
>
> So, Rawls cannot be criticized for ϕ-ing badly.
>
> But it is important to ϕ.
>
> We should be trying to ϕ.
>
> So, Rawls should be criticized for not even trying to ϕ in the first place.

So, the obvious question then is, What is ϕ-ing? And the answer (not to keep you in suspense) is the following:

Φ-ing: Developing a theory of justice for modern Western liberal societies of all kinds, both racist and nonracist.

And why is Rawls not trying to φ?

Because (in his own mind) he doesn't have to; the class of racist modern Western liberal societies is empty. No modern Western liberal society is racist. Therefore, the United States is not racist. Rawls's theory of justice only applies to nonracist modern Western liberal societies, but since (Rawls believes) the United States is not racist (no modern Western liberal society is), this is not a problem. If, on the other hand, you believe as I do, and as various other people do, that the United States *is* racist, then we get, straightforwardly, the counterintuitive conclusion earlier stated: Rawls's theory of justice does not apply to the United States.

Let us name these premises about the scope of Rawls's theory and the nature of the United States:

TJ(R&~R): Rawls's theory of justice applies both to racist and nonracist
(Western liberal) societies.

TJ(~R): Rawls's theory of justice only applies to nonracist
(Western liberal) societies.

USA(~R): The United States is not a racist (Western liberal) society.

USA(R): The United States is a racist (Western liberal) society.

(The point of specifying "Western liberal" throughout is because of the further
complication that Rawls's theory might be taken to apply to racist Western
liberal societies but not to racist non-Western nonliberal societies.)

Obviously, then, people could disagree with me on multiple grounds. They could insist that Rawls is indeed trying to φ, endorsing TJ(R&~R), and then either accept or reject USA(R). Or they could agree that Rawls is not trying to φ, endorsing TJ(~R) but rejecting USA(R).

Let us start with TJ(~R). What evidence do I have for this seemingly extraordinary claim? It is most clearly stated in his last book, *Justice as Fairness*,[27] where he is summarizing his theory. But I would contend that it has been implicit all along, if not recognized, in his initial characterization of the societies he takes as his reference point and indeed (more generally) in the very structural assumptions of social contract theory.

In *Justice as Fairness*, Rawls says in the preface that his two main aims in the book are "to rectify the more serious faults in *A Theory of Justice* that have obscured the main ideas of justice as fairness" and "to connect into one unified statement the conception of justice presented in *Theory* and the main ideas found in my essays beginning with 1974."[28] The book's editor, Erin Kelly, in her editor's foreword, reports that because of his illness, Rawls was "unable to rework the manuscript in its final state, as he

148   *The Tanner Lectures on Human Values*

had planned." But she goes on to emphasize that "most of the manuscript was nearly complete" and that the most unfinished sections were parts 4 and 5 (out of five sections total).[29] One could infer with a high degree of confidence, then, that passages from the early, presumably finished, sections of the book state his final definitive version of his theory. Well, what does he say there? In part 1, he announces the scope of his theory: "Justice as fairness is a political conception of justice for the special case of the basic structure of a modern democratic society."[30] And a few pages later, he clarifies, "From the start, then, we view a democratic society as a political society that excludes a confessional or an aristocratic state, not to mention a caste, slave, or a racist one."[31]

So, the inference is, I would claim, absolutely straightforward. It is not a matter of translation from another language and the claim that previous translations had been misleading (though there is, of course, Rawls's Harvard colleague Burton Dreben's famous joke that *Theory* read as if it had been translated from the original German). It is not a matter of the discovery of a later, previously unknown manuscript that corrects earlier versions. It is not a matter of reading between the lines to uncover a point hitherto unnoticed. Rawls is informing us directly and unambiguously, in a book that appeared nearly two decades ago, that his theory of justice is not meant to apply to racist societies: TJ($\sim$R). He is not trying to ϕ. So if, contra Rawls's view, the United States is indeed a racist society, USA(R), then the further implication is that Rawls's theory of justice does not apply to the United States.[32]

Why This Reading Has to Be Wrong (but Actually Isn't)

But surely (you object) this could not be correct. I have not kept up with the Rawls literature—I don't know if it is even possible to do so—but I am not aware of any secondary text, whether article or book, that states this restriction on his theory. Even if most American (or other) Rawlsians don't work on race, one would expect them to indicate somewhere—if this reading is correct—that, by the way, Rawls's principles do not apply to racist societies and then explain (if they're American) why they do not believe the United States is a racist society. Or more generally, one would look for a caveat to that effect in the numerous handbooks, companions, and introductions to Rawls that have appeared in the last fifteen years or so or in the online *Stanford Encyclopedia of Philosophy* entry on Rawls. So, this would seem to suggest that TJ($\sim$R) is false and that, in fact, I am misinterpreting Rawls somehow. As the two

[MILLS] *Theorizing Racial Justice* 149

passages stand, the inference does indeed seem straightforward, but my reading of them has to be wrong.

OBJECTION I: You're just misreading what is the familiar ideal theory / nonideal theory distinction.

Here's one obvious suggestion: far from my startling and unfamiliar conclusion following, Rawls is merely making his utterly familiar point that his theory of justice is located within ideal theory, and for it to be applied to racist societies, one would need first to derive the necessary principles of nonideal theory from it.[33] Thus he says explicitly in *Theory* that "the intuitive idea is to split the theory of justice into two parts," the "first or ideal part" assuming strict compliance, the second or nonideal part "worked out [only] after an ideal conception of justice has been chosen." The latter is then conceptually subdivided into two further sections, "one consist[ing] of the principles for governing adjustments to natural limitations and historical contingencies, and the other of principles for meeting injustice."[34]

So, dealing with racist societies and their injustices would require principles of the latter kind, the second subset of nonideal theory, and would presumably include what Rawls refers to as "compensatory justice."[35] As I emphasized, Rawls never actually derives them. In *Political Liberalism*, two decades later, he concedes that problems of race and ethnicity (as well as gender) "may seem of an altogether different character calling for different principles of justice, which *Theory* does not discuss," and in *Justice as Fairness*, likewise, he admits that "the serious problems arising from existing discrimination and distinctions based on gender and race are not on [*Theory*'s] agenda."[36] Nor have subsequent generations of Rawlsians taken up this challenge.[37] But the answer from Rawlsians (insofar as they bother to reply) would presumably be the same: the fact that we have not chosen to do this doesn't mean that it can't be done. You, Charles Mills, are claiming (originally) that this neglect shows that Rawls, as well as we subsequent Rawlsians, are doing a bad job of it. But whether or not this is true, there is no doubt that Rawls is ϕ-ing.

This response is a natural one and is, I think, probably modal. But I now believe that it is mistaken. (Two alternative explanations would be [a] to a significant extent, our interests shape what we pay attention to, and since most Rawlsians aren't interested in race in the first place, they don't even notice the possible implication of these linked *Justice as Fairness* passages; and [b] many—perhaps most?—white readers of the book *agree* with USA[~R], so even if TJ[~R] is true, it doesn't matter for the application of the theory to the United States.)

Here is my *reductio* of the claim in the objection. Rawls does not single out racist societies for special mention but includes them as part of a longer list of "excluded" social orders: theocratic (more familiar today than "confessional"), aristocratic, caste, slave, racist.[38] So what goes for racist societies then presumably goes for the others also. But the implication would then be that all we need to do to make Rawls's theory applicable to *all* these societies is simply to switch to nonideal theory versions of his principles. So in actuality, Rawls's stipulation about the restrictive scope of his theory would not then exclude *any* of them! His famous shift from "comprehensive" to "political" liberalism, from a theory applicable to all societies *sub specie aeternitatis* (at least past a certain stage of technological development and demarcated by Humean boundaries)[39] to a theory only meant for modern Western liberal democracies, would have been revealed to be no shift at all. Modern or premodern, Western or non-Western, all societies meeting this minimal standard would be covered by Rawls's principles. But obviously, this is absurd and in direct contradiction with what he says (and is standardly interpreted as saying in the secondary literature).

I suggest, then, that this attempt to reaffirm the conventional interpretation does not work. Rawls really means, I believe, to exclude racist societies from the ambit of his theory, whether in its ideal version or hypothetical extrapolated nonideal versions, just as he meant to exclude all those other kinds of society.

OBJECTION II: OK, maybe, but even if you're right, it's an isolated conceptual gaffe, probably resulting from his illness, and clearly disconnected from the rest of his body of work.

So, consider now another possible riposte. As noted earlier, the final polished version of *Justice as Fairness* was never completed because of Rawls's illness. Suppose someone were to draw on this fact to argue that so much interpretative weight should not be put on an isolated passage so disconnected (putatively) from the rest of Rawls's work. The mention of racist societies was a slip that Rawls would have ultimately corrected had he been in better health.

But the problem with such a claim is that the exclusion of racist societies, far from being the conceptual gaffe of an ill man late in his life,

[MILLS] *Theorizing Racial Justice*

follows directly from Rawls's initial stipulation three decades earlier in the opening pages of *Theory* about the intended scope of his theory of justice. Readers have simply failed to take with sufficient seriousness his foundational characterization of society there and how conceptually straitened it is, whether as (an ill-considered) definition or (a confused) demarcation of the range of applicability of his principles. For Rawls, society is "a cooperative venture for mutual advantage" governed by rules "designed to advance the good of those taking part in it."[40] Note that this is not an idealized *well-ordered society*—that comes in the next paragraph. So as I have recently observed elsewhere, it means that even before we get to the idea of a perfectly just, utopian society, we are already operating with a highly idealized notion of societies, one completely discrepant with the long depressing history of actual post-hunter-gatherer social orders.[41]

It seems bizarre to conclude that, over his professional lifetime, Rawls believed all societies were really like this, which would in any case be in flagrant contradiction with the later listing in *Justice as Fairness*, not to mention his discussion of "outlaw states" and other oppressive regimes in *The Law of Peoples*.[42] (But it is noteworthy that Samuel Freeman, Rawls's student and preeminent Rawls scholar, does in fact attribute this view to him.)[43] So I suggest that the most charitable reading, in the light of the later *Law of Peoples* discussions and *Justice as Fairness* passages, is to interpret these opening pages in *Theory* as a muddled first-try demarcation by Rawls of the *kinds* of society to which his theory of justice was applicable rather than a *definition* of society. And such a reading would, of course, be consistent with his revival of social contract theory, which classically represents the creation of society and the polity in consensual and mutually beneficial terms. As he says in *The Law of Peoples*, "We seek a political conception of justice for a democratic society, viewed as a system of fair cooperation among free and equal citizens."[44] And "the notion of social cooperation," as he clarifies in *Political Liberalism*, "is not simply that of coordinated social activity efficiently organized and guided by publicly recognized rules to achieve some overall end."[45] After all, a slave society would meet these criteria. What is additionally required is the idea of "fair terms," involving "reciprocity and mutuality," so that "all who cooperate must benefit."[46] By contrast, in a slave economy, for example, "their system of law [does not] specif[y] a decent scheme of political and social cooperation."[47]

152   *The Tanner Lectures on Human Values*

So this interpretation would resolve the seeming contradiction between the early and later Rawls's framing of "society." Yet this consistency is purchased at a heavy cost, which is that the scope of his theory of justice is thereby revealed to be limited to nonoppressive societies. That is why—we can immediately see—theocratic, aristocratic, caste, slave, and racist societies are all excluded. None of these societies can plausibly be represented in terms of voluntary (informed) consent and the consequent institutionalization of reciprocally beneficial rules of cooperation. The passages in *Justice as Fairness* only spell out what was implicit in Rawls's framework of assumptions from the very start: the adoption of a social contract model famously predicated on universal and symmetrical inclusion is limited in its scope to societies meeting these criteria.

> OBJECTION III: Your reading couldn't be correct because at various locations, if admittedly never elaborated upon at any of them, Rawls allows for the possibility of his theory being applied to race (and in any case, it's just crazy to think that—conscientious liberal that he was— he would have deliberately devised a theory of justice that couldn't be so applied).

And that brings me to the third and final objection. I am claiming that Rawls's theory of justice was not intended by him to extend to corrective justice for racist societies. But while race is not explicitly mentioned, *Theory* gives an account of civil disobedience that is arguably inspired by the American civil rights movement. The later paperback edition of *Political Liberalism* allows for "new groups" with "new questions related to ethnicity . . . and race" developing "political conceptions that . . . will debate the current conceptions," and *Justice as Fairness* while conceding that *Theory*'s nontreatment of race was an "omission," expresses confidence that the "political values" expressed in the book will be able "to deal with these questions," since otherwise, its "resources" would be "seriously defective."[48] Moreover, the passage from *Theory* I myself earlier cited specifically mentions (if never to be discussed in detail anywhere) "principles for meeting injustice."[49] Surely, then, these passages from three different texts make clear that Rawls did indeed envisage nonideal theory as potentially covering this issue (for example, via the "four-stage sequence" of *Theory* §31), even if neither he himself nor his followers would ever choose to pursue the matter. And consider, in the end, as a

[MILLS] *Theorizing Racial Justice* 153

related closing rebuttal, how obviously implausible—indeed absurd, and in addition, some might say, insulting—it is to think that a Rawls who had lived through the racial tumult of the 1960s, and mentions Martin Luther King Jr. in his later work, would be so indifferent to racial injustice as to devise a theory excluding its correction.

The mistake here, I would contend, is the failure to recognize the difference between what we could term "a society with racism" and "a racist society." Drawing on Rawls's overarching theorization, albeit not applied to race, a society with racism could be so characterized because of the racist views of many of its members, their resulting private practices and private institutions, and even perhaps some superficial impact on some of the institutions of the "basic structure." But it does not count as a racist society unless racism significantly shapes, in a *deep* way, these latter institutions. So, my reply to the third objection is that the passages cited from Rawls do indeed indicate an awareness of, and concern about, racism, and an indication, perhaps, of how he might have tried to tackle it by further developing his theory (as with his brief cryptic reference in *Justice as Fairness* to "a special form of the difference principle").[50] But he is, I claim, presupposing throughout a society whose racism does not extend to fundamentally shaping the basic structure itself, which is why there is no inconsistency between his extensive direct discussion of race on pages 64–66 of *Justice as Fairness* (the most extensive in his entire body of work) and his earlier denial on page 21 of the very same book that his principles apply to racist societies.[51] These are implicitly two different categories for him.

Moreover, the point is strengthened once one realizes the need for an internal conceptual partitioning of the nonideal within the category of the unjust (as against the zone of constraint by "natural limitations and historical contingencies").[52] The literal sense of "ideal" is, of course, "perfect," admitting no further improvement or bettering. So, an ideal well-ordered society is a perfect society. The slightest deviation from ideality would then mean that you have immediately crossed over into the zone of the nonideal. Imagine, as in figure 2, the ideal as graphically represented by a large bold I, I for ideal, on the left-hand margin of the page, with rightward horizontal deviations from this norm of successively greater distance indicating, by a one-dimensional metric, increasing degrees of badness.

Everything to the right of I counts as nonideal. So, unless we draw internal demarcations within this zone, then hypothetical societies just

DIFFERENTIATING THE NON-IDEAL

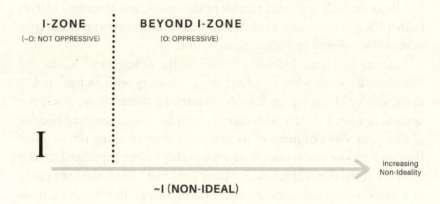

marginally short of perfection (just to the right of I) and deeply oppressive societies (all the way over to the right-hand margin) would both, in an undifferentiated fashion, fall into the same category, ~I. Obviously, such undiscriminating conceptual inclusivity would be very unsatisfactory and inimical to an appreciation of the real and important differences within this wide range of possible social systems. One way of thinking of the philosophical work the contract model is doing for us, then, is as a principled demarcation, within the realm of the ideal/nonideal, of the border between imperfect but still basically good societies (with sound basic structures), which can be modeled as "cooperative ventures for mutual advantage," and bad societies (with oppressive basic structures), which cannot. Theocratic, aristocratic, caste, slave, and racist societies are all far to the right and thus beyond this principled demarcation.

We can then immediately see why, in his discussion in *Theory* of the nonideal issues of civil disobedience and conscientious refusal, Rawls specifies that he is presupposing throughout "the special case of a nearly just society, one that is well-ordered for the most part but in which some serious violations of justice nevertheless do occur, . . . a more or less just democratic state."[53] In the later *Political Liberalism*, likewise, we find "a nearly just democratic society, . . . a more or less just constitutional regime."[54] Similarly, in the *Law of Peoples*, he refers to "a reasonably just domestic society, . . . a reasonably just constitutional democratic society (hereafter sometimes referred to simply as a liberal society), . . . a reasonably just constitutional democratic government," and "a reasonably just (though not necessarily a fully just) constitutional democratic

[MILLS]   *Theorizing Racial Justice*   155

government."[55] Finally, in *Justice as Fairness*, he speaks of "a reasonably just, though not perfect, democratic regime, . . . a perfectly just, or nearly just, constitutional regime," and "democratic regimes as we know them,"[56] thus conceding their real-life flaws but nonetheless affirming their "democratic" character withal.

"Nearly just," "more or less just," "reasonably just" though not "fully just," "not perfect"—these locutions make clear that Rawls is consistently taking for granted as his political reference group liberal democratic societies that are close to I, in the I-zone, so to speak, not societies that are beyond it. *His theory of liberal domestic justice*—including nonideal "compensatory" justice—*only applies to liberal states whose injustices do not exceed these bounds*. Once these (overlapping) ambiguities are cleared up—the difference between liberal societies merely with racism and supposedly "liberal" societies that are racist, the difference between mildly and deeply unjust societies, and more generally, the difference between the slightly and the radically nonideal—we can understand why TJ($\sim$R) could be true despite its seeming incongruity with Rawls's scattered references to racism and condemnation of racist practices. He simply did not regard the United States as a racist society—that is, a society with a racist basic structure that negated its self-designation as a liberal constitutional democracy. So for Rawls, TJ($\sim$R) was true, but USA($\sim$R) was false. Any nonideal "principles for meeting injustice" potentially derivable from his ideal principles would, by his tacit stipulation, be restricted to liberal states in the "nearly just" I-zone, whose injustices were at worst mild ones.

Has the United States Ever Been a Racist Society?
If So, Is It Still a Racist Society?

So that brings us naturally to the question of whether Rawls, and other political philosophers who also endorse USA($\sim$R), was right about this belief. We could distinguish various possible claims: (a) the United States was never a racist society, (b) the United States was once a racist society but had ceased to be one by the period of Rawls's lifetime (1921–2002), (c) the United States was a racist society for part of Rawls's lifetime but then ceased to be such at some unspecified date during his lifetime, or (d) the United States was a racist society before Rawls's birth and in Rawls's lifetime and continues to be a racist society today. (There is also [e]: the United States was not a racist society in Rawls's lifetime but became one after his death. But I assume this is too silly to require discussion.)[57]

How do we adjudicate this question? Well, remember the presumptive criterion we are working with is whether or not race and racism affect in a deep and significant way the "basic structure." According to Rawls, the basic structure consists of the "main political and social institutions": "The political constitution with an independent judiciary, the legally recognized forms of property, and the structure of the economy . . . as well as the family in some form, all belong to the basic structure."[58] Can we say that they were deeply and significantly affected—let's use the term "racialized" as a convenient shorthand: Can we say that they were racialized over any of these time periods?

The very posing of the question reveals its absurdity. The more appropriate variant would be, Was there any time period when they were *not* racialized? Consider, in rebuttal of (a) (if it needs rebuttal), the time before Rawls's birth when the United States was a slave society. The "legally recognized forms of property" then included property in Black human beings: racial chattel slavery. The late Ira Berlin (1941–2018), celebrated as one of American slavery's leading historians, drew a famous distinction between "societies with slaves," where slavery is institutionally cabined and siloed, and "slave societies," where the "peculiar institution" pervades, directly or indirectly, the entire social order, in effect rendering the whole society "peculiar." For him, the United States was a prime example of the latter: "Slavery stood at the center of economic production, and the master-slave relationship provided the model for all social relations: husband and wife, parent and child, employer and employee, teacher and student."[59] The "structure of the economy" was thus the structure of a slave economy, in which the supposedly "free" North was deeply complicit.[60] Not much room for ambiguity about possible racialization there, in a system that lasted nearly 250 years and that fundamentally shaped the Constitution, not merely in the infamous three-fifths clause but in many other aspects also.[61]

Moreover, the crucial issue—and this, of course, is the pertinent consideration from (a) through (d), from the antebellum to the postbellum period—is really always how the Constitution is *interpreted* and the role of race as a hermeneutical lens for reading it.[62] The passage of the Civil War Amendments, for example, including the Thirteenth Amendment's putative ending of slavery and "involuntary servitude," would not save African Americans from the new "Age of Neoslavery," based on convict lease labor, lasting from 1865 till the beginning of World War II, documented by Douglas Blackmon in his Pulitzer Prize–winning exposé, *Slavery by*

[MILLS] *Theorizing Racial Justice* 157

Another Name.[63] Nor would the "Equal Protection Clause" of the Fourteenth Amendment protect them from the "separate but equal" 1896 Supreme Court *Plessy v. Ferguson* decision, which formally legitimated Jim Crow as the law of the land, not to be overturned till *Brown v. Board of Education* in 1954.[64] And of course, racial segregation, both educational and residential, has since then, post-*Brown*, remained the practice of the land, if not the law of the land, so deeply entrenched in the polity that it clearly merits categorization as itself a "social institution" of the "basic structure," if one unacknowledged by Rawls and Rawlsians, lost as they are in the world of ideal theory.[65] Likewise, the right of African American men to vote, supposedly guaranteed by the Fifteenth Amendment, would quickly become a dead letter in the South via a systematic policy of disenfranchisement not deemed by the Supreme Court to justify federal intervention until the 1965 Voting Rights Act nearly a century later.[66]

So—returning to the sequential list of alternatives—what about (b)? Can we plausibly say that the legacy of slavery and postbellum Jim Crow had been cleaned up by the time of Rawls's 1921 birth? Again, as we have just seen, absurd even to ask it. We are still in the epoch of the betrayal of Reconstruction, separate-but-equal that is really separate-and-unequal systemic disenfranchisement, thousands of unpunished lynchings and the repeated defeat in Congress of attempted antilynching legislation, and in general, widespread discrimination reducing Blacks to second-class status.[67] A slave economy has been replaced by a Jim Crow economy, in which, to cite a famous essay by Cheryl Harris, whiteness itself functions as "property."[68] The state and the juridical system—presumably among the "main political and social institutions"—create, recreate, and protect "whiteness" and its privileges, further consolidating race at the foundation of the polity.[69] Indeed, the discriminatory Jim Crow regime was so impressively organized and juridically embedded that the Nazis—looking around the world in the early 1930s for a legal role model to set up the *Rassenstaat*, the racial state, and design and institute the anti-Semitic Nuremberg Laws—took it as their exemplar, an admiring tribute on their part to what they regarded as the leading racial state on the planet at the time, the United States.[70]

Clearly, then, (b) is not remotely a defensible position. Well, can we point, as in (c), to some crucial event, some historic turning point in Rawls's lifetime, after which the United States ceased to be a racist society, for example, the "Second Reconstruction" of the 1950s–60s? But six decades on, it would be pretty difficult to do this, considering all the depressing

158   *The Tanner Lectures on Human Values*

contemporary socioeconomic indicators most of us who work on race know so well: continuing residential and educational segregation (as earlier mentioned), ongoing nation-wide practices of de facto discrimination, new techniques of disenfranchisement and voter suppression greenlighted by the 2013 Supreme Court *Shelby v. Holder* decision, the wealth gap (illustrating the enduring racialization of the economy), mass incarceration and the prison-industrial complex, the pattern of police killings of unarmed Black men and women, and so forth.[71] In 1968, the Kerner Commission established by President Lyndon Johnson in response to the 1960s civil disorders issued its famous damning report that "our nation is moving toward two societies, one Black, one white—separate and unequal."[72] Fifty years later, in 2018, Fred Harris, the sole surviving member of the commission, coauthored a *New York Times* Op-Ed reviewing the progress (not) made over the intervening half a century whose discouraging conclusion was summed up in its title: "The Unmet Promise of Equality."[73]

Finally, it is important to realize that the family, part of the "basic structure" for Rawls, is also racially affected throughout this whole period. Because of the demography of the profession, discussions of the family in the Rawls literature have been overwhelmingly shaped by the concerns of white feminism. But during slavery, of course, the nonrecognition of slave families and the inferior social status even of free Black families made the white family the real domestic pillar of the nation.[74] As Dorothy Roberts points out, Black women have historically been systematically denied equal "reproductive rights."[75] And relatedly, the role of antimiscegenation custom and law—the latter not deemed unconstitutional until the 1967 *Loving v. Virginia* Supreme Court decision—was crucial to safeguarding the "purity" of the white race and thus naturalizing a social ontology of domination. Though not simultaneously, at one time or another, no less than forty-one states had antimiscegenation prohibitions on the books. In the judgment of Peggy Pascoe's *What Comes Naturally*, "[Anti-]miscegenation law was a kind of factory for the production of race,"[76] thereby producing and reproducing the polity *as* a white-dominated one. Whatever the ambiguities of the abstract "colorless" family's location in Rawls, as debated by white feminists over the past few decades—whether it is fully or not fully part of the basic structure for him—the real-life white family has functioned unequivocally in the basic structure to perpetuate white political rule.

So, it would seem that (d), the United States as historically and still currently a racist society, is indeed the judgment validated by the evidence. USA(R) is true. In conjunction with TJ($\sim$R), we have therefore

[MILLS]   *Theorizing Racial Justice*   159

now finally arrived at the evidence for my (seemingly) startling claim. Rawls's theory of justice does not apply to the United States.

The Implications of TJ(~R)

Let me now emphasize, if they are not immediately apparent, how shocking the implications of TJ(~R) are.

Implications for Theorizing Corrective Racial Justice

To begin with, it means that the few attempts to use Rawls's apparatus to theorize the correction of racial injustice in the United States (but arguably in the "West" more broadly) have been misguided from the beginning. To repeat the points from the start of this section, my original critique, and that of (at least some of) that very small number of us interested in developing the theory in this direction, had been that Rawls is doing a bad job of constructing a theory able to deal with the nonideal issue of corrective racial justice. Hence my arguments over the years are that he needed to recognize the existence of white supremacy, he needed to show how his principles would have to be modified or extrapolated to become rectificatory ones, and so forth. But it now turns out that this critique was based on a false premise. Insofar as Rawls assumed his theory had the resources to handle corrective racial justice, it was only for the close-to-ideal category of a United States with racism, not a racist United States with a white-supremacist basic structure.[77] Rawls simply did not view the United States that way, so he would have seen no need to develop such a theory.

Here is a way of representing the implications for justice theory, ideal and nonideal. Elsewhere, I have suggested that a simple way of depicting Rawls's two principles of justice is by the following formula, where the arrows indicate lexical ordering:

$$BL \to (FEO \to DP)$$

Acronyms: BL: Basic liberties (to vote, run for office, have freedom of speech, liberty of conscience, the right to hold personal property, etc.);[78] FEO: Fair equality of opportunity (formal equality of opportunity [antidiscrimination] + resources to equalize for class disadvantage);[79] DP: Difference principle (socioeconomic inequalities to be arranged for the greatest benefit of the least advantaged, for example, those disadvantaged because of having a thin bundle of natural talents).[80] So, translated into prose, that gives us that the first principle of justice, the guarantee of equal basic liberties, is lexically dominant (must be satisfied first) over the second principle, in which, in a subordinate lexical ordering, fair equality of opportunity is lexically dominant over the difference principle.[81]

Now these are, of course, principles of distributive (not allocative)[82] justice, PDJ_I, for an ideal well-ordered society, I, one that is "perfectly just."[83] So, let us enclose them within brackets to make this (highly restricted) scope clear:

$$PDJ [BL \to (FEO \to DP)]_I$$

Principles of nonideal theory for "meeting injustice" in nonideal societies, ~I—let us call them principles of corrective justice, $PCJ_{\sim I}$—are then different from PDJ_I.[84] But the implication of my earlier reading of Rawls was that these principles of corrective justice could be derived from the ideal principles in some ordering (the uncertainty indicated by asterisks), even though Rawls himself had not explained how nor had subsequent Rawlsians taken up the issue.

$$PCJ [PCJ1^*PCJ2^*PCJ3]_{\sim I}$$
$$\text{somehow derivable from } PDJ [BL \to (FEO \to DP)]_I$$

So, that was the main burden of my previous criticism: Why had Rawls and Rawlsians, given their ostensible commitment to remedying the "pressing and urgent matters" of social injustice, here racial injustice, not tackled this project? But my assumption was still that such a derivation from Rawlsian principles was possible.

However, the implication of my new reading, as indicated above, is that we need to demarcate within ~I societies those that are still within the I-zone and those that are outside it.

I-zone societies, being close to I ("nearly just" though not "fully just"), are still roughly representable by the social contract model as cooperative ventures for mutual advantage; societies outside the I-zone, on the other hand, being structurally oppressive, are not. Let us call the former ~I(~O) societies (not ideal but not structurally oppressive) and the latter ~I(O) societies (not ideal and structurally oppressive). Then respecting this demarcation, we have the following:

$$PCJ [PCJ1^*PCJ2^*PCJ3]_{\sim I(\sim O)} \text{ versus } PCJ [PCJ4^*PCJ5^*PCJ6]_{\sim I(O)}$$

| Within the I-zone | Outside the I-zone |

So, summing it all up, $PCJ_{\sim I(\sim O)}$ may be derivable from Rawls's PDJ, but $PCJ_{\sim I(O)}$ is not. One will need a rethinking of the liberal justice apparatus

[MILLS] *Theorizing Racial Justice* 161

to theorize corrective justice for such societies, since they are not cooperative ventures for mutual advantage in the first place.

Implications for Theorizing Social Justice More Generally

But as should now be evident, the repercussions extend far more broadly than antiracist corrective justice theorizing. Critical theorists of race and "whiteness" have long pointed out that one of the interesting cognitive phenomena associated with white domination is that under certain circumstances, whites disappear as a "race" and simply become coextensive with humans. Or alternatively phrased, whiteness becomes humanness. Issues of "race" are then tacitly or overtly thought of by whites as really having to do with *nonwhites* as a group, not the "raceless" and "universal" whites.[85]

So, one mistaken reaction to my claim from the overwhelmingly white constituency of Rawlsian philosophers might be that while it is unfortunate that racial justice cannot be theorized by the apparatus, it does not affect social justice theorizing "in general." But the point is that *all* Rawlsian philosophy aimed at prescribing social justice for the United States is likewise affected, not just that tiny subsection of Rawlsianism working on racial justice. For whatever the area of focus, all such work is operating with the mistaken assumption that Rawls's theory of justice applies to the United States. But since the United States is a racist society, this assumption is false. And that holds retroactively, of course, for the past half century's volume of work on Rawls and the United States also.

As can be appreciated, then, the implications are really very dramatic ones.

How Rawls Went Wrong

If I am correct, it means that in Rawlsian theorizing, a deep injustice has been done to "justice" as a concept. If we start from the reasonable premise that any theoretical apparatus, whether dealing with the physical or moral or mathematical or whatever world, needs to be adequate to the (world-relative) "reality" it is theorizing, then Rawlsian theory, insofar as it is supposed to be designed for the United States and other modern Western liberal democratic societies, is a spectacular failure. (I have focused on the United States in this lecture, but I would claim that my argument goes through generally for most or all "Western" nations, insofar as their modern history has been one of imperialism, colonialism, racial enslavement, and expropriative white settlement—all under

162   *The Tanner Lectures on Human Values*

the banner of the racial superiority of Europeans. So, since Rawls's theory excludes racist societies, it excludes them also.) It is a theory based on not a recognition of the racial realities of the development of Western modernity but rather the opposite: their systematic denial.

But methodological inadequacy is not its most important failing. After all, "injustice" to a concept can only be metaphorical. Far more important are the epistemic and moral injustices of a *literal* kind done to the humans so urgently in need of justice in this modern Western world, above all, of course, the people of color subordinated by the West in modernity. A Western theory of justice that by its very architecture precludes even the acknowledgment, let alone the remedying, of "basic structure" racial injustice, white supremacy, is in effect a theory of complicity with injustice. So, we need to ask the obvious question: How did this happen? For this silence is not at all idiosyncratic to Rawls. Rather, as I have documented elsewhere, it is *typical* of Western political philosophy, not just across the liberal Anglo-American spectrum, left to right, Rawls to Nozick, but in the communitarian and "Critical Theory" traditions also.[86] Nowhere in this multifaceted, multipolitically oriented body of work do we find any systematic engagement with the history of European expansionism and the resulting creation of global white domination.[87] So, in seeking an answer to the question of why Rawls went wrong, we are really asking a *general* question about a certain community. It is not individual, not (in general) peculiar to Rawls's own identity and personal trajectory through the world, but social-structural. However, in keeping with the overall theme of the lecture, I will focus here on the liberal philosophical mainstream.

I suggest there are multiple factors at work that together combine in an overwhelming way for an "over"-determined outcome, given that each individually would be arguably close to sufficient in itself.

Ideological Socialization and Illusions about the United States

Rawls is in one sense our contemporary, insofar as his philosophical corpus is very much alive and well and still shaping the debate. But in another sense, he is very much from a different epoch, born in 1921, nearly one hundred years ago, and growing up in the United States and a predecolonization world where white domination would pretty much have been taken for granted in the circles in which he would have been moving. What kind of sociopolitical education would he have received in high school and university? Certainly *not* one that framed the United States

[MILLS] *Theorizing Racial Justice* 163

as a racist society. Rogers Smith's 1997 *Civic Ideals*, a book I have cited repeatedly over the years, documents how deeply entrenched in accounts of American political culture is the picture of a historically liberal egalitarian United States in which racism is at most an "anomaly."[88] This was the vision of Alexis de Tocqueville, Louis Hartz, and even Gunnar Myrdal's Carnegie Corporation–commissioned 1944 study of American racism, *An American Dilemma: The Negro Problem and Modern Democracy.*[89] As various Black radical scholars pointed out at the time, and as Stephen Steinberg has reminded us more recently, the very title announces its theoretical tendentiousness, given that Myrdal's conceptual framing was massively contradicted by the data in his huge thirteen-hundred-plus-page work.[90] The 1960s and '70s would see the incursion into even mainstream thought of more radical framings, but Rawls would not adopt them. His view of the United States is fully in the "anomaly" tradition, as against Smith's own "multiple traditions" analysis or the Black radical diagnosis of racism as "symbiotic" with liberalism. Thus, the presumption is that the United States is at worst a society with racism rather than a racist society. (Nowhere in Rawls's work will you find even by now respectable concepts like "institutional racism," let alone the phrase "white supremacy" as an overall characterization of the American social order.)[91]

European Social Democracy and the "Social Question"

One must also take into account his personal experience. The timing (1971) of Rawls's book would naturally lead one to think that Lyndon Johnson's 1960s "Great Society" was a central influence. But as Katrina Forrester has revealed in her impressive overview of the postwar formation of "liberal egalitarianism,"[92] the foundations of Rawls's theory were actually established much earlier. A 1952 trip to Oxford had put him in dialogue with Oxford academics who were members of the British Labour Party, which was trying at the time to institutionalize the postwar social-democratic welfare state. Forrester writes, "He [Rawls] moved left in line with the debates about equality and social justice that preoccupied the revisionist wing of the British Labour Party. . . . It was social democratic Britain as much as Cold War America that provided the political theories and orientation that shaped Rawls's own."[93]

But twentieth-century Western European social democracy had its origins in the nineteenth-century debates over what used to be called "the social question." Stimulated by the social unrest over the huge and growing divisions between rich and poor in (Western) Europe created by the new industrial capitalist economy, the social question centered on what an equitable division of the social product would be between capital and labor: in other words, the familiar left-right spectrum of liberalism. So, "class" justice and injustice were the issue, certainly not gender (that was the separate "Woman Question") or race ("the Colonial Question," "the Native Problem"). Duly imported into the United States by Rawls, and ignoring "the Negro Problem" of his own country, this body of theory essentially made "social justice" coextensive with "class justice"—which should instantly render understandable for us Rawls and Rawlsianism's marginalization of both gender and race. Indeed, if you carry out the simple thought experiment—as a preliminary to Rawls's own proposed thought experiment—of mentally renaming the book *A Theory of Class Justice*, you will, I suggest, immediately see how much more accurate and apropos a characterization of the whole project it is. It was never about "social" justice in any comprehensive sense in the first place. Rather, it was "social justice" = "class justice," where "classes" were conceived of as composed solely of white males. Hence the apparatus's deep-rooted resistance to being adapted to the theorization of either gender or race. Its very design is inimical to tackling these issues because they were not part of its mandate to begin with.

Racially Defining the Modern "Western" Political Tradition

Moreover, these material origins, as any contextualization of Western social justice theory should lead us to expect, are manifest in the broader discipline's "origins" story as well. In the standard "just so" narrative, Anglo-American analytics tell one another and (more unfortunately) their students that I briefly mentioned earlier that Western political philosophy was on its deathbed in the 1950s, limited to the boring ordinary-language analysis of political terms, until dramatically revived by Rawls's work. So, Rawls deserves the credit not merely for this resurrection but for shifting the normative focus of political theory from our obligations to the state to the issue of social justice.

But how is "Anglo-American" or, more broadly, the "West" being defined? Is it geographical (national, continental, imperial)? Is it civic (membership in Anglo-American or other Western states)? Is it linguistic (speaking English, or some other "Western" language)? Surely it isn't, surely it couldn't be, *racial*?! But then if it isn't, why is the "tradition" defined so as to exclude people like Frederick Douglass and Martin Delany and W. E. B. Du Bois and Ida B. Wells and Ralph Ellison and

[MILLS] *Theorizing Racial Justice* 165

James Baldwin? Aren't they English-speaking citizens of the United States? Mightn't an ex-slave like Douglass conceivably have something worthwhile to say about freedom (a central liberal value, so we are told)? Mightn't a victim of separate-but-equal Jim Crow like *Invisible Man* author Ellison have some insights about equality (another one)?[94] But it would never occur to Rawls or his disciples, or white American political philosophers in general, that there is a long-standing African American political tradition that—long before Rawls's vaunted reorientation of the field—had made the question of racial justice, and sometimes, if not often enough, gender justice, central.[95] The Jim Crowing of everyday American life extends to the American academy and its conceptual space as well. It comes "naturally" to Rawls and Rawlsians to construct a narrative that makes Anglo-American or, more broadly, Western political philosophy coextensive with the theorizing of its *European* and *Euro-American* spokespersons and not their African and African American slaves and ex-slaves, who might just possibly have had some contrary thoughts on (i) and (ii) above (how we should think of the United States and what we should include in "social justice"). Above all, of course, they would have frontally and militantly challenged a conceptualization of justice that completely marginalized historic injustice and the corresponding need for corrective justice, as Rawls's apparatus does.

Committing Epistemic Injustice in Theorizing Social Justice

Once you put these various failures together, you should immediately be able to see how deep an injustice Rawls is committing against the victims of American racial injustice. (My focus here has been on Black Americans, but in the case of Native Americans, it is even more striking, because of course the "cooperative venture for mutual advantage" characterization, insofar as it ignores the perspective of the Indigenous peoples upon whose land this "venture" is being launched, is paradigmatically, one could say definitionally, a white settler colonial conceptualization. Perhaps noncoincidentally, while Blacks make at least a fleeting appearance in Rawls's work, Native Americans are completely absent from the two thousand pages of his five books.) Philosophers have long pointed out the relations between epistemology and ethics, whether in terms of homologous concepts (epistemic and moral duties and prohibitions, epistemic and moral goods, virtuous epistemic and moral agents) or the epistemology of ethics (intuitionism, universalization, the ideal observer) or other connections. Elsewhere, I have suggested what I think might be a new relation hitherto unnoticed, or perhaps, more modestly, insufficiently noticed: the idea that we might sometimes, or even routinely, be committing epistemic injustice *in* our theorization of social justice.[96]

Here, of course, I am referring to the very influential work of my colleague Miranda Fricker.[97] The claim would be that—in the light of what we know about the subordination of the majority of the population in post-hunter-gatherer societies—we should be particularly diligent in trying to come up with appropriate theories of social justice about seeking out the voices of those subordinated by our society so as not to simply recapitulate in more sophisticated form apologist concepts hegemonic in the social discourse of the time. In other words, we can ask (what should have been) the obvious question: Why didn't Rawls see that by *not* engaging African Americans and Native Americans, he was committing a testimonial and hermeneutical injustice against them? And the answer is, of course, that he was part of a dominant Euro-American social group ("whites") and a dominant intellectual tradition that simply took such exclusions for granted. It is not a matter of Rawls's personal deficiencies but rather the structural determinants, socioeconomic, cultural, and racial, that shaped his perspective, his worldview, that made it so "natural" for him (a social naturalness, of course) to proceed in this way.

In a retrospective essay looking back at her book and its reception, Fricker reemphasizes that epistemic injustice should be clearly demarcated from intellectual fraud, gaslighting, and other forms of deliberate deception; the causality here is *structural*.[98] It is because of the circles in which he was moving—very small circles, Forrester points out; a tiny cohort of theorists, largely male and overwhelmingly white, at three elite institutions, Harvard, Princeton, and Oxford[99]—and their embedded ignorances that what we now know as liberal egalitarianism has the architecture it does. To give just one example repeatedly mentioned by Forrester: Rawls was consistently attracted throughout his career to the idea of representing society as a game.[100] Think of that: *a game*! Can you seriously imagine anybody but a member of the ruling white male social group finding such a figuring anything but completely ludicrous? Are slavery, Indigenous expropriation, colonial subjugation, Jim Crow, apartheid, or white supremacy to be regarded as "games"? But it is thus that our preferred metaphors reveal us and make clear who and what we are.[101] Given his beliefs about the United States, and the West more generally, John Rawls simply saw no need to develop a theory of justice for societies of structural racial domination. In effect, people of color were simply

LIBERAL RACIAL JUSTICE

denied the status of equal team players in the model "games" he and his colleagues were playing with one another.

So that brings us, finally, to the challenge of determining what liberal principles of racial justice would in fact be. If the interpretation of part 2 is correct, Rawls's theory of justice only applies to Western societies in the I-zone, not racist Western societies beyond the I-zone, such as the United States. Here it is not a matter of a "deviation" from a "basic structure" that is essentially sound but rather a basic structure that is itself racialized, unfairly privileging the dominant race (call them the R1s) at the expense of the subordinate race or races (call them the R2s). Obviously, then, this is not a society to be conceived of as a "cooperative venture for mutual advantage," since there is no reason why the R2s would have voluntarily signed on to such an agreement in the first place. Rather, it is a society that needs to be understood as an "exploitative venture for R1/white advantage." So, one can immediately see why the orthodox contract apparatus, classical or updated, is an inappropriate metaphor—iconography, story, model, thought experiment, device of representation, what have you— for capturing the realities of such a sociopolitical order, since, rather than inclusion being the norm, systemic racial exclusion is the norm. As I have argued elsewhere, the more appropriate metaphor is the idea of a "domination contract," an exclusionary contract among members of the privileged group to limit institutionalized equality to themselves while subordinating others. Generalized from Rousseau's demystificatory "class contract" of *Discourse on the Origin of Inequality*, Carole Pateman's "sexual contract," and my own "racial contract," the "domination contract" as a revisionist model seeks to provide both a more accurate *factual* portrayal of modern illiberal "liberal" society and a superior *normative* "device of representation" for deriving principles of justice for modern illiberal "liberal" society.[102]

When I first advanced this suggestion more than a decade ago, I was, as emphasized, still assuming the conventional interpretation in the profession of Rawls's project—namely, that his theory of justice was meant to apply both to racist and nonracist modern Western societies. So, my criticism was that the mainstream contract would have to be radically modified to take account of race. But now, as a result of my new interpretation, I would claim that my case has, in effect, been made for me by Rawls himself. *A racist society cannot be modeled by a consensual contract, nor can the updated Rawlsian version be a "device of representation" for deriving the principles of justice appropriate for it.* In effect, we can now see, these are two different projects. For the category of racist (modern Western) societies, we need to shift ground to the radically different terrain of societies that are *nominally* liberal but in fact structured in a systemically illiberal way. Referring back to the discussion in part 1, the task of liberal social justice will then be to "liberalize" this illiberal state of affairs by dismantling the structure of group domination in question.

That structure will, of course, be multifaceted, containing overlapping and intersecting constituents (class, gender, sexual orientation, etc.). So, abstracting out race as an identity and racial justice as a goal, as I am trying to do here, will necessarily be somewhat artificial. But assuming that this is possible, we then have—in contrast to the mainstream contract—a social ontology, (b), of individuals as racial group members—R1s and R2s, whites and nonwhites—in relations of domination and subordination; a conceptual cartography, (c), of an R1-dominant, white-supremacist American polity, with all the consequent ramifications for its constituent social institutions; and a historical account, (d), of the past that has brought such a polity into existence, requiring attention to the dynamics of European settler colonialism and Atlantic slave societies standardly ignored in the political philosophy literature.[103] Only on this basis will we then be properly positioned to determine, (e), what the schedule of (racially differentiated) rights, protections, and freedoms should be for the (racialized) individuals in this society to achieve, (a), their moral equality, freedom, and self-realization.

So how do we derive these principles? The recommendation I have made elsewhere, which I will repeat here, is that we perform a modified version of the Rawlsian thought experiment. We imagine ourselves behind the Rawlsian "veil of ignorance," choosing principles of justice on prudential, self-interested grounds but with crucial differences from his own version.[104] The contrasting projects are illustrated in figure 3:

In both cases (Rawls's original on the left, the consensual contract; my modified version on the right, the domination contract), we are choosing principles of justice consistent with liberal values, V, using the "contract" as a "device of representation." But to begin with, the alternative setting of my version makes it an exercise in nonideal normative theory and not "nonideal but close to ideal" (within the I-zone) but quite remote from it. We are choosing principles of justice for a racially oppressive, ill-ordered, R1-supremacist society, in which the R1s

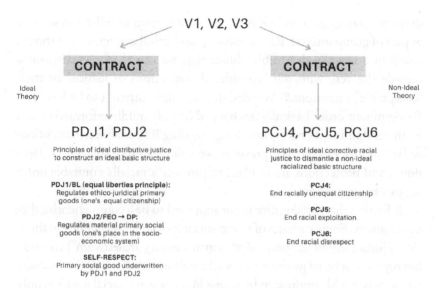

dominate the R2s, as modeled by the racial domination contract. So, the principles of justice we are seeking are principles of corrective rather than distributive justice and, in addition, principles PCJ4, PCJ5, and PCJ6 for structurally oppressive societies rather than principles PCJ1, PCJ2, and PCJ3 for societies that are basically sound with some unfortunate "partial compliance" deviations. For racist societies, the phrase "partial compliance" misstates the situation. It implies that the original intention *was* to fully include the "inferior" races, the R2s (racism as an "anomaly"), when in reality their exclusion was a matter of principle so that what is actually involved *is* "full compliance" but with a racialized set of norms (racism as structural).

Correspondingly, the appropriate normative metric here is not ideal theory but the actual norms that regulated the treatment of the R1s to be suitably modified, "deracialized," so as to include the R2s both formally and substantively and revised where necessary to correct for previous and ongoing structural R2 subordination. Behind the veil, then, one will be choosing primarily *as* a group member a potential R1 or R2, not in the sense that one knows one's R-membership (since such knowledge is blocked by the veil) but in the sense that one's overriding concern is not to be disadvantaged, once the veil lifts, by one's R-identity. (Though the veil is thin enough to admit knowledge of the historically R1-supremacist nature of the society, it blocks knowledge of R1/R2 demographic proportions, thereby ruling out the maximization of expected utility as a prudential decision strategy.) So, as in Rawls, the combination of self-interest (here as part of group interest, R_1/R_2 interest) and stipulated ignorance should result in a morally defensible choice that we can then compare, once outside the veil, with our "considered convictions of justice" or their "acceptable" extensions.[105] Worried that we might turn out to be R_2s in an R_1-dominant order basically unchanged or only mildly reformed or R_1s in an R_2-dominant order where long-standing R_2 racial *ressentiment* can at last find its vindictive expression, we will make sure that rights, freedoms, and protections are in place to produce a racially equitable order for us whatever we are.

It follows that racial justice is not supposed to be a comprehensive theory of justice. Some varieties of feminism claim to offer self-sufficient theories of justice meant to compete with mainstream ("malestream") theories, but my view of racial justice is not at all ambitious in that way. So, a racially just society could continue to be unjust in other ways; racial justice is only a part of justice. Drawing on Andrew Valls's recent book, one way of thinking of this project, referring back to figure 2, is as an exercise in transitional justice,[106] moving us from locations far outside the I-zone to locations somewhat closer to it (depending, of course, on what other systems of structural group domination exist in the society). Because my focus has been on race throughout, it might seem that I am suggesting a sequence of temporal priority and action (first, race; then . . .). But as emphasized from the start, the singling out of race has been motivated by its underdiscussion and undertheorization in the literature. In practice, a multidimensional social justice project to overcome illiberal group domination would be what is politically called for, with "racial justice" being brought into synthesizing a relationship with other corrective measures along other axes, thereby making "social" justice as a concept genuinely inclusive, which it is currently not.

In previous work, I have suggested that racial injustice has at least six dimensions—juridico-political, economic, cultural, cognitive-evaluative, somatic, ontological—that can be illuminatingly gathered under three basic categories, corresponding to one's civic political status (the first), one's entitlement to fair (race-independent) professional and economic opportunities for careers and the accumulation of wealth (the second), and one's socially recognized personhood (the remaining four).[107] In other words, in a racist society, the R_2s will, de jure or de facto, be second-class citizens, be exploited through the denial to them of equal economic access and wealth opportunities, and be viewed as less than full persons, with inferior cultures, inferior cognitive capacities, inferior bodies, and

[Mills] *Theorizing Racial Justice* 171

inferior moral status, all on the grounds of race. Correspondingly, my three suggested principles of corrective racial justice that I am claiming would be prudentially converged upon by choosers behind the veil and that would match our moral convictions, immediate or extended, outside the veil are the following:

> PCJ4: End racially unequal citizenship
> PCJ5: End racial exploitation
> PCJ6: End racial disrespect

Note that, as pointed out from the start, one does not have to be a left-liberal to recognize the wrongs being targeted here as violations, since they constitute infringements on basic rights that are supposed to be affirmed across the liberal spectrum. Racial justice is thus conceptually distinct from Rawlsian social-democratic justice and should in theory be endorsed by right-liberals also. But in practice, right-wing and libertarian ideological hostility to the concept of a constraining "basic structure" that shapes people's lives—especially when extrapolated to include *nonjuridical* "material" obstacles that justify (I am claiming) coercive state intervention to restructure it—means that left-liberals will be its natural constituency.

Yet for both left and right, this seeming parallelism might encourage the criticism that in the end, these principles are hardly different from Rawls's own, so my claim to be engaged in a quite different exercise turns out to be false. But remember, to begin with, that insofar as I am self-consciously working within a liberal framework, drawing on liberal values, V, and a deontological contractualist vocabulary of rights, liberties, and duties, there will inevitably be a certain normative convergence. If the principles were totally unfamiliar, they could hardly be liberal ones! In terms of key differences, note that (1) there is no difference principle, DP (racial justice requires closing the R_1/R_2 gap, but it is not the case that the DP has ever been implemented in the United States, or other modern Western liberal societies, so for race it is irrelevant); (2) PCJ6 requires the correction for institutional racial disrespect, which does not even exist in Rawls's ideal society, predicated as it is on the reciprocal equal recognition of the "contractors," whereas systemic disrespect is structurally foundational for the nonidealized domination contract, for whom the R_2s are not equal contractors in the first place; (3) PCJ5 mandates ending racial exploitation,[108] but since exploitation does not even exist in Rawls's idealized "cooperative venture for mutual advantage," the concept is completely untheorized by him, whether for race or any other identity;[109] and finally, (4) the realization of PCJ4 will necessitate a correction not just of the deficient basic liberties, BL, of the R2s but also of the unequal and asymmetrically superior BL of the R1s, which will be *reciprocally related* to the R2s' inferior BL, for example, an "equal protection" that in effect embeds differential R1 racial privilege at R2 expense or a schedule of property rights in which whiteness/R1-ness has effectively functioned as "property."[110] So a liberal deracializing of the illiberal domination contract to redress past and ongoing illicit structural R1 advantage and R2 disadvantage is not the same as a liberal prescribing of equal rights and opportunities for a society of equals that was never racialized to begin with.

As we saw, Rawls's principles of justice are lexically ordered, PDJ $[BL \rightarrow (FEO \rightarrow DP)]_1$, and in his brief discussion of corrective justice, he seems to be suggesting that principles of the latter kind should also have a lexical ordering, insofar as the most "grievous" injustices should be addressed first.[111] But he was really thinking of societies that were flawed yet still close enough to ideal that their situation could be thought of in terms of "partial compliance." With a racist society, the situation is different, in that, as emphasized, the real problem is more or less "full compliance" *with* racist principles. Whether the issue is second-class citizenship, racial exploitation, or denied personhood, the refusal to admit the equal humanity of the R2s is the common factor throughout. I suggest, then, that in the case of such societies, the principles of corrective justice, PCJ4, PCJ5, and PCJ6, should be regarded as conjunctively rather than lexically operative—that is, as having equal priority. For in each area, institutionally recognized R2 personhood is being violated: the "inferior" ontological status of the R2s, their socially disrespected standing, is what justifies their second-class citizenship and the denial of equal economic opportunities. So the principles should be seen as jointly rather than lexically imperative for us to fulfill: PCJ $[PCJ4.PCJ5.PCJ6]_{\sim 1}$.

Another point worth noting is that the R2 category, being just the negation of R1 ("nonwhite"), will include different racial groups, with different histories and different claims to justice. Recent work in critical race theory has warned of the dangers of trying to squeeze all racial relations into the "black-white binary."[112] Anti-Latinx, anti–Asian / Asian American, and anti–Native American racism have historically taken different forms, with different dikailogical remedies arguably being called for. In the case of Native Americans in particular, demands for, say, land

[MILLS] *Theorizing Racial Justice*   173

and sovereignty are quite different from African American demands for affirmative action or reparations. My hope is that the principles are articulated at a sufficiently high level of abstraction so that these differences can be accommodated once the particular racial histories are taken into account. Intersectionality—and its complication of what "racial" justice would mean, as in the famous Black feminist manifesto of the Combahee River Collective—has not been addressed here.[113] But elsewhere, I have made suggestions about modifying the "domination contract" to include both race and gender in what I believe is a useful way that could be applied to these and other "intersecting" identities.[114] And note that dealing with such challenges will be a general problem for *all* theories of corrective justice, so it is certainly not the case that my recommended modified racial contractualism is uniquely or distinctively disadvantaged in this respect.

Finally, as an interestingly inverted variant on an earlier objection, it might be claimed that these principles are not (tacitly) Rawlsian and thus controversial (for those not on the left) but in fact essentially trivial, the justice equivalent of Mom and apple pie. *Of course* we should end second-class citizenship, exploitation, and institutional ontological inferiority for any thus affected groups—who could disagree with that? But first, one must demur—in a time of resurgent racism for which the epoch of "color blindness" is a distant memory—that significant sections of the white population do not in fact endorse such putative truisms and do actually disagree. So unanimous or near-unanimous acceptance cannot be taken for granted. For this subset of the population, affirming such norms, even without further specification, is not at all an uncontroversial matter.

Second, and more importantly, once the actual content of the principles is specified, as determined by an informed recognition of what life is actually like for the R2s in an R1-dominant social order, their substantive, and thus controversial, prescriptive implications (all legally coercible, remember) will immediately become apparent. First-class R2 citizenship, for example, would arguably require not merely the obvious *formal* granting of equal civic status, which people of color (nominally) already have, but such substantive measures as a rethinking of the threshold for Supreme Court "strict scrutiny" where race is involved, the rescinding of the 2013 *Shelby County v. Holder* Supreme Court decision, the ending of felon disfranchisement because of its hugely racially disparate impact, the redrawing of racially gerrymandered voting districts and prohibition of other related practices of voter suppression, exploration of the role of the Electoral College and the Senate in perpetuating white

174   *The Tanner Lectures on Human Values*

majoritarianism, massively increased funding for the effective implementation of existing antidiscrimination law and extension into other areas of society of such law, structural reform of the criminal justice system, the dismantling of the urban ghetto and other manifestations of national segregation, a rebuilding of an American educational program that systemically handicaps students of color, and many other measures. Ending racial exploitation would mean not just, say, prohibiting unequal pay for equal work, banning sweatshop labor, and abolishing the (in actuality if not designation) national racial division of labor but initiating a refurbished and aggressive affirmative action program across the country as well as reparative measures to correct for the huge wealth advantage whites have accumulated over the years at the expense of people of color through "unjust enrichment," a concept not usually so broadly defined in liberal jurisprudence but arguably manifest in the long history of discrimination in hiring and promotion, federal backing of restrictive covenants, mortgage discrimination, the racist postwar implementation at the local level of the G.I. Bill, inferior education (again—though here in its economic implications) in segregated inner-city schools that denies Blacks and Latinx an equal chance to develop human capital, and so forth.[115] "Ontological" equalization (as socially recognized and institutionalized respect)[116] would require far more than getting rid of public racist imagery in the form of mock–Native American team names and mascots, the Confederate flag, and Civil War monuments and statues glorifying the "Lost Cause" and its "heroes" but would also demand federal apologies, the reconstitution of national memory, and the reimagining of national iconographies and could extend to rewriting textbooks to emphasize the historically white-supremacist nature of the polity, the devising of early childhood educational programs to combat the development of "implicit bias" in children, and the resulting stigmatization—once these children become adults who will discriminate in the public sphere—of nonwhite cultures, testimonies, bodies, and personhood as unworthy, not credible, ugly, and inferior. In sum, once one thinks through, in their darkly impressive multiplicity and multidimensionality, how many different ways race affects us, one should also be able to see how sweeping the corrective measures would need to be to achieve genuine racial justice.

If such measures appear strange and illiberal to those familiar only with the discursive world of the segregated white forums of mainstream liberal social justice theory—that is, of course, my point. Racial liberalism as idealizing white liberalism has not merely bleached the actual world

[MILLS]   *Theorizing Racial Justice*   175

but whited out an objective perception of what would be required to right its wrongs. I would contend that, however unfamiliar, the alternative liberalism I have sketched here is indeed truly to be characterized as such and is in fact more faithful to the liberal ideal than its currently hegemonic pretenders and usurpers. As the country moves toward a nonwhite demographic majority for the first time in its history, we can confidently predict that the demands for racial justice are only going to get louder.[117] Philosophical liberalism with nothing to say to such claimants will continue to be, albeit more sophisticatedly than in the degraded intellectual universe of Twitter and the blogosphere, racial liberalism in all but name and a betrayal of the tradition at its (infrequent) best.

NOTES

1   New July 2020 endnote: This talk was originally given at the University of Michigan on February 12, 2020, more than three months before George Floyd's killing by the Minneapolis police on May 25, 2020, would ignite national and then global protests around the issues of police brutality, racism, and systemic racial injustice. In that respect, my lecture turned out to be tragically timely. But it must be reiterated, as emphasized in my introduction, that these issues are not recent but long-standing ones, and white mainstream political philosophy's ignoring of them is likewise a deep-rooted and long-enduring case of the disciplinary malfeasance of the profession. For important pioneering work on the subject by two now-retired Black philosophers, see Bernard R. Boxill, *Blacks and Social Justice*, rev. ed. (Lanham, MD: Rowman & Littlefield, 1992); and Howard McGary, *Race and Social Justice* (Malden, MA: Blackwell, 1999).

2   Plato, *The Republic*, ed. G. R. F. Ferrari, trans. Tom Griffith (New York: Cambridge University Press, 2000).

3   John Rawls, *A Theory of Justice*, rev. ed. (1971; repr., Cambridge, MA: Harvard University Press, 1999).

4   For documentation, see Charles W. Mills, *Black Rights/White Wrongs: The Critique of Racial Liberalism* (New York: Oxford University Press, 2017).

5   Duncan Bell, "What Is Liberalism?", *Political Theory* 42, no. 6 (December 2014): 682–715.

6   Desmond King, *In the Name of Liberalism: Illiberal Social Policy in the USA and Britain* (New York: Oxford University Press, 1999); Uday Singh Mehta, *Liberalism and Empire: A Study in Nineteenth-Century British Thought* (Chicago: University of Chicago Press, 1999); Duncan Ivison, *Postcolonial Liberalism* (New York: Cambridge University Press, 2002); Jennifer Pitts, *A Turn to Empire: The Rise of Imperial Liberalism in Britain and France* (Princeton, NJ: Princeton University Press, 2005); Domenico Losurdo, *Liberalism: A Counter-History*, trans. Gregory Elliott (New York: Verso, 2011); Duncan Bell, *Reordering the World: Essays on Liberalism and Empire* (Princeton, NJ: Princeton University Press, 2016).

7   Mary Wollstonecraft, *A Vindication of the Rights of Men* and *A Vindication of the Rights of Woman*, ed. Sylvana Tomaselli (New York: Cambridge University Press, 1995); John R. Cole, *Between the Queen and the Cabby: Olympe de Gouges's Rights of Woman* (Montreal: McGill-Queen's University Press, 2011); Abigail Adams, *Letters* (New York: Library of America, 2016).

8 Carole Pateman, *The Sexual Contract* (Palo Alto, CA: Stanford University Press, 1988).

9 Charles W. Mills, *The Racial Contract* (Ithaca, NY: Cornell University Press, 1997).

10 Marilyn Lake and Henry Reynolds, *Drawing the Global Colour Line: White Men's Countries and the International Challenge of Racial Equality* (New York: Cambridge University Press, 2008), chap. 12.

11 Losurdo, *Liberalism*.

12 My thanks to Tyler Zimmer for his technical graphic expertise in constructing the three figures.

13 But see chap. 2, "Occupy Liberalism!," of Mills, *Black Rights/White Wrongs*.

14 Ann E. Cudd, *Analyzing Oppression* (New York: Oxford University Press, 2006).

15 Mills, *Black Rights/White Wrongs*.

16 See, for example, Elizabeth Anderson, *The Imperative of Integration* (Princeton, NJ: Princeton University Press, 2010).

17 Mehta, *Liberalism and Empire*; Pitts, *Turn to Empire*; Andrew Valls, ed., *Race and Racism in Modern Philosophy* (Ithaca, NY: Cornell University Press, 2005); John M. Hobson, *The Eurocentric Conception of World Politics: Western International Theory, 1760–2010* (New York: Cambridge University Press, 2012); Inder S. Marwah, *Liberalism, Diversity and Domination: Kant, Mill and the Government of Difference* (New York: Cambridge University Press, 2019).

18 Srdjan Vucetic, *The Anglosphere: A Genealogy of a Racialized Identity in International Relations* (Palo Alto, CA: Stanford University Press, 2011).

19 Samuel Freeman, *Rawls* (New York: Routledge, 2007).

20 Thomas Hobbes, *Leviathan*, rev. student ed., ed. Richard Tuck (New York: Cambridge University Press, 1996); John Locke, *Two Treatises of Government*, student ed., ed. Peter Laslett (New York: Cambridge University Press, 2013); Jean-Jacques Rousseau, *"The Social Contract" and Other Later Political Writings*, 2nd ed., ed. and trans. Victor Gourevitch (New York: Cambridge University Press, 2019); Immanuel Kant, *The Metaphysics of Morals*, rev. ed., trans. Mary Gregor, ed. Lara Denis (New York: Cambridge University Press, 2017).

21 Michael Lessnoff, *Social Contract* (Atlantic Highlands, NJ: Humanities, 1986); David Boucher and Paul Kelly, eds., *The Social Contract from Hobbes to Rawls* (New York: Routledge, 1994); Stephen Darwall, ed., *Contractarianism/Contractualism* (Malden, MA: Blackwell, 2003).

22 Rawls, *Theory*, 6–10.

23 Rawls, *Theory*, 8.

24 Rawls, *Theory*, 8, 309.

25 Charles W. Mills, "Rawls on Race/Race in Rawls," in Mills, *Black Rights/White Wrongs*, chap. 8.

26 Rawls, *Theory*, 8.

27 John Rawls, *Justice as Fairness: A Restatement*, ed. Erin Kelly (Cambridge, MA: Harvard University Press, 2001).

28 Rawls, *Justice as Fairness*, xv.

29 Erin Kelly, foreword to *Justice as Fairness*, xii.

30 Rawls, *Justice as Fairness*, 14.

31 Rawls, *Justice as Fairness*, 21. An interesting point about this list is that at one stage or another, the United States would arguably have qualified for at least three of the excluded categories (caste, slave, racist), thus rendering Rawls's offhandedness about the issue even more striking.

[MILLS] *Theorizing Racial Justice* 177

32 In a November 2019 presentation of this second section of my talk as a self-contained lecture at Harvard University, I was corrected in the audience Q&A by T. M. Scanlon, who said that my interpretation was wrong and that Rawls had indeed thought of the United States as a racist society. Never having even met Rawls, I am certainly in no position to counter Prof. Scanlon's recollections of Rawls (his doctoral supervisor and friend) with my own. But I would then raise the question I originally dismissed: Why would Rawls, an American citizen, self-consciously devise a theory of justice inapplicable—by his own stipulation—to his own country? Clearly to attribute such a project to him is prima facie very implausible. Note also that in *The Law of Peoples* (Cambridge, MA: Harvard University Press, 2001), Rawls characterizes the United States of 1945—long before the civil rights victories of the 1950s–60s (the "Second Reconstruction"), with the nation's postwar Jim Crow regime still solidly in place and after an antifascist war fought with a segregated military—as "a liberal democratic people" (101), which would seem to be incompatible with any simultaneous diagnosis on his part of national racism. So the textual evidence does not appear to support Scanlon's claim. But in any case, whatever Rawls's own illusions or possible inconsistencies, the real issue is that by his own prescriptions about the restrictive scope of "political liberalism," the most important Western liberal social justice theory of the twentieth century does not cover racist societies, thereby, I would claim, vindicating my contention about the continuing "racial" character of Western liberalism, here in the non-acknowledgment of the actual racist history of the West.

33 Before my theoretical epiphany (if indeed it is such), this was in fact what I reflexively assumed myself.

34 Rawls, *Theory*, 246.

35 Rawls, *Theory*, 8, 309.

36 John Rawls, *Political Liberalism* (New York: Columbia University Press, 1993), xxviii; Rawls, *Justice as Fairness*, 66.

37 For documentation, see Mills, *Black Rights/White Wrongs*.

38 Rawls, *Justice as Fairness*, 21.

39 Rawls, *Theory*, 109–10.

40 Rawls, *Theory*, 4.

41 Charles W. Mills, "Through a Glass, Whitely: Ideal Theory as Epistemic Injustice," Central Division Presidential Address, February 23, 2018, *Proceedings & Addresses of the American Philosophical Association* 92 (November 2018): 43–77.

42 Rawls, *Justice as Fairness*, 14, 21, 101; Rawls, *Law of Peoples*, 4–5, 65, 80–81, 90–91.

43 Freeman, *Rawls*, 106, 483.

44 Rawls, *Law of Peoples*, 31.

45 Rawls, *Political Liberalism*, exp. ed. (New York: Columbia University Press, 1996), 300.

46 Rawls, *Political Liberalism*, exp. ed., 300.

47 Rawls, *Law of Peoples*, 66.

48 Rawls, *Theory*, chap. 6; Rawls, *Political Liberalism*, liii; Rawls, *Justice as Fairness*, 66.

49 Rawls, *Theory*, 216.

50 Rawls, *Justice as Fairness*, 66.

51 Rawls, *Justice as Fairness*, 64–66, 21.

52 Rawls, *Theory*, 216.

53 Rawls, *Theory*, 363.

54 Rawls, *Political Liberalism*, exp. ed., 15n17, 15.

55 Rawls, *Law of Peoples*, 11, 12, 23, 24.

56 Rawls, *Justice as Fairness*, 4, 13, 43n5.

57 New July 2020 endnote: In the wake of Floyd's death—with the ongoing vastly differential racial impact of the COVID-19 pandemic being daily manifested (both in mortality rates and economic fallout) and after two months of huge multiracial demonstrations across the country and innumerable news stories, Op-Eds, online PDFs, TV shows, documentaries, and podcasts exposing the ubiquity and multidimensionality of structural and institutional racism in all spheres of U.S. society, from the economy and criminal justice system to the worlds of fashion and classical music—the following discussion will inevitably have a somewhat tonally odd and dated character. After all, nine out of the top ten books on the recent (as I write) *New York Times*'s nonfiction bestseller list were on race and racism, and on July 13, 2020, George Soros's Open Society Foundation promised $220 million to the cause of realizing racial equality. The reader may wonder, Why work so hard to prove the obvious? But remember that the (largely white) audience I was addressing in February 2020 was very different from the present one, and for them, and the white political philosophy establishment more broadly, these claims were *not* (or at least could not be assumed to be) obvious. And in any case, given my philosophical engagement with Rawls specifically, the connection between race and Rawls's "basic structure" concept still needs to be demonstrated, being crucial to my overall argument.

58 Rawls, *Justice as Fairness*, 10.

59 Neil Genzlinger, "Ira Berlin, 77, Historian Whose Books Upended Notions of Slavery, Dies," *New York Times* (print), June 9, 2018, obituary, section B, 6. The quote is from Ira Berlin's *Many Thousands Gone: The First Two Centuries of Slavery in North America* (Cambridge, MA: Harvard University Press, 1998).

60 Anne Farrow, Joel Lang, and Jenifer Frank, *Complicity: How the North Promoted, Prolonged, and Profited from Slavery* (New York: Ballantine, 2006).

61 George William Van Cleve, *A Slaveholders' Union: Slavery, Politics, and the Constitution in the Early American Republic* (Chicago: University of Chicago Press, 2010); David Waldstreicher, *Slavery's Constitution: From Revolution to Ratification* (New York: Hill and Wang, 2010).

62 Donald E. Lively, *The Constitution and Race* (Westport, CT: Praeger, 1992); Kimberlé Crenshaw, Neil Gotanda, Gary Peller, and Kendall Thomas, eds., *Critical Race Theory: The Key Writings That Formed the Movement* (New York: New Press, 1995).

63 Douglas A. Blackmon, *Slavery by Another Name: The Re-enslavement of Black Americans from the Civil War to World War II* (New York: Doubleday, 2008). See also the 2016 Netflix documentary by Ava DuVernay, *13th*.

64 Lawrence Goldstone, *Inherently Unequal: The Betrayal of Equal Rights by the Supreme Court, 1865–1903* (New York: Walker, 2011); Tina Fernandes Botts, *For Equals Only: Race, Equality, and the Equal Protection Clause* (Lanham, MD: Lexington Books, 2018); Mark Golub, *Is Racial Equality Unconstitutional?* (New York: Oxford University Press, 2019).

65 Douglas S. Massey and Nancy A. Denton, *American Apartheid: Segregation and the Making of the Underclass* (Cambridge, MA: Harvard University Press, 1993); Gary Orfield and Susan E. Eaton, *Dismantling Desegregation: The Quiet Reversal of "Brown v. Board of Education"* (New York: New Press, 1996); Anderson, *Imperative of Integration*; Erica Frankenberg and Gary Orfield, eds., *The Resegregation of Suburban Schools: A Hidden Crisis in American Education*

[MILLS] *Theorizing Racial Justice* 179

(Cambridge, MA: Harvard Education Press, 2012); Tommie Shelby, *Dark Ghettos: Injustice, Dissent, and Reform* (Cambridge, MA: Harvard University Press, 2016); Richard Rothstein, *The Color of Law: A Forgotten History of How Our Government Segregated America* (New York: W. W. Norton, 2017); Jessica Trounstine, *Segregation by Design: Local Politics and Inequality in American Cities* (New York: Cambridge University Press, 2018).

66   Ari Berman, *Give Us the Ballot: The Modern Struggle for Voting Rights in America* (New York: Farrar, Straus and Giroux, 2015).

67   Philip Dray, *At the Hands of Persons Unknown: The Lynching of Black America* (New York: Modern Library, 2003); Desmond King, *Separate and Unequal: African Americans and the U.S. Federal Government*, rev. ed. (New York: Oxford University Press, 2007); Eric Foner, *The Second Founding: How the Civil War and Reconstruction Remade the Constitution* (New York: W. W. Norton, 2019); Henry Louis Gates Jr., *Stony the Road: Reconstruction, White Supremacy, and the Rise of Jim Crow* (New York: Penguin, 2019).

68   Cheryl I. Harris, "Whiteness as Property," *Harvard Law Review* 106, no. 8 (June): 1709–91.

69   Anthony Marx, *Making Race and Nation: A Comparison of the United States, South Africa, and Brazil* (New York: Cambridge University Press, 1998); King, *Separate and Unequal*; Ian F. Haney López, *White by Law: The Legal Construction of Race*, rev. 10th anniversary ed. (New York: New York University Press, 2006); Gloria J. Browne-Marshall, *Race, Law, and American Society: 1607 to Present*, 2nd ed. (New York: Routledge, 2013).

70   James Q. Whitman, *Hitler's American Model: The United States and the Making of Nazi Race Law* (Princeton, NJ: Princeton University Press, 2017).

71   Melvin L. Oliver and Thomas M. Shapiro, *Black Wealth/White Wealth: A New Perspective on Racial Inequality*, 10th anniversary ed. (New York: Routledge, 2006); Mehrsa Baradaran, *The Color of Money: Black Banks and the Racial Wealth Gap* (Cambridge, MA: Harvard University Press, 2017); Rothstein, *Color of Law*; Carol Anderson, *One Person, No Vote: How Voter Suppression Is Destroying Our Democracy* (New York: Bloomsbury, 2018); Noel A. Cazenave, *Killing African Americans: Police and Vigilante Violence as a Racial Control Mechanism* (New York: Routledge, 2018); Michelle Alexander, *The New Jim Crow: Mass Incarceration in the Age of Colorblindness*, 10th anniversary ed. (New York: New Press, 2020). Because of the aforementioned Rawlsian focus on ideal theory, he has very little to say about the criminal justice system. But obviously, given his categories, it would have to count as part of the basic structure also and—under nonideal conditions—a particularly important one.

72   *The Kerner Report: The National Advisory Commission on Civil Disorders* (Princeton, NJ: Princeton University Press, 2016).

73   Fred Harris and Alan Curtis, "The Unmet Promise of Equality," *New York Times*, accessed May 17, 2020. See also Fred Harris and Alan Curtis, eds., *Healing Our Divided Society: Investing in America Fifty Years after the Kerner Report* (Philadelphia: Temple University Press, 2018).

74   Tera W. Hunter, *Bound in Wedlock: Slave and Free Black Marriage in the Nineteenth Century* (Cambridge, MA: Harvard University Press, 2017).

75   Dorothy Roberts, *Killing the Black Body: Race, Reproduction, and the Meaning of Liberty*, 20th anniversary ed. (New York: Vintage, 2017).

76   Peggy Pascoe, *What Comes Naturally: Miscegenation Law and the Making of Race in America* (New York: Oxford University Press, 2009), 11.

77   For a classic comparativist historical treatment, see George M. Fredrickson, *White Supremacy: A Comparative Study in American and South African*

History (New York: Oxford University Press, 1981); and for a more recent analysis from a political science perspective, David A. Bateman, Ira Katznelson, and John S. Lapinski, *Southern Nation: Congress and White Supremacy after Reconstruction* (Princeton, NJ: Princeton University Press, 2018). The "Southern Nation" of the title does not refer to the South but rather—that's the whole point of the book—to the country as such.

78 Rawls, *Theory*, 53.

79 Rawls, *Theory*, 62–63.

80 Rawls, *Theory*, 64–73.

81 Rawls, *Theory*, 265–67; Rawls, *Justice as Fairness*, 42–43.

82 Rawls, *Theory*, 77; Rawls, *Justice as Fairness*, 50–51.

83 Rawls, *Theory*, 8, 215.

84 Rawls, *Theory*, 215–16.

85 Linda Martín Alcoff, *The Future of Whiteness* (Malden, MA: Polity, 2015); Richard Dyer, *White: Essays on Race and Culture*, 20th anniversary ed. (New York: Routledge, 2017).

86 Charles W. Mills, "Decolonizing Western Political Philosophy," *New Political Science* 37, no. 1 (March 2015): 1–24; Charles W. Mills, "Criticizing Critical Theory," in *Critical Theory in Critical Times: Transforming the Global Political and Economic Order*, ed. Penelope Deutscher and Cristina Lafont (New York: Columbia University Press, 2017); Charles W. Mills, "Racial Justice," *Aristotelian Society Supplementary Volume* 92, no. 1 (2018): 69–89; Mills, *Black Rights/White Wrongs*.

87 For an exception, see Thomas McCarthy, *Race, Empire, and the Idea of Human Development* (New York: Cambridge University Press, 2009).

88 Rogers M. Smith, *Civic Ideals: Conflicting Visions of Citizenship in U.S. History* (New Haven, CT: Yale University Press, 1997).

89 Gunnar Myrdal, *An American Dilemma: The Negro Problem and Modern Democracy*, 2 vols. (New York: Routledge, 2017).

90 Stephen Steinberg, *Turning Back: The Retreat from Racial Justice in American Thought and Policy*, 3rd ed. (Boston: Beacon, 2001).

91 Mills, "Rawls on Race/Race in Rawls," in Mills, *Black Rights/White Wrongs*, chap. 8.

92 Katrina Forrester, *In the Shadow of Justice: Postwar Liberalism and the Making of Political Philosophy* (Princeton, NJ: Princeton University Press, 2019).

93 Forrester, *Shadow of Justice*, 3.

94 Ralph Ellison, *Invisible Man*, 2nd ed. (New York: Vintage, 1995).

95 See Melvin L. Rogers and Jack Turner, eds., *African American Political Thought: A Collected History* (Chicago: University of Chicago Press, 2020).

96 Mills, "Through a Glass, Whitely."

97 Miranda Fricker, *Epistemic Injustice: Power and the Ethics of Knowing* (New York: Oxford University Press, 2007).

98 Miranda Fricker, "Epistemic Injustice and the Preservation of Ignorance," in *The Epistemic Dimensions of Ignorance*, ed. Rik Peels and Martijn Blaauw (New York: Cambridge University Press, 2016).

99 Forrester, *Shadow of Justice*.

100 Forrester, *Shadow of Justice*, 11, 12, 13, 16, 17, 33, 35, 37, 39, 67.

101 George Lakoff and Mark Johnson, *Metaphors We Live By* (Chicago: University of Chicago Press, 2003).

102 Jean-Jacques Rousseau, *The "Discourses" and Other Early Political Writings*, 2nd ed., ed. and trans. Victor Gourevitch (New York: Cambridge University Press, 2019); Pateman, *Sexual Contract*; Mills, *Racial Contract*; Carole

Pateman and Charles W. Mills, *Contract and Domination* (Malden, MA: Polity, 2007), chaps. 3 and 4; Mills, *Black Rights/White Wrongs*. But for a critique of Pateman and myself for our neglect of disability, see Stacy Clifford Simplican, *The Capacity Contract: Intellectual Disability and the Question of Citizenship* (Minneapolis: University of Minnesota Press, 2015), which argues that ableism is actually the more fundamental category.

103   See, for example, Berlin, *Many Thousands Gone*; Van Cleve, *A Slaveholders' Union*; Edward Cavanagh and Lorenzo Veracini, eds., *The Routledge Handbook of the History of Settler Colonialism* (New York: Routledge, 2017); Adam Dahl, *Empire of the People: Settler Colonialism and the Foundations of Modern Democratic Thought* (Lawrence: University of Kansas Press, 2018). Nikole Hannah-Jones, "1619 Project," *New York Times*, August 14, 2019, is also of obvious relevance here. While there has been criticism of some of project creator Nikole Hannah-Jones's claims in particular, the importance of recognizing the role of slavery and corresponding anti-Black racism in American history has generally been conceded even by its critics, at least those on the liberal side of the political spectrum.

104   Pateman and Mills, *Contract and Domination*, chaps. 3 and 4; Mills, *Black Rights/White Wrongs*, epilogue.

105   Rawls, *Theory*, §4.

106   Andrew Valls, *Rethinking Racial Justice* (New York: Oxford University Press, 2018).

107   Charles W. Mills, "White Supremacy as Sociopolitical System," in *From Class to Race: Essays in White Marxism and Black Radicalism*, ed. Charles W. Mills (Lanham, MD: Rowman & Littlefield, 2003), chap. 7; Mills, "Racial Justice."

108   Mills, "Racial Exploitation," in Mills, *Black Rights/White Wrongs*, chap. 7.

109   "The notion of exploitation is out of place here," since "it implies a deep injustice in the background system." Rawls, *Theory*, 272.

110   Botts, *For Equals Only*; Golub, *Is Racial Equality Unconstitutional?*; Harris, "Whiteness as Property."

111   Rawls, *Theory*, 216.

112   See, for example, *Critical Philosophy of Race* 1, no. 1 (2013): Special Issue: Beyond the Black/White Binary.

113   Keeanga-Yamahtta Taylor, ed., *How We Get Free: Black Feminism and the Combahee River Collective* (Chicago: Haymarket, 2017).

114   See Mills, "Intersecting Contracts," in Pateman and Mills, *Contract and Domination*, chap. 6; and also Charles W. Mills, "The Racial Contract Revisited: Still Unbroken after All These Years," *Politics, Groups, and Identities* 3, no. 3 (September 2015): 541–57, esp. 552–55, "Intersectionality and the Contract."

115   William A. Darity and A. Kirsten Mullen, *From Here to Equality: Reparations for Black Americans in the Twenty-First Century* (Chapel Hill: University of North Carolina Press, 2020).

116   Derrick Darby, *Rights, Race, and Recognition* (New York: Cambridge University Press, 2009).

117   Five months later—as I complete this final revision in July 2020—does this point really need any further emphasis?

Active and Passive Citizens

RICHARD TUCK

THE TANNER LECTURES ON HUMAN VALUES

Delivered at

Princeton University
November 6–7, 2019

RICHARD TUCK is the Frank G. Thomson Professor of Government at Harvard University, where he has taught since 1995 as a premier scholar of the history of political thought. He taught at the University of Cambridge from 1973 to 1995, and he is still an Honorary Fellow of Jesus College there. He is also a Fellow of the British Academy and an Honorary Foreign Member of the American Academy of Arts and Sciences. His works include *Natural Rights Theories: Their Origin and Development, Hobbes: A Very Short Introduction, Philosophy and Government, 1572–1651, Rights of War and Peace: Political Thought and the International Order from Grotius to Kant; Free Riding*, and *The Sleeping Sovereign: The Invention of Modern Democracy*. They address a variety of topics—including political authority, human rights, natural law, and toleration—and focus on a number of thinkers, including Hobbes, Grotius, Selden, and Descartes. His current work deals with political thought and international law and traces the history of thought about international politics from Grotius, Hobbes, Pufendorf, Locke, and Vattel to Kant. He is also engaged in a work on the origins of twentieth-century economic thought; in it, he argues that the "free rider" problem was only invented, as a problem, in recent decades. Thus, his interests to a remarkable degree span concerns in all subfields of the discipline.

LECTURE I.
ROUSSEAU AND SIEYÈS

The title of these lectures comes from Abbé Sieyès's address on *The Rights of Man and Citizen*, which he delivered before the National Assembly on July 21, 1789. In the list of the rights of man, he included such things as "liberty, property and security", freedom of expression, freedom to come and go from the state, and freedom to employ one's "strength, industry and capital" in whatever kind of work one might choose, unimpeded by any "individual or association".[1] (Sieyès was a great admirer of Adam Smith—I will say more about this presently.)

But he was not willing to include a right to participate in politics in this list of fundamental rights. He went on to say,

> Up to now we have dealt with the natural and civil rights of the citizens. It remains for us to consider the political rights. The difference between the two kinds of rights lies in the fact that the natural and civil rights are those for the maintenance and development of which the society is formed: and the political rights are those by which the society forms itself. It is better, for the sake of linguistic clarity, to call the first passive rights, and the second active rights.
>
> All the residents of a country [pays] ought to enjoy the rights of a passive citizen: they all have the right to the protection of their person, their property, their liberty, etc., but they do not all have the right to take an active part in the formation of public institutions [pouvoirs]; they are not active citizens. Women, at least as things stand at the moment [du moins dans l'état actuel], children, foreigners, and those who make no contribution to the public establishment ought not to have any active influence on the state.[2] Everyone can enjoy the advantages of the society, but only those who contribute to the public establishment are like the true agents [actionnaires] of the great social enterprise. Only they are truly active citizens, the true members of the association.[3]

This terminology was then used in the first Revolutionary constitution of 1791, drawn up broadly on Sieyèsian lines, in which the category of active citizens consisted instead of French nationals who had paid in tax at least the equivalent of three days' work, were not bankrupt at the time of an election, and were not household servants.[4] It was then picked

[185]

up by Kant, who in both *Theory and Practice* of 1793 and the *Metaphysics of Morals* of 1797 used it to make an entirely Sieyèsian point about the importance for all citizens of a regime of rights and the relative unimportance for them of the management of the state.[5]

I have begun with this passage from Sieyès because it seems to me to embody a profound truth about much of modern political theory. Sieyès's ideas have enjoyed a considerable revival in recent years, and there are good reasons for this. If one wants to find the first person who theorised the modern state in the way many people now think about it, it would be Sieyès.

Indeed, the late Robbie Wokler went so far as to say, extravagantly, that "it may be said that Sieyès is the father of the nation-state, standing to the whole of political modernity as does God to the Creation!"[6] Because so much of Sieyès's theory is appealing to modern readers, his distinction between active and passive citizens has been treated as an embarrassing anomaly, explicable (at least as regards women) by a general prejudice of his time. But I do not think that it is as easy to dismiss it as his modern admirers think; indeed, I think that the fact that he was able to make the distinction reveals something very fundamental about states of a Sieyèsian kind, that in some sense, *all* its citizens are "passive" rather than "active".

The principal reason for the revival of interest in Sieyès is that he combined two things of great appeal to modern theorists. The first, as we have just seen, was his insistence that the primary basis for a political society is its adherence to a specific and far-reaching set of human rights which must be guaranteed to all residents, "passive" as well as "active". These rights should be deeply entrenched, and the Constitution of 1791 made it enormously difficult to revise any article.[7] It was this feature which led Bentham in his mocking attack on "Citizen Sieyès" to describe the Declaration of Rights with which the Constitution began as the rule of the dead over the living: "We the unlawful representatives of the people will govern the people for ages and in spite of ages: we will govern them for ages after we are no more. The only lawful representatives, the first and all succeeding lawful representatives of the nation, the deputies appointed by the people for the time being, shall not govern them as we do, shall not exercise any jurisdiction over them except such as it has been our pleasure to allow".[8] In his return to politics after the Terror, Sieyès also began to theorise a modern constitutional court, "a body of representatives with the special task of judging alleged violations of the constitution", thereby inventing the institution which in

[Tuck] *Rousseau and Sieyès*

modern states has been charged with ensuring the continued entrenchment of the fundamental rights.

The second feature of Sieyès's theory which appeals to modern readers was his equally clear insistence on the necessarily *representative* character of the state. Both Sieyès in his writings and the Constitution of 1791 were clear on this: the Constitution stated plainly that "the nation, from which alone are derived all powers, cannot exercise them except by delegation. The French Constitution is representative". And throughout his works, Sieyès insisted that a large nation could only operate through representation. By this, he did not simply mean that there had to be elected delegates but, much more importantly, that the delegates had to be free to come to their own decisions through a process of deliberation. As he said in another work of 1789, attacking any idea of mandation,

> The Citizens can put their trust in some people chosen from amongst themselves. Without alienating their rights, they delegate their exercise. It is for the common good that they nominate Representatives more capable than themselves of understanding the general interest, and of interpreting in this respect their own wills. . . . [E]ven in the strictest democracy this is the only way to form a common will. It is not in the watches of the night, with everyone in their own houses, that the democrats who are most jealous of their liberty form and fix their individual opinion, to be carried from there into the public space; only to return to their houses to start over again in complete solitude, in the event that no will common to the majority could be extracted from these isolated opinions. We would emphatically say that such a means of forming a common will would be absurd. When people gather, it is to deliberate, to know what other people are thinking, to benefit from mutual enlightenment, to compare particular wills, modify them, reconcile them, and eventually achieve a result which is common to a plurality. I now ask: should what would seem absurd in the most rigorous and jealous democracy be the rule for a representative legislature? It is incontestable that the Deputies have come to the National Assembly not to announce the already formed will of their constituents [Committans], but to deliberate and vote freely following their actual opinion, illuminated by all the enlightenment which the Assembly can furnish to each of them.[9]

In another work the same year, he linked representation to the *division of labour*, arguing that representation was a necessary feature of modernity.

188 *The Tanner Lectures on Human Values*

We cannot now turn our back on the division of labour, which is "the effect and the cause of the increase in wealth and the improvement of human industry. The subject is fully developed in the work of Doctor Smith. . . . It applies to political tasks [travaux] as much as to all kinds of productive labour. The common interest, the improvement of the social State itself, demands that we make of Government a specialised profession".[10] Just as we do not instruct a plumber on how to fix our pipes, we should not instruct our delegates on how to fix our politics.

But his consistent commitment to these two principles—entrenched rights and deliberative representative bodies—meant inevitably that Sieyès had an equivocal attitude to democracy. He made his name in early 1789 with his famous *What Is the Third Estate?* in which he defended the right of the assembly of the Third Estate to remake the French constitution, using what often looked like the language of radical democracy: "What is the Third Estate? Everything. . . . A nation could never have stipulated that the rights inherent in the common will, namely, the majority, could ever be transferred to the minority".[11] But the point of this language in *What Is the Third Estate?* was to deny the right of the privileged classes to have in effect extra votes in the assembly. "In any national representation . . . influence should be in proportion to the number of individual heads that have a right to be represented. . . . A representative body always has to stand in for the Nation itself. Influence within it ought to have the same nature, the same proportions, and the same rules".[12] It was not the case that Sieyès even in *What Is the Third Estate?* supposed that the twenty-six million citizens of France should determine the composition of the assembly by *voting* for it; instead, it had to represent their *interests* and not give a special weight to the interests of a privileged minority. He was willing to say that because "all the States of Europe" are now "nothing but vast Workshops": "You cannot refuse the title of Citizen, & the rights of citizenship, to this uneducated multitude wholly absorbed in their forced labour. Just as they ought to obey the Law like you, they ought also, like you, come together in making it".[13] But on the very next page, he made clear that the "coming together" he envisaged was purely that of "five or six million active Citizens" who in turn "can only hope for a Legislature by representation".

Moreover, one can read all of Sieyès's works, both in print and in manuscript, without finding any clear discussion of the sense in which passive citizens might also be "represented" by an assembly chosen by their active counterparts.[14] The closest one can get, I think, is his account of how the assembly should consult the common interest of all the citizens, and in that sense "represent" them all, but the mechanisms which he proposed to ensure adequate deliberation were expressly designed to admit very little control by the population. But given his fundamental commitments, this is not surprising: while both bodies of rights and representation were in his view integral to civil life *as such*, electoral mechanisms were (so to speak) *epiphenomenal*, of practical but not fundamental significance—they were a kind of safeguard to ensure that the realm of human rights was protected from attack. This is why I said that the category of passive citizen should not simply be seen as a regrettable concession to the prejudices of Sieyès's time: the rights which the passive citizens enjoyed were what really mattered, and the fact that they lacked an *active* role in shaping their politics was relatively unimportant, since very little of significance for the general population would in the end require this kind of active involvement. If everyone was represented, and no one's opinion about a political question could have a direct role in shaping the answer, then, as I said, all citizens were in effect passive.

Sieyès was the great theorist of the kind of state which finally emerged from the French Revolution and of which he had in part been the actual author. The post-Napoleonic states of the nineteenth century exhibited just this combination of entrenched rights, representation, and a belief that their institutions corresponded to a "general will" without a commitment to ensuring that the generality of their citizens actually participated in *creating* the will. This was the state which Benjamin Constant praised, agreeing entirely with Sieyès about the necessary link between the modern economy with its division of labour and political representation;[15] it was the state for which Hegel provided the most elaborate philosophical justification, and it was the state which Marx denounced for its antidemocratic character, with both Hegel and Marx seeing clearly Sieyès's role in its creation.[16]

For a time, this post-Napoleonic state was occluded by the rise of universal suffrage and various kinds of more direct and widespread democracy. The history of referendums in France neatly illustrates this constantly shifting balance. Sieyès's opponents among both the Jacobins and the Girondins were committed to them, but they disappeared after the fall of Napoleon. They were revived for a time under Napoleon III, and though his use of them has often been seen as an argument against referendums, the Second Empire undoubtedly belonged, in a distorted form, to a general democratic moment in European history, manifested most strikingly by what succeeded it for two months in Paris in 1871! Referendums were then abandoned until they were revived under the Fifth Republic, which has used them not infrequently. During the twentieth century, they also became the norm for constitutional ratification in a large number of states. But the Sieyèsian ideal never vanished, and most modern theories of democracy fit much more closely onto a Sieyèsian state than they do onto (let us say) the Paris Commune. And some major modern states, for example, have expressly abjured popular participation in fundamental constitution-making—this is true of both Germany and India. We have been living now for some years in a world where the old theoretical defences of a more radical democracy have worn extremely thin, and to do as I propose to do in these lectures—that is, to defend majoritarian democracy in (I think) rather old-fashioned terms—now seems extremely quixotic.

Marx, who was an extremely acute historian of the French Revolution, put his finger on the reason for this uneasy relationship between democracy and the Sieyèsian state in a remarkable passage in *The Holy Family*:

> Robespierre, Saint-just and their party fell because they confused the ancient, realistic-democratic commonweal based on real slavery with the modern spiritualistic-democratic representative state, which is based on emancipated slavery, bourgeois society. What a terrible illusion it is to have to recognise and sanction in the rights of man modern bourgeois society, the society of industry, of universal competition, of private interest freely pursuing its aims, of anarchy, of self-estranged natural and spiritual individuality, and at the same time to want afterwards to annul the manifestations of the life of this society in particular individuals and simultaneously to want to model the political head of that society in the manner of antiquity!
>
> The illusion appears tragic when Saint-Just, on the day of his execution, pointed to the large table of the Rights of Man hanging in the hall of the Conciergerie and said with proud dignity: "C'est pourtant moi qui ai fait cela". It was just this table that proclaimed the right of a man who cannot be the man of the ancient commonweal any more than his economic and industrial conditions are those of ancient times.[17]

Marx and Engels in the 1840s viewed themselves as the standard-bearers of radical democracy, supporting every movement (such as the

Chartists) which sought to expand the franchise; this was the chief complaint of the Prussian censors in 1843, that Marx's "ultra-democratic opinions [and not his socialist leanings] are in utter contradiction to the principles of the Prussian State".[18] If they had predecessors, they themselves believed, they were only to be found in the Babeufists. But they did have a predecessor, I think, though, like many of their generation, they failed fully to recognise him for reasons I will discuss presently. This was Rousseau.[19]

It is clear that Sieyès's insistence on the necessarily representative character of the state was a deliberate rejection of Rousseau—who had famously said that "sovereignty . . . cannot be represented; it lies essentially in the general will, and will does not admit of representation. . . . The deputies of the people, therefore, are not and cannot be its representatives: they are merely its stewards, and can carry through no definitive acts".[20] Despite this, there has been a tendency in modern scholarship on Sieyès to assimilate him to Rousseau.[21] This is partly because Sieyès's "democratic opinions" have been exaggerated but more that Rousseau's account of democracy has been regularly misunderstood.

The early readers of Rousseau were generally in agreement about what he had said in *The Social Contract* and its ancillary works,[22] whether they were hostile to his views or sympathetic to them. They took him to have argued that the basis of all law must be a general will which is simply a majority vote by the entire population. So obvious was this to them that one of his hostile readers, Guillaume François Bertier, reproved him for *not* saying what later interpreters often thought he had said, that the general will was a kind of bearer of reason that could be detached from voting. What he should have done, Bertier said, was to "compare the general will, in a community of a people, to the light of pure and unspotted [saine] reason in each man taken by themselves. This pure and unspotted reason is always right, always inclines to the true good, and proposes what is of greatest advantage". But instead, he had simply supposed that it was created "by means of general assemblies of all the people, and by way of adding votes".[23] The same was said by one of his most sympathetic readers: writing about the Third Estate in the weeks before it met in a genuinely and explicitly Rousseauian fashion (unlike Sieyès),[24] Jean-Baptiste Salaville proclaimed that "the will of the majority is . . . the expression of the general will; it is the Sovereign; it constitutes the Law. All the other wills should abase themselves before it; and its decrees must have the force of Destiny".[25] And he made clear that the

192   *The Tanner Lectures on Human Values*

deputies of the Third Estate should be chosen by the votes of the twenty-three million citizens, proposing even a weighted system in which larger districts counted for more in the assembly than smaller ones.[26]

The idea that Rousseau was not a radical democrat of this kind appeared first (I have argued elsewhere) in a work by Paul Philippe Gudin de la Brenellerie boldly entitled *Supplément au Contract Social* and clearly intended as a counterrevolutionary reading of Rousseau.[27] In it, he asserted,

> Whatever form the legislative assembly of a nation takes, whether it is all the people or their representatives, what matters is that the laws which it passes should be the expression of the <u>general will</u>, and not of one party which dominates the assembly.
>
> The majority [<u>pluralité</u>] of votes never expresses anything but the will of the most numerous party; but that party is not always that of the generality [<u>généralité</u>] of the citizens.

And he went on to say that "<u>equality of rights, justice in everything</u>; these are the signs by which the citizens can always recognise whether the laws which are proposed come from the general will, or from the wills of a party which has seized the majority of votes".[28] Having argued this, he easily assimilated Rousseau to Sieyès and, even more strikingly, to the physiocrats and their idea that a state should be governed according to the principles of reason—despite the fact that in his famous letter to Mirabeau, Rousseau himself had expressly linked physiocracy to despotism. As I showed, Gudin's reading was picked up in Germany and became extremely influential there, but it is clear that Gudin was pushing against the earlier, common-sense reading of Rousseau's text and that the link he constructed between Rousseau and the physiocrats would have astonished the author of *The Social Contract*.

Nevertheless, the idea that Rousseau was not in fact a theorist of what we might call "active" democracy is still very widespread, so I want to deal with it in some detail. The first point to make is a familiar one, but it needs to be emphasised: Rousseau's fundamental idea was that no law carries an obligation for us unless we have *actually* taken part in making it (what "taking part" means is of course an important question, to which I will return later today and again in my second lecture). In book 3, chapter 15 of *The Social Contract*, he said that "every law the people has not ratified in person is null and void—is, in fact, not a law", and he put it even more plainly in his *Considerations on the Government of Poland*, dealing with the question of whether there should be a concurrent upper house in the Polish Sejm: "The law of nature, that holy and imprescriptible law, which speaks to the heart and reason of man, does not permit legislative authority to be thus restricted [by the concurrence of a senate], nor does it allow laws to be binding on anyone who has not voted for them in person, like the deputies [nonces], or at least through representatives, like the body of the nobility. This sacred law cannot be violated with impunity".[29]

What Rousseau understood by "law", we should remember, is not quite the same as its normal meaning; as I argued in my *The Sleeping Sovereign*, where I traced the distinction Rousseau consistently drew between "sovereign" and "government", the laws which we have to ratify in person are fundamental ones, closer to constitutional articles than to the day-to-day business of a parliament or congress. In particular, they have to be general *in scope* as well as general in origin. It is this which enabled the French Revolutionaries who wanted plebiscitary ratification of their constitutional proposals to view themselves as Rousseauian, while it was also what Sieyès denied, since he believed that *constitutions* as well as all other laws have to be made by representatives freely deliberating.

In the *Considerations on the Government of Poland*, Rousseau was of course dealing with the existing Polish constitution, in which only the—admittedly large—class of *noblesse* voted for the Sejm; the rest of the population, as he understood it, were serfs who lacked personal liberty and were like the slaves or conquered peoples described in book 1, chapter 4 of *The Social Contract*, who were still in effect in a state of war with their masters.[30] The fact that only the nobility were free does not contradict his general principle, that for free men, the law has to be something which they voted for. Rousseau believed that the Polish serfs should be freed, but he recognised the substantial difficulties in doing so; his attitude to them rather resembles his attitude to the slaves of British America. Quizzed by a British abolitionist in 1776 about whether it was appropriate to support the colonists when they were slave owners, Rousseau replied that he was confident that the slaves would soon be freed and that it was important not to undermine the Americans' struggle for liberty.[31] So although it has been said that Rousseau's exclusion of the serfs from the Polish state revealed the limits of his democratic imagination,[32] I think that is misleading: he was concerned with the kind of obligation to the laws which a free man might be under and not with the kind of submission to power which a slave might be forced to make. And his view was clearly that the free men of Poland had personally to take part in the making of law.

This did not mean that they all had to turn up in person to the legislative assembly, but it did mean that they had to *mandate* their delegates. It is often forgotten that Rousseau's hostility to representation was not in fact hostility to the use of delegates, if that were necessary for a large country like Poland, though of course he always expressed a strong preference for mass citizen assemblies if they could be held; as he said in *Poland*, "Representatives of the people are . . . easy to corrupt; and it rarely happens that they are not so corrupted". But he continued,

> I see two means of preventing this terrible evil of corruption, which turns the organ of freedom into the instrument of slavery.
>
> The first . . . is to have the diets elected frequently, for if the representatives are often changed it is more costly and difficult to seduce them. On this point your constitution is better than that of Great Britain. . . .
>
> The second means is to bind the representatives to follow their instructions exactly, and to make them render their constituents a strict account of their conduct in the diet. In this respect I can only marvel at the negligence, the carelessness and, I would even venture to say, the stupidity of the English nation, which, after having armed its deputies with supreme power, has added no brake to regulate the use they may make of that power throughout the seven years of their mandate.[33]

Rousseau was perfectly aware of the fact that his ideas could apply to a modern state, despite his preference for city republics; indeed, in addressing the citizens of Geneva in the "Ninth Letter" from *Letter from the Mountain*, he anticipated Sieyès in his awareness of the nature of modernity: "Ancient Peoples are no longer a model for modern ones; they are too alien to them in every respect. You above all, Genevans, keep your place. . . . You are neither Romans, nor Spartans; you are not even Athenians. . . . You are Merchants, Artisans, Bourgeois, always occupied with their private interests, with their work, with their trafficking, with their gain".[34]

When the French writers debated mandation in 1788–89, they had had the passage from the *Considerations on the Government of Poland* in front of them since 1782, when it was first published. As I observed in *The Sleeping Sovereign*, it is curious that Rousseau nowhere considered the favourite solution of the French radicals to the problem of participation in a large country—namely, the plebiscite—but it was only in the year of Rousseau's

[TUCK] *Rousseau and Sieyès*

death, in 1778, that such a thing was tried anywhere, in Massachusetts as it happens. And even after the introduction of plebiscites, radicals continued to look to mandation as the means of mass participation—Marx, for example, praised the provisional constitution produced in the Paris Commune for specifying that "each delegate [to the National Delegation] [had] to be at any time revocable and bound by the <u>mandat imperatif</u> of his constituents".[35] Mandation had actually been much more common in the political life of pre-Revolutionary Europe than we often realise; MPs in England were frequently mandated by the same gatherings in which they were elected (something of which Rousseau was apparently unaware),[36] and delegates to the Estates General in France had traditionally arrived with *cahiers de doleance* voted on by their constituents.[37]

If Rousseau genuinely believed that all free men had personally to take part in the making of law if the laws were to carry any obligation for them, an obvious question is the familiar one: Did they have to be *men*? And furthermore, did they have to be *citizens* as distinct from resident aliens— who were not serfs or slaves? If so, then for all the rhetoric of participation, Rousseau was not proposing anything very different in practice from Sieyès; and indeed, his theory would be less consistent than Sieyès's, since Sieyès did not believe that his passive citizens were under some different kind of obligation to the laws from that of the active citizen: all that mattered to both active and passive citizens was that their rights were secure and their interests represented.

The standard answer to these questions has been that Rousseau certainly assumed that women were not full citizens, and it has been supposed that he thought the same about foreigners. But these are more difficult issues than they seem at first sight. Helena Rosenblatt has called on us, for example, to be cautious about how we interpret Rousseau's remarks about women in the *Letter to D'Alembert* which was firmly rooted in Genevan social conflicts,[38] but few people have been willing to suppose that *citoyen* in Rousseau's political writings also denotes *citoyenne* and *habitant*, resident alien. Nevertheless, we have good evidence that he certainly believed that all *habitants* should be citizens, and there are reasons not to presume that he excluded women.

He addressed the question of *habitants* in *The Social Contract*, book 4, chapter 2:

> If there are opponents outside the social compact [lors du pacte social], their opposition does not invalidate it, but merely prevents

them from being included in it; they are foreigners among the citizens. When the State is instituted, residence constitutes consent; to dwell within its territory is to submit to its sovereignty. This should of course be understood as applying to a free state; for elsewhere family, goods, lack of a refuge, necessity, or violence may detain a resident [habitant] in a country against his will; and then his dwelling there no longer by itself implies his consent to the contract or to its violation.[39]

At first glance, this might seem to be rather like Locke's well-known argument in the *Second Treatise* that voluntary residence in a country expresses tacit consent to its laws. But in Locke's case, tacit consent was to be distinguished from express consent, a formal act of association which gave the person taking it full rights of citizenship; this distinction was critical to his whole political project, since it allowed him to say that Catholics (who would not take the oath of allegiance, which he clearly had in mind, since it required them to abjure papal authority) were like foreigners in their own land and could be excluded from citizenship— and this would apply to a Catholic monarch. But Rousseau did not say this: the plain reading of the passage is that anyone who resides in a free state has given consent to *the contract* and not merely to the laws promulgated by the contractors. That is, they are full members of the state, since there is no other way of signing up to the contract than residence in such a state.

That this is what he thought is confirmed by a remark in his *History of Geneva*.[40] As we all know, Rousseau repeatedly said that Geneva was (or more properly, had been) the model for *The Social Contract*.[41] And in the *History of Geneva*, he looked back nostalgically to the period in the city's history when it was "as democratic as was possible":[42]

There was no inequality of rights in the Bourgeoisie. For at that time the difference between Citizens and Bourgeois did not exist [footnote: "The word citizen, which one finds in ancient acts is only a literal translation of the word cives, and has no other meaning than that of the word Bourgeois, which cannot be rendered in Latin"] and everyone could equally attain offices. Nevertheless there were habitants who were not bourgeois; newcomers were not supposed at first to share the rights of the children of the house. But the sons of the habitants became bourgeois by their birth, and the word natif was no more known than that of citizen.

> Sometimes even the <u>habitants</u> entered into the General Council, above all when it was composed only of heads of families; for then all who were heads entered into it indiscriminately.

The legal categories in the Geneva of Rousseau's day were *citoyen*, with full voting rights in the General Council, the biannual meeting to vote in legislation and elect magistrates, and the right to stand for election, *bourgeois*, a new resident who paid a sum to be allowed to vote and have some economic privileges (the relic of a guild system of the kind familiar in cities across Europe) but could not stand for office, *habitant*, who was simply a resident alien, and *natif*, the son of an *habitant*. As can be seen from this passage, however, Rousseau believed that in the great days of democracy, none of these distinctions applied and, in particular, that resident aliens had been able to play a full part in its proceedings.

The belief that resident aliens must be able to vote for the laws under which they lived was in some respects a touchstone of whether or not someone subscribed to what I am calling "active democracy". We find it accordingly in Jeremy Bentham (who once said that he had been fascinated by Rousseau "to the highest pitch of fascination"),[43] who argued in his *Plan of Parliamentary Reform* that "aliens" should have the vote (though he added that their numbers were likely to be so few that "though they were all enemies, no sensible practical mischief could ensue").[44] We find it in the Paris Commune, where a resident alien, Leo Frankel, was famously elected to the central committee and became the Minister of Labour, something praised by Marx: "The Commune admitted all foreigners to the honor of dying for an immortal cause".[45] And we find it in the early United States, something I will return to in my second lecture. If it was true that everyone had to take part in the making of the laws which obliged them, then this was an inevitable conclusion to draw.

As for women, the question of what Rousseau thought has been compromised by the widespread assumption that the kinds of constraints on women's political activity which were characteristic of almost all countries in the nineteenth century had been in place for centuries and that anyone who thought that women should be able to vote therefore had to say so *explicitly*. But as we are now beginning to understand, the actual history is much more complicated and remarkable. We have in fact an extremely good piece of evidence for this, from precisely the moment I am concerned with. When the Estates General were summoned in 1789 for the first time since 1614, the rules for election to the Third Estate specified that the electors should be "habitants . . . born in France or naturalised, aged twenty-five or over, with a permanent address [domiciliés] and included on the tax rolls".[46] Although even distinguished historians such as François Furet have assumed that this meant male *habitants*,[47] it is clear from detailed work on the *cahiers* produced by the local meetings of voters that very many women participated—in some parishes in the Périgord, which has been most closely studied, up to a fifth of voters were women. In most places, it was heads of households who were on the tax rolls and who were called to vote, but heads of households could frequently be women, especially (but not exclusively) widows, and in some places, other female members of the household voted.[48] To a very high degree, the last Estates General was elected on the basis of near-universal suffrage, something not merely countenanced but positively welcomed by the royal government and the Assembly of Notables which was advising it.[49] Not until the constitutional proposals of 1793 did women *lose* the vote in France—and we now know that in the plebiscite on the new constitution which was to take away their vote, many women voted under the old rules for the last time until 1945.[50]

Eighteenth-century France was by no means unusual in this respect: in England, before the so-called Great Reform Act of 1832, women who met the various property qualifications could—and did—vote, though not in numbers comparable to French women in 1789.[51] Again, women lost the vote in 1832. And if we look at the other nations in which Rousseau was interested, Corsica was famous for having full female suffrage,[52] and it has even been alleged that noblewomen in Poland took part in the Sejms.[53] In Geneva itself, though, this seems not to have been the case—though the ubiquity of the principle in Western Europe that heads of households could include widows, and the fact that they so often took part in political activity alongside men, would suggest that if it was not so in Geneva, then the city was rather unusual.

How would the economic interests of the often sizable concerns headed by widows have been represented on the General Council if widows were excluded? Widows were certainly enrolled on the register of *habitants*, something Rousseau must have known when he praised the fact that *habitants* had once voted on the General Council.[54]

If all this is correct, then there is no reason not to think that Rousseau genuinely believed in universal participation as a basis for a legal order. And those who took some inspiration from him clearly thought the same; Bentham, to use him again as an example, produced one of the

[TUCK] *Rousseau and Sieyès*

most powerful defences of female suffrage in his *Projet of a Constitutional Code for France*, which was targeted precisely at the active/passive citizen distinction written into the Constitution of 1791.[55] While another of the advocates of female suffrage at this moment, Pierre Guyomar, a faithful Rousseauian, said expressly in 1793 that "in my opinion women ought to be included in The Social Contract".[56] However, this has not been enough for many modern readers of Rousseau. From two directions, they have called into question the radical character of his democratic theory. One direction is pioneered by Gudin: on this view, Rousseau's "general will" represents the general good and is in principle detachable from the actual process of voting—so that a vote can in effect be nullified if it clashes with what is independently specifiable as the common interest. The other direction was actually first hinted at (I think) by Kenneth Arrow in his *Social Choice and Individual Values* in 1951 but has since become very popular:[57] it is the idea that the general will is authoritative because it is an instance of "epistemic democracy", in which a large number of people asking a question about something will tend to cluster in their answers around the correct one. While this preserves the point of voting, it still presumes that there is a correct answer to a political question and that it is the *correctness* of the answer and not the fact that it was *voted* for which makes the outcome authoritative. Neither view sits very well with a commitment to universal suffrage; this is obviously true of the first, but it is also true of the second, since *universality* has no special role in an epistemic theory: a large number is enough to give us the correct result, and adding votes beyond that number will not make any significant difference and may represent a disutility. But both, I think, are hard to square with Rousseau's actual texts.

The first view largely rests on the most famous and important passage in *The Social Contract*, book 2, chapter 3:

> It follows from what has gone before that the general will is always right and tends to the public advantage; but it does not follow that the deliberations of the people are always equally correct. Our will is always for our own good, but we do not always see what that is; the people is never corrupted, but it is often deceived, and on such occasions only does it seem to will what is bad.
>
> There is often a great deal of difference between the will of all and the general will; the latter considers only the common interest, while the former takes private interest into account, and is no more

200   *The Tanner Lectures on Human Values*

than a sum of particular wills: but take away from these same wills the pluses and minuses that cancel one another, and the general will remains as the sum of the differences.

To this, people often add the passage in book 2, chapter 6 in which Rousseau explains why a "legislator" might be necessary to convert a "multitude" into a civil society: "Of itself the people wills always the good, but of itself it by no means always sees it. The general will is always in the right, but the judgment which guides it is not always enlightened. It must be got to see objects as they are, and sometimes as they ought to appear to it.... The individuals see the good they reject; the public wills the good it does not see. All stand equally in need of guidance".

Behind both these passages stands a distinction most familiar to modern readers from Hobbes, between a "people" and a "multitude". As we now understand, following the work of Bruno Bernardi and Mike Sonenscher, the term *volonté générale* came into Rousseau from the 1706 Barbeyrac translation of Pufendorf's *De Iure Naturae*.[58] At VII.5.5, where Pufendorf was discussing the nature of democratic sovereignty in explicitly Hobbesian terms, he said that "in moral Considerations there is no manner of Absurdity in supposing, that those particular Wills [volontez particulières], which unite and conspire to make up the Will of the Community [Corps Moral], should want some Power or Quality which the general Will [volonté générale] is possess'd of ".[59] He also said, "It requires no Depth of Parts to apprehend the Difference between all in general, and each in particular; between the Assembly of the People in Democracies, and private Men dispers'd according to their respective Habitations". The will of "private Men dispers'd" is what Rousseau termed in this passage "the will of all", and the "general will" is the will of the assembly as a single body.

We should not be too fixated on this terminology: Rousseau, followed by his early readers, was quite prepared to use the phrase "will of all" as a synonym for "general will": thus in the *Letters from the Mountain* ("Letter Six"), where he was summarising *The Social Contract*, he stated, "The will of all is thus the order, the supreme rule, and that general and personified rule is what I call the Sovereign".[60] The reason for this looseness is that—as the famous remark about taking away the pluses and minuses illustrates—the general will *is* the will of all, with an appropriate mathematical transformation performed on it. The transformation is most easily understood as a rather elaborate description of calculating where

[TUCK] *Rousseau and Sieyès*

the majority opinion is to be found; for example, if one hundred people vote "Yes" on a measure and ninety vote "No", the ninety "No" votes are "cancelled" by ninety "Yes" votes, leaving ten "Yes" votes to determine the general will. He said something similar in *Poland*: "The law, which is only the expression of the general will, is properly a resultant of all the particular interests combined and balanced in proportion to their number".[61] There is no suggestion in these passages that the building blocks (so to speak) of the general will are anything other than particular wills and private interests; the generality comes, as it did (for example) in Hobbes on democracy, from each citizen's willingness to make the majority will of the society his own, once the vote has taken place.[62]

The discrepancy which Rousseau feared between the general will and the "deliberations of the people" which might be corrupted in some way is explained in all these passages not by the ignorance or poor judgement of the individual citizens but (once a civil society has come into being) by the existence of *partial association*. The paragraph which immediately follows the famous passage in book 2, chapter 3 makes this absolutely clear. It reads,

> If, when the people, being furnished with adequate information, held its deliberations, the citizens had no communication one with another, the grand total of the small differences would always give the general will, and the decision would always be good. But when factions arise, and partial associations are formed at the expense of the great association, the will of each of these associations becomes general in relation to its members, while it remains particular in relation to the State: it may then be said that there are no longer as many votes as there are men, but only as many as there are associations. The differences become less numerous and give a less general result. Lastly, when one of these associations is so great as to prevail over all the rest, the result is no longer a sum of small differences, but a single difference; in this case there is no longer a general will, and the opinion which prevails is purely particular.

This reminds us that Rousseau was as hostile to *deliberation*, and as scared of the power of orators, as Hobbes—his plea that citizens should have "no communication one with another" is what, I think, Sieyès was attacking in the remarks I quoted earlier, ridiculing the democrats who fixed their individual opinions "in the watches of the night, with everyone

202 *The Tanner Lectures on Human Values*

in their own houses". There can be no disputing that it is only this aggregation of individual interests into partial associations which Rousseau believed to be the means by which the general will might be prevented from emerging from a vote. He said exactly the same after the equivalent passage in *Poland*: "The law, which is only the expression of the general will, is properly a resultant of all the particular interests combined and balanced in proportion to their number; but corporate interests, because of their too great weight, would upset the balance, and ought not, in their collective capacity, to be included in it. Each individual should have a vote; no corporate group of any kind should have one".[63]

As for the legislator, there is a well-known problem in all these kinds of social contract theories about how a disunited "multitude" can be turned into a "people", and Rousseau was clearly drawing *inter alia* on Cicero's account in the *De Inventione* I.2 of how men "scattered in the fields and hidden in sylvan retreats" could be fashioned by "a man—great and wise I am sure" into a single people. The essence of a "multitude" was that its members' wills were not *united*, *union* (as in Hobbes) being the subordination of their own wills to that of the majority, and without this commitment, there could be no effective or stable general will. Rousseau solved the Hobbesian problem of how to get men in a state of nature to agree to agree (so to speak) by positing a legislator of the Ciceronian kind. But we should always remember that the legislator has no actual political *authority*: "He . . . who draws up the laws has, or should have, no right of legislation, and the people cannot, even if it wishes, deprive itself of this incommunicable right, because, according to the fundamental compact, only the general will can bind the individuals, and there can be no assurance that a particular will is in conformity with the general will, until it has been put to the free vote of the people".[64]

The epistemic democrats (to turn to them) can agree with all this, however, and still deny that Rousseau's general will is *in itself* the source of legitimacy in the state. This is because for them also, partial associations corrupt the general will, since the general will arises from the unconstrained expression of opinion about a political question by a very large number of independent voters. These interpreters of Rousseau instead lean heavily on some passages in book 4 of *The Social Contract*—in particular, one in chapter 2:

When in the popular assembly a law is proposed, what the people is asked is not exactly whether it approves or rejects the proposal, but

[Tuck]   *Rousseau and Sieyès*   203

whether it is in conformity with the general will, which is their will. Each man, in giving his vote, states his opinion on that point; and the general will is found by counting votes. When therefore the opinion that is contrary to my own prevails, this proves neither more nor less than that I was mistaken, and that what I thought to be the general will was not so. If my particular opinion had carried the day I should have achieved the opposite of what was my will; and it is in that case that I should not have been free.

To this can be added a remark in chapter 1, where Rousseau says of a man who sells his vote that "he does not extinguish in himself the general will, but only eludes it. The fault he commits is that of changing the state of the question, and answering something different from what he is asked. Instead of saying, by his vote, 'It is to the advantage of the State,' he says, 'It is of advantage to this or that man or party that this or that view should prevail.'"

It is easy to see why these look like epistemic arguments. But one must be careful. Rousseau nowhere says that the point of gathering "opinions" about the general will is to arrive at the right answer to a political problem, and in the climactic passage of *Letters from the Mountain* in which he appealed to the citizens of Geneva, he said expressly that this was *not* his idea: "Above all come together. You are ruined without resource if you remain divided. And why would you be divided when such great common interests unite you? . . . In a word, it is less a question of deliberation here than of concord; the choice of which course you will take is not the greatest question: Were it bad in itself, take it all together; by that alone it will become the best, and you will always do what needs to be done provided that you do so in concert".[65] "Were it bad in itself, take it all together; by that alone it will become the best" is the key to Rousseau's thought: the generality of the general will *makes* it the right answer; it does not *detect* it. Rousseau did not believe that the correct course of action for a republic of his kind could be independently specified—only after the vote would such a thing come into existence. What mattered was the capacity of citizens to act together without dissension at the point of action, even if there had been great dissension before the final decision was made; and the union after the decision had been taken required a general acceptance of the vote as the deciding factor and the acceptance by the minority that they would commit themselves to what the majority wished to do.

In the first of these "epistemic" passages, Rousseau was, I think, in fact concerned primarily with the problem of why an individual should subordinate his will to that of the majority, as in Richard Wollheim's old "paradox".[66] The quotation from chapter 2 is explicitly an answer to the question: "How a man can be both free and forced to conform to wills that are not his own. How are the opponents at once free and subject to laws they have not agreed to?" And when he said that people are not exactly asked whether they approve or reject a measure, I think that he was saying what the level-headed responses to Wollheim, such as Ross Harrison's, said: that is, what you are asked is what your *provisional* view is but not what in the final analysis you will be committed to, since that will only be known when the general will is ascertained.[67] It is an "opinion" in the sense that it is provisional and revisionable.

Importantly, this is perfectly compatible with it being the case that people vote in their own interests, as Rousseau frequently said, for example, in the passage from *Poland* quoted earlier—the law is "a resultant of all the particular interests combined and balanced in proportion to their number". I am not required to think about the common good when I decide what to vote for, since my commitment to the common good is satisfied simply by my willingness to subordinate my interest to that of the majority of my fellow citizens. The ballot tells us where the majority interest lies precisely *because* we have each followed our private interest in our vote. This does not preclude our having wishes for the collectivity and voting accordingly, but equally, it does not preclude our voting in our own interests on straightforward matters of personal concern, such as tax proposals. The key thing is that when we lose, we make the policy supported by our fellow citizens genuinely our own.[68]

The second of the two epistemic passages, about the vote seller, is slightly different. It occurs in the context of a further discussion of the danger of partial association, and the point which Rousseau seems to be making is that if I choose to belong to a partial association with coordinated voting (this, after all, is what a man who sells his vote agrees to), then I have ipso facto lost interest in the general will and am treating the voting process as a means to a partial victory. Again, this is different from a requirement on me *when I vote as an individual and not as a member of an association* that I should not vote in my own interests; indeed, precisely what is wrong with partial associations (in Rousseau's eyes) is that they commit me to subordinate my own interest to the interest of the group (or if I simply sell my vote to one other person, to the interest of that person).

If what I have been saying so far is correct, we have in Rousseau the first and possibly the greatest theorist of the kind of radical democracy which

[TUCK] *Rousseau and Sieyès*

was espoused by those in the nineteenth century who were profoundly opposed to the modern state and who succeeded in refashioning their institutions upon democratic lines. But as I said at the beginning of this lecture, in many ways, this process has gone into reverse, for reasons which I do not have time to discuss now but which merit more discussion than they have usually received. Chief among them, I would put the disappearance of a mass labour force which, between 1850 and 1950, produced the material conditions of common life and then went to war to preserve it. This has now gone and, with it, a widespread sense that we *need* all of our fellow citizens. Instead, the rhetoric of many modern democrats is that we have to *help* them, and charity is not a strong enough principle to sustain genuine democracy; apart from anything else, as a long tradition from the ancient world to the eighteenth century recognised, the recipients of charity can come to hate their benefactors, since the acts of benevolence merely reveal ever more clearly the power differential between the people concerned.[69] But our fellow citizens are still there, and their capacity to transform our lives through their actions is still there, and in my next lecture, I propose to outline a modern version of the Rousseauian theory (as I have described it) which vindicates this.

NOTES

1 *Préliminaire de la Constitution. Reconnaissance et exposition raisonnée des Droits de l'Homme et du Citoyen. Lu les 20 et 21 Juillet 1789, au Comité de Constitution*, 1st ed. (Paris: Chez Baudouin, 1789), 25–27 (my translation).

2 *Sur la chose publique*, Abbé Sieyès's own term for the *respublica* (*Political Writings*, ed. Michael Sonenscher [Indianapolis, IN: Hackett 2003], xxi). Sonenscher elsewhere translates it as "public functions" (xxviii and 48).

3 *Préliminaire de la Constitution*, 20–22 (my translation).

4 The Constitution of 1791 did not expressly limit the vote to men, giving it to "Ceux qui sont nés en France", and so on, and women did in fact vote in the plebiscite on the Jacobin Constitution of the Year I (1793; Serge Aberdam, "Deux occasions de participation féminine en 1793: le vote sur la constitution et le partage des biens communaux", *Annales Historiques de la Révolution Française* 339 [2005]: 17–34). It was the Constitution of the Year I, in a famous historical irony, which restricted it for the first time to "hommes", understood as males. The terms "active" and "passive" disappeared from public documents with the coming of universal male suffrage after the Insurrection of 10 August 1792 and did not reappear with the repeal of universal suffrage in 1795, but even when universal male suffrage was reinstated, as it was under Napoleon and, finally, in 1848, the *category* of passive citizen persisted, since both women and foreigners continued to be "inactive"—in France, in the case of women, down to 1945, and in the case of foreigners, down to the present day. Sieyès himself continued to use the terminology: in his proposals for the constitution of the Year VIII after the Eighteenth Brumaire in 1799, he said that "the political association consists only of the <u>active</u>

206   *The Tanner Lectures on Human Values*

citizens, those who are engaged in the common project" (*Emmanuel Joseph Sieyès: The Essential Political Writings*, ed. Oliver W. Lembecke and Florian Weber (Leiden: Brill, 2014), 194).

5 See, for example, his remarks in the *Metaphysics of Morals*:

> This inequality is, however, in no way opposed to their freedom and equality as men, who together make up a people; on the contrary, it is only in conformity with the conditions of freedom and equality that this people can become a state and enter into a civil constitution. But not all persons qualify with equal right to vote within this constitution, that is, to be citizens and not mere associates in the state. For from their capacity to demand that all others treat them in accordance with the laws of natural freedom and equality as passive parts of the state it does not follow that they also have the right to manage the state itself as active members of it, the right to organize it or to cooperate for introducing certain laws. (Immanuel Kant, *The Metaphysics of Morals*, trans. Mary Gregor [Cambridge: Cambridge University Press, 1991], 126)

The examples of passive citizens he gave there included "the blacksmith in India, who goes into people's houses to work on iron with his hammer, anvil, and bellows, as compared with the European carpenter or blacksmith who can put the products of his work up as goods for sale to the public" and who would therefore count as *active* (like, it should be said, Kant's father, a harness maker and citizen of Konigsberg). He did acknowledge, though, that "the concept of a passive citizen seems to contradict the concept of a citizen as such". For Kant's (rather complicated) intellectual relationship with Sieyès, see, for example, François Azouvi and Dominique Bourel, *De Konigsberg à Paris: La Réception de Kant en France (1788–1804)* (Paris: Vrin, 1991), 77.

6 "Contextualizing Hegel's Phenomenology of the French Revolution and the Terror", *Political Theory* 26, no. 1 (1998): 39.

7 Later in his life, Sieyès proposed a constitution which could not be amended at all. See Richard Tuck, *The Sleeping Sovereign* (Cambridge: Cambridge University Press, 2016), 178–79.

8 *Rights, Representation, and Reform*, ed. Philip Schofield, Catherine Pease-Watkin, and Cyprian Blamires (Oxford: Oxford University Press, 2002), 272.

9 *Dire . . . sur la question du Veto Royal* (Paris, September 1789), pp. 17–18; my translation.

10 *Observations sur le Rapport du Comité de Constitution, concernant la nouvelle Organisation de la France* (October 1789), pp. 34–35; my translation.

11 Emmanuel Joseph Sieyès, *Sieyès: Political Writings*, ed. Michael Sonenscher (Indianapolis: Hackett, 2003), 98, 142.

12 *Sieyès: Political Writings*, 142.

13 *Dire . . . sur la question du Veto Royal*, 14–15; my translation.

14 See on this question Nadia Urbinati, *Representative Democracy: Principles and Genealogy* (Chicago: University of Chicago Press, 2006), 151. In general, Urbinati's book is the best discussion of the Sieyèsian distinction.

15 "The representative system is nothing but an organisation by means of which a nation charges a few individuals to do what it cannot or does not wish to do herself. Poor men look after their own business; rich men hire stewards". Benjamin Constant, *Political Writings*, ed. Biancamaria Fontana (Cambridge: Cambridge University Press, 1988), 325–26.

[TUCK] *Rousseau and Sieyès* 207

16 In his essay on the English Reform Bill, Hegel praised Sieyès for having devised the constitutional structure of post-Jacobin France, the constitution which Hegel treated in his *Philosophy of Right* as the paradigm of a modern state (*Hegel's Political Writings*, trans. T. M. Knox, ed. Z. A. Pelczynski [Oxford: Oxford University Press, 1964], 322), while Marx observed in *The Holy Family* IV.4 that Proudhon "for the first time makes a real science of political economy possible. Proudhon's treatise <u>Qu'est-ce que la propriété?</u> is as important for modern political economy as Sieyès' work <u>Qu'est-ce que le tiers état?</u> for modern politics" (Karl Marx and Friedrich Engels, *Collected Works of Marx and Engels*, vol. 4 [Lawrence and Wishart, 1975], 32).

17 *The Holy Family*, chap. 6, sec.3c, *Collected Works of Marx and Engels* IV (Lawrence and Wishart 1975), 122. He went on to give a fascinating interpretation of Napoleon:

> It was not the revolutionary movement as a whole that became the prey of Napoleon on 18 Brumaire . . . ; it was the liberal bourgeoisie. One only needs to read the speeches of the legislators of the time to be convinced of this. One has the impression of coming from the National Convention into a modern Chamber of Deputies.
>
> Napoleon represented the last battle of revolutionary terror against the bourgeois society which had been proclaimed by this same Revolution, and against its policy.
>
> Napoleon, of course, already discerned the essence of the modern state; he understood that it is based on the unhampered development of bourgeois society, on the free movement of private interest, etc. He decided to recognise and protect this basis. He was no terrorist with his head in the clouds. Yet at the same time he still regarded the state as an end in itself and civil life only as a treasurer and his subordinate which must have no will of its own. He perfected the Terror by substituting permanent war for permanent revolution.

Napoleon then fell for the same reason as the Jacobins, defeated by bourgeois society: "French businessmen took steps to anticipate the event that first shook Napoleon's power. Paris exchange-brokers forced him by means of an artificially created famine to delay the opening of the Russian campaign by nearly two months and thus to launch it too late in the year". (122–23) He will have got this idea from reading Philippe de Ségur's *Histoire de Napoléon et de la grande-armée pendant l'année 1812* (Paris: Baudouin Frères, 1825), 73, where Ségur says,

> Cependant une famine s'annonçait en France. Bientôt la crainte universelle accrut le mal par les précautions qu'elle suggéra. L'avarice, toujour prête à saisir toutes les voies de fortune, s'empara des grains, encore à vil prix, et attendit que la faim les lui redemendât au poids de l'or. Alors l'alarme devint générale. Napoléon fut forcé de suspendre son départ: impatient il pressait son conseil; mais les mesures à prendre étaient graves, sa présence nécessaire; et cette guerre où chaque heure perdue était irréparable, fut retardée de deux mois.

The ambiguity Marx diagnosed in Napoleon is one that can be seen repeatedly in these kinds of European rulers; it was true, for example, of the

208   *The Tanner Lectures on Human Values*

interwar dictators, who combined a rhetoric of anticapitalism with support for large private capitalistic enterprises. One might also say that to some extent this Napoleonic ambiguity remains true of the French state down to the present day.

18   Franz Mehring, *Karl Marx: The Story of His Life* (London: Allen and Unwin, 1936), 51.

19   For a sympathetic account of the much-discussed question of the intellectual relationship between Marx and Rousseau, see David Leopold, *The Young Marx* (Cambridge: Cambridge University Press, 2007), 262–71.

20   Rousseau, *The Social Contract*, bk. 3, chap. 15. All quotations from *The Social Contract* are from the G. D. H. Cole translation, which to me is still Rousseau speaking in English. It was first published as an Everyman edition in 1913, reprinted with amendments and additions by J. H. Brumfitt and J. C. Hall in 1973, and again with a new introduction by Alan Ryan in 1993.

21   For example, Sonenscher in his introduction to *Sieyès: Political Writings*, xlvi–xlvii.

22   I mean by this the *Considerations on Poland*, the sketch for Corsica, and in particular, the *Letters from the Mountain* together with the draft *History of Geneva*.

23   Guillaume François Bertier, *Observations sur Le Contrat Social de J. J. Rousseau* (Paris: Chez Mérigot le jeune, 1789), 66–71. This was published posthumously; Berthier had died in 1782. The *Avertissement de l'editeur* (v–vii) says that the work was begun as soon as the *Social Contract* appeared.

24   See p. 74: "Nous allons voir des Etats-Généraux". While the Estates General did not meet until May 1789, it was clear from the autumn of 1788 that they were to be summoned, and there was extensive argument over the rights of the Third Estate in late 1788. The chronology of *Considerations*, and its relationship to *What Is the Third Estate?* (which was published in January 1789), is not clear. Despite what Kenneth Margerison says (*Pamphlets & Public Opinion: The Campaign for a Union of Orders in the Early French Revolution* [West Lafayette, IN: Purdue University Press, 1998], 100–101), it is not obvious that Salaville had read Sieyès, and it is quite likely that the two works were written independently of each other, both during the controversy of 1788. One intriguing possibility is that it was the overt Rousseauism of *Considerations* which then provoked Sieyès in his works later in 1789 to deny the possibility of mandation, which was not an issue in *What Is the Third Estate?* The anonymous editor (allegedly Jean-Joseph Rive) of a third edition of the *Considerations* in 1789 (itself suggestive of an early date for the first edition) described Salaville's discussion of representation as "tout-à-fait neuve" (69).

25   Jean-Baptiste Salaville, *De l'organisation d'un état monarchique, ou Considérations sur les vices de la monarchie françoise, & sur la nécessité de lui donner une constitution* (Paris, 1789), 53–54. See Barny, *Le triomphe du droit naturel: La constitution de la doctine révolutionnaire des droits de l'homme (1787–1789)*; and *Annales Litteraires de l'Université de Besançon* 622 (1997): 124–26. Jean-Paul Rabaut Saint Etienne provided a rather different explanation of the role of the majority in establishing the general will: each voter recognises that the general will expresses the common interest, but he votes in accordance with his own *amour de soi*. The plurality of votes expresses the "preponderant" interest, and in the absence of "privilege", the preponderant interest is the general will. *Question de droit public: Doit-on recueillir les voix, dans les états-généraux, par ordres, ou par têtes de délibérans?* ("En Languedoc", 1789),

9–16. For further examples of the use of Rousseau in the debates of 1789, see Tuck, *Sleeping Sovereign*.

26 "What is a Representative? It is a Man to whom the Represented say: 'We cannot ourselves come to the National Assembly; but we charge you to carry our votes which are to be counted with yours'; and so whether they express their will by instructions which they give him, or by the trust which they put in their Representative, they decide on what he is going to vote for [ils adoptent d'avance le voeu qu'il formera lui-même]; their wills are made one [identifiées], but not their votes: they ought always to be counted in the sum total of votes from which comes the national will [voeu national]. . . . [T]he Representative of a larger number of Represented brings to the Assembly a larger number of effective votes [voix effectives]; &, since all the votes have the same degree of value, he ought necessarily to outweigh a Representative who only has the votes of a smaller number of Represented". Tuck, *Sleeping Sovereign*, 76–78.

27 Though it was not printed until 1791, the dedication to the National Assembly is dated October 30, 1790 (p. xii), and it was accepted by the Assembly on December 16 (p. 299). See Richard Tuck, "From Rousseau to Kant", in *Markets, Morals and Politics: Jealousy of Trade and the History of Political Thought*, ed. Béla Kapossy, Isaac Nakhimovsky, Sophus Reinert, and Richard Whatmore (Cambridge, MA: Harvard University Press, 2018), 82–110.

28 Paul Philippe Gudin de la Brenellerie, *Supplément au Contract [sic] Social* (Paris, 1791), 20–21.

29 *Political Writings*, trans. and ed. F. M. Watkins (Edinburgh: Nelson, 1953), 185.

30 See, for example, his remark that "the institution of serfdom in Poland makes it impossible . . . for the peasants to be armed immediately; arms in servile hands will always be more dangerous than useful to the state" (*Political Writings*, 239).

31 For an account of this fascinating encounter, see Thomas Bentley, *Journal of a Visit to Paris, 1776*, ed. Peter France (Brighton: University of Sussex Library 1977), 59–60. Some further details are recorded (at second hand) by David Williams in his *Incidents in My Own Life Which Have Been Thought of Some Importance*, ed. Peter France (Brighton: University of Sussex Library 1980), 20–22.

32 For example, Wilmoore Kendall in his edition of *The Government of Poland* (Indianapolis: Hackett, 1985), xiv.

33 *Political Writings*, 192–93.

34 Jean-Jacques Rousseau, *Collected Writings of Rousseau*, vol. 9, ed. Christopher Kelly and Eve Grace, trans. Christopher Kelly and Judith R. Bush (Hanover, NH: Dartmouth College, 2001), 293.

35 *The Civil War in France*, Address III, *Collected Works of Marx and Engels*, vol. 22 (Lawrence and Wishart, 1975), 332. And see the *Manifeste du Comité des Vingt Arrondissements*, in *Affiches, Professions de Foi, Documents Officiels, Clubs & Comités pendant la Commune*, ed. Firmin Maillard (Paris: E. Dentu, 1871), 114, calling for "La souveraineté du suffrage universel, restant toujours maître de lui-même et pouvant se convoquer et se manifester incessamment; Le principe de l'élection appliqué a tous les fonctionnaires ou magistrats; La responsabilité des mandataires, et par conséquent leur révocabilité permanente; Le mandat impératif, c'est-à-dire précisant et limitant le pouvoir et la mission du mandataire".

36 In 1620, the City of York appointed a fifteen-man committee to draw up the instructions, and similar practices are documented in Berwick, Great

Yarmouth, Southwark and many other boroughs—above all, London. Even in county elections, with much larger electorates and no institutional structures like a town council to manage the drafting of instructions, the voters could agree to issue specific commands to their members: in Cheshire in 1624, the presiding officer, the sheriff, after urging the voters to choose two able candidates, also urged them to "go a little further and . . . command your knights that if there be occasion offered they shall in the name of their country, and as by special command of the country, make public protestation against a toleration of religion or the repealing of laws formerly made against recusants". This suggests that "going a little further" than simply electing a representative was a perfectly familiar feature of seventeenth-century elections, and it certainly continued into the eighteenth century. See *The History of Parliament: The House of Commons 1604–1629*, vol. 1, ed. Andrew Thrush and John P. Ferris (Cambridge: Cambridge University Press, 2010), 456; and the article on Bristol in *The History of Parliament: The House of Commons 1754–1790*, vol. 1, ed. L. Namier and J. Brooke (London: Secker and Warburg, 1964).

37 While Bentham was rather hostile to mandation, he was an enthusiast for the recall of deputies when their electors believed that they had not represented their wishes properly. See *Constitutional Code*, chap. 4, article 2, in *Constitutional Code*, vol. 1, ed F. Rosen and J. H. Burns (Oxford: Oxford University Press, 1983), 26. It should also be noted that in addition to this, he advocated for annual elections.

38 "On the 'Misogyny' of Jean-Jacques Rousseau: The Letter to d'Alembert in Historical Context", *French Historical Studies* 25 (2002): 91–114. The other "misogynist" text is of course *Emile*, but there too the issue is complex: much of the denunciation of women is a denunciation of the way that, like men, they have been corrupted by modern society, and there is one passage where he applauds their role in politics: "Every great revolution began with the women. Through a woman Rome gained her liberty, through a woman the plebeians won the consulate, through a woman the tyranny of the decemvirs was overthrown; it was the women who saved Rome when besieged by Coriolanus". *Emile, or Education*, trans. Barbara Foxley (London: J. M. Dent, 1921), 354.

39 Cole translated Rousseau's "lors du pacte social il s'y trouve des opposans" as "opponents when the social compact is made", implying that it is restricted to the formation of the society. Last sentence is a footnote.

40 His unfinished *History of the Government of Geneva* seems to belong broadly with his *Letters from the Mountain*, though it was not published until 1861.

41 "That primitive Contract, that essence of Sovereignty, that empire of the Laws, that institution of Government, that manner of confining it in various degrees in order to balance authority with force, that tendency to usurpation, those periodic assemblies, that skill in getting rid of them, finally that imminent destruction that menaces you and that I wished to prevent; isn't this stroke for stroke the image of your Republic, since its birth up to this day?" *Sixth Letter from the Mountain*, in Kelly and Grace, *Collected Writings of Rousseau*, 9:233.

42 *Collected Writings of Rousseau*, 9:113–14. Kelly and Bush translate "aussi démocratique qu'il était possible" as "as democratic as possible", but this is subtly different from the French.

43 Letter to Etienne Dumont, May 14, 1802, in *The Correspondence of Jeremy Bentham*, vol. 7, ed. J. R. Dinwiddy (Oxford: Oxford University Press, 1988), 26.

44 *Plan of Parliamentary Reform* (London, 1817), 9. He appears to have thought something similar in his earlier *Projet of a Constitutional Code for France*: "By a

French citizen is to be understood 1. all such as have had their birth on French ground: 2. all such as shall have thought proper to inscribe their names in the register of any parish in France, renouncing at the same time their allegiance to every other state". *The Collected Works of Jeremy Bentham: Rights, Representation, and Reform: Nonsense upon Stilts and Other Writings on the French Revolution*, ed. Philip Schofield, Catherine Pease-Watkin, and Cyprian Blamires (Oxford: Oxford University Press, 2002), 231. "Every man ought at all times to be free, upon proper notice, to chuse what state he will belong to. It is much more material to individuals to enjoy this right uncontrouled, than it can be to the community to controul it" (pp. 249–50). Any foreigner could simply put their name on the electoral roll whenever they chose.

45 *Civil War in France*, 338. The commission for elections on March 26, 1871, is pronounced as follows in answer to the question, "<u>Les étrangers peuvent-ils être admis à la Commune?</u>":

> Considérant que le drapeau de la Commune est celui de la République universelle Considérant que toute cité a le droit de donner le titre de citoyen aux étrangers qui la servent;
>   Que cet usage existe depuis longtemps chez des nations voisines Considérant que le titre de membre de la Commune étant une marque de confiance plus grande encore que le titre de citoyen, comporte implicitement cette dernière qualité,
>   La commission est d'avis que les étrangers peuvent être admis et vous propose l'admission du citoyen Frankel.

Firmin Maillard, ed., *Affiches, Professions de Foi, Documents Officiels, Clubs & Comités pendant la Commune* (Paris: E. Dentu, 1871), 146.

46 *Recueil de documents relatifs à la convocation des États généraux de 1789*, vol. 1, ed. Armand Brette (Paris: Imprimerie Nationale, 1894), 77.

47 François Furet, "The Monarchy and the Procedures for the Elections of 1789", *Journal of Modern History* 60 (1988): 67.

48 See the detailed study by René Larivière: "Les femmes dans les assemblées de paroisses pour l'élection aux Etats Généraux de 1789", *Bulletin d'Histoire Economique et Sociale de la Révolution Française* 1974. 123–56; figures for Périgord are on p. 138, including the observation that the voters were "veuves le plus souvent, mais aussi femmes mariées avec ou representant leur époux, mères avec leur fils ou célibataires". In the small Norman village of Crulai in 1708, 66 out of 310 *chefs de famille* were widows and on the tax rolls. Jacques Dupâquier, "Des roles de tailles a la démographie historique: L'exemple de Crulai", *Population* 24 (1969): 98.

49 Furet, "Monarchy and the Procedures", 64–65. The electorate for earlier meetings of the Estates-General was studied by J. Russell Major in *The Deputies to the Estates General in Renaissance France* (Madison: University of Wisconsin Press, 1960). He concluded that, as in 1789, there was a great deal of local variation, but by the sixteenth century, the suffrage was often very extensive (pp. 125–27); he did not investigate the question of women voting.

50 Serge Aberdam, "Deux occasions de participation féminine en 1793: le vote sur la constitution et le partage des biens communaux", *Annales Historiques de la Révolution Française* 339 (2005): 17–34. As both he and Larivière observe, women were expressly given the vote in 1793 in the assemblies which were charged with dividing up the old common lands, so they were not entirely excluded from political processes.

210   *The Tanner Lectures on Human Values*

51   See Derek Hirst, *The Representative of the People? Voters and Voting in England under the Early Stuarts* (Cambridge: Cambridge University Press, 1975): 18–19.

52   Pierre Antonetti, *Histoire de la Corse* (Paris: Editions Laffont, 1973), 267.

53   Lynn Lubamersky, "Women and Political Patronage in the Politics of the Polish-Lithuanian Commonwealth", *Polish Review* 44 (1999): 269.

54   The first few pages of the first volume of the *Livre des Habitants* yield a number of widows' names: for example, Ysabeau Monon, *relaissée* of Charles Quinal (p. 3), Janne *relaissée* "d'ung nommé Langloisse" (p. 10) and Pernette Marchant *relaissée* of Jehan Le Gras (p. 23). *Livre des Habitants de Genève Tome I 1549–1560*, ed. Paul-F. Geisendorf (Geneva: Librairie Droz, 1957).

55   *Collected Works of Jeremy Bentham*, 246. Although the editors date this to 1789 and regard it as a response to the "Articles of the Constitution" promulgated in October 1789, this dating is not absolutely convincing. The radical character of the proposals has more the tone of something produced in 1792, and it also seems to track the structure and contents of the actual constitution as issued in September 1791. It is tempting to associate the *Projet* with the invitation issued to *savants* across Europe in October 1792 to produce new constitutional proposals. As we know from a report on these proposals in April 1793 (Jean-Denis Lanjuinais, *Rapport lu le lundi 9 avril 1793, à la Convention nationale, au nom du Comité des six, établi pour analyser les projets de constitution: Sur le titre II du projet du Comité des neuf, concernant l'état des citoyens & les conditions nécessaires pour en exercer les droits* [Paris, 1793]), many of them had proposed female suffrage, including David William's *Observations sur la dernière constitution de la France*, one of the few which were printed. Although the expressed intention in September 1792 was to abolish the monarchy, the Constitution of 1791 with a king was still in force, and the fact that Bentham's *Projet* includes a king is not conclusive evidence against a later date; Williams's *Incidents in My Own Life Which Have Been Thought of Some Importance*, ed. Peter France (Brighton: University of Sussex Library, 1980) records that his own invitation was "only to write down my objections to the Constitution of 1791" (p. 28). Nor is the fact that Bentham refers to a proposal in 1789 to have staggered elections to the assembly proof that the *Projet* was drafted before the 1791 Constitution took its final shape, as the editors thought. It is also worth noting that the *Projet* deals in some detail with the divisions of territory, something the *savants* seem to have been asked to consider. See Lanjuinais, *Rapport fait a la Convention nationale au nom de son Comité des six, établi pour analyser les projets de constitution: Sur le titre premier du projet du Comité des neuf, concernant la division du territoire de la République* (Paris, 1793).

56   Pierre Guyomar, *Le partisan de l'égalité politique entre les individus* (Paris, 1793), 14. See also his strongly majoritarian remarks to the assembly in 1795, attacking the system of indirect election under the directory (and incidentally drawing the kind of parallel between America and France which I discussed in *The Sleeping Sovereign*):

> C'est à la majorité, et non à la minorité, de faire les élections dans le vrai système représentatif. En effet, les représentants, nommés par les électeurs, ne sont pas les élus du peuple, mais les délégués des corps électoraux. Une fois que le peuple aurait nommé ses électeurs, il ne serait plus rien, tandis qu'il doit être dans le système représentatif, la source immédiate d'où doivent découler tous les pouvoirs. Forcé par l'étendue du territoire de déléguer le droit

de faire des lois, il est contraire au système représentatif de con-
fier à d'autres le droit d'élection. Bref, réduire le droit de cité à
nommer des électeurs, c'est le réduire à fort peu de choses, c'est
pour ainsi dire l'anéantir. En effet, la volonté ne se représente pas;
aussi, à la majorité seule du peuple appartient le droit d'accepter
ou de rejeter le pacte social. À la majorité du peuple aussi appartient le droit immédiat d'élection. Les Américains, fidèles au vrai
principe du système représentatif, ont conservé le droit immédiat
d'élection; ils sont nos frères aînés en Révolution, leur République est florissante.

Bernard Gainot, "Pierre Guyomar et la revendication démocratique dans
les débats autour de la constitution de l'an III", in *1795, pour une République
sans Révolution*, ed. Roger Dupuy (Rennes: Presses Universitaires de Rennes,
1996), 261–73.

57 Kenneth J. Arrow, *Social Choice and Individual Values*, 2nd ed. (Yale University
Press, 1963), 85 and 24n. See Brian Barry, *Political Argument* (Routledge,
1965), 292–93; Bernard Grofman and Scott L. Feld, "Rousseau's General
Will: A Condorcetian Perspective", *American Political Science Review* 82
(1988): 567–76; David M. Estlund, Jeremy Waldron, Bernard Grofman, and
Scott L. Feld, "Democratic Theory and the Public Interest: Condorcet
and Rousseau Revisited", *American Political Science Review* 83 (1989): 1317–
40. For the most thoughtful discussion of the argument, though one that is
broadly in sympathy with it, see Joshua Cohen, *Rousseau: A Free Community
of Equals* (Oxford: Oxford University Press, 2010), 78–82.

58 Bruno Bernardi, *La Fabrique des Concept: Recherches sur l'Invention Concept-
tuellew de Rousseau* (Paris: Champion, 2006), 421; Michael Sonenscher, *Sans-
culottes: An Eighteenth-Century Emblem in the French Revolution* (Princeton,
NJ: Princeton University Press, 2008), 117.

59 "Enim vero in moralibus hautquaquam absurdum eft, particulares illas volun-
tates, ex quarum conspiratione voluntas universitatis resultat, destitui aliqua
facultate, qua huic inest". Similarly, at VII.2.5, the Barbeyrac Pufendorf talks
of the "resolutions" of the sovereign which "passent pour la volonté de tous
en général & de chacun en particulier"; this is, I think, an unacknowledged
quotation from du Verdus's translation of Hobbes's *De Cive* (1660), which also
talks about the will of the sovereign being taken for "la volonté de tous eux en
general, & de chacun en particulier" (vol. 6), a translation of *omnes et singuli*
which Sorbiere in his more widely read translation of 1649 did not use.

60 "La volonté de tous est donc l'ordre, la règle suprême; & cette règle générale &
personnifiée est ce que j'appelle le souverain". For one of the first of Rousseau's
followers saying the same, see Guillaume-Joseph Saige, *Catéchisme du citoyen:
Ou, élements du droit public françois, par demandes et par réponses* (published
and then immediately condemned in 1775): "By the essence of the civil state,
sovereign authority can only legitimately reside in the body of the people, since
the will of all [volonté de tous] is the only thing which invariably tends to the
main purpose of a political institution". Keith Baker, "A Classical Republican
in Eighteenth-Century Bordeaux: Guillaume-Joseph Saige", in *Inventing the
Revolution*, ed. Keith Baker (Cambridge: Cambridge University Press, 1990),
128–52; Roger Barny, "Prélude Idéologique à la Révolution Française: Le
Rousseauisme avant 1789", *Annales Litteraires de l'Université de Besançon* 315
(1985): 101–20. The letters were published at the end of 1764, both as a defence
of *The Social Contract* and as an intervention in Genevan politics; they have

214 *The Tanner Lectures on Human Values*

been remarkably neglected by writers on Rousseau's political ideas, with the conspicuous exception of Joshua Cohen.

61 "La Loi, qui n'est que l'expression de la volonté générale, est bien le résultat de tous les intérêts particuliers combinés & balancés par leur multitude". Rousseau, *Oeuvres Complètes*, vol. III, ed. Michel Launay (Paris: Editions du Seuil, 1971), 541.

62 "When men have met to erect a commonwealth, they are, almost by the very fact that they have met, a <u>Democracy</u>. From the fact that they have gathered voluntarily, they are understood to be bound by the decisions made by agreement of the majority. And that is a <u>Democracy</u>, as long as the convention lasts, or is set to reconvene at certain times and places. For a convention whose will is the will of all the citizens has <u>sovereign power</u>. And because it is assumed that each man in this convention has the right to vote, it follows that it is a <u>Democracy</u>". Hobbes, *De Cive*, bk. 7, chap. 5, in *On the Citizen*, trans. Michael Silverthorne, ed. Richard Tuck (Cambridge: Cambridge University Press, 1998), 94.

63 *Political Writings*, 199.

64 Rousseau, *Social Contract*, bk. 3, chap. 7.

65 *Collected Writings of Rousseau*, 9:306. I would like to thank Nathaniel Hiatt for helping me see the significance of this passage.

66 "A Paradox in the Theory of Democracy", in *Philosophy, Politics and Society*, ed. Peter Laslett and W. G. Runciman (Oxford: Basil Blackwell 1962), 71–87.

67 "No Paradox in Democracy", *Political Studies* 18 (1970): 514–17.

68 This was Salaville's view also: he quoted just this passage on giving opinions and explained it by saying that when I vote, "I can be wrong and consequently vote against my will, which is aimed at the maintenance and prosperity of the association. It is just the same, whatever the number of votes allied to mine, if the majority is not on my side" (p. 54).

69 See, in particular, Hobbes's remark in chapter 11 of *Leviathan*: "Benefits oblige; and obligation is thraldome; and unrequitable obligation, perpetuall thraldome; which is to ones equall, hatefull" (ed. Richard Tuck [Cambridge: Cambridge University Press, 1996] 71). This drew on Seneca's essay *De Beneficiis*, with its remarks such as "Repeated reference to our services wounds and crushes the spirit of the other. He wants to cry out like the man who, after being saved from the proscription of the triumvirs by one of Caesar's friends, because he could not endure his benefactor's arrogance, cried 'Give me back to Caesar!'" (Loeb ed. II.11).

LECTURE II.
ACTIVE DEMOCRACY

I want to begin this lecture by reminding you of what I said in my first one. In it, I drew a distinction between what I think are the two most powerful theories of a modern state. The first I associated with the Abbé Sieyès, though also with Constant and Hegel. On this account, the key features of the state are, first, that it protects the fundamental rights of all its residents and, second, that it has an institutional structure designed to represent the interests of the residents in the process of political decision-making without putting direct control in their hands. As I said, it is no coincidence that Sieyès in the course of his theorising should have distinguished between "active" and "passive" citizens; *activity*, from a Sieyèsian perspective, is not a particularly salient feature of politics and indeed might endanger the structures set up to provide protection for rights and the responsible discussion of political questions. Modern theorists of a Sieyèsian sort will not go as far as he did in resisting (or as I showed, in fact, *abolishing*) universal suffrage, but the vote in practice means almost as little to them as it did to Sieyès, since it is hemmed in by all sorts of limitation on what it can achieve. And many of them are quite prepared to leave in place a distinction between "active" citizen and "passive" resident alien, one of Sieyès's two principal examples of "passivity", the other of course being women.

The second theory I associated with Rousseau, but also with Bentham and Marx, and the tradition of radical democracy in the nineteenth century exemplified by the Paris Commune. The central convictions of writers and activists in this tradition have been, first, that if I have not played a part in legislating, laws have no authority over me (I shall turn to what "playing a part" might mean later), and second, that democracy is best understood as a means of collective *action*, giving human beings the capacity radically to transform the conditions of their lives. On this view, the essential characteristic of democratic politics is that the citizens think of themselves as engaged in constructing this common activity and are willing to allow the wishes of a majority to override their own wishes and their (possibly quite correct) belief that the majority of their fellow citizens are wrong. As Rousseau said in his striking remark at the end of *Letters from the Mountain*, which I quoted last time, "It is less a question of deliberation here than of concord; the choice of which course you will take is not the greatest question: Were it bad in itself, take it all together; by that alone it will become the best".

[215]

216 *The Tanner Lectures on Human Values*

This theory plainly implies universal suffrage—that is, suffrage for anyone whose daily life is under the authority of the state (i.e., anyone other than the most temporary visitor), and we duly find this being argued for by most of these theorists. Even Rousseau, I claimed, should be read in a generous fashion to include among his *citoyens* both resident aliens and (I recognize more controversially) women. Indeed, I think that universal suffrage was in practice a touchstone for this attitude to the modern state, and the slowness of the extension of the franchise in almost all countries from the 1830s to the 1940s is testimony not so much to the difficulty of changing social prejudices (though clearly, that was part of it) as to the force of a quite modern idea about the state, of a broadly Sieyèsian kind, which as I said, made universal suffrage unnecessary or undesirable. The shift in attitudes to the suffrage between Bentham and J. S. Mill is an illustration of this—Bentham's confidence was replaced by Mill's caution, not because Mill was clinging to pre-Benthamite prejudices, but because he was much more open than Bentham had been to ideas of a Sieyèsian type, as we see in his admiration for Tocqueville.

What I want to do today is to defend a theory of this Rousseauian kind against its modern critics. And the best way to bring out its distinctive features, I think, is to compare it with a set of theories of democracy which have been popular for some time with professional philosophers and which are increasingly becoming popular with political activists, ideas which can be classified under the general heading of theories of *sortition*. Their essential characteristic is the idea that a lottery of some kind should be used in many instances where we would otherwise use voting; their advocates tend to call in aid the practices of ancient Athens, where sortition was treated as a natural feature of a democracy. Aristotle, in fact, observed that "the appointment of magistrates by lot is thought to be democratical, and the election of them oligarchical".[1] It should be said that while sortition was indeed used extensively in Athens in choosing officials, it was always alongside majority voting on other matters, including legislation. It should also be said that it was not used in Rome, though Rome was much closer in character to our mass democracies. In Rome, sortition was only used (as it is in our societies) to choose juries: otherwise, everything was decided by majority voting, though often of a complex kind.

We still live, more or less, in political societies of the Roman and not the Athenian type, and the oldest of our institutions to use majority voting to make decisions, the Catholic Church, traces its institutional origins straightforwardly back to its beginnings in Rome.[2] Rousseau, as is well known, was profoundly interested in the politics of Rome and in its various voting methods but was rather contemptuous of Athens, which he described as not a democracy but an aristocracy of orators.[3]

The most thorough discussion of sortition as an alternative to election has been in the work of Alexander Guerrero.[4] He has argued that a lottery would be a better means of choosing the members of a legislature than a vote, since it would respect more than voting does the essential principle of *equality* among the citizens. This is so (according to Guerrero) not merely because of the formal respect in which elections do not cleave closely to the principle of equality—that is, the simple fact that not all citizens can be candidates—but also because a lottery might substantively render politics more equal, since it would not be vulnerable to the manipulation by social power and wealth which is such a familiar feature of elections. The idea that a *legislature* might be chosen by lot is, of course, a radical one, but a preference for lotteries over elections is to be found also in the growing enthusiasm for citizen juries to play a role in policy-making.

There are two aspects to a citizen jury: one is that it listens to the arguments of experts on various aspects of the question presented to it in an organised fashion, but this can also be a feature of an elected assembly (committees in Parliament and Congress regularly do this, after all). The more distinctive feature is that the jury, like a jury in a criminal trial, is chosen by lot, and it is this which (in the eyes of the advocates for citizen juries) gives the institution its special character.

The point of a lottery, however, is not merely to preserve the principle of democratic equality: implicit in it (and often explicit) is the idea that it can be more *representative* of the population, in the sense that its composition can mirror the composition of the entire society with regard to what can be thought of as its relevant characteristics, such as wealth or ethnic identity. Two notions of representation coexist uneasily in modern political thought, as my friend and colleague at Harvard Eric Nelson has recently observed in a brilliant piece of historical reconstruction.[5] One is the idea that we should choose people to represent us in an assembly where we cannot be present. We might want to give these representatives carte blanche to do what they think best, or we might want to keep them under our own control; this is the most obvious difference between Sieyès and Rousseau. But the other notion of representation, which is very prominent today but which was also familiar to the nineteenth century, is that the assembly should *mirror* the population.[6] In this picture, the fact that the representatives are chosen by the electorate, though possibly desirable, is less significant than their possession of an appropriate social character and may indeed conflict with it (hence all-women shortlists now, or what amounted to all working-class shortlists with the rise of Labour a century ago). The mirror picture has little or nothing in common with the Rousseauian idea,[7] but it does overlap with the Sieyèsian one, since on the Sieyèsian account, the fact of choice is also really secondary to the characteristics of the representatives—as Sieyès himself acknowledged, the election might be a practical necessity in a modern state, but he thought that it should be severely circumscribed in its effects. The revival of sortition has brought out the difference between these two kinds of representation very vividly, since a system of sortition is intensely concerned with mirroring, but has abandoned electoral choice.

Because of this feature, a citizen jury has at the very least to be a large number of people: the principle of equality would be preserved, strictly speaking, by a lottery which produced a single person, but no one thinks that such a system would be democratic if the random dictator were to be given any political power. (A friend of mine once suggested that the Queen of England should be replaced by a citizen chosen annually by lot, but not even Guerrero has supposed that the President of the United States could be chosen in such a way.) A very large number of people chosen entirely at random might succeed in being representative, but most advocates of citizen juries have usually supposed that something like the techniques of modern opinion polling should be used to put the jury together. These techniques in fact depend on mirroring the population: they do not nowadays consist merely of randomly sampling the entire population but instead use a careful selection of relevant characteristics to put together a sample which will adequately represent the population. On the whole, these techniques have proved remarkably successful, and one interesting reason for the resurgence of sortition might be the availability of sophisticated polling, something unknown until the mid-twentieth century. But even in antiquity, it was assumed that a lottery for magistrates should be designed to have some representational character of this kind—Aristotle (again) said that "it is . . . a good plan that those who deliberate should be elected by vote or by lot in equal numbers out of the different classes",[8] which looks like an attempt to make sure that class divisions were represented in the deliberative body.

[TUCK] *Active Democracy* 219

The fact that modern polling techniques would be needed to construct an appropriate jury also points to the possibility that one could select policies *simply* on the basis of polling, without the additional element of a jury sitting to hear evidence. The two features are separable, and it would be perfectly feasible for an advocate of sortition to argue that if it is true that opinion polling works as a means of representing the views of a population, then we should treat it as at least as authoritative as the result of a plebiscite or general election—and indeed as more authoritative, in that it would not have been corrupted by an electoral process. The fact that we do not, and that there is an important distinction in most people's minds between a "mere" opinion poll and an actual vote, is, I think, a good illustration of the central problem of sortition as the vehicle for democratic politics, and I shall return to this point presently.

There is another quite fashionable democratic theory which has an affinity with sortition, though it has normally been treated as different from it. This is the "epistemic" theory, which I discussed in my first lecture in the context of the interpretation of Rousseau. On the face of it, the epistemic theory is committed to majority voting and not to sortition, but in reality, it is only an ersatz form of majoritarianism. This is first and most obviously because the authority of the decision rests not on the fact that the majority voted for it but on the fact that it is the right course of action, and the vote is merely evidence for that and conceivably not the only or the best kind of evidence. But equally important is the fact that, as I said in my first lecture, *universality* is not at all a necessary aspect of an epistemic theory. *Equality* is, since a vital aspect of the epistemic theory is that the participants all have an equal chance of answering the question correctly, but a suitable lottery of voters would work just as well at securing the epistemic result as universal suffrage and indeed in most circumstances would work much better. So the epistemic theory is in its essence quite close to the idea of sortition, since each theory is interested in reaching a political decision through a process in which people are given an equal chance of something—either an equal chance of participating in legislation or an equal chance of arriving at the right answer to a political question. It is not an accident that the epistemic theory has its roots in Condorcet's theory not of an electorate but of a *jury*.

Sortition is a particularly clear-cut alternative to a Rousseauian theory, since it is an unusually pure example of what we might call representation without agency. It has revived because Sieyèsian representation has come to seem unrealistic—modern assemblies do not consist of wise and responsible individuals deliberating judiciously over the future of their country but of hacks and placemen put into the assembly through the power of money or the power of a party. But the turn to sortition has patently been a turn away from electoral democracy *as such*, and by playing down the significance of the vote, it leaves the mass of citizens with no *active* role at all; each one *passively* awaits the result of the lottery, in the hope (or maybe the fear) of being called to participate in law-making. It is the purest version of representation, in which there is no agency on the part of the citizens at all, and in this respect, it corresponds to, but goes even further than, the other constraints on the vote, such as entrenched constitutions which, as I said in my first lecture, have been characteristic of modern politics since the 1790s.

There are two principal reasons why contempt for modern electoral politics has led people right back to sortition and not back simply to the eighteenth and nineteenth centuries' traditions of plebiscites and mandation. One is a general fear of mass political action and the consequences of strong majoritarianism, a fear I will return to later. The other reason is deeper and more theoretically interesting: it is a belief that the central idea in an active or agentive view of politics—that when I vote, I am actually *effecting* something—is simply false. From the 1950s onward, political scientists took it for granted that an individual's vote, or any other contribution to a large-scale enterprise, is extremely unlikely to make any difference to the outcome. The classic illustration of this is the so-called pivotal voter theory, according to which a rational agent would only vote for instrumental reasons if the chances of their being "pivotal"—that is, it is their vote which turns the election—were reasonably high.

Implicit in the pivotal voter theory is the assumption that I would vote for the same sort of reason that I would hand over money in a market—that is, that without doing so, I would not receive the good I am paying for. And indeed, an analogy between an election and a market has been quite pervasive in modern literature, beginning with Mises in the 1932 edition of his book *Socialism: An Economic and Sociological Analysis*: "When we call a capitalist society a consumers' democracy we mean that the power to dispose of the means of production, which belongs to the entrepreneurs and capitalists, can only be acquired by means of the consumers' ballot, held daily in the market-place. Every child who prefers one toy to another puts its voting paper in the ballot-box, which eventually decides who shall be elected captain of industry".[9] Mises even drew an explicit comparison between Mill's plural votes and the extra leverage which wealth gives in this "electoral" process. The same rough analogy between voting and a market has been drawn by various other people, including Kenneth Arrow and, above all, Anthony Downs. For most people other than Mises, it should be said, it is only an *analogy*; they recognise that in an election, the voter is voting with a deliberate and expressed intention to bring about a *collective* outcome, and the vote is merely the means to do this. As I said in my first lecture, this is not the same as saying that the voter is thinking about the common good in a *disinterested* fashion. He may support a certain kind of outcome for purely self-interested reasons, but it is still a collective outcome which he has in view. But in a market, this is evidently not the case—Mises's child would be astonished to be told that it was voting for a captain of industry rather than choosing the toy it wanted. Nevertheless, the idea that a vote operates rather like money in a market is quite widespread at a popular level and has led to a strange distortion of people's attitudes to voting; in the aftermath of Trump's election, I heard an interview on NPR with a protester against the new president, who said in tones of outrage, "I didn't vote for this"—as if Amazon had failed to deliver the goods they had ordered.

Since in normal elections, no one is likely to be a pivotal voter, most modern theorists of democracy have supposed that, if they are acting rationally, voters must intend something else by voting rather than actually to bring about a desired outcome. The most favoured candidate for their intention is that they are *expressing* themselves; what is striking about this explanation, however, is that it either puts the act of voting into the same category as other kinds of self-expression—such as carrying banners, etc.—or treats it as a kind of private smugness; either way, it downgrades the distinctive character of the *vote*. The voter, on a Rousseauian account, believes that he is involved in making a collective *decision* when he votes, but an expressive account disregards the distinctively decisive character of the vote; it has to, after all, since it denies that in normal circumstances, a vote *can* be decisive. It is perfectly possible, for example, to engage in all these expressive acts in a state where decisions are made through sortition: I may wish to influence the citizen jury or the experts who testify before it, but I will not be one of the groups which finally make the decision. An unwillingness to take votes entirely seriously—manifested in this country by the recent tendency of state legislatures to undermine or ignore popular plebiscites[10] and in Britain (of course) by the struggle over Brexit—may be a consequence of thinking of them as expressive, since it treats them as just another kind of evidence about popular opinion, to be balanced against other considerations rather than being accorded the decisiveness with which traditional democratic theory viewed them.

Another candidate is that the voters are acting out of a sense of fairness—they do not want other citizens to go through the effort of voting while they stay at home enjoying the benefits of the process (either the victory of their side or the general benefits of a stable political system). The problem with this interpretation is that fairness is—so to speak—a secondary quality. If a system of collective action is in place, it might well be true that I ought to contribute to it. But fairness cannot be an explanation of why the system was chosen in the first place: I can be perfectly fair toward my fellow citizens under a regime of sortition or indeed under any method of making political decisions. There has to be some point to the choice of a *voting* system, and some motivation for people to vote, other than the principle of a just distribution of burdens. And for a Rousseauian, that point is the fact that I am self-legislating: when I take part in the vote, I am actually contributing to the formation of the laws I live under.

Some years ago, I published a book in which I explored the assumptions behind the idea that only pivotal voters can think of themselves as bringing about an outcome.[11] What I argued there was that the implicit assumption in this account of voting is that the only situation in which I have an instrumental reason for voting is one where my vote is *necessary* to achieve the outcome I desire. But in fact, it is also possible for me to have an instrumental reason if my vote is *sufficient*, though in that situation, I have to have the further or "meta" desire that it should be I who is bringing about the result. This sounds subtle and complex, but it can be understood fairly easily through the example of a serial vote, in which one after another, we step up to vote for one of two candidates or legislative measures. At some point, there will be a majority for one of the options, and we can imagine that we stop counting the votes at that point (Roman elections were rather like this). The last voter's vote decided the election, and so (we can say) he certainly had an instrumental reason for casting his ballot. By the same token, all the earlier voters who cast their ballots for the winning candidate can pride themselves on equally contributing to the outcome—each vote was decisive, conditional upon the other votes being cast. However, suppose that there were still a lot of voters in line waiting to vote when the ballot was stopped. Many of them *would have* voted for the winning candidate, so if the last voter had not bothered to turn up, the result would have been the same. His vote

[TUCK] *Active Democracy*

was not pivotal, in the sense of being necessary to secure the outcome, but it was sufficient. And if he wanted to be someone who actually made a difference to the result, he could do so by voting; though if he did *not* want to be that kind of person, he had no particular reason to vote, even though he wanted the outcome of the ballot. In other words, he could choose to be an agent and act in order to secure his goal, or he could choose merely to be a passive recipient of it.

Serial voting of the kind I have imagined is now very rare in practice, but in premodern voting systems, it was quite common. Any election which takes the form of an assembly in which people step up to register their vote in public will have this character, and that was the shape elections took in both England and France before the coming of the secret ballot in the late nineteenth century.[12] But the underlying logic is still the same in modern systems, and indeed it can be quite vividly experienced in the British system. Many of us have watched the count in a constituency and seen the paper ballots piling up for each candidate. At some point in the evening, it can become clear that enough ballots for one of them have been counted to guarantee that that candidate has won. If my ballot is in that pile, I can feel just like the voter in the serial vote—*my* piece of paper is part of the sufficient set of ballots. If it has not yet been counted, I will not be able to feel quite like that; but if I have voted for a winning candidate, the chance that my ballot is part of the sufficient or effective set in a two-person race must by definition be more than 50 percent. This is a vivid example, but the same reasoning applies even in an American-style election with voting machines: if there are enough people who vote like me, I can think of myself as having a high probability of contributing effectively to an electoral outcome and certainly a probability high enough to make it worth my while to vote, given my desire to play a real and effective part in the process.

This is the point which has largely been overlooked in the modern theory of voting and is the key reason why, in the end, there can be no real analogy between market behaviour and voting. In a market, there is no point in my handing over money if I am going to get the thing for free, whereas there could be an instrumental point in my voting even if someone else would step up in my place and secure the election of my candidate. It might be a matter of great importance to me in a political context that it was *I* who brought about the result. There is of course an element of what might be thought of as expressiveness in this, in that I am motivated by the value of the action; but it is only of value to me *because* it

224   *The Tanner Lectures on Human Values*

is instrumental, and because I can rightly think I am achieving something directly through my vote.

There is a question which in its general form has not received as much attention as it deserves: In what circumstances do I want to bring about a result myself, even if someone else is morally certain to bring it about if I do not? For most economists, my desire to do something myself is merely an extra desire added to the wish to possess a particular good and can be treated simply as a matter of personal taste—some people (including me) like DIY; some don't. But there are areas where this looks implausible; the one which has received philosophical attention is charity or altruism, where it seems odd to say that I passionately want the hungry to be fed, but I would rather someone else did it.[13] I think that it is a fundamental feature of human existence that we *do* things: there is something very alien about the idea of a way of life in which we simply receive goods without actively *getting* them.[14] But we do not need to go into that more general issue here, since our participation in democratic politics looks like a very good instance of something where my agency is critical. If Rousseau and the other radical democrats were right in saying that laws have no full authority over me—or to put it another way, that the state is in some sense alien to me—unless I have taken part in making its collective decisions, then I cannot as a democrat look on my participation as being like a preference for making my own coffee table rather than buying one.

On an agentive view of this kind, majoritarianism will arise very naturally. On the one hand, if a vote required unanimity, then clearly, there would be very few times that any collective action could actually be agreed upon. Each time it was, I would indeed have taken a full part in determining the result, but because there would be so few occasions on which we could do anything, my overall agency—my capacity to transform the world in some way—would not be very great. And on the other, if a minority regularly got its way, then by definition, any particular member of the community would be likely to have less agency than if the decision was taken in accordance with the wishes of the majority.

This account seems to me to be more plausible than the most serious recent argument for majoritarianism, put forward by Jeremy Waldron.[15] Waldron has argued that the attraction of majoritarianism is that it is a decision procedure which respects both the principle of equality and the principle that "the fact that a given member of the group holds a certain view" has "positive decisional weight". The latter principle can be rephrased as *all other things being equal*; one member can decide the matter, and

[TUCK] *Active Democracy*

each of us could be that member—it is not specified in advance who it should be. Waldron had to propose this rather odd principle because a few pages earlier, he had assumed that a vote makes no difference to the outcome, has no "positive decisional weight", unless it is pivotal. There are two problems with his view, however. First, why should the mere possibility that a pivotal voter could decide an outcome be a reason for me to accept a majoritarian decision where there was *not* a majority of only one vote? But second, and I think more interesting, what would Waldron say about a well-organised process of sortition?[16] As we have seen, it certainly meets his fundamental test of equality among the citizens; a majoritarian form of sortition, as in a jury, also meets the condition of an equal chance of being pivotal. But it is, I think, not the kind of majoritarian democracy which Waldron wanted to defend.

Supermajorities, on the "active" account of democracy, are a matter of judgement (as indeed Rousseau said):[17] to require a supermajority is to render the proposed course of action less likely, but it does ensure that a larger group of people support the proposal. In general, however, there is a good reason to support a straight majority as a decision procedure, perhaps *especially* on important matters: a population which thinks that the status quo is unduly privileged, and that a minority of the population can block urgent change, may come to feel a general hostility to their political institutions. The experience of America with regard to its constitutional constraints, such as the difficulty in overturning the Citizens United judgement, is not reassuring.

Political scientists have often been puzzled by the so-called bandwagon effect, but on this account, it is entirely rational (given, as I said, my desire to take part) to join a bandwagon which corresponds more or less to what I want, this is the natural origin of political parties, which so many modern political theorists treat with a kind of high-minded disdain.[18] Furthermore, if my vote is a means of doing things and not merely a way of expressing a preference, it makes sense to think about *bargaining* with it, or forming coalitions with other voters who may want different things from me. Again, we must assume that I *want* to be effective in some way and do not *need* to be; but with that caveat, I can think about different ways of being effective, and some of those ways may not simply be voting for what I want. If it is possible for us to think of our vote as having an effect, it must be possible for us to think strategically about it. So a stark contrast between getting what I want and failing to get it may be misleading; there will almost always be new possibilities for me to get

226   *The Tanner Lectures on Human Values*

some of what I want if I can ally in some way with enough of my fellow citizens.

Moreover, any defeat is often likely to be temporary and provisional, a feature of democratic politics of the utmost importance; it is the temporary nature of any defeat which damps down the violent passions of the losers, since they live to fight again another day.

Compare the politics of abortion in the United States and the UK; indeed, I might say (though I am of course parti pris) that the history of the UK at least down to the 1970s is an often overlooked vindication of rather pure majoritarianism. One might not have expected that the country with the least constraints on its legislature of any in the world should have had a (relatively) stable and tolerant history, but I would say that it is precisely *because* there were no constraints that it had this history. The passions unleashed by Brexit illustrate what happens when a tradition of this sort is broken, and one side thinks it can have a near-permanent victory by entrenching in the UK the kind of economic policies embodied in the EU treaties.

This possibility, that an unconstrained electorate might, counterintuitively, be a more reliable basis for civil peace than a system of entrenched rights, should receive more attention from the defenders of what is often called "liberal" democracy than it does. Most clear cases of illiberal democracy in fact involve taking the vote away from minorities, either formally, through denying them citizenship, or informally, through corruption of the voting process, and this is actually testimony to the fact that majoritarianism, as long as it respects the clear condition that everyone should always have the vote, is not as potentially illiberal as people often imagine. In reality (as distinct from the abstract fears of antimajoritarians), a tyrannical majority can never be confident that coalitions of voters cannot be constructed to oppose them unless they deny the minority the vote. An obvious example is the way Reconstruction in the American South was brought to a halt, but even the Nazi war on Jews began with the Denaturalisation Law of 1933 and the Citizenship Law of 1935.[19]

The possibility that a democracy might pass laws of this kind is, however, sometimes used as an argument against the principle of majoritarianism, but this is to miss the point. It is rather like the equally mistaken idea that a fundamental problem with the principle of toleration is that it entails tolerating the intolerant. If doing so destroys the possibility of living in accordance with the principle, most people recognise, then it does not follow that the intolerant should be tolerated. From the Rousseauian perspective, the fundamental criterion for the authority of law is the universality of its origin in the popular will, and a democracy which deprived some of its citizens of the vote would simply have ceased to be a democracy and could claim no legitimacy for its acts. Its leaders would have staged a coup, and there would be no difference between this and a democracy simply handing over all its power to a single ruler. In his discussion of this process in book 3, chapter 10 of *The Social Contract*, Rousseau referred to it as *usurpation*. No known political system can in the end guard against coups; if the judges of the supreme court of a country with a completely entrenched constitution choose to interpret it in an illegitimate fashion, what recourse is left to the citizens? The most relevant question is, What kind of political system is least likely to engender the kind of hostilities which might lead to a coup? (Bearing in mind that political systems of any kind may not in the end be all that powerful against overwhelming social forces). And a perfectly plausible answer to this question is a system which offers the maximum scope for a relatively rapid change of policy, such that no one feels permanently prevented from getting something of what they want politically.

Practical considerations of this kind have played an important part in the intuitive hostility many people feel to a Rousseauian account of democracy, but there is another more theoretically salient doubt which is often expressed. It can be phrased as, In what sense is the result of a vote in which I have taken part of *my action* if I have in fact been outvoted? The answer to this question which Rousseau and the other early theorists of democracy (including, in this respect, Hobbes) always gave was, it is my action if I have agreed beforehand that I will accept the result of a majority vote. As Rousseau said in book 1, chapter 5 of *The Social Contract*, "If there were no prior convention, where, unless the election were unanimous, would be the obligation on the minority to submit to the choice of the majority? How have a hundred men who wish for a master the right to vote on behalf of ten who do not? The law of majority voting is itself something established by convention, and presupposes unanimity, on one occasion at least".

But there is a major problem with this way of putting the thought, and it comes out clearly through a comparison with Hobbes. Hobbes had said in *De Cive* (where he thought most deeply about democracy), like Rousseau, that "if the move towards formation of a commonwealth is to get started, each member of a crowd [multitudo] must agree with the others that on any issue anyone brings forward in the group, the wish of

228   *The Tanner Lectures on Human Values*

the majority shall be taken as the will of all; for otherwise, a crowd will never have any will at all, since their attitudes and aspirations differ so markedly from one another".[20] Unlike Rousseau, however, he believed that this majoritarian democracy could pass its authority on to an aristocracy or monarchy, since he took the relationship of the individual citizen to the democratic assembly of which he was part to be the same as his relationship to a monarch. In each case, the citizen had agreed that whatever the assembly, or the monarch, should decide, the decision would count as his own will. On this view, the outvoted member of an assembly is no different from a citizen who takes no part in its proceedings, nor indeed from a citizen of a country where there is no democracy: anyone who is willing to abide by the constitutional structure has given this general authority to the sovereign to act on their behalf. But if this is the basis for saying that the action of a majority is "mine" even though I am outvoted, then by the same token, the action of the majority is "mine" even though I did not vote at all, and that seems to undermine completely the force of the Rousseauian thought that we must all take part in an active fashion in making our laws.

But the way Rousseau himself phrased the point about prior unanimity made it (I think) too Hobbesian; what he had in mind was in reality closer to *posterior* unanimity than *prior* unanimity. The difference between the two comes out most clearly in what I called in my first lecture the most level-headed responses to Richard Wollheim's so-called paradox, such as Ross Harrison's. What these responses pointed out is that my initial vote is *provisional*: as a democrat, I agree that once the majority view is known, I accept it as my own. This democratic commitment is indeed prior to the vote, as Rousseau thought, but the alignment of my will with the will of the majority (to use the Rousseauian language) is posterior: henceforward I will act on the basis of a belief that the correct course of action *for me* is to do what the majority of my fellow citizens have expressly voted for.[21]

An important implication of this was brought out by Condorcet in his *On the Necessity of a Ratification of the Constitution by the Citizens* of August 1789, in a passage which also confirms that this is the right way to interpret a Rousseauian position:

> Any law accepted by the plurality [pluralité] of the inhabitants of a nation can be taken as having unanimous support: given the need to accept or to reject the law and to follow the plurality opinion

[TUCK] *Active Democracy*

[l'opinion du plus grand nombre], anyone who rejects a proposed law will already have decided to abide by it if it is supported by the plurality. This kind of unanimous approval will continue for as long as those who were alive at the time continue to form a plurality, since they were all able to consent to live by this law for this length of time. But such approval becomes meaningless as soon as these individuals cease to form a plurality of the nation.

Thus, the length of time for which any constitutional law [loi constitutionnelle] can remain in force is the time it takes for half of the citizens alive when the law was passed to be replaced by new ones. This is easily calculated, and takes about 20 years if the age of majority is fixed at 21, and 18 years if the age of majority is 25 [given a much lower life expectancy in eighteenth-century France than in the twenty-first century U.S. or U.K.].

The same is true of constitutions which are produced by a Convention, because then, once again, the plurality (and by extension all) of the citizens agree to abide by this constitution.

I consider it very important to set a maximum period for which a law can remain irrevocable. People no longer dare claim that there can legitimately be perpetual laws.[22]

Thomas Jefferson said exactly the same as Condorcet in his well-known letters from Paris to James Madison and Richard Gem in 1789, concluding that nineteen years was the appropriate time to revisit the constitution. He had presumably just read Condorcet's pamphlet.[23]

In this view, the actual implementation of a vote by an assembly is unanimous; at the point at which (for example) the resolution of an assembly becomes law, there *is* no minority. An important feature of this approach is that it avoids the theoretical—and indeed metaphysical—problems implicit in the idea of group agency as distinct from joint agency (to use the helpful distinction, for example, in Pettit and List).[24] The assembly for Condorcet or Jefferson is simply a set of individuals who have a common goal, and it is no different from a mob each of whom has the same desire, say, to tear down the gates of the Bastille. Indeed, one way of capturing what is implied in the agentive view is that it takes democracy to be in effect a kind of civilised and domesticated version of a mob—and that should not alarm us. Human beings, when they gather together physically, can effect great changes; it is not an accident that famous revolutionary moments are cases of mass action, such as the storming of the Bastille

230 *The Tanner Lectures on Human Values*

or the Winter Palace. And even in our own time, the major changes in world politics have been signalled by people actually meeting in large numbers and physically taking action, from the Paris streets in May 1968 through the Gdansk shipyard, the tearing down of the Berlin Wall, and Tiananmen Square to the Maidan and Tahrir Square. Beneath our placid democratic procedures, there is still this ancient fact. The great discovery of democracy was that people could accept a simple head count as the basis for the transformation which they might otherwise have effected through physical action and, potentially, violence. Obviously, legislative assemblies do not in general directly transform their surroundings, but the fact that there is a complicated set of conventions or laws which allow the actions of the assembly to be enforced does not (on a Condorcet or Jefferson understanding of the situation) transform the essential character of the assembly itself; the question of whether the object is directly material—the gates—or not (or only indirectly material) is a contingent one and does not affect the character of the joint action.

This generation of democrats feared a strong idea of group agency because, as Condorcet said, they feared the idea of perpetual laws. Or as Jefferson said, returning to the subject in 1816,

> It is now forty years since the constitution of Virginia was formed. [The tables of mortality] inform us, that, within that period, two-thirds of the adults then living are dead. Have then the remaining third, even if they had the wish, the right to hold in obedience to their will, and to laws heretofore made by them, the other two-thirds, who, with themselves, compose the present mass of adults? If they have not, who has? The dead? But the dead have no rights. . . . This corporeal globe, and everything upon it, belongs to its present corporeal inhabitants, during their generation. They alone have a right to direct what is the concern of themselves alone, and to declare the law of that direction; and this direction can only be made by their majority.[25]

Remember what I said in my first lecture about Bentham's attack on Sieyès for his desire to govern France "for ages after we are no more". They also feared perpetual, or at least prolonged, *debt*: their arguments applied not only to constitutional measures but also to public debt. On their account, a debt was contracted by the individuals acting in concert in the same fashion as it would have been by an individual acting alone, and it expired in the same way; the fact that (speaking metaphorically) an assembly might live forever did not mean that its debts could continue in perpetuity. The practical point of their argument was then that no assembly could bind its successors for longer than twenty years—it could of course repeal normal laws within this time period, but if it asserted that the law had some special status and degree of permanence, like a constitution, it could not make it last longer than twenty years. The dream of permanent laws has somewhat receded (except in Germany), but public debt remains a good example of how a state can commit itself to an obligation which it cannot rescind at any time of its choosing. On Condorcet's or Jefferson's account, however, an assembly could not undertake a debt with an expiry date of more than twenty years.

If we apply Condorcet's reasoning to a modern state such as the UK, the time limit is about forty-two years,[26] which oddly enough, is almost exactly the interval between the first EU referendum and the second! It is as if people possess an intuitive sense of when a major constitutional provision should be reopened. It is also the case that on the whole, governments do not nowadays borrow on a timescale of more than thirty years (e.g., the longest standard U.S. Treasury bond is thirty years), just as many of us have mortgages for the same period. This was by no means true even in the recent past, and governments still issue some undated bonds.[27] But if we exclude such cases, we can in practice get many of the features for which we might suppose a strong theory of group identity was necessary without having to postulate anything more than what we might term Condorcet agency.

A theory of collective agency of this kind answers the "Hobbesian problem" I raised earlier. However, unwilling I may first have been to take part in the action of a mob, if I do take part, I am actually effecting something in a way that the bystanders are not, even if they agree wholeheartedly with what the mob is doing. I am not "represented" by the other members of my mob, but the bystanders are. If we translate this to a legislative assembly, we can think of the laws it passes as the action of the entire body; that is indeed still the formal character of laws passed by the UK Parliament, which technically take the shape of petitions in the name of both houses to the queen to legislate,[28] to which she can (in theory) reply "La reine s'avisera": "We'll see". The assembly can represent the rest of the citizens, but the majority in the assembly does not represent the minority.

A theory of this kind also avoids the various problems connected with social welfare functions, of which the most famous is the so-called

232   *The Tanner Lectures on Human Values*

impossibility theorem of Kenneth Arrow. The fundamental idea behind an Arrovian social welfare function is that there could be a collective decision which corresponded in some more or less precise fashion to the interests or wishes of the citizens, with the collective decision looking like the same kind of thing as an individual decision—it should, for example, exhibit the same kinds of traits which an individual's judgement might be expected to display, such as noncyclicity in a ranking of alternatives. This is really a kind of representation of the citizens' preferences, in which the individual's wishes are independent of the function—that is, as Arrow himself put it, "individual values are taken as data and are not capable of being altered by the nature of the decision process itself".[29] Arrow contrasted his social choices with those made through strategic behaviour on the part of the citizens, or with the alteration of the citizens' preferences to fit in with the need to come to a decision, which would not exhibit the same contradictions, and he himself suggested that a Rousseauian approach would avoid his problems.[30]

As I have already stressed, a Rousseauian view of democracy has as a natural implication, universal suffrage and, in particular, suffrage for *habitants, resident aliens*. Very few modern states now allow this, though in the United States at least, it was widespread in the first thirty years or so of the new Republic. As Jamie Raskin has observed, it was not until after 1812 that it began to be abandoned, though exceptions continued throughout the nineteenth century; it finally disappeared from all states and from all elections at any level in 1928. But it has never been declared unconstitutional, and in recent years, a number of American municipalities have revived it.[31] An Illinois case of 1840 put the argument very clearly: the right of suffrage belongs "to those who, having by habitation and residence identified their interests and feelings with the citizen, are upon the just principles of reciprocity between the governed and governing, entitled to a vote in the choice of the officers of the government, although they may be neither native nor adopted citizens".[32] Aliens had to establish a certain degree of residence, but no more than one would have to do in order to appear on the electoral register after moving from Boston to New York.

In the United States, as this quotation illustrates, the practice of permitting aliens to vote could be seen as compatible with the idea of exclusionary citizenship, but that is a hard balance to maintain. If the vote, of all rights, is in the hands of noncitizens, why should they not count as citizens and the entire distinction between resident alien and citizen

[TUCK] *Active Democracy*

be abandoned? Indeed, something like this thought probably lay behind the disappearance of alien voting: with universal adult citizen suffrage after 1920, the only way to maintain an exclusionary kind of citizenship was to restrict the vote to citizens and not residents. But no theory of "active" democracy can countenance this distinction: the laws concerning our common life must be made by all those who are taking part in it, and residence is the only convincing test of whether someone is taking part—as is understood almost universally when it comes to questions of which citizens should have a voice in local government.

This is something Michael Walzer recognised in *Spheres of Justice* when he observed that "the rule of citizens over non-citizens, of members over strangers, is probably the most common form of tyranny in human history".[33] Walzer has been criticised for arguing from this that what he called "communities of character" must be free to decide who joins them from outside, and I think it is fair to say that the position espoused by Joseph Carens, that there should in general be open borders, is now much more popular even among political activists. But it was critical to Walzer's case that there should not be a distinction between citizen and resident, and he understood that this was something which might be difficult to square with open borders. Carens, strikingly, is less concerned with this issue and talks in *The Ethics of Immigration* in quite conventional terms about the process of naturalisation;[34] the idea that an immigrant should be a citizen within a few months of moving does not figure in his account, and one can see why. Both in theory and, even more, in practice, open borders really rely on a distinction between citizen and resident and on the relative powerlessness even of citizens; would employers in the United States still welcome large numbers of immigrant workers if they knew that these workers could immediately have political power over them? If all residents are to vote, it seems to me that *some* kind of immigration policy is necessary, though it should be as liberal as possible. At the moment, the bottleneck for citizenship is (so to speak) internal, but it makes better sense from the point of view of radical democracy for it to be at the border. To say this is not, however, to endorse a rich notion of "community" of the Walzerian kind. My own view is that the *only* thing that binds democratic citizens together is that they are engaged in creating through law and politics the conditions of their common life. No ethnic, linguistic or cultural criteria are relevant; indeed, I would say that the emphasis on *national* identity as it developed in the nineteenth century was inherently *antidemocratic*, since it required something other

234 *The Tanner Lectures on Human Values*

than the activity of democracy to be what united citizens, and by doing so, it devalued the activity.

NOTES

1 Aristotle, *Politics*, bk. 4, chap. 9.

2 The pope is technically elected by the clergy of the city of Rome, though the clergy are now cardinals drawn from all around the world. Since 1179, there has usually (but not invariably) been a supermajority requirement. An interesting contrast can be drawn with the choice of the pope of the Coptic Church, where a boy draws one of three names out of a chalice—a survival of sortition in part of the old Hellenistic world. The geographical distribution of majority voting, or indeed voting of any kind, deserves further study. It seems not to have been used in ancient China; it does not figure in the Old Testament, and examples in ancient India which have been described as "election" turn out on inspection to be cases of sortition. Sortition seems to be close to universal in human societies, but majority voting is (on the global scale) an unusual phenomenon, testimony perhaps to its psychological difficulty.

3 In his *Discourse on Political Economy*, Everyman ed. (1973), 122. The Roman comitia was not fully deliberative but a mechanism for permitting a very large body of citizens to vote after hearing a rather limited set of addresses from private citizens. See Andrew Lintott, *The Constitution of the Roman Republic* (Oxford: Oxford University Press, 1999), 45–46.

4 See in particular his pathbreaking article "Against Elections: The Lottocratic Alternative", *Philosophy & Public Affairs* 42 (2014): 135–78. Footnote 19 on p. 157 is a good survey of the modern literature on sortition, but it does not include Bernard Manin's important account of the history of the turn from sortition to election, *The Principles of Representative Government*.

5 "Representation and the Fall", *Modern Intellectual History* (2018).

6 See Greg Conti, *Parliament the Mirror of the Nation* (Cambridge: Cambridge University Press, 2019). And Philip Pettit, "Representation, Responsive and Indicative", *Constellations* 17 (2010): 426–34.

7 Except in the sense that it might be evidence for some kind of distortion in the electoral process that an assembly consists entirely of one sort of person. But on the Rousseauian account, it is not conclusive evidence, nor is it intrinsically undesirable, as long as the mandates of the electors are obeyed by the delegates.

8 Aristotle, *Politics*, bk. 4, chap.14.

9 *Socialism: An Economic and Sociological Analysis*, trans. J. Kahane (Indianapolis: Liberty Fund, 1981), 12.

10 See, for example, Dave Denison, "Defeating the Voters", *Baffler*, May 14, 2019.

11 *Free Riding* (Cambridge, MA: Harvard University Press, 2008).

12 The Romans managed to combine a secret ballot with serial voting by (in effect) announcing a rolling count and withdrawing candidates when they secured a majority; this was also a practical way of avoiding Condorcet cycling in elections, such as those for the tribunate where there were multiple candidates.

13 See Kenneth J. Arrow, "Gifts and Exchanges", in *Altruism, Morality, and Economic Theory*, ed. Edmund S. Phelps (New York: Russell Sage Foundation, 1975): 17–18; and Thomas Nagel, "Comment", in Phelps, *Altruism, Morality, and Economic Theory*, 65. Arrow's paper was also published in *Philosophy & Public Affairs* 1 (1972): 343–62. Later discussions are by James Andreoni, "Giving with Impure Altruism: Applications to Charity and Ricardian Equivalence", *Journal of Political Economy* 97 (1989): 1447–58; James Andreoni, "Impure

[Tuck] *Active Democracy* 235

Altruism and Donations to Public Goods: A Theory of Warm-Glow Giving",
Economic Journal 100 (1990): 464–77; and Robert Goodin, *Reasons for Welfare*
(Princeton, NJ: Princeton University Press, 1988), 155–57. Goodin coined the
appealing term "agency altruism"—see, for example, Nancy Flobre and Robert
Goodin, "Revealing Altruism", *Review of Social Economy* 62 (2004): 1–25.

14 In this context, there is a persistent and revealing confusion in the literature on
choice between "choice" and "preference". Preference does not imply action,
so I can (for example) have preferences with regard to the past—I prefer the
Girondins to the Jacobins. But I cannot *choose* the Girondins over the Jacobins
(unless I am being asked to do something now, such as rank them in a quiz).

15 *Law and Disagreement* (Oxford: Oxford University Press, 1999), 113–14.

16 He rejected a simple coin toss as a means of making a decision, but a representative sample of citizens seems, as I say, to meet his criteria.

17 Rousseau, *Social Contract*, bk. 4, chap. 2. On supermajorities in general, see the
appropriately critical remarks by Melissa Schwartzberg in *Counting the Many*
(Cambridge: Cambridge University Press, 2013).

18 Nancy Rosenblum being an exception. See her *On the Side of the Angels: An
Appreciation of Parties and Partisanship* (Princeton, NJ: Princeton University
Press, 2008).

19 The first took the vote away from naturalised Jews (about a quarter of the German Jewish population), and the second from all Jews. A less vicious but still
pertinent example would be the way the Protestant ruling class of Northern
Ireland in the 1970s used an archaic property franchise in the local government of the province to ensure a large Protestant majority, at a time when the
rest of the UK had moved (in 1945) to universal suffrage in local government.

20 Rousseau, *Social Contract*, bk. 4, chap. 2.

21 Daniela Cammack has drawn my attention to a remarkable passage in Demosthenes, which Rousseau (who admired Demosthenes) will have known. In it,
Demosthenes attacked the Athenians for being "double-dealers" because "they
praise the Spartans in all other respects, they do not imitate the most admirable of all their practices, but rather do the very opposite. For they say, men of
Athens, that among them [the Spartans] each man airs any opinion he may
have until the question is put, but when the decision has been ratified, they all
approve it and work together, even those who opposed it. Therefore, though
few, they prevail over many and by actions well timed they get what they cannot get by war". *Exordium*, Loeb ed., 35:2–3.

22 *Sur la necessité de faire ratifier le constitution par les citoyens*, Condorcet, *Oeuvres* IX (Paris, 1847), 415, translated in *Condorcet: Foundations of Social Choice
and Political Theory*, trans. and ed. Iain McLean and Fiona Hewitt (Aldershot:
Edward Elgar, 1994), 272.

23 *The Papers of Thomas Jefferson*, vol. 15, ed Julian P. Boyd (Princeton, NJ: Princeton University Press, 1958), 379–99.

24 Christian List and Philip Pettit, *Group Agency: The Possibility, Design and Status of Corporate Agents* (Oxford: Oxford University Press, 2011). It is worth
bearing in mind that a characteristic of many of these early democrats (especially Bentham and Marx) was a fear of "fictions" or "reifications". I would
say the same was true of Hobbes, despite the frequent attribution to him of a
notion of corporate identity; as in the case of his ideas on democracy, he was
much more ambiguous than is often recognised.

25 Letter to Samuel Kercheval, *The Writings of Thomas Jefferson*, vol. 15, ed. Albert
Ellery Bergh, "The Memorial Edition" (Washington, DC: Thomas Jefferson
Memorial Association, 1907), 42–43.

26   The UK has an electorate of forty-five million and a death rate in the adult population of about 540,000 p.a., so half the current electorate will be dead after approximately 42.5 years.

27   The British government finally paid off the last of its National War Bonds, issued in 1917, in 2015. Shortly afterwards, it paid off some Consols which contained debts incurred at the time of the South Sea Bubble, the Napoleonic Wars, etc.

28   Each bill that goes to the queen begins, "Be it enacted by the Queen's most Excellent Majesty, by and with the advice and consent of the Lords Spiritual and Temporal, and Commons, in this present Parliament assembled, and by authority of the same, as follows: 'Once assented to, the Act simply begins "An Act to"'".

29   Kenneth J. Arrow, *Social Choice and Individual Values*, 2nd ed. (New Haven, CT: Yale University Press, 1963), 7.

30   "The belief in democracy may be so strong that any decision on the distribution of goods arrived at democratically may be preferred to such a decision arrived at in other ways, even though all individuals might have preferred the second distribution of goods to the first if it had been arrived at democratically". Footnote: "Cf. Rousseau . . . : 'The law of plurality of votes is itself established by agreement, and supposes unanimity at least in the beginning.'" Arrow concluded that this "would require that individuals ascribe an incommensurably greater value to the process than to the decisions reached under it, a proposition which hardly seems like a credible representation of the psychology of most individuals in a social situation" (*Social Choice and Individual Values*, 2:90–91). But he was not, I think, aware of Rousseau's remark at the end of *Letters from the Mountain*—"Were it bad in itself, take it all together; by that alone it will become the best". He also thought that Rousseau was an epistemic democrat (p. 85 and 24n), something he may have been the first to suggest; he traced a version of epistemic democracy back to Frank Knight's 1935 essay on "Economic Theory and Nationalism".

31   See Jamin B. Raskin, "Legal Aliens, Local Citizens: The Historical, Constitutional and Theoretical Meanings of Alien Suffrage", *University of Pennsylvania Law Review* 141 (1993): 1391–1470.

32   Raskin, "Legal Aliens", 1405.

33   *Spheres of Justice: A Defense of Pluralism and Equality* (New York City: Basic Books, 1983), 62.

34   See his discussion in chapter 3 of *The Ethics of Immigration* (Oxford: Oxford University Press, 2013); on p. 60, he accepts that a country might legitimately require up to ten years residence before granting citizenship to an immigrant.

     The title of my Stanford lecture was "The Evolution of Societal Patriarchy."

The Evolution of Institutional Patriarchy

RICHARD W. WRANGHAM

THE TANNER LECTURES ON HUMAN VALUES

Delivered at

Stanford University
March 1–3, 2022

RICHARD W. WRANGHAM is the Ruth B. Moore Research Professor of Biological Anthropology in the Department of Human Evolutionary Biology at Harvard University. He received his PhD in zoology in 1975 from Cambridge University and conducted postdoctoral research in the Department of Psychology (Bristol University), Department of Psychiatry (Stanford University) and King's College Research Centre (Cambridge University). He taught in the Department of Anthropology at the University of Michigan prior to joining the faculty at Harvard in 1989. He has studied ecology, nutrition and social behaviour in various primates in the wild, including vervet monkeys and gelada, but his principal work has been on the ecological and behavioural comparisons of chimpanzees and humans. He has served as a trustee to several important primatological research organizations—including the Dian Fossey Gorilla Fund, the Jane Goodall Institute, and the Great Ape World Heritage Species Project—and is a past president of the International Primatological Society. Awards and fellowships include a MacArthur Foundation Fellowship (1987), the Royal Anthropological Institute Rivers Medal (1993), an American Academy of Arts and Sciences fellowship (1993), the Baron-von-Swaine Award (University of Würzburg 2000) and a British Academy fellowship (2013). Together with Elizabeth Ross, he cofounded the Kasiisi Project in 1997 and serves as an ambassador of the Great Apes Survival Partnership (GRASP). Among his many publications are *Demonic Males: Apes and the Origins of Human Violence* (with Dale Peterson), *Catching Fire: How Cooking Made Us Human*, and *The Goodness Paradox: The Strange Relationship between Virtue and Violence in Human Evolution*.

THE EVOLUTION OF INSTITUTIONAL PATRIARCHY

"If all Men are born free," Mary Astell asked in her best-selling *Some Reflections upon Marriage* (1700), "how is it that all Women are born slaves?"[1] Her question was a justified dig at the many Enlightenment thinkers whose concern for political equality was focused on men almost to the exclusion of women. Women as a group were subordinated, and the reasons were unclear.

Little has changed. For all their gains, women generally remain, in Simone de Beauvoir's words (1953), the second sex. And despite an immense scholarship, no explanations have been widely accepted for their subjugation.

In this essay, I address one facet of Astell's question—namely, institutional patriarchy. I define institutional patriarchy as "institutional arrangements that privilege males such that men (as a group) dominate women (as individuals or as a group)." I contrast it with "behavioural patriarchy," defined here as "relationships within the face-to-face community such that individual men dominate individual women."

Institutional patriarchy and behavioural patriarchy are intertwined because each strongly influences the other: "The personal is the political," as feminists have stressed since the 1960s. Laws in the United States used to permit men to rape their wives, but now they make marital rape illegal. Personal experiences might lead individuals to advocate either for or against institutional sexism. But even though institutional and behavioural patriarchy are intimately related, they work differently. Institutional patriarchy connotes arrangements, not behaviour, and is produced by institutions such as law. Behavioural patriarchy describes what actually happens when individuals interact, albeit individuals who are aware of the nature and power of law.

My aim is to understand why institutional patriarchy occurs, how it originated, and what implications it has for patriarchy as a whole. Curiously, despite much work on the impact of institutions on women's status (Pateman 1980; MacKinnon 2005, 2012; Hudson et al. 2020) and on the evolutionary biology of male domination (Smuts 1995), few efforts appear to have been made to explain the evolution of institutional patriarchy separately from behavioural patriarchy. The origins of patriarchy are undertheorized in general, and the distinction between the two types of patriarchy has been made only occasionally (Hunnicutt 2009, 2021). Nevertheless, a promising line of investigation is readily apparent. Institutions

[239]

240   *The Tanner Lectures on Human Values*

that are responsible for institutional patriarchy tend to be dominated by males. So an obvious question is how males came to dominate human social institutions.

Conventional approaches invoke three main sex differences in biology that interact with environmental factors such as social and economic forces to leave men on top (e.g., Wood and Eagly 2002). Men are stronger than women; thanks to mating competition and war, they are more aggressive; and women are constrained by their reproductive roles. The significance of these points is routinely disputed, however (Pateman 1980, 1988). Slave populations remind us that physical strength does not always predict social power. The men who use their institutional power to direct war are rarely involved in fighting. In other species, mating competition among males can lead to their being larger and better adapted for aggression without their dominating females (e.g., bonobos, *Pan paniscus*; Furuichi 2011; Surbeck and Hohmann 2017). And reproductive constraints do not stop females from dominating males in a variety of primates and other mammals (Lewis 2018). Such observations led Harari (2011, 172) to express his puzzlement about "why almost all cultures valued manhood over womanhood. We do not know what this reason is. There are plenty of theories, none of them convincing." Harari's assessment indicates that the field has advanced relatively little since 1949, when de Beauvoir (1953, 49) wrote, "Biology alone cannot provide an answer to the question that concerns us: why is woman the *Other*?"

In this essay, I offer a new solution to the problem of why women are not only "the other" but are also subjugated. My answer is evolutionary, but it does not refer to sex differences in anatomy, physiology or aggressiveness. It is based instead on sex differences in coalitional psychology. I argue that the ultimate source of the coalitions among males that underlie institutional patriarchy is that males are more fearful of being dominated by a tyrannical male than females are.

The approach builds on work by Christopher Boehm, who drew attention to an influential type of social network found throughout human societies but absent in all nonhumans (Boehm 1993, 1999, 2012a, 2012b, 2017, 2018). Boehm (1999, 8) called the novel phenomenon a "moral community." I prefer the term "alpha alliance." I define it as a set of individuals who collaborate successfully in support of each other's dominance over the rest of their group (Fig. 1).[2]

In small groups, such as nomadic hunter-gatherers, the alpha alliance can be the only alliance. In larger groups, such as state societies, the

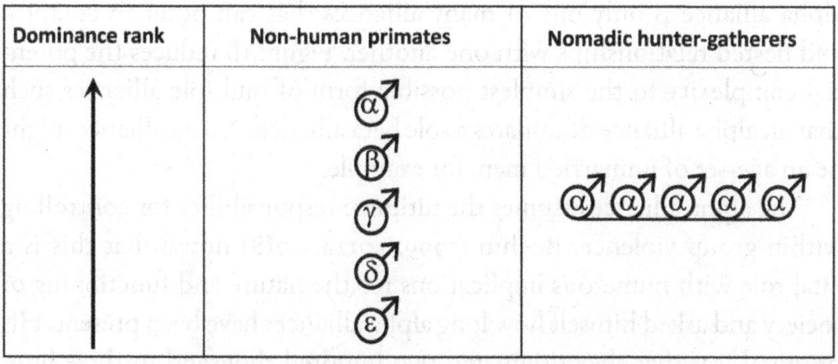

Dominance rank	Non-human primates	Nomadic hunter-gatherers
↑	♂(α) ♂(β) ♂(γ) ♂(δ) ♂(ε)	♂(α) ♂(α) ♂(α) ♂(α) ♂(α)

FIGURE 1A. Concept of male-dominance hierarchy in
nonhuman primates and nomadic hunter-gatherers.

The figure portrays groups with five adult males. In most nonhuman primates, male–male aggression generates a clear alpha who can defeat all his rivals in physical conflict, and natural selection favours individual fighting ability. Examples are chimpanzees, bonobos, gorillas and chacma baboons. Below the alpha, other males often form an approximately linear aggressive dominance hierarchy. In nomadic hunter-gatherers, by contrast, there is no alpha. The hunter-gatherer scheme represents societies with such a strong egalitarian ethic that no leader is recognized (e.g., !Kung San or Ju/'Hoansi; Lee, 1979). The line linking the men indicates that they are allied. Natural selection favours the ability of males to cooperate in forming and using their alliance. Their alliance enables them to resolve conflicts within the group in their own favour and to set self-interested norms.

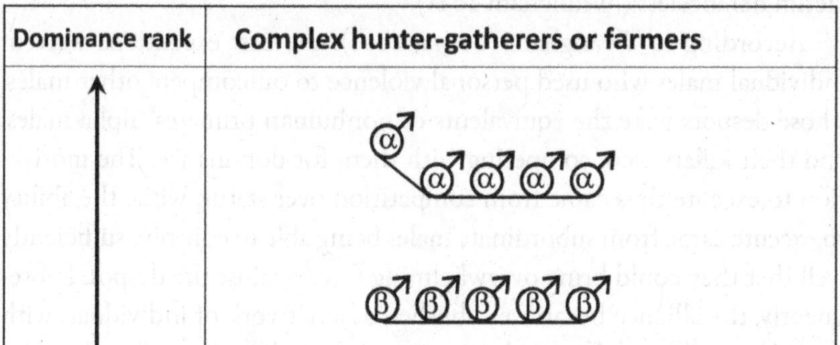

Dominance rank	Complex hunter-gatherers or farmers
↑	♂(α) ♂(α) ♂(α) ♂(α) ♂(α) ♂(β) ♂(β) ♂(β) ♂(β) ♂(β)

FIGURE 1B. Concept of male-dominance hierarchy in larger human groups.

The figure portrays a group with ten adult males in two alliances. Males of the alpha alliance use cultural institutions to dominate males of the beta alliance (e.g., in religion, law, control of police). Within each alliance, there can be formal or informal recognition of some individuals as leaders. Here, the alpha alliance is shown as having a leader. He is not an alpha, however, because his authority depends on support from his allies, not on his personal fighting ability. Even the most domineering human leader can lose his position if his allies desert him.

Only two alliances are portrayed in this figure, but in reality, most societies include numerous alliances that have complex relationships with one another, including nested alliances, alliance networks (alliances among alliances), and individuals who are members of more than one alliance.

alpha alliance is only one of many alliances that can occur in complex and nested relationships with one another. Figure 1b reduces the potential complexity to the simplest possible form of multiple alliances such that an alpha alliance dominates a sole beta alliance. A beta alliance might be an age-set of unmarried men, for example.

The alpha alliance assumes the ultimate responsibility for controlling within-group violence. Boehm (1999, 2012a, 2018) noted that this is a vital role with numerous implications for the nature and functioning of society and asked himself how long alpha alliances have been present. His proposal was that they originated two hundred thousand to three hundred thousand years ago in the Middle Pleistocene and have played the same control role ever since. However, he did not find a way to test that hypothesis.

In a refinement of Boehm's argument, I hypothesize that the alpha alliance achieved its dominance over the rest of society by virtue of its evolving a mechanism for safely killing other adults. The mechanism was targeted conspiratorial killing (TCK), a skill that was previously unknown in the ancestry of humans or any other vertebrate. The ability to plan and safely conduct executions was made possible by language becoming so sophisticated that killers could conspire to render a chosen victim defenceless (Wrangham 2021).[3]

According to Wrangham (2019a, 2021), the first executions were of individual males who used personal violence to outcompete other males. Those despots were the equivalents of nonhuman primates' alpha males, and their killers were competing with them for dominance. The motivation to execute thus came from competition over status, while the ability to execute came from subordinate males being able to conspire sufficiently well that they could bring overwhelming force against the despot. Subsequently, the alliance became established as a network of individuals with shared interests, and they used execution to control any group member who threatened the alliance's interests. The individual alpha male duly came to be replaced in the human dominance hierarchy by an alpha alliance.

According to this execution hypothesis, killing by the alpha alliance underlays two types of genetic change (Fig. 2).

First was selection against the kind of aggressiveness that made a male a successful alpha—namely, reactive aggression. This resulted in self-domestication (Wrangham 2019a, 2021).

Second was selection in favour of the psychological underpinnings that allowed a moral sense of right and wrong, where "right" meant

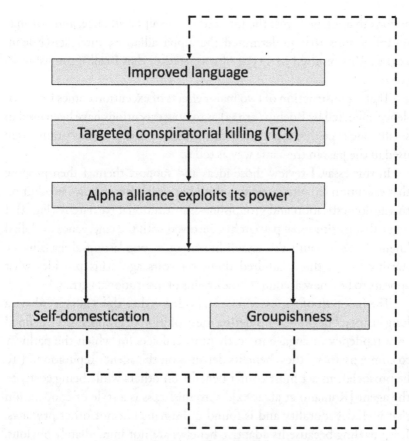

FIGURE 2. Evolutionary effects on self-domestication and groupishness of the ability to execute.

The figure shows the hypothesized consequences of an ability to conduct targeted conspiratorial killing (TCK), which is thought to have originated shortly before three hundred thousand years ago. *Homo sapiens* is the only vertebrate species known to have this ability (Wrangham 2021). The emergence of TCK is inferred to be due to sufficient improvement in linguistic ability that individuals could conspire to create a dangerous plan of killing the alpha male and enact it safely. The source of the supposed improvement in language skills is unknown. TCK benefited males in the alpha alliance who therefore used it regularly, leading to self-domestication and groupishness among other consequences. The dashed line indicates that as *H. sapiens* became more tolerant and cooperative, individuals would have become increasingly skilled at communicating, including through improved language. As a result, they would have become more skilled at conspiring and using their social power, leading to a positive feedback loop. See text for details and evidence. Figure created by Amar Sarkar using BioRender.com.

actions that aligned with the interests of the alpha alliance, and "wrong" meant actions that undermined the alpha alliance's interests (Boehm 2012a). This resulted in a type of cooperation that I call "groupishness" (below).

That reconstruction of two major effects of execution comes from evidence collected by Boehm (2012a) as to how executions have been used in small-scale societies, together with the assumption that executions were used in the past in the same way as today.

In this essay, I review those ideas and support them. I then propose that execution led ultimately to a third big social consequence in addition to self-domestication and groupishness: institutional patriarchy (Fig. 3). I argue that institutional patriarchy coevolved with the emergence of skilled linguistic ability and the establishment of a long-lasting alpha alliance starting before three hundred thousand years ago. This provides what appears to be a new account of the origins of institutional patriarchy.

The first part of the essay reviews evidence that alpha alliances have a long history. I begin by considering the evolution of groupishness, defined as "a tendency to engage in costly prosocial acts for which the pathway to compensatory fitness benefits depends on the agent's reputation." (To be prosocial, an act must confer benefits on others while being costly to the agent [Romano et al. 2022].) Groupishness is a style of cooperation that includes morality and is found in humans but not other primates. It is puzzling because its adaptive benefits are not immediately obvious. Lightly amending Boehm's proposal for explaining morality (a major form of groupishness), I argue that his core explanation is plausible. Specifically, I conclude that human groupishness evolved due to the enforcing actions of alpha alliances that rewarded cooperation and punished noncooperation. However, I also note that no way has been found to test the execution hypothesis for the evolution of groupishness directly.

In part 2, I turn to human self-domestication as a test of the execution hypothesis. Since Boehm did not consider self-domestication as part of his argument, the test is strengthened by being *a priori*. I show that data on self-domestication conform tidily to the hypothesis that the ability to execute arose shortly before 315,000 years ago. I conclude that the self-domestication data provide strong support for Boehm's theory, whereas no competing theories are satisfactory. Accordingly, I conclude that the capacity for execution, the loss of alpha males, the emergence of alpha alliances, and the sufficient ability to use language to establish norms all began shortly before three hundred thousand years ago.

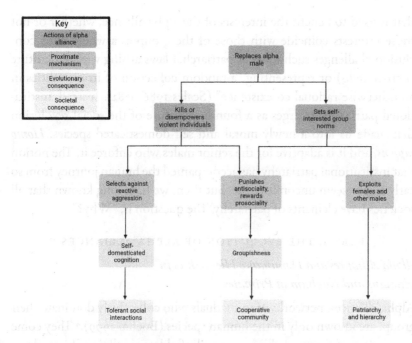

FIGURE 3. Simplified pathway showing three major social consequences of the evolution of alpha alliances.

The scenario begins with an alpha alliance replacing the alpha male atop the within-group dominance hierarchy. The second row portrays two major consequences for the social group: the alpha alliance uses its killing power to eliminate competitors, and it uses language to set norms for behaviour within the group. The third row shows the short-term behavioural consequences of enforcement by the alpha alliance. Selection against reactive aggression leads to a "self-domesticated cognition," including more cooperative communication, reduced impulsiveness, and greater docility (Hare 2017), while selection against norm violators and in favour of norm followers leads to an evolved tendency for groupishness. By contrast, no evolutionary effects on psychology have been proposed as having resulted from the alpha alliance's exploitation of other individuals. The social consequences shown in the bottom row are only those relevant to understanding the evolution of institutional patriarchy. See text for details and evidence. Figure created by Amar Sarkar using BioRender.com.

In the third part, I assume that the execution hypothesis is correct and consider its implications for the evolution of patriarchy. To anticipate my conclusion, I propose that the institutional subjugation of women has its origins in the alpha alliance's control of within-group violence among males, which then evolved into systems of law. According to this idea, legal norms originated in the Middle Pleistocene as a mechanism organized by males to protect themselves from being dominated by a tyrant (an individual alpha). Ever since, the law has been a dominant social institution that is used to benefit the interests of the alpha alliance, whether or not those interests coincide with those of the group as a whole. This conclusion challenges such ideas as patriarchal laws arising with agriculture (Lerner 1986) or representing "a random collection of irrationalities in an otherwise rational co-existence" (Scales 1986, 1382). Instead, institutional patriarchy emerges as a founding feature of the social revolution that made us into a newly moral and self-domesticated species, *Homo sapiens*, and it is adaptive for the senior males who enforce it. The notion that institutional patriarchy has accompanied the human journey from so early might seem uncomfortable, but then, we have long known that all societies have elements of patriarchy. The question is, "Why?"

PART I. THE EVOLUTION OF ALPHA ALLIANCES

Alpha Alliances and Dominance Hierarchies in Humans and Nonhuman Primates

Alpha alliances, networks of individuals who collectively dominate their group, are known only in the human species (Boehm 1999).[4] They come in a variety of forms, such as a council of elders, a religious hierarchy, a parliament, a senate, an oligarchy, or a monarchy. They are found in every human society, with wide variation in their size, composition, complexity, stability, and relationships with subordinate alliances.

In smaller groups, the members of alpha alliances are all male or mostly male. In larger groups, a male bias in composition is also almost always present, but there are often opportunities for females to belong. Alpha-alliance males are typically older than the average adult male in the group, making human societies generally both patriarchal and gerontocratic. Females who become part of the alpha alliance are also typically relatively old, past their conceptive years. Alpha alliances can be led by individual females, but those in which females outnumber males are vanishingly rare. The first national example of an alpha alliance numerically dominated by women was the Rwandan parliament, which, since 2008, has had more females than males (Bauer 2012). However, in practice, Rwanda in many ways remains deeply patriarchal.

The critical sense in which alpha alliances are politically dominant is that they regulate within-group violence, which they achieve by punishing those who violate norms of nonviolence, including by authorizing their execution. They also organize policies and activities in relation to other societies, whether peace or war. Following Boehm (1999), I assume that alpha alliances evolved from the typical systems of male dominance found in the nonhuman primates most closely related to humans—namely, the Catarrhini (old-world monkeys and apes). I therefore begin by briefly describing the Catarrhine system of male dominance.

Adult males present a persistent threat of violence to one another in the twenty or so Catarrhine species that live in multimale groups (Port et al. 2018). The nature and intensity of male–male combat are well understood as being ultimately adapted to competition for mating opportunities. Selection in favor of the most successful mating strategies has led to the evolution of superior fighting abilities in males. Compared to females, males have larger bodies, bigger and more dangerous weapons, and/or higher propensities for reactive aggression. Although these traits evolved by male–male competition, they can also be used in other contexts, such as against females, prey, or predators (van Schaik 2016).

An important social consequence of male–male aggression in nonhumans is the formation of a generally stable dominance hierarchy that predicts which of two competing males will win future conflicts. The hierarchy benefits both opponents by allowing them to avoid fights that are potentially costly to both despite having a highly predictable outcome. Accordingly, an unambitious subordinate tends to signal to the alpha that he accepts the alpha's dominant status. Subordinates who fail to signal their acceptance of being low status face a high risk of being challenged or attacked (e.g., Goodall 1986). Much male–male conflict is therefore over dominance status rather than over immediate opportunities to mate or feed.

The hierarchy is topped by a single male, the alpha, who has defeated all rivals in physical fights. The alpha tends to father a disproportionate share of offspring, resulting in his having high genetic fitness compared to other males (Ishizuka et al. 2018; McCarthy et al. 2020). There is therefore a strong selection pressure in nonhuman primates in favour of the kind of aggressive behaviour that enables a male to become an alpha.

Human political systems are both similar to and different from the male-dominance systems of nonhuman primates. They are similar in being headed by the most socially powerful individuals, in regulating the expression of violence within groups, and in enabling higher-ranking individuals to achieve higher genetic fitness. In contrast to nonhuman primates, however, in humans, there is no primate-style alpha, because when human political networks are headed by a single individual, he or she does not acquire their top-ranked status by defeating all rivals in one-on-one combat. Instead, the human leader's ability to achieve and maintain the top-ranked position is due to support from members of his or her alpha alliance. Such leaders can be very skilled at manipulating their supporters and rivals so as to protect their status, but they cannot control everything. During the 1,200 years between 600 and 1800 CE, about 15 percent of European monarchs died by being murdered, for example (Eisner 2011). In the words of Kokkonen et al. (2021, 146), "All regimes, even the most repressive, build on the cooperation of myriad individuals; the autocrat is simply the person at the top of the pyramid. Without the loyalty or obedience of the people under him, he is powerless." Even such autocrats as Stalin, Julius Caesar, or Genghis Khan are thus not alphas in the primate sense.

Admittedly, in some primates, such as chimpanzees, the alpha male can form an alliance with a subordinate male. This "alpha–subordinate" alliance benefits the alpha by giving him coalitionary support in aggressive interactions, while in return, the subordinate is allowed more mating opportunities than he could otherwise expect (Duffy et al. 2007; Feldblum et al. 2021). The alpha–subordinate alliance is thus valuable in reducing the alpha's effort to defend his status. It is not vital, however. Chimpanzees do not travel in permanent associations, so an alpha sometimes meets rivals without any of his allies being present. He must then be able to defeat any rival individually even without the help of a subordinate supporter (Goodall 1986). The equivalent is true of all other nonhuman primates with the possible exception of bonobos (Surbeck et al. 2019). In nonhuman primates, the alpha's alliances are luxuries, not necessities.

In human social groups, by contrast, a leader's ability to dominate depends (almost always) entirely on his or her being a member of an alpha alliance. Furthermore, members of the alpha alliance owe allegiance to one another. Human groups come in two types, those without or with a leader (Fig. 1).

Groups without a leader (acephalous societies) include most nomadic hunter-gatherers and some small-scale farming societies. Acephalous groups are characterized by anthropologists as egalitarian, a term that refers to relationships among mature men (Fig. 1a; Woodburn 1982; Flanagan 1989). Note that "egalitarian" does not refer to relationships between men and women, which vary from being relatively equal to highly patriarchal (see part 3). Nor does it imply that males are necessarily uninterested in power. It means only that among breeding males, there are "no sharp divisions of rank, status and wealth" and that "distinctions of rank and status are of minor significance" (Flanagan 1989, 245–46).

In other societies, including complex hunter-gatherers, states, and many small-scale subsistence groups, leaders occur and often take advantage of their power, occasionally translating it into extraordinary reproductive success (Betzig 1982, 2012). But again, because they are subject to the power of their alpha alliance, leaders are not alphas (Fig. 1b).

The alpha alliance functions both to constrain tyrannical behaviour and, when conflicts arise, to cooperate in subjugating other members of their social group whether by personal action (in small groups) or by delegation to others such as a kin group, the military, or police (in large groups). Adults who are institutionally subjugated can include both members and nonmembers of the alliance (Fig. 1b). In small groups, consistently subordinated males are mostly bachelors. With increasing group size, alliances that rank below the alpha alliance might include individuals grouped by factors such as age, sex, gender, ethnicity, economic class, professional activity, sexual identity, religion, and so on.

The human style of hierarchy has been termed "reverse-dominance" (Boehm 1993) or "counter-dominance" (Erdal and Whiten 1994). Note that these phrases are not intended to mean that the hierarchy has been eliminated or reduced in importance. They refer merely to the fact that the fortunes of any would-be alpha male have been reversed or countered by the alpha alliance. The dominance hierarchy itself continues to exist, albeit in a changed form.

Uniquely in humans, in sum, the alpha male has been replaced in the dominance hierarchy by an alpha alliance.

The Execution Hypothesis for How Alpha Alliances Evolved

Why do humans, but no other primates, have alpha alliances instead of alpha individuals? To answer this question, Boehm (2012a) argued that we should look to nomadic hunter-gatherers. Nomadic hunter-gatherers live in small groups and form alpha alliances often without any recognized leader. The fact that alpha alliances occur in all nomadic hunter-gatherers suggests that this pattern of male-dominance relationships has long characterized our ancestors.

The alpha alliance is puzzling at first glance because any male hunter-gatherer who went against tradition by becoming a primate-style alpha would appear likely to achieve evolutionary benefits. As an individual alpha, he could father the majority of offspring in his group, as happens in gorillas (*Gorilla beringei*) and other primates (Stoinski et al. 2009), instead of sharing paternity relatively equally, as happens in human societies in general (Betzig 2012). But according to ethnographies reviewed by Boehm (2012a), even an ambitious male hunter-gatherer does not normally vie to become an alpha male because he fears the reaction of his peers. Marlowe's (2010, 44–45) observation about Hadza men seems to capture the typical situation: "The Hadza certainly are egalitarian. This does not mean that there are no individuals who would like to dominate others and have their way. It is simply difficult to boss others around."

Boehm's (2012a) review of hunter-gatherer ethnographies illustrates why it is "difficult to boss others." Boehm found occasional cases of male hunter-gatherers trying to dominate access to resources within their group by fighting other males for their wives or meat. Efforts of this type ended with the would-be tyrants being killed by members of the alpha alliance. Such killings were conducted either by individuals acting alone or by a coalition and could be authorized in advance or legitimized post hoc, but whatever the mechanism, executioners received tacit or explicit approval from the alpha alliance. Boehm (1999, 2012a) concluded that socially approved executions explain why humans have alpha alliances instead of primate-style alpha individuals.

Thus, Boehm's idea for why alpha individuals are absent among humans is that any male who persisted in bullying all others into submission, as primate alphas do, would eventually be killed by his peers. At least five points support this argument.

First, so far as is known, capital punishment by ruling bodies (alpha alliances) is a human universal (Otterbein 1986; Boehm 1999). It is well known among state societies and other farmers. It has been recorded in nomadic hunter-gatherers in every continent, and although it has not been documented in every hunter-gatherer society (such as the Andamanese), the exceptions are easily explained by the ethnographic record being too limited (Boehm 2012a).

Second, ethnographies indicate that the absence of would-be tyrants does not result from a lack of ambition. Many men are greedy, and some even act on their desires, but most are afraid to do so. Liberman (1985, 259) was explicit about Australian hunter-gatherers: "It is not so much the absence of a desire for social power as it is a fear of the social consequences of their appearing to presume that they are better than their fellows."

Third, among nomadic hunter-gatherers, there is no method other than execution to stop a determined aggressor. A violent, selfish man who behaves without empathy or regard for moral norms is sometimes not deterred by such efforts to reform him as being ridiculed, cajoled, shouted at, exiled, or ostracized. In the absence of prisons or police, the renegade cannot be escaped. In these circumstances, force is the only solution. An alternative that has occasionally been suggested is that the entire group might hide from the tyrant (Endicott 1988). However, hunter-gatherers clearly have the skills to track and find each other.

Fourth, the fact that alpha alliances are not found in nonhuman primates is readily explained because humans are the only species capable of conducting capital punishment. Boehm (2012a, 2017, 2018) was mistaken about this point. He observed that within-group killings occur among chimpanzees (*Pan troglodytes*), and based on an erroneous idea that the victims tended to be alpha males, he suggested that chimpanzees are capable of executing alpha males. But alpha males are not the typical targets of within-group killings by chimpanzees. Only one killing of an alpha male has been reported, and the case was clearly unplanned. Usually, one of the killers is the alpha male, so within-group killings tend to reinforce the status of the alpha male rather than challenge it. Within-group killings among chimpanzees are therefore not equivalent to capital punishment (Wrangham 2021). Humans are the only vertebrate species known to be capable of deliberately putting an alpha to death.

Fifth, the question of why humans but no other species conduct capital punishment is answered by the consideration of how such killings happen. The key is that the killings take place only if they incur vanishingly little risk for the killers. After a decision to execute has been made, the intended killers accordingly wait for an opportunity when the victim cannot fight back, such as when the victim has no weapons or allies with him or can be shot in the back with an arrow.

Nonhumans such as chimpanzees are unable to share their intentions to kill a member of their own community and are therefore unable to assess their relative power over a target victim. Admittedly, a party of several male chimpanzees who cooperate with one another is easily able to overwhelm single adult males, as shown by scores of reports of their killing lone members of neighbouring communities, and they are able to make those intergroup kills safely by always having a substantial advantage of numbers, averaging eight attackers per victim (Wilson et al. 2014). With so many attackers, the victim is immobilized, and terrible damage is applied, from hitting and biting to ripping the thorax or twisting limbs until muscles tear (Goodall 1986; Wilson et al. 2014).

But those successes depend on each attacker being confident that his group mates will support him. Confidence in shared aggressive motivations is no problem when the victim belongs to another community because a simple rule of hostility to out-groups allows male chimpanzees to invariably treat members of different communities as "others." On the other hand, if a subordinate male chimpanzee was motivated to kill the alpha of his own group, he would have no basis for being sure how others would react to him initiating an attack. Although some might join him, others might side with the alpha, and others again might abstain. The uncertainty would mean that a large imbalance of power in favour of the attacker could not be guaranteed, so starting a fight would be risky. This difficulty in predicting how coalitions would be composed appears sufficient to explain why within-group executions are not undertaken among chimpanzees or any other mammal.

The essential problem is that chimpanzees have a relatively limited ability (compared to humans) to share and assess one another's intentions. Executions among humans, by contrast, depend on a dominant network approving the act. Such approval seems inconceivable without the use of language (Wrangham 2021).

In sum, the reason that humans are the only primate that has a dominance hierarchy headed by an alpha alliance rather than an alpha individual is attributable to humans being the only species capable of collaborating to safely kill even the most intimidating member of their own group.

The Groupishness Problem

Boehm's focus on alpha alliances emerged from his efforts to solve a problem of human cooperation. In Boehm's words, referring to humans, "Why do so many members of a supposedly egoistic and nepotistic species in some contexts become quite giving to people they aren't related to and sometimes don't even know?" (Boehm 2012a, 10). This problem has classically been described as a puzzle about the evolution of cooperation and has been intensely debated ever since Darwin (1871) first raised it.

Boehm's remarkable proposal differed radically from the conventional approaches, which are reviewed below, that had dominated the discussion for more than a century and had left the problem without a canonical solution. He hypothesized that a genetically based tendency for prosocial behaviour towards nonkin was selected because, for around a quarter of a million years, antisocial individuals were executed by alpha alliances. Meanwhile, prosocial behaviour was positively selected because the alpha alliance set norms for prosocial behaviour and punished norm violators. The combination of selection against antisocial tendencies and for prosocial tendencies fostered the evolution of the uniquely human style of cooperation that I call "groupishness."

Boehm himself never discussed patriarchy, but because his account of the evolution of groupishness required him to explain the existence of alpha alliances, it can potentially explain a vital contribution to institutional patriarchy. I will argue that that promise is realized. Specifically, I conclude that groupishness evolved out of the behaviour of alpha alliances and that alpha alliances created institutional patriarchy.

A confident understanding of why humans have institutional patriarchy therefore requires us to consider the evolution of groupishness and alpha alliances. To appreciate and assess Boehm's hypothesis, we must consider how other scholars have tackled the problem of groupishness, why it has been difficult to solve, and why Boehm's solution, with appropriate modifications, is appealing. This process requires us to understand groupishness in some detail.

I apologise for introducing the term "groupishness," a play on "selfishness." "Groupishness" is essentially a new term in this context. It is far from ideal, but a new word is needed because despite the much discussion by evolutionary theorists of this kind of behaviour, amazingly, the behaviour has never been given a convenient descriptor. Instead, people refer to it by terms that either describe the system (such as "cooperation among unrelated individuals"; Gintis et al. 2001, 103) or refer to the behavioural tendency with a phrase (e.g., "being prone to engage in a system of indirect reciprocity"; Sigmund 2013, 202). Haidt (2012, 223) used "groupishness" to refer to an "ability to transcend self-interest and lose ourselves in something larger." My definition follows the spirit of Haidt's "transcending immediate self-interest" while being precise about the evolutionarily relevant mechanism. Thus, I define groupishness as a tendency to engage in costly prosocial acts for which the pathway to compensatory fitness benefits depends on the agent's reputation.

Groupishness can be contrasted with all other kinds of evolved social behaviour, including not only competitive interactions but also prosocial investments in mates, offspring, kin or nonkin alliance partners, whether involving direct reciprocity, pseudoreciprocity or generalized reciprocity (Connor 2010; Taborsky et al. 2021). As explained below, those "nongroupish" acts could equally be called "second-party behaviour," while nongroupish prosociality would be "second-party prosociality."

In some respects, groupishness and nongroupishness are functionally identical. Considering only prosocial acts, both types of behaviour are altruistic (that is, they confer a benefit to another individual at a cost to the actor's reproductive value). Equally, theorists assume that both types of behaviour tend to be adaptive (tending to maximize the agent's fitness), which means that in an evolutionary sense, both are selfish. Thus, in those respects, groupishness and nongroupishness cannot be differentiated.

Instead, the critical difference between them is how the return benefit is gained. Nongroupishness is a simpler system. In that case, the return benefit to be derived from a prosocial act comes from the recipient (which is why nongroupishness can be called "second-party behaviour"). If an agent invests in a nonkin ally, for example, the return benefit might come from that ally giving coalitionary support to the agent. The return benefit need not be behavioural. When an agent donates food to its offspring, the return benefit comes from a probable increase in the offspring's condition, favouring the agent by kin selection. An important feature of return benefits being reciprocated directly is that agents can assess for themselves the likelihood of their prosocial act leading to a return benefit and can therefore adjust their level of investment rather precisely so as to maximise the probable net gain (Taborsky et al. 2021).

The more opaque system, groupishness, is defined by the return benefits coming from the actions of a third party who observed the agent's prosociality themselves or else heard about it from gossip. To understand why the agent would first benefit an unrelated second party from whom they can expect no return benefit, we assume that a third party predictably tends to provide a return benefit. A vital question, therefore, is why the third party can be expected to give anything to the prosocial agent (Trivers 1971). Proposed explanations focus on the agent's reputation having been enhanced by the evidence of their prosociality. They fall into two types.

The first is indirect reciprocity, which was traditionally supposed to be the most important but which now seems relatively unimportant. I follow Roberts et al. (2021) in defining indirect reciprocity as occurring when the third party pays a cost to benefit the prosocial agent. Economic experiments show that people tend to give to those with good reputations (Wedekind and Milinski 2000; Wedekind and Braithwaite 2002; Milinski et al. 2001; Milinski et al. 2002; Rotella et al. 2021). This supports the idea that indirect reciprocity can explain groupish acts because it suggests that when third parties pay to provide a return benefit, they do so in the expectation that investment in reciprocity with the groupish agent is likely to be beneficial.

The fact that the third party pays a cost is critical: it means that the third party's behaviour is an investment rather than being immediately self-serving. When defined in this way as involving a cost paid by the third party, the term "indirect reciprocity" refers to a restricted subset of what was once thought of as "a catch-all term for benefitting through third parties," regardless of whether a cost was paid (Roberts et al. 2021, 2). For example, Alexander (1987, 85) was one of those who used "indirect reciprocity" as a catchall term. He regarded indirect reciprocity as occurring whenever "the return is expected from someone other than the recipient of the beneficence . . . [that is,] from essentially any individual or collection of individuals in the group." Because Alexander paid no attention to whether the third party paid any costs (like many others, for example, Nowak and Sigmund 2005), he inadvertently encompassed in his concept of indirect reciprocity both the more restricted definition of indirect reciprocity used here and a very different explanation for groupishness—namely, signalling.

Signalling the agent's quality is the second, and only alternative, explanation for why third parties are expected to respond positively to an agent's enhanced reputation. Evidence that the agent is high quality supposedly leads third parties to choose to interact positively with the agent, which they do for their own selfish reasons, without paying a cost to do so. For example, a third party who is already in search of a mating partner might choose the agent as their mating partner in preference to some other individual. That particular form of signalling has been called Return-Benefit-Partner-Choice, or RBPC (Roberts et al. 2021). Signalling theories would thus explain the third party's beneficence towards the prosocial agent as being immediately self-serving, unlike indirect reciprocity (which involves an investment). Signalling now appears to be a much more important mechanism than indirect reciprocity for explaining groupishness (Roberts et al. 2021).

Why, then, in the light of indirect reciprocity and signalling theories, was groupishness favoured in human evolution? Evidence that indirect reciprocity actually occurs among humans is very limited in naturalistic contexts. Only in lab experiments, which are of course unnatural in many ways, has indirect reciprocity been favoured as an explanation of groupishness (Bshary and Raihani 2017). This makes indirect reciprocity an unlikely explanation for the evolution of groupishness.

The presence of alpha males at the time when groupishness originated would have added severely to the difficulty. Indirect reciprocity depends on the punishment of free riders being effective. But alpha males would be expected not only to act as free riders (taking without giving) but also to be impervious to attempts to punish them (Phillips 2018), unless they could be stopped by a coalition.

By contrast, individuals' motivation to signal their quality to a partner has often been shown to lead them to manipulate their reputation (Bshary and Raihani 2017). Signalling theories are therefore clearly favoured, and Boehm's is the only signalling theory that has been advanced to explain why being groupish would benefit the agent.

The reputational signal that Boehm (2012a) argued as being critical for the evolution of groupishness is evidence of conforming to norms set by the alpha alliance. His hypothesis was that the alpha alliance, presumably through the use of language, set norms that benefitted its interests and used execution or the threat of execution to punish norm violators. The ability of the alpha alliance to kill cheaply meant that it paid every group member (including those in the alpha alliance) to avoid being perceived as a norm violator. Groupishness, accordingly, is seen as having evolved as a signal of willingness to follow group norms.

That is the key takeaway. When groupishness is appropriately defined as behaviour that is favoured via its effects on the agent's reputation, explanations that invoke indirect reciprocity are inadequate. Groupishness evolved as an adaptation to the imposition of group norms, which implies the existence of an alpha alliance setting the norms.

In sum, groupishness is a motivational tendency to be generous towards nonkin. Its evolution is best explained by signalling theory, such that prosocial behaviour that is unexpectedly generous or self-sacrificial signals an individual's commitment to group norms. This conforms to the idea, which is strongly supported in general, that the evolution of cooperation is often favoured by an enforcement mechanism suppressing noncooperators (Frank 2003, 2013; Ågren et al. 2019). The execution hypothesis suggests that groupishness is favoured because the alpha alliance tends to act as an enforcer, rewarding prosocial behaviour and punishing antisocial behaviour.

As an aside, a fascinating aspect is that nongroupish and groupish motivations are necessarily in conflict with each other, as Durkheim (1973) noted: individuals will often have to decide whether to be selfish in the short-term (in other words, be nongroupish) or to invest in their reputation (i.e., be groupish). This means that a theory is needed to explain which tendency an individual will follow on any particular occasion. Unfortunately, the important criterion for deciding to engage in a groupish act is expected to be the act's predicted impact on the agent's reputation, which means that the decision involves guesswork. The problem is that agents will only rarely be able to estimate how their reputation will be affected. Among the uncertainties are whether the recipient will tell others about being aided, how honest the recipient will be, and how many third parties will notice the aid.

Agents therefore have too little information to know with any precision how groupish they should be. The difficulty is illustrated by moral dilemmas. The preferred solution to a moral dilemma is sometimes deontological, meaning that people decide according to their internalized moral rules. But sometimes the solution might be utilitarian, meaning that the agent tries to maximise the beneficial outcome for society as a whole. Overall, there appear to be no general rules beyond an effort to build or maintain a positive reputation (Nowak and Sigmund 2005).

Given this state of inevitable ignorance, agents seem to develop their own individual principles for modulating their degree of groupishness, as seen in the wide range of individual tendencies for being groupish, from "saints" to "sinners." The "saint" strategy is low risk with regard to being punished by the alpha alliance but is unlikely to lead to high resource acquisition. Conversely, the "sinner" strategy is high risk with regard to incurring punishment while creating more opportunities for resource gain (by being more nongroupish than groupish). Whether individuals act as saints or sinners might have as much to do with personality traits or fighting abilities as with the immediate context (cf. Sell et al. 2012).

The evolution of groupishness therefore produced a species in which individual behaviour is especially unpredictable. This unpredictability can be expected to contribute to individual variation in attitudes to moral issues, including patriarchy.

Similar Concepts to Groupishness

Groupishness, as I have defined it, is closely related to various similar terms or concepts concerned with characterizing puzzling forms of nonkin cooperation found in humans compared to other mammals, including strong reciprocity, extrafamilial generosity, generalized altruism, prosociality, a morality of fairness, norm psychology, ultrasociality and hypercooperation. To justify the use of groupishness as a term, and

258   *The Tanner Lectures on Human Values*

to clarify the differences among terms, here I review their similarities and differences.

This section thus serves merely to explain how groupishness is related to similar concepts and why all other terms that have been used are unsatisfactory. Nonspecialists can omit it without loss.

We have already seen in the previous section that "indirect reciprocity" differs from groupishness. Groupishness is a behavioral tendency, whereas indirect reciprocity is a mechanism that might explain how the tendency is rewarding. Furthermore, indirect reciprocity is only one such mechanism. Another is signalling.

Groupishness is very similar to "strong reciprocity." Both describe a costly psychological tendency for which the route to receiving rewards is unknowable (Gintis 2000). Strong reciprocity has been described as "a predisposition to cooperate with others and to punish those who violate the norms of cooperation, at personal cost, even when it is implausible to expect that these costs will be repaid" (Gintis et al. 2003, 153), or "the essential feature of strong reciprocity is a willingness to sacrifice resources for rewarding fair and punishing unfair behavior even if this is costly and provides neither present nor future material rewards for the reciprocator" (Fehr et al. 2002, 3). Those definitions, which are typical, differ from my "groupishness" because they imply that there are no future rewards at all. "Strong reciprocity" also has the difficulty of being an inappropriate word for describing the agent's initial behaviour, which, although possibly performed in the expectation of reciprocity, is not itself an act of reciprocity. Further confusion involving the term "strong reciprocity" comes from its being used to describe both the behavioural tendency and a specific explanation for that tendency (based on group selection; Bowles and Gintis 2004; West et al. 2011).

Boehm (2012a, 9) used "extrafamilial generosity" to mean "being generous to people lacking any blood ties to the generous party." That concept has the disadvantage that its key criterion is the kin relationship of recipients rather than the route by which return benefits are received. As a result, it confounds prosocial acts towards nonkin that are relatively easy to explain (those directed towards allies or mates—that is, second-party prosociality) with others that are puzzling (those directed towards individuals who are unlikely to reciprocate directly).

"Generalized altruism" has been used in a somewhat similar way to "extrafamilial generosity" to mean "prosocial behaviour toward unidentified 'others,'" but it has a different proviso of excluding altruism directed towards members of the actor's social group ("group solidarity"; Baldassarri 2015, 359). Like "extrafamilial generosity," "generalized altruism" so defined refers to who it is directed to rather than to the ability of the actor to assess how or whether the altruism will be repaid. It can be a useful definition for conducting empirical studies.

"Prosociality," defined as "a costly act that confers benefits on other people" (Romano et al. 2022) includes both groupishness and a wide range of nongroupish behaviours such as investments in kin and alliance partners.

"Moral behaviour" is often used to mean "behaviour guided by a sense of right and wrong," but it has also been defined, similarly to my definition of "groupishness," by its underlying evolutionary mechanism. For example, Alexander (1987, 77) stated that "moral systems are systems of indirect reciprocity." If "indirect reciprocity" is taken to mean "returns from third parties" (which would include signalling), that definition could in theory be identical to groupishness. However, many scholars would find Alexander's definition too limited, since morality can come in two forms, a "morality of sympathy" and a "morality of fairness." A "morality of sympathy" involves generosity expressed within dyadic relationships of nonkin and is found in various animals, including great apes (de Waal 2006). By contrast, only humans are considered to have a "morality of fairness" motivated by a sense of justice (Tomasello 2016; Engelmann et al. 2017; McAuliffe and Santos 2018).[5] Morality can also be delimited as "natural," meaning "prosocial attitudes independent of what [individuals] learn from culturally elaborated norms" (Li and Tomasello 2021, 101). A natural morality of fairness is thus similar to evolved groupishness. However, groupishness is a larger concept than morality, since it allows for other prosocial traits such as spirituality and collective effervescence (Xygalatas et al. 2011; Páez et al. 2015).

"Norm psychology" connotes a set of mechanisms responsible for moral behaviour. It has been defined as "a suite of psychological adaptations for inferring, encoding in memory, adhering to, enforcing and redressing violations of the shared behavioural standards of one's community" (Chudek and Henrich 2011, 218). Norm psychology is thus an important mechanism underlying a major component of groupishness—namely, a morality of fairness.

"Parochial altruism" is defined as a combination of altruism towards nonkin of "one's own ethnic, racial, or other group" together with hostility towards members of other groups (Choi and Bowles 2007). It is thus a specific type of groupishness expressed in the context of intergroup aggression.

Terms such as "hypercooperation" or "ultrasociality" have been used to refer to humans' exceptional prosociality towards nonkin and are sometimes apparently intended to capture the same essential features as what I am calling groupishness (Burkart et al. 2014; Tomasello 2014; Gintis et al. 2015; Kessler et al. 2018; Henrich and Muthukrishna 2021). However, groupishness is only one major source of hypercooperation. Others are humans' exceptional cognitive abilities that enable complex systems of punishment, reward and reciprocity (West et al. 2011), and culturally transmitted patterns, including those that result from group-structured cultural selection (or cultural group selection; Henrich and Muthukrishna 2021). Cultural selection for cooperation results from social arrangements that are the product of norms, norm enforcement, institutions, et cetera, rather than being evolved psychological tendencies derived from genetic selection.

The difference between nongroupish and groupish tendencies drawn here is very similar to the difference that Durkheim (1973) drew between what he called egoism and altruism, found in his writings after 1895 (Hawkins 1977; Fish 2013).

Past usages of groupishness have varied widely. For Evans et al. (2019), "groupish" groups were those that exerted a particularly strong effect on their members, such that the expected range of behaviours was very narrow, and any deviation from them was seen as illegitimate. Miller (1998, 1502) used "groupish" to refer to "a propensity to combine with others in collective, simultaneous, and instantaneous mobilization of survival drives directed to survival of the group." For Collins (1983), "groupishness" was a collective orientation (in that case, characteristic of Japanese society). None of those usages has become widespread. They should not be confused with my definition. I previously defined groupishness as "a tendency to cooperate and be prosocial in ways that appear to transcend genetic self-interest" (Wrangham 2021, 1). That definition is compatible with the definition that I use here but is less precise.

Note that the psychological tendencies underlying both groupish and nongroupish behaviour can be either evolved or learned. The primary concern of this essay is with evolved groupishness.

Evidence for Groupishness Being an Evolved Trait

Groupishness includes giving to strangers, donating in anonymous settings, rewarding good deeds, punishing norm violators and self-sacrificing on behalf of a perceived moral right (Fehr and Fischbacher 2004; Choi and Bowles 2007; Sigmund 2013). A canonical example comes from cross-cultural experiments: in various economic games, humans are more generous than a nongroupish theory of selfishness would predict, whether hunter-gatherers, small-scale horticulturalists or individuals in state societies (Henrich et al. 2005).

Evidence for groupishness being genetically based comes from social emotions that are expressed in the context of reputation management. Shame and pride, which are known only in humans, are found to be strongly linked with concern about reputation (Sznycer et al. 2016; Sznycer et al. 2017). Importantly, shame is associated with blushing, which is an involuntary display also linked to embarrassment and maintenance of reputation and found in all human populations but not in nonhumans (Crozier 2010; aan het Rot et al. 2015). The close association of an uncontrollable signal with concern about reputation is strong evidence of groupishness being partly genetically encoded.

Numerous experiments have also compared individuals' tendencies for social behaviour when in the presence or absence of eye cues, such as stylized images of human eyes. A meta-analysis of fifteen studies found that eye cues reduced antisocial behaviour by an average of 35 percent (Dear et al. 2019). A positive effect of eye cues has also been reported on prosocial behaviour, but the effect varies substantially according to experimental context (Rotella et al. 2021).

In keeping with the above evidence for genetic influences on groupishness, prosociality in human infants suggests that human tendencies to be more cooperative than other primates are evolved traits. As expected, chimpanzees (and presumably all other animals) are not concerned about their reputations (Engelmann et al. 2016). Thus, human infants exhibit components of norm psychology earlier in life than is easily explained by cultural learning (Graham et al. 2013; Tomasello 2016). By three years old, children intervene to enforce a norm of avoiding harm, and they tend to discriminate against norm violators (Yucel and Vaish, 2018). Individuals start managing their behaviour at around five years old in ways that enhance their reputation (Engelmann et al. 2012).

Cultural input is evidenced when groupishness is associated with indoctrination or other environmental factors. For example, indoctrination appears to explain self-sacrifice in war. That kind of heroism has rarely been documented in hunter-gatherers but is reported relatively often in societies with a militarized culture (Wrangham 2019a). Fear of supernatural punishment appears responsible for religious believers increasing their prosocial behaviour after being reminded about their God (Shariff et al. 2016). Cross-cultural studies of the ultimatum game find that larger offers are made towards anonymous recipients in societies with more experience in markets (Henrich et al. 2005). These examples show groupishness originating in or being strongly influenced by culture. Note that they do not invalidate evidence that groupishness is also an evolved tendency.

West et al. (2011) noted that many nonhuman species display altruism towards nonkin and can use punishment to enforce cooperation. They therefore argued that there is nothing special about human tendencies for prosociality, which is as selfish as it is in other species. Admittedly, all adaptive behaviour is ultimately selfish. However, altruistic tendencies can be positively selected as either nongroupish or groupish behaviour, and only humans are known to be groupish via a system of third-party behaviour.

In sum, while some forms of groupishness are purely cultural, others are evolved. This means that groupishness needs an evolutionary explanation.

Proposed Explanations for Groupishness

In *The execution hypothesis for how alpha alliances evolved*, I described how Boehm's execution hypothesis aims to explain the evolutionary loss of alpha males in humans. Below, I consider how the same hypothesis also accounts for the evolution of groupishness. First, I briefly review the three principal approaches that have been taken to date.

Consideration of groupishness as an evolutionary problem began with Darwin's (1871) analysis of why people behave in ways that are considered to be morally right. The theoretical challenge comes from the fact that moral behaviour such as aiding nonkin incurs self-sacrifice by the moralist. Darwin concluded that if selfish individuals cheat moralists by accepting benefits while offering nothing in return, ordinary natural selection theory could not explain the evolution of moral behaviour. His analysis has been universally accepted, leading to continuing debate about how to solve the problem. The critical difficulty is to explain why cheating (free riding) is not favoured.

Like many subsequent theorists, Darwin favoured a solution invoking genetic group selection (Darwin 1871; Hamilton 1975; Sober and Wilson 1998; Choi and Bowles 2007; Wilson 2012). The essential claim of this approach is that cooperation within the group can have such beneficial effects in improving between-group competitive ability that from an evolutionary perspective, self-sacrificial cooperators gain more than they lose. However, although conditions under which this process could operate have been theorized (Choi and Bowles 2007), they have not yet been shown to be realistic for human evolution (West et al. 2011; Dyble 2021). For example, rates of intergroup migration among humans appear to be too high to allow sufficient group stability for group selection to be significant (Langergraber et al. 2011). A specific context in which the benefits of within-group cooperation have been argued to be large enough to explain the evolution of groupishness is war, based partly on the idea that human warfare is more lethal than intergroup aggression in nonhumans (Alexander 1990; Flinn et al. 2005; Choi and Bowles 2007). However, other species are now known to experience rates of death in intergroup aggression that overlap with those among hunter-gatherers, suggesting that human war is not as evolutionarily unique as once thought (Johnstone et al. 2020; Wrangham 2021). Overall, since humans do not fulfil the stringent criteria for group selection to operate, multilevel genetic selection theories for the evolution of groupishness remain debatable at best (West et al. 2007; Boomsma 2016).

A second approach invokes the cultural evolution of cooperative norms, which could eventually lead to genetic selection for mechanisms underlying groupish behaviour, including norm psychology (Boyd and Richerson 2005; Richerson et al. 2016). Cultural evolution can occur in a variety of ways. Major mechanisms include powerful individuals imposing new rules on their group, existing norms being lost due to environmental disasters, or cultural differences in cooperation contributing to success or failure in between-group competition (Singh et al. 2017; Henrich and Muthukrishna 2021).

Cultural selection theory would see groupishness as having been favoured initially by novel behaviours, especially punishment of norm violators, that were themselves enabled by increasing cognitive abilities (Richerson et al. 2016). Such punishment, which appears to be a cultural universal (Henrich et al. 2006), would have stabilized cooperation (Fehr and Fischbacher 2004; Gavrilets et al. 2008; Boyd et al. 2010). After a tendency to punish norm violators arose, it could in theory have spread by cultural selection, even if it were costly for the punishers, as a result of benefits at the group level. Genetic selection would subsequently add to its effectiveness by making appropriate elements of a norm psychology innate (Henrich and Muthukrishna 2021). Similar arguments invoking gene-culture evolution can be imagined for moral emotions, such as shame and embarrassment. Like genetic group selection, cultural selection theory for the evolution of cooperation remains controversial. It is hard to test and is argued by some to be unnecessary (Krasnow and Delton 2016; Burton-Chellew et al. 2017).

Humans' exceptional cognitive abilities are essential components of both genetic group selection and cultural selection theories, but they have also been proposed to favour the evolution of groupishness purely by individual selection, as noted above ("The Groupishness Problem"). One version of this approach notes that systems of indirect reciprocity could emerge by modification of abilities involved in direct reciprocity that would enable individuals to monitor, respond to and communicate about one another's reputations. Once those cognitive abilities evolve, intelligent individuals could supposedly create a system of indirect reciprocity that is self-serving despite the need to conduct costly punishments (Alexander 1987, 1990; Flinn et al. 2005; Nowak and Sigmund 2005; Sigmund 2013). The idea is supported by experiments. When agents in small groups perceive that someone who fails to cooperate in one context is likely to be a noncooperator in general, they tend to punish spontaneously and benefit from doing so (Krasnow et al. 2015). Other things being equal, therefore, systems of indirect reciprocity can in theory evolve by individual selection, at least in some contexts (Romano et al. 2022). But when we compare contemporary subjects with the population of human ancestors in which groupishness arose, it seems unlikely that "other things are equal." In particular, aggressive dominance was likely to have been present in the form of a selfish and powerful alpha male. This undermines the theoretical plausibility of indirect reciprocity being able to evolve (Phillips 2018).

In sum, genetic group selection, cultural selection and individual selection are the main candidate mechanisms that have classically been used to explain the evolution of groupishness, and all are debatable. Strikingly, even though in each case, the main goal is to explain why free riding is not favoured, none of them directly addresses the alpha-male problem. Instead, they implicitly regard human society as having been sufficiently egalitarian by the time that groupishness evolved that free-riding tyrants could not easily have coerced resources from others in their group in the way that happens routinely among nonhuman primates. That omission is of vital importance because if alpha males were present when groupishness first evolved, the difficulty of explaining the constraints on free riding is greatly increased (Phillips 2018). On the other hand, if alpha males are supposed to have been absent when groupishness first evolved, their disappearance needs to be explained (Wrangham 2019b). At some point in human or prehuman ancestry, alpha males were lost, and whenever this happened, the loss should have greatly facilitated the evolution of cooperation. Knowing when alpha males were lost, therefore, should provide vital clues about the evolution of third-party systems of prosociality.

The Execution Hypothesis for Groupishness

Boehm's solution for the evolution of groupishness is unusual in treating the nature of the male-dominance hierarchy as a significant theoretical challenge (Boehm 1999, 2012a, 2012b, 2014, 2017, 2018). As we have seen, Boehm argued that alpha-style behaviour was selected against as a result of subordinate males becoming sufficiently skilled in coalitionary behaviour that they could safely kill the alpha. Anyone who tried to outcompete others would have been vulnerable to being killed in their turn, as evidenced by Boehm's ethnographic survey. The winning coalition of originally subordinate males therefore supposedly stabilized into a long-term alliance that kept any of its members from becoming alpha themselves.

It was the selfish behaviour of this alpha alliance, in enforcing norms that benefited themselves, that Boehm suggested led to groupishness. If the alpha alliance had the coalitionary skills to eliminate the alpha male (the most intimidating member of any group), it was clearly able to intimidate any other group member. Based on behaviour in small-scale societies, Boehm argued that the alpha alliance would have punished those who acted "wrongly," meaning against the alpha alliance's interests, and rewarded those who acted "right." Individual selection would accordingly have favoured individuals who followed alliance-imposed norms (Fig. 3). Punishment by the alpha alliance supposedly included execution as well as a series of lesser sanctions that would have had lesser fitness consequences.

Warner's (1958) study of the Murngin hunter-gatherers in Australia illustrates an alliance's readiness to punish a norm violation with execution: "If a young man chances upon an old man engaged in making a totemic emblem, the former is killed. . . . A Mandelpui boy came upon two old Liaalaomir men making a totemic emblem. When they saw him they said, 'Come look,' and with smiles and gestures indicated their approval of his having a closer view of their totem. This was to put him off his guard; a few days later they ambushed him and killed him" (Warner 1958, 159–61).

The young man in that case would have been a subordinate member of the group, not yet having joined the alpha alliance (which Warner called "the superordinate male group"). But members of the alliance were also subject to sanctions, as Warner (1958, 394) made clear:

> The superordinate male group, made sacred through the ritual initiation of its individual members into the sacred group, and maintained as a unit by continual participation in the rituals, subordinates the female group which is united by virtue of exclusion from the ceremonies and of ritual uncleanliness. . . . Within this mystery lies one of the strongest and most effective sanctions found in Murngin society. . . . The ceremonial mysteries of the male group, then, help subordinate not only the women and younger boys but also the men themselves, since they too cannot profane the sacred mysteries by some impure and illegal act; if they do, the male group feels obliged to act. . . . It is in the ultimate sanctions of the totemic system that Murngin society finds its final unity.

The execution hypothesis is consistent with a rich set of data from contemporary ethnographies of nomadic hunter-gatherers and larger-scale societies showing that the group (in other words, the alpha alliance) both controls despotic male tendencies and maintains moral norms by punishments that include killing (Boehm 1999, 2012, 2018; Otterbein 1986). It also fits the fact that decisions to be moral are often taken in relation to a fear of punishment (DeScioli and Kurzban 2009) and that people tend to show strong conformity to the norms of the group with which they identify (Sunstein 2019).

The hypothesis has other merits. It accounts for males in small-scale societies having egalitarian social relationships in the form of the alpha alliance (Boehm 1993; Erdal and Whiten 1994). It fits the inference that Pleistocene *Homo* were already skilled killers of large animals (Ben-Dor and Barkai 2020), suggesting that well-planned kills of group members would have been low risk for executioners. The idea that Pleistocene *Homo* were capable of within-group killing is also supported by the fact that coalitions of chimpanzees make adaptive kills of conspecifics from other groups, although chimpanzees appear incapable of planning lethal attacks on members of their own community (Wrangham 2021). The execution hypothesis thus has much in its favour.

Against it, however, the execution hypothesis for groupishness is difficult to test because the frequency and context of Pleistocene executions are unknown, and groupishness leaves no known traces in the fossil record. When and how rapidly groupishness was influenced by the proposed selection pressure therefore cannot be estimated directly.

With regard to the skills necessary for execution, two main explanations have been advanced to explain where they came from: lethal weaponry or sophisticated language.

The weapons idea is that spears or thrown rocks enabled coalitions of individually subordinate males to exert increased control over alpha males by killing them more easily and safely than before. A shift from handheld to projectile weapons could also have played a role. Such weaponry supposedly reduced the benefits of individual fighting prowess and gave power to the disadvantaged by making killing efficient (Gintis et al. 2015, 327). Variations of this argument were made by Woodburn (1982), Bingham (2001), Okada and Bingham (2008), Boehm (2012a), Phillips et al. (2014) and Chapais (2015).

Weapons or other tools (e.g., rope) are almost always used in executions, but whether they are either sufficient or necessary is questionable. If they were sufficient, we would expect executions to have been carried out by many or all species of *Homo* and certainly by *Homo heidelbergensis*, Neanderthals and Denisovans, but those species show no signs of selection against reactive aggression. Weapons do not seem to be necessary either, given that alliances of animals such as chimpanzees, wolves and lions can efficiently kill lone victims (Wrangham 2019b).

The focus on sophisticated language comes from the evidence described earlier that although chimpanzees have the cognitive ability to make coalitionary kills of males from other groups, they are unable to kill alphas in their own group. The carrying out of a planned execution requires that the killers share explicit intentions with one another. This capacity, shared intentionality, is unique to humans (Tomasello 2016). Chimpanzees cannot communicate to others that they wish to kill a particular individual, let alone justify their desire, find out if their partner feels the same way or plan to meet at some future time at a specified place in order to carry out the deed. Those kinds of abilities depend on a sophisticated form of language (Wrangham 2019a, 2021).

Many, perhaps all, species of *Homo* presumably had some level of linguistic ability. But this idea suggests that *H. sapiens* was the only species with sufficient language skills for execution. The art of forming lethal coalitions would have been dangerous. The skills they needed would include the ability to make subtle suggestions and plausibly deny accusations of

268 *The Tanner Lectures on Human Values*

making threatening plans. How such abilities evolved is unknown, like the evolution of language in general. Note that the conclusion that males found language especially valuable for forming dangerous conspiracies does not imply anything about sex differences in the long-term development of linguistic skills.

In sum, evolved groupishness occurs in humans and no other primates. Traditional theories of genetic group selection, cultural group selection or cognitive skills have failed to consider how alpha-male behaviour was selected against and have not yet produced convincing explanations for groupishness evolving. Compared to those three approaches, Boehm's execution hypothesis differs by being the only one that purports to explain how selfish behaviour by alpha males would have been selected against (Boehm 1999, 2012; Wrangham 2019a).

The problem with the execution hypothesis is that with regard to groupishness, it seems impossible to test because signals of groupishness are psychological: they do not fossilize. A test is possible, however, when a second major consequence of execution is considered—namely, self-domestication.

PART 2. SELF-DOMESTICATION AS A TEST OF THE EXECUTION HYPOTHESIS

Self-Domestication as a Test

This section presents data on self-domestication as a test of the execution hypothesis. I define self-domestication as a reduction in a species' propensity for reactive aggression that occurs without any other species being involved (Wrangham 2021; cf. Theofanopoulou et al. 2017). Since a high propensity for reactive aggression enables alpha males to achieve and maintain their dominant status, the execution of alphas is expected to have selected against the propensity for reactive aggression or, in other words, to have produced self-domestication. Fortunately, self-domestication can in theory be recognized in the fossil record from changes in cranial and skeletal anatomy. This means that the fossil record should be able to provide a test of two predictions from Boehm's execution hypothesis.

First, the hypothesis predicts that a self-domestication syndrome emerged during the evolution of *Homo*. If there is no evidence of a *Homo* ancestor having experienced selection against reactive aggression, the evolutionary loss of alpha males must have happened before the origin of *Homo*, such as during an australopithecine phase (between roughly seven and two million years ago). Such an early loss of alpha males would essentially invalidate the idea that executions were responsible for groupishness, because it is highly unlikely that australopithecines, whose brains were barely larger than those of living great apes, had sufficient cognitive skills to monitor reputations adaptively.

Second, Boehm (2012a) cited archaeological evidence that meat came to be more widely shared starting around 250,000 years ago and suggested that this signal of increased sociality showed the evolution of a morality of fairness. If Boehm was right, a self-domestication syndrome should be detectable 250,000 years ago.

Self-Domestication as a Biological Phenomenon

Domesticated mammals often differ from their ancestors or closest wild relatives in characteristic ways, including changes in size, pigmentation, skull anatomy, physiology, reproduction and social behaviour. These biological correlates of domestication were first described by Darwin (1883) and are known as the "domestication syndrome." More than forty traits have been proposed to be part of the domestication syndrome (Price 1999; Wilkins et al. 2014; Lord et al. 2020).

Confusingly, the domestication syndrome is unpredictable with regard to the traits found in any specific individual, population or even species. For example, domesticated animals such as cats, dogs, horses and goats are more likely than their wild relatives to have a white "blaze" on their forehead or white tips on their legs. Yet despite this overall trend, many individuals within those species do not have a white blaze on their forehead or white tips on their legs, and in some other domesticates such as llamas and gerbils, such features are rare or entirely absent (Sánchez-Villagra et al. 2019; Lord et al. 2020). The unpredictability of the combination of traits means that the domestication syndrome can easily be defined out of existence (Lord et al. 2020). However, when defined as a "repeated occurrence in domesticated mammals of a set of distinctive traits, none of which were deliberately selected," it is a robust phenomenon (Wilkins 2020, 143; Trut et al. 2020; Zeder 2020).

In 1959, Belyaev (1969) launched research aimed at understanding why the domestication syndrome occurs. He observed that all domesticated animals are tamer than their wild ancestors and duly hypothesized that the biological correlates of domestication resulted from selection for tameness. By selecting captive foxes (*Vulpes vulpes*) based on how closely juveniles would allow a human to approach before they showed an aggressive or fearful response, he produced results that strongly supported the idea (Belyaev and Trut 1975; Trut 1999; Trut et al. 2009; Dugatkin and Trut 2017). Results have been replicated in mink, rats, mice and chickens (Singh et al. 2017; Agnvall et al. 2018; Geiger et al. 2018; Katajamaa and Jensen 2020). In these studies, selection for tameness or docility led to a rapid increase in the frequency of traits belonging to the domestication syndrome.

In those experiments, as with most cases of domestication, the selection pressure for tameness was imposed by humans. The principle that selection for tameness generates a domestication syndrome, however, does not depend on humans being responsible. Evolution is not expected to be affected by whether the selection pressure is exerted by another species (such as humans) or by within-species interactions. All that is expected to matter is that selection acts against reactive aggression and favours a more docile personality.

Accordingly, wild animals that have experienced selection for reduced reactive aggression are expected to show a domestication syndrome. This prediction has been examined in detail for bonobos (Hare et al. 2012). Male bonobos show reduced adaptations for reactive aggression compared to chimpanzees, which provide a model of their common ancestor (Muller et al. 2017). Bonobos also show numerous elements of the domestication syndrome, including short faces, smaller teeth, smaller brains, reduced sexual dimorphism in teeth, reduced body mass, reduced brow ridges, increased play, increased gregariousness, increased tolerance, delayed cognitive development and neotenous crania compared to chimpanzees (Hare et al. 2012; Hare 2017; Rosati 2019; Wrangham 2021). The many convergences between bonobos and domesticated mammals indicate that subsequent to their splitting from a chimpanzee-like ancestor about one million years ago, bonobos have "self-domesticated." The cause of their self-domestication is uncertain, but an ecological hypothesis has been proposed based on reduced interspecific competition for food among bonobos than chimpanzees (Hare et al. 2012). Regardless of why bonobos self-domesticated, they provide extraordinary support for the prediction that selection against reactive aggression leads to a domestication syndrome (which in their case is more properly called a "self-domestication syndrome").

Other potential cases of self-domestication that have been reported recently come from wild marmosets, *Callithrix jacchus* (Ghazanfar et al. 2020), urban populations of red foxes, *Vulpes vulpes* (Parsons et al. 2020), and the evolution of dogs from wolves, *Canis lupus* (Coppinger and Coppinger 2000).

Human Self-Domestication

As long ago as Aristotle, writers have observed that humans are exceptionally docile compared to wild animals and have deduced that humans are more like domesticates (Wrangham 2019a). In 1795, the "father of anthropology" Johann Blumenbach argued that humans really were domesticated, and a century later, Bagehot (1872) and Boas (1938) applied the term "self-domesticated" to humans (Boas 1938, 76). However, it was not until 2003 when Helen Leach reviewed the anatomical evidence that the idea of human self-domestication was investigated scientifically. Since then, much relevant evidence has appeared.

The argument began with anatomy. Leach (2003) noted that archaeologists are sometimes uncertain whether the fossil skeletons of early Middle Eastern domesticates—especially cattle, sheep and goats—represent wild or domesticated populations. To decide the question, they tend to rely on a combination of features that characterize domesticates compared to their wild ancestors, especially "reduction in size and stature, cranial gracilization, changes in post-cranial robusticity, shortening of the face and jaws, tooth crowding and malocclusion, and tooth-size reduction and simplification" (Leach 2003, 355). Strikingly, all of these criteria were found in humans by the end of the Pleistocene. This suggested to Leach that humans had experienced an evolutionary process that was akin to domestication. As she pointed out, it was surprising that the strongly domestication-like features of human ancestry had not previously provoked any search for an overarching explanation.

When exactly the domestication-like changes began has not been identified. Probably the earliest dates will prove to be different for different traits. However, the changes that Leach (2003) noted as characterizing humans are all associated with the species *Homo sapiens*, which is generally less heavily built than its ancestors. It is because of this that when Hublin et al. (2017) found fossil crania from Morocco dated at ~315,000 years ago having a slightly less protruding face, smaller chewing teeth and less prominent brow ridges than ancestral forms, they assigned them to *H. sapiens*. Hublin et al.'s judgement made the Moroccan material the earliest evidence of *H. sapiens*, which marks it also as the earliest appearance of the recent human self-domestication syndrome.

Cieri et al. (2014) studied how two aspects of human cranial anatomy assumed to be part of the domestication syndrome—namely, brow ridge projection and the shape of the upper face—have changed over the last two hundred thousand years. They found that over time, brow ridges were progressively reduced and faces progressively narrowed and shortened (Fig. 4). Overall, the craniofacial changes reflected a tendency for feminization, meaning that characteristically male features changed in the direction of female features.

The long-term reduction in facial width is particularly enlightening because variation in facial width among living individuals has been studied extensively in relation to a series of indices of aggressive behaviour. Facial width is typically indexed by a ratio of bizygomatic width to height (nasion-to-prosthion; facial width-to-height ratio, or FWHR). Relatively wide faces (higher FWHR) are found in men compared to women, in larger compared to smaller men and in lower compared to higher SES (socioeconomic strata), but they do not differ by race or by whether men have a beard (Short et al. 2012; Geniole and McCormick 2015; Noser et al. 2018). In meta-analyses, higher FWHR has also been found to be associated with more threatening behaviour, more antisocial behaviour and more fighting, as well as with higher fighting ability (Geniole et al. 2015; Haselhuhn et al. 2015). In a smaller sample, FWHR was also found to be positively associated with psychopathy in males, as measured by a combination of fearless dominance, self-centred impulsivity and cold-heartedness (Anderl et al. 2016). The decrease in facial width thus suggests

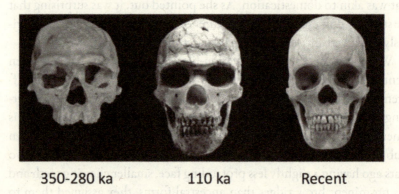

FIGURE 4. Cranial changes in *Homo sapiens*.

The leftmost picture shows a facsimile of a skull from Jebel Irhoud in Morocco dated at ~315,000 years ago (Hublin et al. 2017). The central skull is an adult male, Skhul 5, found in Israel and dated to 110–90 thousand years ago. On the right is a recent African male (*right*). Note the large brow ridges and wide masculinized face characteristic of the left two (Middle Pleistocene) humans. The two more recent specimens were scaled to the same nasion-bregma height and aligned on those landmarks. Photographs © David Brill (Cieri et al. 2014; Fig. 1) and Natural History Museum, London (Stringer and Galway-Witham 2017).

that the tendency for aggression has been consistently reduced throughout the approximately three hundred thousand years of *H. sapiens*.

The two most recent close relatives of *H. sapiens* are Neanderthals (*H. neanderthalensis*) and Denisovans (which do not yet have a formal binomial name). These two species split from the *H. sapiens* lineage by around five hundred thousand years ago. In neither case is there any evidence of self-domestication. Neanderthal crania are well known and have relatively large, wide faces (Fig. 5). No fossil crania are known for Denisovans, but their face shape has been reconstructed based on their DNA methylation maps in comparison with Neanderthals and chimpanzees. Like Neanderthals, Denisovans were reconstructed as having a wide face (Fig. 5; Gokhman et al. 2019). Other evidence that Neanderthals were not domesticated comes from comparisons with *H. sapiens* of their cranial growth pattern (more paedomorphic in *H. sapiens*), prognathism (longer face in Neanderthals), brow ridges (larger in Neanderthals), teeth (larger in Neanderthals) and brains (larger in Neanderthals; Theofanopoulou et al. 2017). Given the many similarities between Neanderthals and *H. sapiens*, the implication of Neanderthals not being self-domesticated is that their use of language was less skilled than in *H. sapiens*. The putative difference in linguistic skill may have been relatively small, but it was enough to allow *sapiens* to conduct capital punishment adaptively in a way that Neanderthals could not.

The difference in evidence of self-domestication means that Neanderthals, and to a lesser extent Denisovans, offer the opportunity for a genetic test of the proposal that *H. sapiens* have undergone self-domestication. The prediction is that *H. sapiens* differ genetically from those two close cousins in the same way as domesticated mammals tend to differ from their closest wild relatives.

This question has been approached by first comparing genomes of dogs, cats, horses and cattle with their close wild relatives (Theofanopoulou et al. 2017). Genes undergoing positive selection in the four domesticated species were compared across species. There were enough similarities to indicate that the researchers had found a set of genes associated with the domestication syndrome. Those "domestication genes" were then compared with genes that had been positively selected in *H. sapiens* compared to Neanderthals. Significant overlap was found between the mammalian "domestication genes" and those that had been positively selected in *H. sapiens* compared to Neanderthals. These data thus provide support for *H. sapiens* having been self-domesticated (reduced in reactive

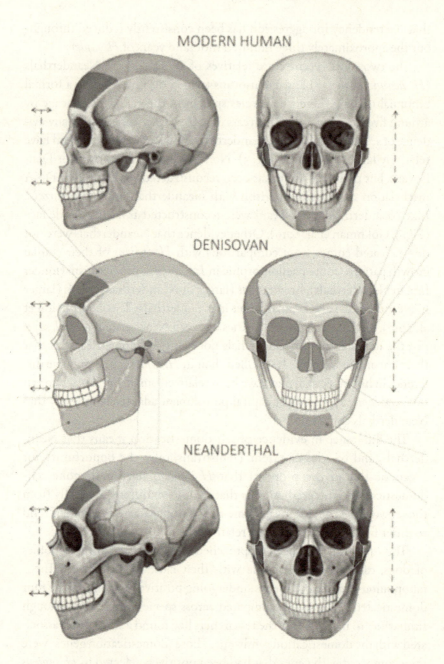

FIGURE 5. Facial width in three recent species of *Homo*.
Modern humans (*H. sapiens*) have a narrower face than Neanderthals or reconstructions of Denisovans. The figure is taken from Gokhman et al. (2019).

aggression) at some point after about five hundred thousand years ago (Theofanopoulou et al. 2017).

The specific genetic pathways that generate the domestication syndrome are still not well known, but a leading candidate is a mild neurocristopathy—that is, a reduction in the rate of migration and/or total number of neural crest cells (Wilkins et al. 2014; Rubio and Summers 2022). Effects of a neurocristopathy are well established in the production of unpigmented hair at terminal sites of melanoblast migration (tips of feet, tail and forehead), a common feature of domesticated animals (San-Jose and Roulin 2020). In other cases of domestication-linked traits—such as floppy ears, short face, reduced brain size and increased tameness itself—the putative effects of neurocristopathy are plausible but unproven (Wilkins et al. 2014; Wilkins 2017). However, supportive evidence for the neurocristopathy hypothesis has been found in comparisons of at least eight domesticated mammals with their relatives, from cats and rabbits to buffalo and camels (Wrangham 2021).

The idea that a mild neurocristopathy contributes to the domestication syndrome is therefore certainly plausible. Researchers have accordingly examined genetic differences between *H. sapiens* and Neanderthals to find out whether they are related to neural crest cell migration. The hypothesis of a domestication syndrome in *H. sapiens* is again supported because compared to Neanderthals, genetic changes in *H. sapiens* have been found in gene BAZ1B, a major regulator for neural crest migration affecting hundreds of relevant genes (Theofanopoulou et al. 2017; Zanella et al. 2019; Andirkó et al. 2022). Self-domestication has been estimated from this analysis to have begun between five hundred thousand and three hundred thousand years ago (Andirkó et al. 2022).

In sum, the hypothesis that selection against reactive aggression occurred during the existence of the genus *Homo*, which originated around two million years ago or earlier, is supported by fossil evidence of a self-domestication syndrome starting around three hundred thousand years ago. The conclusion that the cranial anatomy of *H. sapiens* represents a transition towards self-domestication is supported in turn by genetic data because *H. sapiens*, but not Neanderthals or Denisovans, exhibit similar genetic changes to those found in domesticated mammals.

To recapitulate, the execution hypothesis predicts that a self-domestication syndrome would be found. Anatomical and genetic data on self-domestication in *Homo* ancestry offer a test of the execution hypothesis, and the prediction is upheld.

276   *The Tanner Lectures on Human Values*

Boehm's idea, based on studies of cut-marked bones from animals that *Homo* had killed, was that the self-domestication syndrome would be seen around 250,000 years ago. That prediction is supported too, since self-domestication is evidenced by ~315,000 years ago.

The evidence for self-domestication in *H. sapiens* thus provides remarkable support for the execution hypothesis and places the timing of execution rather precisely, shortly before three hundred thousand years ago.

The Potential Role of Females in Human Self-Domestication

So far in this essay, I have discussed evidence that the self-domestication syndrome in *H. sapiens* was caused by the emergence of an ability to execute safely, that an alliance of males killed the alpha and that the motivation for the original formation of the killing alliances was competition among males. That scenario is inferred from the assumption that the present is the key to the past: in other words, the behaviour of contemporary nomadic hunter-gatherers is seen as a continuation of prehistory. The supposed responsibility of males for initiating the process is also justified by the claim that subordinate males would have derived large fitness benefits from the elimination of the alpha-male role.

But of course, males are not the only ones affected by the male-dominance hierarchy. If other explanations can be found for human self-domestication, they will call the execution hypothesis into question. Here I consider the potential for female–female coalitions and female choice of mating partners to have contributed to self-domestication and the loss of the alpha-male role.

Female–female coalitions are especially thought-provoking because they are thought to have contributed to self-domestication in bonobos (Hare et al. 2012; Hare and Wrangham 2017). Male bonobos show reduced adaptations for aggression compared to male chimpanzees, prompting the question of why selection has acted against bonobo aggression (Hare et al. 2012). A frequent context in which aggression by male bonobos appears to be maladaptive is male–female conflict: males who attempt to coerce or fight females are almost always overwhelmed by a defensive coalition of females, a pattern that is rare among chimpanzees (Tokuyama and Furuichi 2016). This suggests that selection against male aggressiveness in bonobos (in other words, self-domestication) could have resulted from males being dominated by female–female coalitions.

Unfortunately for their potential value as a model for the evolution of human behaviour, however, bonobos have alpha males. According

[WRANGHAM] *The Evolution of Institutional Patriarchy*

to current data, alpha-male bonobos obtain as disproportionate a share of paternity as alpha-male chimpanzees do (Surbeck et al. 2017). This means that female–female coalitions in bonobos neither eliminated the alpha-male role nor reduced its reproductive significance. Therefore, they cannot help explain how those changes happened in humans.

A different aspect of self-domestication that bonobos could in theory help explain is a reduction of male aggressiveness towards females. In bonobos, males are so relatively unaggressive towards females that the average female and male have approximately equal dominance status, and females often occupy the top ranks (Surbeck and Hohmann 2013). The system is fascinating, but unfortunately, it has little relevance for humans given that humans exhibit persistent male dominance over females. Thus, the social relationships of bonobos and humans are too different for any direct parallels to be instructive about human self-domestication.

Given that the path toward self-domestication in bonobos is unhelpful, it makes sense to consider how female–female coalitions could have contributed in a way specific to humans. Ideally, female coalitional behaviour would explain the reduced paternity success of alpha males, as well as the emergence of an alpha alliance. I see three difficulties with the idea.

First, it is unclear why females would be motivated to be aggressive to the alpha male, since their interests would ordinarily align with his. Mountain gorillas illustrate the point. In the gorilla mating system, an alpha male fathers the great majority of offspring, and he protects them from the dangers of predation and infanticide (Stoinski et al. 2009). Females prefer males that win male–male fights, choosing to bond and mate with males whose impressive physical qualities signal their likely effectiveness as a protector (Geary 2021). Since the females and alpha male have little cause for conflict, the alpha is hardly ever sexually aggressive towards females.

In a similar way, among humans, females have repeatedly been found to prefer males who are competitively successful, often through fighting but also through other routes such as wealth, sports and intellectual pursuits (Smuts 1995; Buss and Schmitt 2019; Gorelik 2022). If the groups of *Homo* prior to *H. sapiens* had alpha males who were as dominant as they are in gorillas, there would have been no obvious reason for females to ally against him.

Second, it is hard to see how females could have contributed positively to the establishment of the alpha alliance, assuming that it was a network composed primarily of males and serving male interests, as happens today.

Third, the regular use of female–female coalitions in the Pleistocene might have been expected to leave relevant traces in the psychology or behaviour of contemporary humans. But cross-culturally, very little use of female–female coalitions against bullying males has been recorded among nomadic hunter-gatherers or anywhere else (Smuts 1995). For example, female–female coalitions have rarely been reported to be used to physically stop a male from rape or sexual intimidation. In bonobos, by contrast, female–female coalitions against males are so frequent that male coercion is essentially absent (Paoli 2009). Among humans, the contemporary rarity of female–female coalitions and subordinate status of females imply that if females in the past had a greater ability to control aggressive males, they subsequently lost it.

There is thus little support for the idea that female–female coalitions provide an alternative to male–male coalitions as an explanation for human self-domestication. The other main mechanism by which females might have selected against alpha males is their choice of mating partners.

In theory, females could have undermined the selective advantage of alpha-male behaviour by mating preferentially with less aggressive, more docile males (Cieri et al. 2014; Gleeson and Kushnick 2018). In favour of this suggestion, female choice of mating partners is a widely distributed and well-studied phenomenon that can be an important selective factor in birds and mammals, including humans (Clutton-Brock and McAuliffe 2009; Gorelik 2022).

Gleeson and Kushnick (2018) found support for the idea by investigating variations in the social status of females across human populations. Females with higher status were assumed to have more freedom to choose their mates and were therefore predicted to choose less aggressive men. The measure of male aggressiveness was stature. Gleeson and Kushnick (2018) found that across populations, higher female status was indeed correlated with shorter males. They concluded that female choice among humans could have favoured the local evolution of reduced male aggressiveness.

Whether or not such effects are important in contemporary society, however, female choice theories for the evolution of human self-domestication face a major difficulty when applied to the past. The problem is to explain how a female preference to mate with less aggressive males could have overcome the strategy of an alpha male at a time when the alpha's power to coerce females was much less constrained than among males nowadays.

Primates illustrate the problem. In large groups that contain multiple males, such as in chimpanzees and savanna baboons, there tends to be a conflict in mate choice between females and males. Females make efforts to mate with many or all of the males, whereas males attempt to monopolize mating access to females. Female preference to mate with diverse males is apparently a strategy to reduce the risk of infanticide (van Schaik 2016). Paternity data show that the conflict in mate choice tends to be resolved in favour of the most aggressive males, and in chimpanzees and chacma baboons, the mechanism responsible is clear: males use violence to intimidate females into mating with them more often than the females prefer (Muller et al. 2011; Feldblum et al. 2014; Baniel et al. 2017). Thus, in these primates, the female preference to mate with less aggressive males is defeated by the domineering strategies of more aggressive males. Males are highly aggressive to females, and the male hierarchy continues to include an alpha.

Among contemporary humans, a species in which the propensity for male reactive aggression is relatively low, it is possible that female choice of caring, less aggressive males can favour more docile males. But even though there are no alpha males in today's human groups, females often prefer competitively successful and more aggressive males, probably because they feel better protected from physical threats as well as receiving more investment for offspring (Smuts 1995; Gorelik 2022).

To compound the difficulty, rape or intimidation of females routinely restricts female choice in humans today despite the propensity for male reactive aggression having apparently declined for around three hundred thousand years. The power of Middle Pleistocene females to consistently refuse to mate with bullying males would seem to have been much more limited than in living humans. This means that when self-domestication began, mate choice by individual females seems very unlikely to have exerted a significant influence on the direction of selection for male aggressiveness.

In sum, the primate evidence indicates that either female and male interests were aligned in maintaining the alpha-male role, or females would have been coerced by male aggression into accepting the status quo. There are therefore no obvious models for imagining how female behaviour would have played a significant role in selecting against alpha males in the *Homo* lineage.

Other Proposed Sources of Human Self-Domestication

Female behaviour is not the only alternative proposal to the execution hypothesis for explaining human self-domestication. Others invoke social selection by the male choice of cooperative partners, self-control and high population density. Although all these ideas offer reasons why cooperative, unaggressive behaviour might be favoured, they share a common difficulty: like female alliances and female choice, none of them explains how or why selection would act against the alpha (Wrangham 2019b).

Take social selection by male choice of cooperative partners. A specific version of this idea, the "interdependence hypothesis," was presented by Tomasello (2016) as an explanation for the evolution of morality and included a proposal for the reduction of aggressiveness in *H. sapiens*.

According to the interdependence hypothesis, a human style of morality originated around four hundred thousand years ago as a result of an ecological change—namely, a "disappearance of individually obtainable foods" (Tomasello 2016, 136). Tomasello (2016) then envisaged two processes that could have been responsible for shifting early humans away from a primate-style male-dominance hierarchy.

First, individuals were forced to collaborate in the food quest rather than forage on their own as they had until then. The result was a new kind of interdependence. Individuals who were more collaborative fed better, for instance, than those who were not chosen as foraging partners and defended better against predators. Effective cooperation depended on a reduction in selfishness and aggressiveness and on a concomitant increase in sympathy and shared intentionality.

Second, pair-bonding was initiated. As a result, males recognized their offspring and spent time with them. Selection favoured a low propensity for male aggression because aggressive fathers risked hurting their offspring.

Tomasello (2016) also considered that cooperative breeding, a social system in which individuals help rear others' offspring at a cost to their own reproductive effort, was an important feature of early *Homo* society and selected for increased social tolerance. Like Burkart et al. (2009) and Hrdy (2009), he assumed that *Homo* began to breed cooperatively around two million years ago.

According to Tomasello (2016, 43), "It was thus this pair-bonded, child-caring, relatively tolerant and gentle creature—a self-domesticated great ape—who entered into the new and still more collaborative lifeways that we will be positing as the evolutionary origins of uniquely human cooperation and morality." The difficulty with this hypothesis is that Tomasello does not discuss what would stop a determined, physically powerful alpha male from exerting his fighting ability at the expense of others in his group. Suppose that teamwork indeed became more important in the food quest, that the alpha male would have been excluded as a partner and that as a result, the alpha would have become a less effective forager than his cooperating peers. Tomasello's implied conclusion is that the despot would feed poorly, and that as a result, he would lose fitness: perhaps he would become so weakened that females would reject him. By analogy with nonhuman primates such as chimpanzees or savanna baboons, however, an alternative conclusion must be considered. The despotic male would improve his lot by seizing the choicest foods that others produced: his physical dominance would allow it. Like a male lion feeding off the kills brought down by females, the determinedly aggressive and effective fighter would continue to have high fitness thanks to his ability to commandeer food, mates or other resources from others in the group. His ability to use force to intimidate or rape females would mean that in terms of genetic success, any injury that his high propensity for aggression caused to his offspring would be easily compensated. But anyway, no injuries would be expected to be caused to their own offspring by even the most aggressive males, to judge from the tolerant relationships of males with their offspring among species that have a high capacity for aggression, such as chimpanzees, gorillas, baboons or lions.

In short, whether or not a hypothesis of social selection for unaggressive partners applies to the evolution of cooperation, it does not explain why alpha-male behaviour would have been selected against. Tyrants using brute force for personal gain would have been favoured unless they were stopped by community action, as the execution hypothesis proposes and contemporary ethnographies demonstrate.

A second approach suggests that the evolution of self-domestication could have been promoted by an increased ability for self-control, one result of which would have been less use of reactive aggression (Hare 2017; Shilton et al. 2020). This idea builds on the evidence that brain size was rising shortly before the approximately three-hundred-thousand-year-old signal of self-domestication and that brain size is strongly correlated with the control of prepotent responses (MacLean et al. 2014). Thus, the ability to control reactive aggression is thought to have been increasing as *H. sapiens* evolved. But a similar problem applies as it does to the social selection of cooperative partners. An increased capacity for self-control does not explain how alpha males would be stopped from taking advantage of their power to dominate others.

A third suggestion is that increasing population density could have been responsible for increasing selection pressures against reactive aggression (Cieri et al. 2014; Marean 2015). In one scenario, a rise in the population density of *Homo* selected for increased social tolerance towards unfamiliar individuals, an extension of social networks and more sharing of acquired foods. Again, however, alpha males would be expected to exploit the social tolerance of others in their group.

In sum, the execution hypothesis is the only proposal made to date that appears capable of explaining the evidence that shortly before three hundred thousand years ago, selection started acting against the propensity for reactive aggression.

Groupishness and Self-Domestication: Significance for the Evolution of Alpha Alliances

Up to this point, my goals have been to describe the execution hypothesis and to test it using data on self-domestication. Here I briefly rehearse how this approach is intended to contribute to understanding the origins and maintenance of institutional patriarchy.

My ultimate question is why human social institutions have a strong tendency to be dominated by men and male values. Perhaps the most widely accepted traditional answer is that societies were originally more gender balanced, and then around ten thousand years ago, they transitioned into patriarchies. According to that view, cultural influences such as agriculture, complex warfare or patriarchal ideology are held responsible for the supposed changes (Lerner 1986; Hudson et al. 2020).

The contrasting proposal that I explore in this essay is that a major component of patriarchy—namely, institutional patriarchy—arose much earlier. Instead of emerging around ten thousand years ago, I suggest that it evolved around the time when *Homo sapiens* first appeared three hundred thousand years ago, coincident with language that was sufficiently sophisticated that it allowed the formation of an alpha alliance and the imposition of social norms. This idea stems from the argument that executions began around that time, associated with the emergence and consolidation of alpha alliances. If the execution hypothesis is correct, as I have argued that it is, an obvious possibility is that alpha alliances have exerted a patriarchal influence since their origin.

PART 3. INSTITUTIONAL PATRIARCHY AS A CONSEQUENCE OF THE SELF-INTERESTED BEHAVIOUR OF ALPHA ALLIANCES

The Implication of Alpha Alliances for the Evolution of Institutional Patriarchy

A core message of Boehm's 1999 book *Hierarchy in the Forest* is that in order to understand the evolution of human cooperation, it is vital to consider the nature of the male-dominance hierarchy. Unfortunately, most subsequent discussions of the evolution of human cooperation have ignored Boehm's warning (e.g., Boyd and Richerson 2005; Axelrod 2006; Hrdy 2009; West et al. 2011; Haidt 2012; Tomasello et al. 2012; Hawkes 2014; Sapolsky 2017; Henrich and Muthukrishna 2021). Nevertheless, the argument that the presence of alpha males would have constrained the evolution of groupishness seems inescapable.

First, the evolution of what I am calling groupishness is widely agreed to depend on "punishment of those who free-ride or otherwise engage in anti-social behavior" (Gintis et al. 2001, 116). But if an alpha male is present, he is such a powerful individual that he is essentially an unpunishable free rider with a very high ability to take resources from cooperators for his own benefit. The marginal gains that subordinate individuals might otherwise acquire from cooperation among one another are therefore vulnerable to being lost to the alpha. The presence of a highly asymmetric dominance hierarchy, as indicated by the presence of an alpha male, is accordingly expected to mean that groupishness will not evolve via indirect reciprocity (Phillips 2018).

The evolution of cooperation by signalling has a more complicated relationship to the presence of a free-riding alpha male. For humans, the signalling hypothesis is that group members behave prosocially, and refrain from behaving antisocially, to show their commitment to norms imposed by the alpha alliance. The supposed reward is escaping punishment by the alpha alliance. The same dynamic would in theory seem to work when the sanctioning party is an alpha male instead of an alpha alliance, but the costs of punishment would be higher for a single male than for a set of allies.

In support of this conjecture, in Catarrhine groups, alpha males and some other high-ranking individuals can use their power to police conflicts among lower-ranking group members. They do so by intervening aggressively to stop the conflict. Their policing results in increased cooperation and more sociopositive behaviour (Flack et al. 2005; Flack et al. 2006).[6] Flack et al. (2005) found that policing was more likely in monkey species with only one breeding male than when multiple males were present. They suggested that policing tends to occur where power is distributed more asymmetrically and where there is less of a collective action problem for the punishers. Policing among nonhuman primates is not known to involve norm enforcement, but parallel costs and benefits would nevertheless seem to apply to the human punishers. Thus, since the human alpha alliance holds extremely asymmetric power (being able to execute) and is united in its goals of norm enforcement, it can be expected to have lower costs and higher benefits from policing compared to an alpha individual. This suggests that other things being equal, the replacement of alpha individuals by alpha alliances would lead to increased policing of conflicts.

In short, the nature of the male-dominance hierarchy is vital. This conclusion raises critical questions. When did alpha males disappear from human ancestry? How were they suppressed? And what were the consequences for society?

According to the execution hypothesis reviewed in parts 1 and 2, we can now answer some of those questions with considerable confidence. Alpha males disappeared in a process that started sometime shortly before three hundred thousand years ago when coalitions of subordinate males developed the ability to safely kill even their most intimidating peers. Several major consequences for society would have followed. I have already discussed three of them.

First, alpha males were replaced at the top of the dominance hierarchy by alpha alliances (or in Boehm's phrase, "moral communities").

Second, alpha alliances served their own interests by establishing social norms and punishing antisocial behaviour. Individuals who failed to follow moral norms would have been ostracized, exiled or killed, leading to a reduction in their fitness. This generated selection for groupishness and led to the evolution of moral emotions and moral cognition, such as a conscience.

Third, the control of violence by alpha alliances generated selection against the propensity for reactive aggression. The result was self-domestication, with numerous biological and psychological effects. A particularly important result was a reduction in aggressiveness, which promoted increased opportunities for communication and cooperation and thus led to a positive feedback loop between reduced aggressiveness and increased cooperation.

Several other large consequences can be predicted also.

Fourth, after the loss of the alpha-male system, paternity would have become more evenly distributed across multiple males. Most likely this led swiftly to the pattern found in nomadic hunter-gatherers. In other words, long-term bonds emerged between each senior male and one or more females, and relationships between alliance males typically included respect for each other's mating bonds, also known as marriages. Hamadryas baboons provide a partial model for this arrangement (Swedell and Plummer 2012).

Any such change in the breeding system from alpha-dominated polygyny to multiple male–female bonds would have affected female relationships. In alpha-male systems such as gorillas and hamadryas baboons, female–female competition tends to be relatively muted, and males invest little in females other than protection from other males. If the loss of the alpha male indeed led to all male members of the alpha alliance forming pair-bonds with females, females would be expected to compete more with one another. Selection for reproductive females being attractive to males should therefore have intensified. Meanwhile, males would have competed with one another less by violence (which would be proscribed) and more by investment in females and their offspring. Thus, a mating system much more like the contemporary human arrangements can easily be imagined as a consequence of the loss of alpha males.

Fifth, language skills would have already been sufficiently high quality to allow targeted conspiratorial killing. Linguistic ability would then have continued to improve as increasing groupishness and self-domestication made face-to-face communication more efficacious among group members, resulting in a positive feedback loop (Fig. 2; Progovac and Benítez-Burraco 2019). Improvements in language would also have made social norms, rules and institutions increasingly elaborate. Those cultural acquisitions would have contributed to making alliances and their hierarchical relationships predictable and long-lasting. It might be argued, given the high level of linguistic skill that would have been necessary for allies to organize the confident killing of a tyrant, that early forms of norms, rules and institutions could have preceded the emergence of the alpha alliance. Even if such early forms occurred, however, their nature and operation in a society tyrannized by an alpha male would surely have been very different from their contemporary familiar versions.

The final expected impact of the development of capital punishment, to be considered here in more detail, is its influence on institutional patriarchy. The alpha alliance's dominant position within early *H. sapiens* societies, combined with cognitive mechanisms that enabled them to conspire together, would have allowed them to act so as to favour their shared interests as a group of breeding males. Those interests would have included two major categories of behaviour conducted by any member of the group. Both would have been adaptive for the males in the alpha alliance but in different ways. One category brought benefits to the alliance at others' expense. The other brought benefits both to the alliance and to the group as a whole.

Norms such as "male alliance members should get the best food," "females should be punished more than males for mating outside the marriage bond," or "bachelors should not be allowed near married women after dark" would not necessarily have benefited the group as a whole. They would have benefited alliance males, however, in relation to males who were not members of the alpha alliance. Such norms are expected to have emerged to promote the values held by males in the alpha alliance.

By contrast, norms such as "no taking without permission," "share food when you have more than enough," or "do not hit another's child" would have tended to suppress conflict and therefore to benefit not only members but also nonmembers of the alpha alliance. These group-level benefits would thus have given rise to "morality-as-cooperation" (Curry et al. 2019).

Note that according to this proposal, group-level benefits were favoured by the enforcement of norms rather than by group selection of individual behavioural tendencies. Enforcement by a selfish power was possible only because a stable alliance had emerged, which occurred for reasons unrelated to the spread of group-beneficial norms. However, after institutions were in place, it is easy to imagine that norm variants spread or died out through various processes of cultural transmission, including group-structured selection.

The above inferences suggest how society changed following the loss of alpha males. In many ways, the proposed transition is to a society indistinguishable from conventional concepts of nomadic hunter-gatherers: a largely monogamous set of pair-bonds, males acknowledging one another's marriages, females competing for mates, no formal leadership of the group, and decisions affecting the group taken by a network of senior male individuals.

In other ways, however, the transition envisages a more cynical use of power by breeding males than is normally thought to characterize nomadic hunter-gatherers. In line with the clearly selfish use of power by alpha males in nonhuman primates, I have suggested that the males who formed the alpha alliance would have used their social dominance for equivalently selfish reasons. The result would include a system of patriarchy through the use of language-based institutions.

Obviously, we cannot assess how patriarchal *H. sapiens* has been from its origins to the present day. In order to test whether alpha alliances can be expected to have imposed patriarchal values on society, therefore, I assess whether the nature and distribution of patriarchy in living humans conform to the prediction that alpha alliances use their dominant position to promote their own interests, predominantly those of senior males.

Institutional versus Behavioural Patriarchy

In the introduction to this essay, I proposed the value of recognizing two types of patriarchy, institutional and behavioural. The distinction echoes prior divisions such as "political dominance" versus "informal dominance" (Rogers 1975), "patriarchy" versus "male dominance" (Goldberg 1993), and "macro-level patriarchy" versus "micro-level patriarchy" (Hunnicutt 2009). I suggested that institutional patriarchy is a promising target of investigation because it focuses attention on a specific question—namely, why males dominate the relevant institutions.

The distinction is useful for a second reason also because it suggests a new answer to an old, vexed question. The question is whether patriarchy is a valid concept for humans as a whole, given that relations between men and women vary widely both across and within societies (Hunnicutt 2009). The answer suggested by considering institutional and behavioural patriarchy separately is that of the two types, only institutional patriarchy is sufficiently characteristic to warrant recognition as a universal feature of our species.

By contrast, behavioural patriarchy varies so much in its intensity that it does not allow for easy generalizations across populations. Violence against women illustrates the problem. In many countries and societies, women have traditionally been beaten, raped, claustrated, scarred or killed by men far more often than the other way round, so the international community recognizes violence against women as an important public health, social policy and human rights concern (Devries et al. 2013). A survey of 141 studies in 81 countries showed that 30 percent of women aged fifteen and over have experienced physical and/or sexual intimate partner violence (Devries et al. 2013). Hudson et al.'s (2020) systematic analysis of data from 176 countries leaves no room for doubt that globally, violence against women is a persistent problem.

Nevertheless, Rogers (1975) argued that male dominance is often a myth because in peasant societies, domestic relationships are often not patriarchal at all. Similarly, Blumberg (2004) reported that at the behavioural ("micro-") level, societies range from highly patriarchal (such as "warrior-complex" societies) to gender-egalitarian (such as some hunter-gatherer and horticultural societies; see also Leacock 1978; Hayden 1986; Kent 1995; Keen 2006; Hrdy 2009; Hudson et al. 2020). This means that the evolution of behavioural patriarchy requires a detailed analysis of economic, political and other factors to understand its variation across different societies, and in some societies, females and males are so equal in economic and political power that behavioural patriarchy is barely detectable (Endicott and Endicott, 2008).

Furthermore, even within societies in which males are generally very dominant over females, domestic relationships can vary widely. The Bena Bena, a small group in the New Guinea Highlands, had an ethic of "hard" men who were often at war and regarded women as polluting. But some wives dominated their husbands, as Robbins (1982) illustrated:

> Pu'a [was] a quiet, tongue-tied, shy young man in his middle twenties in 1962. Pu'a had somehow been matched with a flirtatious, loud-mouthed, assertive woman. As their house was close to mine, I heard many arguments between them and the tongue lashings she gave him. The ultimate degradation arose when he decided to donate a pig which she did not want killed. Knowing she would attack him in order to prevent him from killing it, he told some men in his pooling unit that he wanted to donate the pig and for them to kill it. They cheerfully did so the morning of the pooling. Pu'a's wife did not interfere and did nothing except avoid him until he came home that evening after the distribution had been completed. As he entered the house, she screamed at him for having killed the pig and hurled vicious insults. He only shouted back at her occasionally. By this time, we all were intently listening in order not to miss any part of the show. Suddenly there was a howl and Pu'a staggered out of the door with his wife flailing at him with a firebrand. Just as he got outside, she smashed him on top of the head, knocking him to his knees. She took one brief look at him, whirled around, and stalked back into the house. He knelt a few seconds, appearing

dazed and then got up and staggered back into the house. Nothing further was heard. (Cited by Langness 1990, 393–94)

Similar examples can be found everywhere. In 1758, John Wesley was the spiritual leader of 150,000 Methodists in Britain, but he would lose arguments with his wife, Mary, sometimes in extreme form. One day, John Hampson, a friend of Wesley, "went into a room and found Mrs. Wesley foaming with fury. Her husband was on the floor where she had been trailing him by the hair of his head; and she herself was still holding in her hand venerable locks which she had plucked up by the roots" (Hattersley 2003, 277).

The contrast between behavioural and institutional relationships was particularly stark in the case of Vyacheslav Mikhailovich Molotov and his wife, Polina. Molotov was premier of the USSR during the 1930s. According to Montefiore (2004, 163), Molotov "was dominated by his wife Polina, to whom he wrote passionate love letters." But "this Soviet Robespierre believed in terror and never regretted signing the death warrants of the wives of his friends."

Thus, even though behavioural patriarchy is rampant, including the fact that many more men kill their wives than women kill their husbands (Rosenfeld 2009), these cases of gender-egalitarian societies and women dominating their institutionally dominant husbands illustrate how difficult it is to generalize about the phenomenon. Cross-cultural surveys support the point. Across societies, husband-beating by wives is found sufficiently often that one study found that it rose with increased gender empowerment and women working more outside the home (Archer 2006). Overall, the point made by Friedl (1967, 103) from a survey of small-scale societies is vital to appreciate: "Women's status can be low in the public domain, but high, even dominant, relative to males in the domestic domain."

Equally, the fact that institutions are run by men does not necessarily mean that women's influences are absent. Innumerable examples can be found of women wielding substantial power within male-run institutions even without having access to jural and formal rights (Rogers 1975, 729).

In short, women's de facto status varies substantially and is often much higher than a blanket assertion of patriarchy might indicate. Much of the variation occurs at the level of behavioural patriarchy, which can be absent within households and also ranges among populations from being intense to essentially absent. Even though in most societies, women tend

290   *The Tanner Lectures on Human Values*

to suffer badly at the hands of men (Hudson et al. 2020), there is nevertheless impressive variation.

With regard to institutional patriarchy, by contrast, there is more consistency.

The Distribution of Institutional Patriarchy

In an assessment of the distribution of institutional patriarchy, it is helpful to consider two categories of society—namely, recent nation-states and all other societies. I consider "all other societies" first.

Occasional claims have been made of societies being matriarchal, but if societal matriarchies are defined as "institutional arrangements that privilege females such that women (as a group) dominate men (as individuals or as a group)," the evidence is clear. No societal matriarchy has ever been discovered. Anthropologist Margaret Mead was unambiguous: "It is true ... that all the claims so glibly made about societies ruled by women are nonsense. We have no reason to believe that they ever existed.... Men everywhere have been in charge of running the show.... Men have been the leaders in public affairs and the final authorities at home" (Mead 1973, 48). Historian Gerda Lerner (1986, 30) agreed: "There is not a single society known where women-as-a-group have decision-making power over men or where they define the rules of sexual conduct or control marriage exchanges." Such claims were reported by Goldberg (1993, 48) to be based on over twelve hundred studies.

A 1974 book, *Woman, Culture, and Society*, edited by two prominent female anthropologists (Michelle Rosaldo and Louise Lamphere) and featuring sixteen female authors, echoed the claim that matriarchy is universally absent in traditional societies and in doing so strongly implied that institutional patriarchy is universal:

> Male, as opposed to female, activities are always recognized as predominantly important ... and cultural systems give authority and value to the roles and activities of men.... Everywhere, from those societies we might want to call most egalitarian to those in which sexual stratification is most marked, men are the locus of cultural value. Some area of activity is always seen as exclusively or predominantly male, and therefore overwhelmingly and morally important. This observation has its corollary in the fact that everywhere men have authority over women, that they have a culturally legitimated right to her subordination and compliance. (Rosaldo 1974, 19–21)

Goldberg (1993) made relevant evidence easily available in an appendix to his book *Why Men Rule*. He reported on forty-one societies for which some confusion has occasionally been written about whether or not they are patriarchal, presenting unambiguous quotations taken mostly from primary ethnographies.

Thus among serious scholars, the pattern of dominance between genders at the institutional level is clear. There are zero matriarchies; institutional patriarchy is the overwhelmingly prevalent pattern and is very likely universal.

Confusion can arise from nomadic hunter-gatherers being described as egalitarian. One problem is that in general, "egalitarianism" in the hunter-gatherer literature refers to relationships among men. For example, when Woodburn (1982, 434) referred to hunter-gatherers as "profoundly egalitarian," he followed his claim with "I have exempted relations between men and women from this sweeping assertion."

A more important conceptual problem is that behavioural and institutional patriarchy are rarely distinguished. The difference is important because hunter-gatherer women often have much greater freedom in terms of ordinary day-to-day interactions than on occasions when men invoke traditional norms. The evidence is striking from Australia, which had no contact with agricultural populations until the eighteenth century and therefore represents some of the best-documented large populations of hunter-gatherers. Ethnographer Catherine Berndt (1965) emphasized that there were strong traditions of female autonomy throughout Australia at the individual as well as the cultural level. Furthermore, the intensity of male power varied widely, being higher in the north, where resources were most abundant (Keen 2006). Nevertheless, across the continent, institutional rules were patriarchal in at least three ways (Hiatt 1996).

First, both men and women could have secret societies reserved only for their own gender. But norm violations by a member of the wrong gender had different consequences depending on whether they were committed by a man or a woman. Women's sanctions against a man were limited to mystical retribution. Men's sanctions against a woman who discovered men's secrets, by contrast, were likely to be gang rape or execution. Even unintended breaking of the rules was punished, as Meggit (1987, 129) reported on the Walbiri: "No women or children may casually enter the men's country lest they intrude on secret activities; they may go there only in company when ordered to attend certain parts of the initiation ceremonies. A woman who breaks these rules is likely to be beaten and raped, even killed."

Second, both genders could have single-gender ceremonies that they arranged independently from each other and often in secret. Men had such ceremonies more often, but the important difference came when either gender wanted some of the opposite gender to attend. Women could not coerce men to join women's ceremonies, but men could command women's presence at men's ceremonies. Women were sometimes terrified of the use that would be made of them. They could be made to dance, provide food, or have sex with partners chosen by the men.

Third, large gatherings involving members from more than one ethno-linguistic group (or "tribe") were an important part of social life, but they could only be initiated and organized by men. There was nothing equivalent for women.

Berndt could justifiably have added a fourth universal rule, that the authority to execute others came from men.

In addition to those features that Hiatt (1996) considered Australia-wide, a variety of other patriarchal practices that were widespread among Australian hunter-gatherers were also supported by the law or religion. They include the monopolization of young wives by older men, females being married as young as babies, adultery sanctions being greater for females than males, menstruation being seen as polluting, females being coerced into sex with their husband's affiliates or to settle a debt, wife-beating being justified by her failure to produce a satisfactory meal, and female transgressions being resolved by her own choice of gang rape or execution (C. Berndt 1965; R. Berndt 1965; Elkin 1938; Flood 2006; Meggitt 1965; Tindale 1974; Warner 1958). Similar practices are recorded from hunter-gatherers in the Arctic, South America and Africa (Burch 2005; Bridges 1948; Shostak 1981).

Despite these obviously patriarchal conventions, with respect to behavioural patriarchy, as indicated above, some hunter-gatherers come very close to gender equality (Friedl 1967; Leacock 1978; Blumberg 2004; Endicott and Endicott 2008). The Batek of central Malaysia, who number around 1500, have been suggested to show particularly equal relationships between the genders (Endicott and Endicott 2008). They are hunter-gatherers who were formerly raided for slaves by dominant farming neighbours and are now somewhat engaged in a market economy. Their domestic lives appear generally to be very gender equal with only occasional glimpses of male dominance, such as household location being determined more by husbands than by wives. The institutional level is less clear. In favour of the idea of gender equality, no bridewealth is paid, camp decisions are said to be made equally by women and men, disputes are reportedly resolved by the group as a whole and there are no significant gender differences in myths. Against it, politically important figures (shamans and natural leaders) are mostly male, women are tabooed from preferred foods during menstruation and around childbirth, wives cook for their husbands and the godlike creator figure is a male (Endicott 1988; Endicott and Endicott 2008). Specific cases of dispute resolution would help elucidate this case, which raises the possibility of genuinely gender-equal norms.

In the absence of any relevant contemporary evidence, matriarchies are sometimes proposed to have occurred in prehistory. The idea is based mainly on the interpretation of figurines and other representational art that feature females. Such reconstructions are inevitably inconclusive, as religion scholar Cynthia Eller observed: "[Prehistoric art] tells us that then, as now, women seemed to be depicted more often than men. But beyond that, we are given precious little information about the status of either divine or human women in prehistory; it shows us nothing that would contradict the alternative hypothesis that male dominance flourished throughout the prehistoric times from which these works survive" (Eller 2000, 156).

I have reserved separate comments for recent nation-states because in their formal constitutions, most of them have committed themselves to gender equality by guaranteeing that women and men have roughly equal legal status, economic opportunities and political rights. This gives a misleading impression, however, because most other important social institutions are dominated by males, including law, religion, government and business. In the words of Catharine MacKinnon (2012, 404), "[although] 184 of 194 countries have written constitutions guaranteeing gender equality . . . the reality of gender equality exists nowhere." Nevertheless, dramatic changes in the official rights of women during the last century have at least produced theoretical cases in which institutional patriarchy at the highest level has been eroded. The same rarely applies to family law, however (MacKinnon 2012, 2017).

In sum, behavioural patriarchy varies widely, from strong to weak or even neutral at the societal level. With regard to the institutional construct of gender relations, however, humans are overwhelmingly, and possibly universally, patriarchal. Since the alpha alliance is responsible for relevant norms, rules and institutions, this obviously implies that actions of the alpha alliance account for institutional patriarchy. No other concept makes sense. Females can hardly be expected to have constructed institutional patriarchy.

Previous Explanations of Institutional Patriarchy

The execution hypothesis suggests that institutional patriarchy originated in men using violence or the threat of violence to impose their will on all others in the group, including females whom they used for sexual, political and other purposes. A case of "power corrupts," in other words.

Comparison between the execution hypothesis and previous theories is difficult partly because most traditional efforts have treated behavioural and institutional forms of patriarchy as a combined phenomenon. Nevertheless, in an attempt to set the execution hypothesis in context, I briefly abstract some major ideas relevant to the evolution of institutional patriarchy.

Primatologist and evolutionary biologist Barbara Smuts (1995) presented the most detailed and sophisticated application of evolutionary theory to patriarchy to date. She hypothesized that patriarchy originated in male efforts to control and coerce females for sexual and reproductive goals. That idea is derived from sexual selection theory and finds extensive support from primates and many other species (Smuts and Smuts 1993; Hrdy 1997). Some social scientists have similarly assumed that patriarchy originated in male efforts to control female sexual behaviour, on the basis that sexual control by males is a prominent feature of humans (e.g., MacKinnon 1987).

Smuts (1995) found that compared to nonhuman primates, humans exhibit more extensive male dominance and in particular, more complete male control of female sexuality. She accordingly tested six hypotheses derived from evolutionary theory that might explain this human exceptionalism. She found support for all six. (1) Female–female alliances are relatively poorly developed in humans, whereas (2) male–male alliances are relatively strong. (3) Males tend to control critical resources, and (4) as male alliances develop in strength, men at the top can gain power over both other men and women. (5) Females often favour domineering males because those males control valuable resources. Finally, (6) language facilitates ideologies of male supremacy and female inferiority.

Smuts's analysis proposes important explanations for why male dominance is more extreme in humans than in other primates. In doing so, she raised further questions such as why male–male alliances tend to be strong, why female–female alliances tend to be weak, and why female–male mating bonds are so important to both sexes, albeit in different ways. As Smuts (1995) pointed out, her identification of these targets as critical foci of research conforms to much feminist analysis. In many ways, it also fits with the execution hypothesis. But the execution hypothesis differs by giving more credit to the alpha alliance, and specifically its ability to back up threats by killing, as the ultimate source of human exceptionalism. Smuts (1995) admittedly concluded that language contributes to patriarchy by enabling ideologies that value males. That claim is surely fair, but the execution hypothesis also proposes an even more important consequence of language: it enabled the formation of the male–male alliances that became institutions serving male interests.

Overall, Smuts's (1995) conclusion that human males are more patriarchal and dominant than males of other primate species is a vital insight. It provides a further reason, in addition to those cited already, why the human case cannot be explained purely by appealing to features that are ordinary components of primate or mammalian biology, such as males being relatively strong and more aggressive and females being constrained by giving birth and nursing their offspring. It is now clear that patriarchy requires an explanation of features that are specific to humans.

A similar problem applies to another major theory, which is that intergroup aggression and war have been especially important in promoting the evolution of male–male alliances that lie at the root of patriarchy (Smuts 1995; Hudson et al. 2020). The intergroup aggression hypothesis sees the alpha alliance as necessary for groups to defend themselves in the face of intergroup competition. Successful conflict by the alliance is therefore supposedly good for both male and female interests, causing females to be predisposed to give high value to aggressive male alliances as well as males in general.

In support of this idea, much evidence supports an association between violence and patriarchy. Among small-scale societies, those with a "warrior complex" tend to be intensely patriarchal, whereas famously gender-egalitarian societies like the Batek are strikingly nonviolent (Blumberg 2004; Endicott and Endicott 2008). With respect to nation-states, Hudson et al. (2020) surveyed all 176 countries that have a population of at least two hundred thousand. They compared an index of patriarchy (the Patrilineal/Fraternal Syndrome) with a measure of violence and

296   *The Tanner Lectures on Human Values*

instability and found a highly significant positive correlation (0.773). The direction of causation probably goes both ways. Patriarchal ideology can be easily envisaged as readying a society for war, and warriors who have successfully used coalitionary violence might be expected to use it to dominate females within groups.

As an explanation for human exceptionalism, however, a problem with this idea is that male–male alliances in the context of intergroup aggression are found to be as important in some other species as they are in humans but without alliances being used to dominate females. Chimpanzees are the obvious example. Male chimpanzees kill members of other groups in intergroup aggression, with the resulting death rate being similar to the death rates from war among hunter-gatherers (Wrangham et al. 2006). Male chimpanzees also use their power to coerce females sexually (Muller et al. 2011). However, male chimpanzees bully females as individuals, not as male–male alliances. This implies that an extra explanation is needed to account for human, but not chimpanzee, "war alliances" being redirected against females.

The intergroup aggression hypothesis echoes Smuts's (1995) conclusion that male–male alliances contribute importantly to patriarchy and is similar to the execution hypothesis in suggesting that male–male alliances that evolved in one context were then used to dominate females. Compared to the execution hypothesis, the main difference is that the intergroup aggression hypothesis explains less. Thus, the intergroup aggression hypothesis does not address the phenomenon of institutional patriarchy or why male–male alliances control male violence within groups, let alone why humans self-domesticated. It also does not explain why humans show more extreme male dominance of females than other species or when and how that exceptionalism developed. In short, the intergroup aggression hypothesis appears more valuable for explaining variation among current societies than for explaining human exceptionalism and the nature of institutional patriarchy.

When behavioural and institutional patriarchy have been considered separately, the normal assumption appears to be that behavioural patriarchy came first. MacKinnon (2012, 410) illustrated the concept: "The sphere called private has been extensively found to be a (perhaps the) crucible of gender inequality, notably of the patriarchal family, labor stratification and the feminization of poverty, denial of reproductive control, and male dominant stereotypical sexual practices and rape ringed with rape myths rationalized as love or culture." That idea that the "private sphere" was the ultimate origin of patriarchy is likely true, given that males in human ancestry, like other male primates, have probably been attempting to control female sexuality forever. Institutional patriarchy, given its dependence on sophisticated language, was undoubtedly a relatively late achievement.

In sum, this brief survey suggests that previous ideas about the evolution of patriarchy have tended to attribute it to biological factors that enabled behavioural patriarchy. When institutional patriarchy is considered, it is ordinarily thought of as an additional mechanism that arose relatively recently to help males in their efforts to control female sexuality. The hypothesis that the relatively extreme form of human male dominance emerged as a consequence of male alliances adapting to control other males has previously been proposed in the context of between-group, but not within-group, violence.

Law as a Principal Source of Institutional Patriarchy

In contrast to more traditional approaches, the execution hypothesis suggests that institutional patriarchy was imposed by male alliances following their initial formation as devices to suppress male violence within the group. This proposal conforms to the fact that societies are invariably headed by alpha alliances (rather than individual alpha males) and that institutional patriarchy is either a cultural universal or very close to it, as discussed above.

The proposal also predicts that all societies have mechanisms for imposing patriarchy. Since institutional patriarchy represents a tendency for males to win formal disputes against females, and since the law is the principal social mechanism that arbitrates disputes, the law is clearly a potential source of patriarchy. By this view, we would expect that law reflects the goals of, and instantiates agreements made among, males belonging to the alpha alliance.

Accordingly, we should expect that there is a legal system in all societies, that legal decisions are made overwhelmingly by males and that legal disputes between the sexes tend to be decided in favour of males. These expectations all appear to be met.

First, law has sometimes been thought of as being only a few thousand years old rather than being a universal feature of *H. sapiens*. If law must be formally codified in writing, for example, it must clearly be recent. But writing is certainly unnecessary for the practice of law. Legal systems vary with the size, complexity and nature of the society (Kar 2012; Gutmann

298 *The Tanner Lectures on Human Values*

and Voigt 2016), so the question is whether any generalized definition of law covers legal systems in all societies.

Anthropologists agree that the answer has to come from understanding how disputes are settled (Gulliver 1969). In a detailed study of the Cheyenne, Llewellyn and Hoebel (1941) were the first to collect data on actual cases, leading to a widely accepted cross-cultural definition of law: "A social norm is legal if its neglect or infraction is regularly met, in threat or in fact, by the application of physical force by an individual or group possessing the socially recognized privilege of so acting" (Hoebel 1954, 27).

Pospisil (1971) studied the applicability of this definition by surveying ninety-five societies, including the Alaskan Nunamiut and New Guinean Kapauku, both of whom he lived with. He concluded that "there is no basic qualitative difference between tribal (primitive) and civilized law" (Pospisil 1971, 342). He used four criteria to recognize the law as a set of principles of institutionalized social control (Pospisil 1971, 95). The principles must be abstracted from decisions passed by the legal authority, they must be intended to have universal application, the parties to which the principles apply must have duties or rights in relationship to one another that they are expected to fulfil and the decision must be enforceable, which in major disputes might require the use of planned "violence by an authorized sub-group within a larger group." Although execution might sometimes be a necessary punishment, Pospisil (1958) emphasized that psychological sanctions—such as ostracism, ridicule, avoidance or denial of favours—could be effective for minor offences. The vital factor was that somehow, an authority could control the behaviour of a disputant.

The nature of the legal authority could vary widely: it might be an informal tribal headman, a formal tribal chief, a ruling oligarchy, a council of elders, a king, an appointed judge and so on. Whatever it is, an essential feature is that both the legal authority and the parties to the dispute belong to the same social group in which the authority has jurisdiction. The law therefore pertains only to specific social groups and subgroups of a society: "There are as many legal systems in segmented or other types of societies as there are functioning groups" (Pospisil 1971, 343). This means that the legal system can be said to define the group: "A group, in a sense, is a group because there is a legal system that expresses and safeguards its vital pattern of prescribed behaviour and induces (or in case of violation, forces) its members to conform to it" (Pospisil 1971, 343).

Thus, all societies have laws and can even be said to be defined by them.

The second expectation is that legal decisions are made principally by males. The relevant question, therefore, concerns the composition of the legal authority in different societies.

General conclusions about the gender composition of legal authorities are elusive. Most ethnographers of nomadic hunter-gatherers do not refer to a legal system at all, presumably because it requires a specialist to recognize it. However, among Australian hunter-gatherers, none of whom had any clearly defined political authority, systems of law and order across the continent were reviewed by Ronald Berndt (1965). He reported that those who exercised authority within groups were the male elders, meaning mostly middle-aged husbands. I have found no contrary indications for other hunter-gatherers for whom conflicts of various kinds were described (e.g., Hill and Hurtado 1996; Marlowe 2010; Burch 2005).

The same applies to groups other than hunter-gatherers. Four book-length anthropological reviews of cross-cultural variations in law make no mention of any legal authorities being dominated by women, or indeed of gender at all (Hoebel 1954; Pospisil 1971; Donovan 2008; Conaghan 2013). These reviews appeared to take it for granted that the legal authority was male or a male-dominated group, as in Pospisil's examples above.

The third expectation derived from the execution hypothesis was that legal disputes would tend to be decided in favour of males or, in other words, that the law favours males. This idea is routinely supported. Conaghan's book *Law and Gender* reported from an analysis of legal practice around the world: "There is ample evidence, historical but to some extent still current, of the collusion of law in the support of a patriarchal social order in which women were positioned as (at best) different from men and therefore occupying a separate social sphere, or (at worst) inferior and therefore cast in the role of serving or amusing men or constituting objects of their property" (Conaghan 2013, 3). "And yet," the author continued, "for the most part, legal scholarship continues to hold on to the view that gender plays little or no role in the conceptual make-up, normative grounding, or categorical ordering of law. The official position is that the *idea* of law and legal fundamentals are, and certainly ought to be, gender-independent" (Conaghan 2013, 7).

Similar findings are widespread. For example, Htun and Weldon (2012) surveyed seventy countries: "Classical Islamic law, the Napoleonic Code, Anglo-American common law, and the customary law of many sub-Saharan African groups and indigenous peoples of the Americas all upheld the notion that men were in charge of family life: they controlled property, were the legal guardians of children, and had the right to restrict their wives' public activities. Women were obliged to obey their husbands, had limited access to divorce, and, in many traditions, fewer inheritance rights than men" (Htun and Weldon 2012, 2).

Family law throughout human history shows the same trends. Adultery has routinely been considered a much greater crime for women than for men, polygyny has often been legal where nonfraternal polyandry was proscribed, divorce has been easier for men than women and marital rape is regularly considered not to be a crime (Hudson et al. 2020). The latter point is not restricted to recent state societies. Anthropologist Jane Collier (1988) found that in foraging societies, the high value of a wife to a man tended to mean that he might legitimately rape, beat, mutilate, torture or kill her for adultery because her affair risked making him into a bachelor (or leading him to raise offspring that were fathered by another man).

In these open-air societies where women cook for men, being a bachelor meant having low status. This accounts for the strength of men's fear that they might lose their wives:

> The most visible [socially created inequality] is that between married and unmarried men. In societies where women not only feed families but also build shelters, tend hearths, and provide sexual services, married men live very different lives than do bachelors and men whose wives have died or left them. Because a man who lives with a wife has a shelter, hearth, and a readily available sexual partner, he can avoid asking other men for anything. In contrast, the man who lacks a wife must either go without a shelter, hearth and sex, or obtain goods and services from his mother, sister, or lover—a woman who is another man's wife or potential wife. (Collier 1988, 21)

The social importance of being married included the status that mattered most to him, his membership of the alpha alliance: "Once he has a wife to keep his fire and build his shelter, he acquires a place in the camp" (Collier and Rosaldo 1981, 284). It is clear why men in the alpha alliance would want to impose rules that gave them control over their wives.

In short, a legal bias in favour of men is certainly widespread. In the absence of any systematic review, it remains conceivable that a few small-scale societies might have legal practices that favour females or, more likely, show no gender bias (Endicott and Endicott 2008). The discovery of such a system would be fascinating. It is not expected, however, given the overall anthropological consensus regarding the universality of institutional patriarchy.

In many societies, law is certainly not the only institution promoting patriarchy. Religion is a cultural universal that frequently has patriarchal rules that impact family law (Htun and Weldon 2012). Among hunter-gatherers, the consistency with which religion promoted patriarchy is unclear. Peoples et al. (2016) surveyed thirty-three hunter-gatherer societies and found that ancestor worship (which is often patriarchal, being normally associated with kin groups and unilineal descent systems) was present in 45 percent of societies. A cross-cultural investigation of the degree to which religion is institutionally patriarchal would be rewarding.

Whether or not religions are found to be as uniformly patriarchal as the law appears to be, however, their societal role seems to be less fundamental than that of the law. In small-scale societies, the function of the law in regulating within-group conflict means that the legal authority necessarily exerts ultimate power over all group members, including the ability to arrange the deaths of offenders. While religious authorities often also have the power to kill group members, they do not have principal responsibility for keeping the peace.

In sum, the view of the law that emerges from the execution hypothesis is in line with MacKinnon's review of legal studies since the 1970s: "Over the last thirty years, the lives of women, newly visible as such, cast a bright critical light on laws constructed by men. Women's insistence that laws respond to them, too, has exposed the sex of those the law empowers as male, in the main, and the gender of laws, even the law itself, as masculine" (MacKinnon 2005, 1). This conclusion that men dominate the law might seem in conflict with the fact that in ancient Egyptian, Greek and Roman mythology, the individuals symbolizing justice were all women, respectively Maat, Themis and Justicia. But the idea of women representing justice seems like a ploy promoting the lie that justice is blind. Men have been gaslighting women for at least four thousand years.

Comparison of the Alpha-Alliance Theory of Law with Conventional Legal Philosophies

The preceding analysis suggests that law has its beginnings in the Middle Pleistocene in the dynamics of male–male competition, emerging when language became sufficiently skilled to allow conspiracies and social norms, and the alpha alliance's control of violent males evolved into an early form of legal authority. Ever since then, males have continued to form alliances to control within-group violence, and as a result, the law has always been dominated by male interests. Male interests, in turn, can be resolved into two major vectors, concerned with benefiting either society as a whole or the lawmakers at the expense of others within the group.

The execution hypothesis has thus led us to a theory of the origins of law. To show how the alpha-alliance theory relates to conventional understanding, here I briefly compare it with two major conventional theories of legal origins: natural law and legal positivism.

First, natural law theory suggests that law originates in fundamental moral truths that are, in Cicero's words, "universal, unchanging and everlasting" and are thus independent of human nature or human society (Wacks 2006; Murphy 2007). Natural law theory is therefore not compatible with the proposal from alpha-alliance theory that law arose in the context of social dynamics that were particular to human society. In a further conflict with alpha-alliance theory, natural law theory entirely ignores law's patriarchal elements.

Natural law ideals have been promoted for at least two thousand years, from Plato, St Augustine, St Thomas Aquinas and Thomas Hobbes to Sir William Blackstone, who declared in the eighteenth century that English laws were derived from natural law. Despite an overall decline in its importance in the last two centuries, natural law still has avid proponents (Fuller 1969; Finnis 2011), and it remains influential.

Natural rights are frequently supposed to be derived from natural law, as in the American Declaration of Independence ("We hold these truths to be self-evident, that all men are created equal, that they are endowed by their Creator with certain unalienable rights"). Twentieth-century appearances of natural law ideals are found in the phrase "crimes against humanity" in the Nuremberg war trials, and in numerous recognitions of human rights, such as in the charter of the United Nations, the Universal Declaration of Human Rights, the Declaration of Delhi on the Rule of Law or the interpretation by the U.S. Supreme Court of the American Bill of Rights (Wacks 2006; Patrick 2023).

Despite its influence, natural law theory has been heavily criticized for almost three hundred years. A major objection is that its legal principles have traditionally been derived from religious sources and therefore depend on faith. Nonreligious justifications have been preferred recently, but even they have subjective components. Finnis (2011) proposed that there are sixteen self-evident objective goods, independent of the specifics of human nature, that natural law should serve to provide. His list of goods includes life, knowledge, play, aesthetic experience, respect for every basic value in every act and following one's conscience. Such lists appear to have no objective justification. Jeremy Bentham, who laid the foundations of legal positivism, regarded natural law as nothing more than "private opinion in disguise" (Wacks 2006, 21).

Legal positivism is the major alternative to natural law theory. It claims that "the validity of any law can be traced to an objectively verifiable source"—in other words, from a law that has previously been posited (Wacks 2006, 18). Legal positivists thus see the law as being the product of power struggles, which means that it can readily accommodate the view of law as a system of social control manipulated by an alpha alliance.

H. L. A. Hart (1961) is said to be the father of modern legal positivism, which he derived from asserting five features of the human condition. Humans have limited access to resources that we need, are subject to being physically attacked, cannot be on our guard at all times, are often selfish and cannot be relied on to cooperate. Given those "frailties," rules have been needed to allow communities to flourish. Hart's position illustrates the positivist view that different laws have evolved culturally to benefit different societies rather than depending on any inherent moral principles. Hans Frank, the German appointed by Hitler as Governor-General of Poland during World War II, illustrated the idea. In a paper given at the Academy for German Law in December 1939, he argued "that law was nothing more than 'that which is useful and necessary for the German nation'" (Sands 2017, 177).

Legal positivism is thus entirely compatible with alpha-alliance theory in recognizing law as a cultural product designed, among other things, to keep the peace and to benefit society as a whole. However, legal positivists were slow to acknowledge that the law is biased in favour of males. Only when critical legal theory developed in the twentieth century, and specifically with the rise of feminist legal theory from the 1970s onwards, did this omission begin to be seriously examined. Catharine MacKinnon (1987, 1989, 1991, 2005, 2012) has been especially crisp in pronouncing the law as essentially serving the interests of a masculine alpha alliance: "The people who can and do make law work for them, who designed it so it would work for them as if they were the whole world, are men—specifically, white, upper-class men." As a result, "sex inequality is diverse empirically, ideologically, and legally, varying in extent, form and degree, with some places far worse for women than others, but nowhere is equality achieved. Equality between women and men, in realms from the institutional to the intimate, remains more dream than fact" (MacKinnon 2005, 32, 44).

The alpha-alliance theory of law thus readily meshes with the assessments of radical feminist lawyers such as MacKinnon. Equally, it fits claims that the law tends to represent the interests of the dominant group within society, as Marxists and others have argued (Murphy 2007), and more generally that the process of defining the law involves advocacy among competing groups rather than the discovery of fundamental truths. In short, the alpha-alliance theory is compatible with much thinking in contemporary legal philosophy. It is novel, however, in proposing a specific mechanism and date for the law's origin and in providing an empirically based explanation for why the law so persistently supports the interests of senior males.

PART 4. AN ANSWER FOR MARY ASTELL

Mary Astell (1700) asked why women are born slaves. Her answer was that women received too little education to allow them to get decent jobs, so poverty forced them to take a husband and accept whatever tyranny he imposed. The solution was obvious. Women should be better educated so that they can earn their own money and choose for themselves whether or not to marry. Astell's proposal was practical, visionary and revolutionary. Encouraging families to spend more on educating their daughters was a shining example of how behavioural patriarchy might be ameliorated.

Astell did not challenge institutional patriarchy, however. Although she insisted that women and men are equally able, her "understanding of Creation as a hierarchically ordered whole" (Bejan 2019, 799) meant that she was comfortable with the Christian principle that women should be subservient to their husbands. For all her rebelliousness, her answer was limited to behavioural patriarchy.

Alpha-alliance theory now offers an opportunity for an additional kind of answer that focuses on institutional patriarchy. Here I briefly review the conclusions from this essay and consider some implications for gender equality.

I have argued that competition among males in the species immediately preceding *H. sapiens* led to the development of a simple version of law in early *H. sapiens*. I have done so by testing Boehm's (2012a) argument that the evolution of groupishness must have depended on alpha males losing their ability to dominate their groups. I described the multiple sources of evidence that humans are a self-domesticated species, meaning that selection has acted against reactive aggression that previously made domineering males evolutionarily successful. Fossils and genes agree in pointing to the Middle Pleistocene, shortly before three hundred thousand years ago, as the time when self-domestication began. The only reasonable explanation for the occurrence of human self-domestication is that alliances of males were able to safely kill aggressive tyrants who behaved in the style of primate alpha males. The self-domestication evidence thus supports Boehm's scenario for the origin of alpha alliances. Sophisticated language would have been necessary for males to conspire successfully to kill the tyrant, and I suggest that the same degree of linguistic sophistication would have allowed the invention and promulgation of social norms. Those norms helped the male alliances to establish themselves as ruling bodies or alpha alliances, replacing individual alpha males in the dominance hierarchy of Pleistocene groups and all subsequent societies. Males in the alpha alliance used their power to benefit their own interests, and one result has been the emergence of institutional patriarchy.

With respect to the institution of law, patriarchy appears to be a human universal or very close to it. The same appears true of government, and likely of religion. By contrast, behavioural patriarchy varies so widely in intensity that in some societies, the genders are virtually equal in power (Friedl 1967; Leacock 1978; Smuts 1995; Wood and Eagly 2002). The reasons why behavioural patriarchy can vary so much are importantly suggested by research that has surveyed variations in patriarchy as a whole. For example, scholars have pointed to the existence of private property, the extent to which males control resources, the ability of female kin to support one another, patriarchal ideology and the importance of war (Lerner 1986; Smuts 1995; Hudson et al. 2020). Given the importance of those kinds of influence, when behavioural patriarchy changes, how predictably does institutional patriarchy change also? Or vice versa? Or why does institutional patriarchy have stronger impacts on women's lives in some settings than others? Variation in the alignment between the two types of patriarchy appears to have been studied little, given that they are rarely considered separately. It would surely be a promising area of inquiry. For example, why is institutional patriarchy sometimes less intense than behavioural patriarchy (as in the United States; MacKinnon 2012) and sometimes more so (as indicated for the Batek; Endicott and Endicott 2008)?

Much research is therefore needed, but even now, it is worthwhile to speculate why institutional patriarchy varies relatively little, as it appears to do.

Two possibilities suggest themselves for why men might fear losing institutional power to women, one more benign but self-deceptive, the other more cynical and accurate. The nicer version sees men as being fearful that gender equality would damage societal function in general. The more cynical idea is that gender equality would threaten the ability of men in the alpha alliance to maintain their status, whether in relation to the hierarchy of gender or the hierarchy of men. Many benefits could be in jeopardy. If women held equal sway, for instance, they might challenge the senior men's rights to exert reproductive control over their women.

The benign and cynical ideas are both supported by the widespread fear that if women were to take over, society would fall apart. Among the Baruya horticulturalists of New Guinea, women were believed to have greater creative powers than men: "But when the women are left to their own devices, these powers engender chaos. The men were forced to step in and restore order, and to do this, they had to inflict violence on the women, kill them, rob them and so forth. In sum, force or cunning was required to separate the women from the sources of their power so that the men might capture and harness it for the benefit of all. . . . That is why chaos would once again erupt if men were ever to relax their hold. The men's struggle against the women is never-ending" (Godelier 2011, 326). Similar views are found among hunter-gatherers in Tierra del Fuego (Bridges 1948), among horticulturalists in Amazonia (Mehinaku [Gregor, 2011]; Mundurucu [Murphy, 1957]) and in Western thought. Pateman (1980) recounts how Western male elites have routinely viewed women as dangerous on the premise that women do not have the requisite nature or natural capacities to properly participate in civil life. "Never has a people perished from an excess of wine," wrote Jean-Jacques Rousseau. "All perish from the disorder of women" (Pateman 1980, 17).

The more benign justification for maintaining the gender hierarchy is that women's psychology is not suitable for administering civil life. Sigmund Freud was explicit: "The first requisite of civilization . . . is that of justice—that is, the assurance that a law once made will not be broken in favour of an individual," but only men had the requisite "instinctual sublimations" for the task (Freud 1989, 49). Society would run more smoothly for everyone if men were in charge. Pateman (1980) discusses the idea in detail.

[WRANGHAM] *The Evolution of Institutional Patriarchy*

The darker explanation for men's fear of institutional gender equality concerns the fact that since men in the alpha alliance make the laws, they are the individuals who we should expect to feel threatened by women gaining more power. If the legal system indeed maintains elite male interests at the expense of other members of society, the threat posed by women's increased participation is not that women are incompetent but that their goals for justice are different from men's: women would not want as patriarchal a society as alpha-alliance men have achieved. Gender equality would therefore undermine alpha alliance interests in controlling women's sexuality and in maintaining a steep dominance hierarchy. This conforms tidily to alpha-alliance theory. The case is complicated, of course, by the fact that women married to high-status men will often benefit from supporting the interests of the alpha alliance.

Institutional patriarchy can plausibly be seen to persist, then, because men in the alpha alliance have evolved a system for controlling the violence of other men: they benefit from that system, they share breeding rights to women among themselves, they are able to use the system to perpetuate their status and they find ways to justify keeping women from gaining power. The power that men gain from being a member of an alpha alliance is far more than any man can acquire by acting independently. As a male grows into membership of his alliance nowadays, he follows rules that have been established for a longer period than he or anyone else can remember. The system, like the power that he acquires simply by maturing into it as the boy becomes the man, appears to feel all too natural.

Traditionally, the apparent naturalness of patriarchy has been ascribed to anatomy and physiology even by liberals and feminists. For John Locke, the husband's will must prevail because he is naturally the "abler and stronger" (Pateman 1980, 121). For Firestone (2003, 8), procreation is "a fundamentally oppressive biological condition" that explains male freedom to dominate. For Ortner (1974), women's biology is claimed by every culture as making women closer to nature than men, and women have therefore been treated as belonging to a lower order of existence than men. Numerous variants of such themes have been proposed (Lerner 1986). Many such ideas seem likely to serve male interests by implying that patriarchy is simply the way things are (Diane Rosenfeld, pers. comm.).

Alpha-alliance theory is similar to conventional theories of patriarchy in invoking evolved sex differences. Instead of referring to biological differences in size, parenting or fighting ability, however, it argues that the critical difference between male and female is psychological: How concerned are men and women about male violence towards other men in the same group? Men are desperately concerned about controlling male–male violence; women are much less interested in that social problem. So the ultimate root of institutional patriarchy, the reason why male–male coalitions are so strong, is that senior men are more fearful than women are that the senior men will lose their status to other men.

For feminists, a positive aspect of this conclusion is that it allows easier routes to a reduced patriarchy than are afforded by a focus on sex differences in fighting ability or reproductive constraints. The critical point is that institutions matter, such that when an enlightened populace increases gender equality by making institutions less biased in favour of males, it is hitting at the very core of patriarchy. History proves the point. Women's lives have been enormously improved since Mary Astell's day. There will doubtless be numerous obstacles to a complete erosion of male bias, both in institutional rules and in the ways that they are enacted. Important reversals are admittedly possible, such as when societal collapse leads to an increase in male–male violence: the militias that flourish in societal chaos such as seen in recent decades in Libya, Syria or the Democratic Republic of the Congo are rarely kind to women. Nevertheless, over the long term, the trends leading to women increasingly sharing power with men can plausibly be imagined to continue and strengthen. The history of female emancipation and many other moves towards gender equality already indicate that biology, in the case of institutional patriarchy, is not destiny. Gender equality may sometimes seem far off, but to the extent that it depends on institutions, the recent trends have been in the right direction. Whether they will continue that way remains to be seen.

ACKNOWLEDGMENTS

I thank Robert Reich and Stanford University's Tanner Committee for the invitation to give the 2019–20 academic year lectures, which were delayed by circumstance until 2022. Deborah Gordon, Richard Klein, Lisa Lloyd and Ian Morris kindly offered comments on my lectures. Joanie Berry, Pam Gordon and Jamie Jones provided much help and hospitality in planning and during my visit to Stanford. I thank Diane Rosenfeld for inviting me to present a draft lecture to her Harvard Law School class on Gender Violence, Law, and Social Justice. For constructive comments on an earlier draft and other kinds of assistance, I am grateful to Joyce Benenson, Richard Connor, Lloyd Demetrius, Chet Kamin, Lisa Lloyd, Rose McDermott, Joan O'Bryan, Diane Rosenfeld, Amar Sarkar and Anna Walker. For long-term collaboration on topics related to self-domestication, I thank Brian Hare and cherish the memory of Christopher Boehm, who died in November 2021.

NOTES

1 Nowadays, Astell's reference to slaves seems insensitive to the realities of chattel slavery, but it was less so in terms of the discourse of the seventeenth century (Bejan, 2019).

2 "Alpha alliance" is a neologism, coined because the term "moral community" is problematic. The word "community" is easily misunderstood because the alpha alliance does not include all members of the social group. The alpha alliance is usually composed primarily or entirely of senior males, and in many societies, it exerts political dominance over other subgroups, such as women, younger husbands, bachelors, immature individuals, adults in networks marked by socially significant features such as ethnicity, sexuality, profession, and so on. The alpha alliance is therefore a "subcommunity" rather than the whole "community." "Moral" is also a problem. According to Boehm's (2012a) hypothesis, human sensitivity to moral rules (including a conscience and a sense of right and wrong) evolved as a result of the actions of these networks. That means that in its early years, the network was not moral; it was merely coalitionary or collaborative.

3 Boehm (2012a) implied that execution had already been practiced for at least six to seven million years before the evolution of the alpha alliance.

4 In some Cercopithecine monkeys, the female-dominance hierarchy is headed by an alliance of closely related kin. However, this "female alpha alliance" dominates only females, not adult males (Bergman et al., 2003).

5 Moral feelings associated with fairness have been argued to be present in nonhumans, notably capuchins (*Cebus apella*) and chimpanzees (*Pan troglodytes*; Brosnan and de Waal, 2003). Experiments show, however, that only humans have a tendency to sacrifice personal gain for the sake of equality, whereas nonhumans' apparent concern for fairness reflects other motivations such as efforts to manipulate an experimenter (Engelmann et al., 2017; McAuliffe and Santos, 2018). Accordingly, traits associated with fairness—including senses of responsibility, obligation, duty, guilt, and shame—appear to be restricted to humans.

6 Whether the increase in cooperation results from signalling has not been reported, but it seems more likely to result from second-party interactions such as reduced aggressiveness among low-ranking individuals.

REFERENCES

aan het Rot, Marije, D. S. Moskowitz, and Peter J. de Jong. 2015. "Intrapersonal and Interpersonal Concomitants of Facial Blushing during Everyday Social Encounters." *PLOS One* 10 (e0118243): 1–19. https://doi.org/10.1371/journal.pone.0118243.

Agnvall, Beatrix, Johan Bételky, Rebecca Katajamaa, and Per Jensen. 2018. "Is Evolution of Domestication Driven by Tameness? A Selective

Review with Focus on Chickens." *Applied Animal Behaviour Science* 205: 227–33. https://doi.org/10.1016/j.applanim.2017.09.006.

Ågren, J. Arvid, Nicholas G. Davies, and Kevin R. Foster. 2019. "Enforcement Is Central to the Evolution of Cooperation." *Nature, Ecology and Evolution* 3 (7): 1018–29. https://doi.org/10.1038/s41559-019-0907-1.

Alexander, R. D. 1987. *The Biology of Moral Systems*. New York: Aldine de Gruyter.

Alexander, R. D. 1990. *How Did Humans Evolve? Reflections on the Uniquely Unique Species*. Special Publication 1. Ann Arbor: University of Michigan Museum of Zoology.

Anderl, Christine, Tim Hahn, Ann-Kathrin Schmidt, Heike Moldenhauer, Karolien Notebaert, Celina Chantal Clément, and Sabine Windmann. 2016. "Facial Width-to-Height Ratio Predicts Psychopathic Traits in Males." *Personality and Individual Differences* 88: 99–101. https://doi.org/10.1016/j.paid.2015.08.057.

Andirkó, Alejandro, Juan Moriano, Alessandro Vitriolo, Martin Kuhlwilm, Giuseppe Testa, and Cedric Boeckx. 2022. "Temporal Mapping of Derived High-Frequency Gene Variants Supports the Mosaic Nature of the Evolution of *Homo Sapiens*." *Scientific Reports* 12 (9937): 1–9. https://doi.org/10.1038/s41598-022-13589-0.

Archer, John. 2006. "Cross-Cultural Differences in Physical Aggression between Partners: A Social-Role Analysis." *Personality and Social Psychology Review* 10 (2): 133–53.

Astell, Mary. 1700. *Some Reflections upon Marriage*. Seattle: Saltar's Point Press.

Axelrod, Robert. 2006. *The Evolution of Cooperation*. New York: Basic Books.

Bagehot, Walter. 1872. "Physics and Politics: Or Thoughts on the Application of the Principles of 'Natural Selection' and 'Inheritance' to Political Society." London: Henry King.

Baldassarri, Delia. 2015. "Cooperative Networks: Altruism, Group Solidarity, Reciprocity, and Sanctioning in Ugandan Producer Organizations." *American Journal of Sociology* 121 (2): 355–95.

Baniel, Alice, Guy Cowlishaw, and Elise Huchard. 2017. "Male Violence and Sexual Intimidation in a Wild Primate Society." *Current Biology* 27 (14): 2163–68. https://doi.org/10.1016/j.cub.2017.06.013.

Bauer, Gretchen. 2012. "'Let There Be a Balance': Women in African Parliaments." *Political Studies Review* 10: 370–84. https://doi.org/10.1111/j.1478-9302.2012.00272.x.

Bejan, Teresa M. 2019. "'Since All the World Is Mad, Why Should Not I Be So?' Mary Astell on Equality, Hierarchy, and Ambition." *Political Theory* 47 (6): 781–808. https://doi.org/10.1177/0090591719852040.

Belyaev, D. K. 1969. "Domestication of Animals." *Science Journal* 5 (1): 47–52.

Belyaev, Dmitri K., and Lyudmila N. Trut. 1975. "Some Genetic and Endocrine Effects of Selection for Domestication in Silver Foxes." In *The Wild Canids: Their Systematics, Behavioral Ecology, and Evolution*, edited by Michael W. Fox, 416–26. New York: Van Nostrand Reinhold.

Ben-Dor, Miki, and Ran Barkai. 2020. "The Importance of Large Prey Animals during the Pleistocene and the Implications of Their Extinction on the Use of Dietary Ethnographic Analogies." *Journal of Anthropological Archaeology* 59 (101192): 1–12. https://doi.org/10.1016/j.jaa.2020.101192.

Bergman, Thore J., Jacinta C. Beehner, Dorothy L. Cheney, and Robert M. Seyfarth. 2003. "Hierarchical Classification by Rank and Kinship in Baboons." *Science* 302 (5648): 1234–36. https://doi.org/10.1126/science.1087513.

Berndt, Catherine H. 1965. "Women and the 'Secret Life.'" In *Aboriginal Man in Australia*, edited by Ronald M. Berndt and Catherine H. Berndt, 238–82. Sydney: Angus and Robertson.

Berndt, Ronald M. 1965. "Law and Order in Aboriginal Australia." In *Aboriginal Man in Australia*, edited by Ronald M. Berndt and Catherine H. Berndt, 167–206. Sydney: Angus and Robertson.

Betzig, Laura. 1982. "Despotism and Differential Reproduction: A Cross-Cultural Correlation of Conflict Asymmetry, Hierarchy, and Degree of Polygyny." *Ethology and Sociobiology* 3 (4): 209–21.

Betzig, Laura. 2012. "Means, Variances, and Ranges in Reproductive Success: Comparative Evidence." *Evolution and Human Behavior* 33 (4): 309–17. https://doi.org/10.1016/j.evolhumbehav.2011.10.008.

Bingham, Paul M. 2001. "Human Evolution and Human History: A Complete Theory." *Evolutionary Anthropology* 9 (6): 248–57. https://doi.org/10.1002/1520-6505(2000)9:6<248::AID-EVAN1003>3.0.CO;2-X.

Blumberg, Rae L. 2004. "Extending Lenski's Schema to Hold up Both Halves of the Sky—a Theory-Guided Way of Conceptualizing Agrarian Societies That Illuminates a Puzzle about Gender

Stratification." *Sociological Theory* 22 (2): 278–91. https://doi.org/10.1111/j.0735-2751.2004.00218.x.

Boas, Franz. (1911) 1938. *The Mind of Primitive Man*. New York: Macmillan.

Boehm, Christopher. 1993. "Egalitarian Behavior and Reverse Dominance Hierarchy." *Current Anthropology* 34 (3): 227–40.

Boehm, Christopher. 1999. *Hierarchy in the Forest: The Evolution of Egalitarian Behavior*. Cambridge, MA: Harvard University Press.

Boehm, Christopher. 2012a. *Moral Origins: The Evolution of Virtue, Altruism, and Shame*. New York: Basic Books.

Boehm, Christopher. 2012b. "Ancestral Hierarchy and Conflict." *Science* 336 (6083): 844–47. https://doi.org/10.1126/science.1219961.

Boehm, Christopher. 2014. "The Moral Consequences of Social Selection." *Behaviour* 151 (2–3): 167–83.

Boehm, Christopher. 2017. "Ancestral Precursors, Social Control, and Social Selection in the Evolution of Morals." In *Chimpanzees and Human Evolution*, edited by M. N. Muller, R. W. Wrangham, and D. P. Pilbeam, 746–90. Cambridge, MA: Harvard University Press.

Boehm, Christopher. 2018. "Collective Intentionality: A Basic and Early Component of Moral Evolution." *Philosophical Psychology* 31 (5): 680–702. https://doi.org/10.1080/09515089.2018.1486607.

Boomsma, Jacobus J. 2016. "Fifty Years of Illumination about the Natural Levels of Adaptation." *Current Biology* 26 (24): R1247–R1271.

Bowles, Samuel, and Herbert Gintis. 2004. "The Evolution of Strong Reciprocity: Cooperation in Heterogeneous Populations." *Theoretical Population Biology* 65 (1): 17–28. https://doi.org/10.1016/j.tpb.2003.07.001.

Boyd, Robert, Herbert Gintis, and Samuel Bowles. 2010. "Coordinated Punishment of Defectors Sustains Cooperation and Can Proliferate When Rare." *Science* 328 (5978): 617–20.

Boyd, Robert, and Peter Richerson. 2005. *Not by Genes Alone: How Culture Transformed Human Evolution*. Chicago: University of Chicago Press.

Bridges, E. Lucas. 1948. *Uttermost Part of the Earth*. London: Hodder and Stoughton.

Brosnan, Sarah F., and Frans de Waal. 2003. "Monkeys Reject Unequal Pay." *Nature* 425 (6955): 297–99.

Bshary, Redouan, and Nichola J. Raihani. 2017. "Helping in Humans and Other Animals: A Fruitful Interdisciplinary Dialogue." *Proc.*

R. Soc. B. 284 (20170929): 1–9. https://doi.org/10.1098/rspb.2017.0929.

Burch, E. S., Jr. 2005. *Alliance and Conflict: The World System of the Inupiaq Eskimos.* Lincoln: University of Nebraska Press.

Burkart, J. M., O. Allon, F. Amici, C. Fichtel, C. Finkenwirth, A. Heschl, J. Huber, et al. 2014. "The Evolutionary Origin of Human Hyper-Cooperation." *Nature Communications* 5 (4747): 1–9. https://doi.org/10.1038/ncomms5747.

Burkart, J. M., S. B. Hrdy, and C. P. van Schaik. 2009. "Cooperative Breeding and Human Cognitive Evolution." *Evolutionary Anthropology* 18 (5): 175–86. https://doi.org/10.1002/evan.20222.

Burton-Chellew, Maxwell N., Claire El Mouden, and S. A. West. 2017. "Social Learning and the Demise of Costly Cooperation in Humans." *Proc. R. Soc. B.* 284 (20170067): 1–9. https://doi.org/10.1098/rspb.2017.0067.

Buss, David M., and David P. Schmitt. 2019. "Mate Preferences and Their Behavioral Manifestations." *Annual Review of Psychology* 70: 77–110. https://doi.org/10.1146/annurev-psych-010418-103408.

Chapais, Bernard. 2015. "Competence and the Evolutionary Origins of Status and Power in Humans." *Human Nature* 26 (2): 161–83. https://doi.org/10.1007/s12110-015-9227-6.

Choi, Jung-Kyoo, and Samuel Bowles. 2007. "The Coevolution of Parochial Altruism and War." *Science* 318 (5850): 636–40.

Chudek, Maciej, and Joseph Henrich. 2011. "Culture–Gene Coevolution, Norm-Psychology and the Emergence of Human Prosociality." *Trends in Cognitive Sciences* 15 (5): 218–26. https://doi.org/10.1016/j.tics.2011.03.003.

Cieri, Robert L., Steven E. Churchill, Robert G. Franciscus, Jingzhi Tan, and Brian Hare. 2014. "Craniofacial Feminization, Social Tolerance, and the Origins of Behavioral Modernity." *Current Anthropology* 55 (4): 419–43. http://www.jstor.org/stable/10.1086/677209.

Clutton-Brock, Tim, and Katherine McAuliffe. 2009. "Female Mate Choice in Mammals." *Quarterly Review of Biology* 84 (1): 3–27. https://doi.org/10.1086/596461.

Collier, Jane F. 1988. *Marriage and Inequality in Classless Societies.* Stanford, CA: Stanford University Press.

Collier, Jane F., and Michelle Z. Rosaldo. 1981. "Politics and Gender in Simple Societies." In *Sexual Meanings: The Cultural Construction of Gender and Sexuality*, edited by Sherry B. Ortner and Harriet Whitehead, 275–329. Cambridge: Cambridge University Press.

Collins, Kevin. 1983. "The Role of Education in Reinforcing the Group Model in Japanese Society." Paper presented at the Annual Conference of the Australian Comparative and International Education Society, Hamilton, New Zealand.

Conaghan, Joanne. 2013. *Law and Gender*. Oxford: Oxford University Press.

Connor, Richard C. 2010. "Cooperation beyond the Dyad: On Simple Models and a Complex Society." *Phil. Trans. R. Soc. B.* 365 (1553): 2687–97. https://doi.org/10.1098/rstb.2010.0150.

Coppinger, Raymond, and Lorna Coppinger. 2000. *Dogs: A Startling New Understanding of Canine Origin, Behavior, and Evolution*. New York: Scribner.

Crozier, Ray. 2010. "The Puzzle of Blushing." *Psychologist* 23 (5): 390–93.

Curry, Oliver Scott, Daniel Austin Mullins, and Harvey Whitehouse. 2019. "Is It Good to Cooperate? Testing the Theory of Morality-as-Cooperation in 60 Societies." *Current Anthropology* 60 (1): 47–69.

Darwin, Charles. (1871) 2005. *The Descent of Man, and Selection in Relation to Sex, from So Simple a Beginning: The Four Great Books of Charles Darwin*. New York: W. W. Norton.

Darwin, Charles. (1883) 1998. *The Variation of Animals and Plants under Domestication*. Baltimore, MD: Johns Hopkins University Press.

Dear, Keith, Kevin Dutton, and Elaine Fox. 2019. "Do 'Watching Eyes' Influence Antisocial Behavior? A Systematic Review & Meta-Analysis." *Evolution and Human Behavior* 40 (3): 269–80.

De Beauvoir, Simone. 1953. *The Second Sex*. New York: Alfred A. Knopf.

DeScioli, Peter, and Robert Kurzban. 2009. "Mysteries of Morality." *Cognition* 112 (2): 281–99. https://doi.org/10.1016/j.cognition.2009.05.008.

Devries, K. M., J. Y. T. Mak, C. García-Moreno, M. Petzold, J. C. Child, G. Falder, S. Lim, et al. 2013. "The Global Prevalence of Intimate Partner Violence against Women." *Science* 340 (6140): 1527–28.

De Waal, F. B. M. 2006. *Primates and Philosophers: How Morality Evolved*. Princeton, NJ: Princeton University Press.

Donovan, James M. 2008. *Legal Anthropology: An Introduction*. New York: Rowman & Littlefield.

Duffy, Kimberly G., Richard W. Wrangham, and Joan B. Silk. 2007. "The Price of Power: Male Chimpanzees Exchange Political Support for Mating Opportunities." *Current Biology* 17 (15): R586–R587.

Dugatkin, Lee, and Lyudmila Trut. 2017. *How to Tame a Fox (and Build a Dog): Visionary Scientists and a Siberian Tale of Jump-Started Evolution*. Chicago: University of Chicago Press.

Durkheim, Émile. (1914) 1973. "The Dualism of Human Nature and Its Social Conditions." In *Emile Durkheim on Morality and Society: Selected Writings*, edited by Robert N. Bellah, 149–63. Chicago: University of Chicago Press.

Dyble, Mark. 2021. "The Evolution of Altruism through War Is Highly Sensitive to Population Structure and to Civilian and Fighter Mortality." *Proceedings of the National Academy of Sciences* 118 (e2011142118): 1–6. https://doi.org/10.1073/pnas.2011142118.

Eisner, Manuel. 2011. "Killing Kings." *British Journal of Criminology* 51 (3): 556–77.

Elkin, A. P. 1938. *The Australian Aborigines: How to Understand Them*. Sydney: Angus & Robertson.

Eller, Cynthia. 2000. *The Myth of Matriarchal Prehistory: Why an Invented Past Won't Give Women a Future*. Boston: Beacon.

Endicott, Kirk. 1988. "Property, Power and Conflict among the Batek of Malaysia." In *Hunters and Gatherers 2: Property, Power and Ideology*, edited by Tim Ingold, David Riches, and James Woodburn, 110–27. Oxford: Berg.

Endicott, Kirk M., and Karen L. Endicott. 2008. *The Headman Was a Woman: The Gender Egalitarian Batek of Malaysia*. Long Grove, IL: Waveland.

Engelmann, Jan M., Jeremy B. Clift, Esther Herrmann, and Michael Tomasello. 2017. "Social Disappointment Explains Chimpanzees' Behaviour in the Inequity Aversion Task." *Proceedings of the Royal Society B* 284 (20171502): 1–8. https://doi.org/10.1098/rspb.2017.1502.

Engelmann, Jan M., Esther Herrmann, and Michael Tomasello. 2012. "Five-Year Olds, but Not Chimpanzees, Attempt to Manage Their Reputations." *PLOS One* 7 (10): e48433.

Engelmann, Jan M., Esther Herrmann, and Michael Tomasello. 2016. "The Effects of Being Watched on Resource Acquisition in Chimpanzees and Human Children." *Animal Cognition* 19 (1): 147–51.

Erdal, David, and Andrew Whiten. 1994. "On Human Egalitarianism: An Evolutionary Product of Machiavellian Status Escalation?" *Current Anthropology* 35 (2): 175–78.

Evans, Robert, Harry Collins, Martin Weinel, Jennifer Lyttleton-Smith, Hannah O'Mahoney, and Willow Leonard-Clarke. 2019. "Groups and Individuals: Conformity and Diversity in the Performance of Gendered Identities." *British Journal of Sociology* 70 (4): 1561–81. https://doi.org/10.1111/1468-4446.12507.

Fehr, Ernst, and Urs Fischbacher. 2004. "Third-Party Punishment and Social Norms." *Evolution and Human Behavior* 25 (2): 63–87. https://doi.org/10.1016/S1090-5138(04)00005-4.

Fehr, Ernst, Urs Fischbacher, and Simon Gächter. 2002. "Strong Reciprocity, Human Cooperation, and the Enforcement of Social Norms." *Human Nature* 13 (1): 1–25. https://doi.org/10.1007/s12110-002-1012-7.

Feldblum, Joseph T., Christopher Krupenye, Joel Bray, Anne E. Pusey, and Ian C. Gilby. 2021. "Social Bonds Provide Multiple Pathways to Reproductive Success in Wild Male Chimpanzees." *iScience* 24 (102864): 1–19. https://doi.org/10.1016/j.isci.2021.102864.

Feldblum, Joseph T., Emily E. Wroblewski, Rebecca S. Rudicell, Beatrice H. Hahn, Thais Paiva, Mine Cetinkaya-Rundel, Anne E. Pusey, and Ian C. Gilby. 2014. "Sexually Coercive Male Chimpanzees Sire More Offspring." *Current Biology* 24 (23): 2855–60.

Finnis, John. 2011. *Natural Law and Natural Rights*. Oxford: Oxford University Press.

Firestone, Shulamith. 2003. *The Dialectic of Sex: The Case for Feminist Revolution*. New York: Farrar, Straus and Giroux.

Fish, Jonathan S. 2013. "*Homo duplex* Revisited: A Defence of Émile Durkheim's Theory of the Moral Self." *Journal of Classical Sociology* 13 (3): 338–58. https://doi.org/10.1177/1468795X13480440.

Flack, Jessica C., Frans B. M. de Waal, and David C. Krakauer. 2005. "Social Structure, Robustness, and Policing Cost in a Cognitively Sophisticated Species." *American Naturalist* 165 (5): E126-E139. https://doi.org/10.1086/429277.

Flack, Jessica C., Michelle Girvan, Frans B. M. de Waal, and David C. Krakauer. 2006. "Policing Stabilizes Construction of Social Niches in Primates." *Nature* 439 (7075): 426–29. https://doi.org/10.1038/nature04326.

Flanagan, James G. 1989. "Hierarchy in Simple 'Egalitarian' Societies." *Annual Review of Anthropology* 18: 245–66.

Flinn, Mark V., David C. Geary, and Carol V. Ward. 2005. "Ecological Dominance, Social Competition, and Coalitionary Arms Races: Why Humans Evolved Extraordinary Intelligence." *Evolution and Human Behavior* 26 (1): 10–46. https://doi.org/10.1016/j.evolhumbehav.2004.08.005.

Flood, Josephine. 2006. *The Original Australians: Story of the Aboriginal People*. Crows Nest NSW Australia: Allen & Unwin.

Frank, Steven A. 2003. "Perspective: Repression of Competition and the Evolution of Cooperation." *Evolution* 57 (4): 693–705.

Frank, Steven A. 2013. "A New Theory of Cooperation." In *Human Social Evolution: The Foundational Works of Richard D. Alexander*, edited by Kyle Summers and Bernard Crespi, 40–47. New York: Oxford University Press.

Freud, Sigmund. (1930) 1989. *Civilization and Its Discontents*. New York: W. W. Norton.

Friedl, Ernestine. 1967. "The Position of Women: Appearance and Reality." *Anthropological Quarterly* 40 (3): 98–105.

Fuller, Lon Luvois. 1969. *The Morality of Law*. New Haven, CT: Yale University Press.

Furuichi, Takeshi. 2011. "Female Contributions to the Peaceful Nature of Bonobo Society." *Evolutionary Anthropology* 20 (4): 131–42. https://doi.org/10.1002/evan.20308.

Gavrilets, Sergey, Edgar A. Duenez-Guzman, and Michael D. Vose. 2008. "Dynamics of Alliance Formation and the Egalitarian Revolution." *PLOS One* 3 (10): e3293.

Geary, David C. 2021. *Male, Female: The Evolution of Human Sex Differences*. 3rd ed. Washington, DC: American Psychological Association.

Geiger, Madeleine, M. R. Sánchez-Villagra, and Anna K. Lindholm. 2018. "A Longitudinal Study of Phenotypic Changes in Early Domestication of House Mice." *R. Soc. Open Sci.* 5 (172099): 1–7. https://doi.org/10.1098/rsos.172099.

Geniole, Shawn N., Thomas F. Denson, Barnaby J. Dixson, Justin M. Carré, and Cheryl M. McCormick. 2015. "Evidence from Meta-Analyses of the Facial Width-to-Height Ratio as an Evolved Cue of Threat." *PLOS One* 10 (7): e0132726. https://doi.org/10.1371/journal.pone.0132726.

Geniole, Shawn N., and Cheryl M. McCormick. 2015. "Facing Our Ancestors: Judgements of Aggression Are Consistent and Related to the Facial Width-to-Height Ratio in Men Irrespective of Beards." *Evolution and Human Behavior* 36 (4): 279–85.

Ghazanfar, Asif A., Lauren M. Kelly, Daniel Y. Takahashi, Sandra Winters, Rebecca Terrett, and James P. Higham. 2020. "Domestication Phenotype Linked to Vocal Behavior in Marmoset Monkeys." *Current Biology* 30 (24): 1–17. https://doi.org/10.1016/j.cub.2020.09.049.

Gintis, Herbert. 2000. "Strong Reciprocity and Human Sociality." *Journal of Theoretical Biology* 206 (2): 169–79. https://doi.org/10.1006/jtbi.2000.2111.

Gintis, Herbert, Samuel Bowles, Robert Boyd, and Ernst Fehr. 2003. "Explaining Altruistic Behavior in Humans." *Evolution and Human Behavior* 24 (3): 153–72. https://doi.org/10.1016/S1090-5138(02)00157-5.

Gintis, Herbert, Carel van Schaik, and Christopher Boehm. 2015. "*Zoon Politikon*: The Evolutionary Origins of Human Political Systems." *Current Anthropology* 56 (3): 327–53.

Gintis, Herbert, Eric Alden Smith, and Samuel Bowles. 2001. "Costly Signaling and Cooperation." *Journal of Theoretical Biology* 213 (1): 103–19. https://doi.org/10.1006/jtbi.2001.2406.

Gleeson, Ben Thomas, and Geoff Kushnick. 2018. "Female Status, Food Security, and Stature Sexual Dimorphism: Testing Mate Choice as a Mechanism in Human Self-Domestication." *American Journal of Physical Anthropology* 167 (3): 458–69. https://doi.org/10.1002/ajpa.23642.

Godelier, Maurice. 2011. "Bodies, Kinship and Power(s) in the Baruya Culture." *Journal of Ethnographic Theory* 1 (1): 315–44.

Gokhman, David, Nadav Mishol, Marc de Manuel, David de Juan, Jonathan Shuqrun, Eran Meshorer, Tomas Marques-Bonet, et al. 2019. "Reconstructing Denisovan Anatomy Using DNA Methylation Maps." *Cell* 179 (1): 180–92. https://doi.org/10.1016/j.cell.2019.08.035.

Goldberg, Steven. 1993. *Why Men Rule: A Theory of Male Dominance*. Chicago: Open Court.

Goodall, Jane. 1986. *The Chimpanzees of Gombe: Patterns of Behavior*. Cambridge, MA: Harvard University Press.

Gorelik, Gregory. 2022. "Domains of Female Choice in Human Evolution." *Evolutionary Human Sciences* 17 (2): 187–208. https://doi.org/10.1037/ebs0000276.

Graham, Jesse, Jonathan Haidt, Sena Koleva, Matt Motyl, Ravi Iyer, Sean P. Wojcik, and Peter H. Ditto. 2013. "Moral Foundations Theory: The Pragmatic Validity of Moral Pluralism." *Advances in Experimental Social Psychology* 47: 55–130. https://doi.org/10.1016/B978-0-12-407236-7.00002-4.

Gregor, Thomas. 2011. "The Torments of Initiation and the Question of Resistance." In *Echoes of the Tambaran: Masculinity, History and the*

Subject in the Work of Donald F. Tuzin, edited by David Lipset and Paul Roscoe, 241–58. Canberra, Australia: ANU Press.

Gulliver, P. H. 1969. "Case Studies of Law in Non-Western Societies: Introduction." In *Law in Culture and Society*, edited by Laura Nader, 11–23. Chicago: Aldine.

Gutmann, Jerg, and Stefan Voigt. 2016. "The Rule of Law: Measurement and Deep Roots." In *ILE Working Paper Series*, no. 1. Hamburg, Germany: University of Hamburg, Institute of Law and Economics (ILE). http://hdl.handle.net/10419/156097.

Haidt, Jonathan. 2012. *The Righteous Mind: Why Good People Are Divided by Politics and Religion*. New York: Pantheon.

Hamilton, William D. 1975. "Innate Social Aptitudes in Man, an Approach from Evolutionary Genetics." In *Biosocial Anthropology*, edited by Robin Fox, 133–57. New York: Wiley.

Harari, Yuval Noah. 2011. *Sapiens: A Brief History of Humankind*. New York: Vintage.

Hare, Brian. 2017. "Survival of the Friendliest: *Homo sapiens* Evolved via Selection for Prosociality." *Annual Review of Psychology* 68: 155–86. https://doi.org/10.1146/annurev-psych-010416-044201.

Hare, Brian, Victoria Wobber, and Richard W. Wrangham. 2012. "The Self-Domestication Hypothesis: Bonobos Evolved Due to Selection against Male Aggression." *Animal Behaviour* 83 (3): 573–85. https://doi.org/10.1016/j.anbehav.2011.12.007.

Hare, Brian, and Richard W. Wrangham. 2017. "Equal, Similar but Different: Convergent Bonobos and Conserved Chimpanzees." In *Chimpanzees and Human Evolution*, edited by M. N. Muller, David Pilbeam, and R. Wrangham, 142–76. Cambridge, MA: Harvard University Press.

Hart, H. L. A. 1961. *The Concept of Law*. Oxford: Clarendon.

Haselhuhn, Michael P., Margaret E. Ormiston, and Elaine M. Wong. 2015. "Men's Facial Width-to-Height Ratio Predicts Aggression: A Meta-Analysis." *PLOS One* 10 (4): e0122637.

Hattersley, Roy. 2003. *The Life of John Wesley: A Brand from the Burning*. New York: Doubleday.

Hawkes, Kristen. 2014. "Primate Sociality to Human Cooperation: Why Us and Not Them?" *Human Nature* 25 (1): 28–48. https://doi.org/10.1007/s12110-013-9184-x.

Hawkins, M. J. 1977. "A Re-examination of Durkheim's Theory of Human Nature." *Sociological Review* 25 (2): 229–52. https://doi.org/10.1111/j.1467-954X.1977.tb00288.x.

Hayden, B., M. Deal, A. Cannon, and J. Casey. 1986. "Ecological Determinants of Women's Status among Hunter/Gatherers." *Human Evolution* 1 (5): 449–74.

Henrich, Joseph, Richard McElreath, Abigail Barr, Jean Ensminger, Clark Barrett, Alexander Bolyanatz, Juan Camilo Cardenas, et al. 2006. "Costly Punishment across Human Societies." *Science* 312 (5781): 1767–70.

Henrich, Joseph, Robert Boyd, Samuel Bowles, Colin Camerer, Ernst Fehr, Herbert Gintis, Richard McElreath, et al. 2005. "'Economic Man' in Cross-Cultural Perspective: Behavioral Experiments in 15 Small-Scale Societies." *Behavioral and Brain Sciences* 28 (6): 795–855. https://doi.org/10.1017/S0140525X05000142.

Henrich, Joseph, and Michael Muthukrishna. 2021. "The Origins and Psychology of Human Cooperation." *Annual Review of Psychology* 72: 207–40. https://doi.org/10.1146/annurev-psych-081920-042106.

Hiatt, Les R. 1996. *Arguments about Aborigines: Australia and the Evolution of Social Anthropology*. New York: Cambridge University Press.

Hill, Kim, and Magdalena A. Hurtado. 1996. *Aché Life History: The Ecology and Demography of a Foraging People*. New York: Aldine de Gruyter.

Hoebel, E. Adamson. 1954. *The Law of Primitive Man: A Study in Comparative Legal Dynamics*. Cambridge, MA: Harvard University Press.

Hrdy, Sarah B. 1997. "Raising Darwin's Consciousness: Female Sexuality and the Prehominid Origins of Patriarchy." *Human Nature* 8 (1): 1–49.

Hrdy, Sarah Blaffer. 2009. *Mothers and Others: The Evolutionary Origins of Mutual Understanding*. Cambridge, MA: Harvard University Press.

Htun, Mala, and Laurel Weldon. 2012. "Sex Equality in Family Law: Historical Legacies, Feminist Activism, and Religious Power in 70 Countries." In *World Development Report: Gender Equality and Development*. Washington, DC: World Bank. http://hdl.handle.net/10986/9204.

Hublin, Jean-Jacques, Abdelouahed Ben-Ncer, Shara E. Bailey, Sarah E. Freidline, Simon Neubauer, Matthew M. Skinner, Inga Bergmann, et al. 2017. "New Fossils from Jebel Irhoud, Morocco and the Pan-African Origin of *Homo sapiens*." *Nature* 546 (7657): 289–92.

Hudson, Valerie M., Donna Lee Bowen, and Perpetua Lynne Nielsen. 2020. *The First Political Order: How Sex Shapes Governance and National Security Worldwide.* New York: Columbia University Press.

Hunnicutt, Gwen. 2009. "Varieties of Patriarchy and Violence against Women Resurrecting 'Patriarchy' as a Theoretical Tool." *Violence against Women* 15 (5): 553–73.

Hunnicutt, Gwen. 2021. "Commentary on the Special Issue: New Ways of Thinking Theoretically about Violence against Women and Other Forms of Gender-Based Violence." *Violence against Women* 27 (5): 708–16. https://doi.org/10.1177/1077801220958484.

Ishizuka, Shintaro, Yoshi Kawamoto, Tetsuya Sakamaki, Nahoko Tokuyama, Kazuya Toda, Hiroki Okamura, and Takeshi Furuichi. 2018. "Paternity and Kin Structure among Neighbouring Groups in Wild Bonobos at Wamba." *R. Soc. Open Sci.* 5 (171006): 1–10. https://doi.org/10.1098/rsos.171006.

Johnstone, Rufus A., Michael A. Cant, Dominic Cram, and Faye J. Thompson. 2020. "Exploitative Leaders Incite Intergroup Warfare in a Social Mammal." *PNAS.* 117 (47): 29759–66. https://doi.org/10.1073/pnas.2003745117.

Kar, Robin Bradley. 2012. "Western Legal Prehistory: Reconstructing the Hidden Origins of Western Law and Civilization." *University of Illinois Law Review* 5: 1499–1702.

Katajamaa, Rebecca, and Per Jensen. 2020. "Tameness Correlates with Domestication Related Traits in a Red Junglefowl Intercross." *Genes, Brain and Behavior* 20 (3): 1–12. https://doi.org/10.1111/gbb.12704.

Keen, Ian. 2006. "Constraints on the Development of Enduring Inequalities in Late Holocene Australia." *Current Anthropology* 47 (1): 7–19. https://doi.org/10.1086/497672.

Kent, Susan. 1995. "Does Sedentarization Promote Gender Inequality? A Case Study from the Kalahari." *J. Roy. Anthrop. Inst. (N.S.)* 1 (3): 513–36.

Kessler, Sharon E., Tyler R. Bonnell, Joanna M. Setchell, and Colin A. Chapman. 2018. "Social Structure Facilitated the Evolution of Care-Giving as a Strategy for Disease Control in the Human Lineage." *Scientific Reports* 8 (13997): 1–13. https://doi.org/10.1038/s41598-018-31568-2.

Kokkonen, Andrej, Suthan Krishnarajan, Jørgen Møller, and Anders Sundell. 2021. "Blood Is Thicker Than Water: Family Size and Leader

Deposition in Medieval and Early Modern Europe." *Journal of Politics* 83 (4): 1246–59. https://doi.org/10.1086/715065.

Krasnow, Max M., and Andrew W. Delton. 2016. "The Sketch Is Blank: No Evidence for an Explanatory Role for Cultural Group Selection." *Behavioral and Brain Sciences* 39 (e43): 31–32. https://doi.org/10.1017/S0140525X15000163.

Krasnow, Max M., Andrew W. Delton, Leda Cosmides, and John Tooby. 2015. "Group Cooperation without Group Selection: Modest Punishment Can Recruit Much Cooperation." *PLOS One* 10 (4): 1–17.

Langergraber, Kevin E., Grit Schubert, Carolyn Rowney, Richard Wrangham, Zinta Zommers, and Linda Vigilant. 2011. "Genetic Differentiation and the Evolution of Cooperation in Chimpanzees and Humans." *Proc. R. Soc. B.* 278 (1717): 2546–52.

Langness, L. L. 1990. "Oedipus in the New Guinea Highlands?" *Ethos* 18 (4): 387–406. http://www.jstor.org/stable/640310.

Leach, Helen. 2003. "Human Domestication Reconsidered." *Current Anthropology* 44 (3): 349–68. https://doi.org/10.1086/368119.

Leacock, Eleanor. 1978. "Women's Status in Egalitarian Society: Implications for Social Evolution." *Current Anthropology* 19 (2): 247–55. https://doi.org/10.1086/204025.

Lee, Richard B. 1979. *The !Kung San: Men, Women and Work in a Foraging Society*. Cambridge: Cambridge University Press.

Lerner, Gerda. 1986. *The Creation of Patriarchy*. New York: Oxford University Press.

Lewis, Rebecca J. 2018. "Female Power in Primates and the Phenomenon of 'Female Dominance.'" *Annual Review of Anthropology* 47: 533–51. https://doi.org/10.1146/annurev-anthro-102317-045958.

Li, Leon, and Michael Tomasello. 2021. "On the Moral Functions of Language." *Social Cognition* 39 (1): 99–116.

Liberman, Kenneth. 1985. *Understanding Interaction in Central Australia: An Ethnomethodological Study of Australian Aboriginal People*. Boston: Routledge & Kegan Paul.

Llewellyn, Karl N., and E. Adamson Hoebel. 1941. *The Cheyenne Way*. Norman: University of Oklahoma Press.

Lord, Kathryn, Greger Larson, Raymond P. Coppinger, and Elinor K. Karlsson. 2020. "The History of Farm Foxes Undermines the Animal Domestication Syndrome." *Trends in Ecology and Evolution* 35 (2): 125–36. https://doi.org/10.1016/j.tree.2019.10.011.

[WRANGHAM] *The Evolution of Institutional Patriarchy*

MacKinnon, Catharine A. 1987. *Feminism Unmodified: Discourses on Life and Law*. Cambridge, MA: Harvard University Press.

MacKinnon, Catharine A. 1989. *Towards a Feminist Theory of the State*. Cambridge, MA: Harvard University Press.

MacKinnon, Catharine A. 1991. "Reflections on Sex Equality under Law." *Yale Law Journal* 100 (5): 1281–1328.

MacKinnon, Catharine A. 2005. *Women's Lives, Men's Laws*. Cambridge, MA: Belknap, Harvard University Press.

MacKinnon, Catharine A. 2012. "Gender in Constitutions." In *The Oxford Handbook of Comparative Constitutional Law*, edited by Michel Rosenfeld and András Sajó, 397–427. Oxford: Oxford University Press.

MacKinnon, Catharine A. 2017. *Butterfly Politics*. Cambridge, MA: Harvard University Press.

MacLean, Evan L., Brian Hare, Charles L. Nunn, E. Addessi, F. Amici, Rindy C. Anderson, Filippo Aureli, et al. 2014. "The Evolution of Self-Control." *Proceedings of the National Academy of Sciences* 111 (20): E2140–E2148.

Marean, Curtis W. 2015. "An Evolutionary Anthropological Perspective on Modern Human Origins." *Annual Review of Anthropology* 44: 533–56. https://doi.org/10.1146/annurev-anthro-102313-025954.

Marlowe, Frank W. 2010. *The Hadza Hunter-Gatherers of Tanzania*. Berkeley: University of California Press.

McAuliffe, Katherine, and Laurie R. Santos. 2018. "Do Animals Have a Sense of Fairness?" In *Atlas of Moral Psychology*, edited by Kurt Gray and Jesse Graham, 393–400. New York: Guilford Press.

McCarthy, Maureen S., Jack D. Lester, Marie Cibot, Linda Vigilant, and Matthew R. McLennan. 2020. "Atypically High Reproductive Skew in a Small Wild Chimpanzee Community in a Human-Dominated Landscape." *Folia Primatologica* 91 (6): 688–96. https://doi.org/10.1159/000508609.

Mead, Margaret. 1973. "Review of Goldberg, Steven (1973). The Inevitability of Patriarchy. William Morrow, NY." *Redbook* 48.

Meggitt, M. J. 1965. "Marriage among the Walbiri of Central Australia: A Statistical Examination." In *Aboriginal Man in Australia*, edited by Ronald M. Berndt and Catherine H. Berndt, 146–66. Sydney: Angus and Robertson.

Meggitt, M. J. 1987. "Understanding Australian Aboriginal Society: Kinship Systems or Cultural Categories?" In *Traditional Aboriginal*

Society: A Reader, edited by W. H. Edwards, 113–37. Melbourne, Australia: Macmillan.

Milinski, Manfred, D. Semman, T. C. M. Bakker, and H. J. Krambeck. 2001. "Cooperation through Indirect Reciprocity: Image Scoring or Standing Straight?" *Proc. R. Soc. B.* 268 (1484): 2495–2501. https://doi.org/10.1098/rspb.2001.1809.

Milinski, Manfred, Dirk Semman, and Hans-Jürgen Krambeck. 2002. "Reputation Helps Solve the 'Tragedy of the Commons.'" *Nature* 415 (6870): 424–26. https://doi.org/10.1038/415424a.

Miller, Eric. 1998. "A Note on the Protomental System and 'Groupishness': Bion's Basic Assumptions Revisited." *Human Relations* 51 (12): 1495–1508.

Montefiore, Simon Sebag. 2004. *Stalin: The Court of the Red Tsar*. New York: Alfred A. Knopf.

Muller, Martin N., M. Emery Thompson, Sonya M. Kahlenberg, and Richard W. Wrangham. 2011. "Sexual Coercion by Male Chimpanzees Shows That Female Choice May Be More Apparent Than Real." *Behavioral Ecology and Sociobiology* 65 (5): 921–33. https://doi.org/10.1007/s00265-010-1093-y.

Muller, M. N., David Pilbeam, and R. Wrangham, eds. 2017. *Chimpanzees and Human Evolution*. Cambridge MA: Harvard University Press.

Murphy, Mark C. 2007. *Philosophy of Law: The Fundamentals*. Oxford: Blackwell.

Murphy, R. F. 1957. "Intergroup Hostility and Social Cohesion." *American Anthropologist* 59 (6): 1018–35.

Noser, Emilou, Jessica Schoch, and Ulrike Ehlert. 2018. "The Influence of Income and Testosterone on the Validity of Facial Width-to-Height Ratio as a Biomarker for Dominance." *PLOS One* 13 (11): e0207333. https://doi.org/10.1371/journal.pone.0207333.

Nowak, Martin A., and Karl Sigmund. 2005. "Evolution of Indirect Reciprocity." *Nature* 437 (7063): 1291–98. https://doi.org/10.1038/nature04131.

Okada, Daijiro, and Paul M. Bingham. 2008. "Human Uniqueness—Self-Interest and Social Cooperation." *Journal of Theoretical Biology* 253 (2): 261–70.

Ortner, Sherry B. 1974. "Is Female to Male as Nature Is to Culture?" In *Woman, Culture, and Society*, edited by Michelle Z. Rosaldo and Louise Lamphere, 67–88. Stanford, CA: Stanford University Press.

Otterbein, Keith F. 1986. *The Ultimate Coercive Sanction: A Cross-Cultural Study of Capital Punishment*. New Haven, CT: HRAF.

Páez, Dario, Bernard Rimé, Nekane Basabe, and Anna Wlodarczyk. 2015. "Psychosocial Effects of Perceived Emotional Synchrony in Collective Gatherings." *Journal of Personality and Social Psychology* 108 (5): 711–29. https://doi.org/10.1037/pspi0000014.

Paoli, Tommaso. 2009. "The Absence of Sexual Coercion in Bonobos." In *Sexual Coercion in Primates and Humans: An Evolutionary Perspective on Male Aggression against Females*, edited by Martin N. Muller and Richard W. Wrangham, 410–23. Cambridge, MA: Harvard University Press.

Parsons, K. J., Anders Rigg, A. J. Conith, A. C. Kitchener, S. Harris, and Haoyu Zhu. 2020. "Skull Morphology Diverges between Urban and Rural Populations of Red Foxes Mirroring Patterns of Domestication and Macroevolution." *Proceedings of the Royal Society B* 287 (20200763): 1–10. http://dx.doi.org/10.1098/rspb.2020.0763.

Pateman, Carole. 1980. *The Disorder of Women*. Stanford, CA: Stanford University Press.

Pateman, Carole. 1988. *The Sexual Contract*. Stanford, CA: Stanford University Press.

Patrick, Carlton. 2023. "Evolution Is the Source, and the Undoing, of Natural Law." *Evolution and Human Behavior* 44 (3): 175–83.

Peoples, Hervey C., Pavel Duda, and Frank W. Marlowe. 2016. "Hunter-Gatherers and the Origins of Religion." *Human Nature* 27 (3): 261–82. https://doi.org/10.1007/s12110-016-9260-0.

Phillips, Tim. 2018. "The Concepts of Asymmetric and Symmetric Power Can Help Resolve the Puzzle of Altruistic and Cooperative Behaviour." *Biological Reviews* 93 (1): 457–68. https://doi.org/10.1111/brv.12352.

Phillips, Tim, Jiawei Li, and Graham Kendall. 2014. "The Effects of Extra-Somatic Weapons on the Evolution of Human Cooperation towards Non-Kin." *PLOS One* 9 (5): e95742.

Port, Markus, Oliver Schülke, and Julia Ostner. 2018. "Reproductive Tolerance in Male Primates: Old Paradigms and New Evidence." *Evolutionary Anthropology* 27 (3): 107–20. https://doi.org/10.1002/evan.21586.

Pospisil, Leopold. 1958. *Kapauku Papuans and Their Law*. Vol. 54, *Yale University Publications in Anthropology*. New Haven: Department of Anthropology, Yale University.

Pospisil, Leopold. 1971. *Anthropology of Law: A Comparative Theory.* New York: Harper & Row.

Price, Edward O. 1999. "Behavioral Development in Animals Undergoing Domestication." *Applied Animal Behaviour Science* 65 (3): 245–71.

Progovac, Ljiljana, and Antonio Benítez-Burraco. 2019. "From Physical Aggression to Verbal Behavior: Language Evolution and Self-Domestication Feedback Loop." *Frontiers in Psychology* 10 (2807): 1–19. https://doi.org/10.3389/fpsyg.2019.02807.

Richerson, Peter, Ryan Baldini, Adrian V. Bell, Kathryn Demps, Karl Frost, Vicken Hillis, Sarah Mathew, et al. 2016. "Cultural Group Selection Plays an Essential Role in Explaining Human Cooperation: A Sketch of the Evidence." *Behavioral and Brain Sciences* 39 (e30): 1–19. https://doi.org/10.1017/S0140525X1400106X.

Robbins, Sterling. 1982. *Auyana: Those Who Held onto Home.* Seattle: University of Washington Press.

Roberts, Gilbert, Nichola Raihani, Redouan Bshary, Héctor M. Manrique, Andrea Farina, Flóra Samu, and Pat Barclay. 2021. "The Benefits of Being Seen to Help Others: Indirect Reciprocity and Reputation-Based Partner Choice." *Phil. Trans. R. Soc. B.* 376 (20200290): 1–10. https://doi.org/10.1098/rstb.2020.0290.

Rogers, Susan Carol. 1975. "Female Forms of Power and the Myth of Male Dominance: A Model of Female/Male Interaction in Peasant Society." *American Ethnologist* 2 (4): 727–56.

Romano, Angelo, Ali Seyhun Sarai, and Junhui Wu. 2022. "Direct and Indirect Reciprocity among Individuals and Groups." *Current Opinion in Psychology* 43: 254–59. https://doi.org/10.1016/j.copsyc.2021.08.003.

Rosaldo, Michelle Z. 1974. "Women, Culture and Society: A Theoretical Overview." In *Woman, Culture, and Society*, edited by Michelle Z. Rosaldo and Louise Lamphere, 17–42. Stanford, CA: Stanford University Press.

Rosati, Alexandra. 2019. "Heterochrony in Chimpanzee and Bonobo Spatial Memory Development." *American Journal of Physical Anthropology* 169 (2): 302–21. https://doi.org/10.1002/ajpa.23833.

Rosenfeld, Diane L. 2009. "Sexual Coercion, Political Violence, and Law." In *Sexual Coercion in Primates and Humans: An Evolutionary Perspective on Male Aggression against Females*, edited by Martin N. Muller and Richard W. Wrangham, 424–50. Cambridge, MA: Harvard University Press.

Rotella, Amanda, Adam Maxwell Sparks, Sandeep Mishra, and Pat Barclay. 2021. "No Effect of 'Watching Eyes': An Attempted Replication and Extension Investigating Individual Differences." *PLOS One* 16 (e0255531): 1–17. https://doi.org/10.1371/journal.pone.0255531.

Rubio, Andrew O., and Kyle Summers. 2022. "Neural Crest Cell Genes and the Domestication Syndrome: A Comparative Analysis of Selection." *PLOS One* 17 (e0263830): 1–10. https://doi.org/10.1371/journal.pone.0263830.

Sánchez-Villagra, Marcelo R., and Carel P. van Schaik. 2019. "Evaluating the Self-Domestication Hypothesis of Human Evolution." *Current Anthropology* 28 (3): 133–43. https://doi.org/10.1002/evan.21777.

San-Jose, Luis M., and Alexandre Roulin. 2020. "On the Potential Role of the Neural Crest Cells in Integrating Pigmentation into Behavioral and Physiological Syndromes." *Frontiers in Ecology and Evolution* 8 (278): 1–9.

Sands, Philippe. 2017. *East West Street: On the Origins of "Genocide" and "Crimes against Humanity."* New York: Vintage.

Sapolsky, Robert M. 2017. *Behave: The Biology of Humans at Our Best and Worst.* New York: Penguin.

Scales, Ann. 1986. "The Emergence of Feminist Jurisprudence: An Essay." *Yale Law Journal* 95 (7): 1373–1403.

Sell, Aaron, Liana S. E. Hone, and Nicholas Pound. 2012. "The Importance of Physical Strength to Human Males." *Human Nature* 23 (1): 30–44. https://doi.org/10.1007/s12110-012-9131-2.

Shariff, Azim F., Aiyana K. Willard, Teresa Andersen, and Ara Norenzayan. 2016. "Religious Priming: A Meta-Analysis with a Focus on Prosociality." *Personality and Social Psychology Review* 20 (1): 27–48. https://doi.org/10.1177/1088868314568811.

Shilton, Dor, Mati Breski, Daniel Dor, and Eva Jablonka. 2020. "Human Social Evolution: Self-Domestication or Self-Control?" *Frontiers in Psychology* 11 (134): 1–22. https://doi.org/10.3389/fpsyg.2020.00134.

Short, Lindsey A., Catherine J. Mondloch, Cheryl M. McCormick, Justin M. Carré, Ruqian Ma, Genyue Fu, and Kang Lee. 2012. "Detection of Propensity for Aggression Based on Facial Structure Irrespective of Face Race." *Evolution and Human Behavior* 33 (2): 121–29.

Shostak, Marjorie. 1981. *Nisa: The Life and Words of a !Kung Woman.* New York: Random House.

Sigmund, Karl. 2013. "The Basis of Morality, Richard Alexander on Indirect Reciprocity." In *Human Social Evolution: The Foundational Works of Richard D. Alexander*, edited by Kyle Summers and Bernard Crespi, 199–208. New York: Oxford University Press.

Singh, Manvir, Richard W. Wrangham, and Luke Glowacki. 2017. "Self-Interest and the Design of Rules." *Human Nature* 28 (4): 457–80. https://doi.org/10.1007/s12110-017-9298-7.

Smuts, B. B. 1995. "The Evolutionary Origins of Patriarchy." *Human Nature* 6 (1): 1–32.

Smuts, B. B., and R. W. Smuts. 1993. "Male Aggression and Sexual Coercion of Females in Nonhuman Primates and Other Mammals: Evidence and Theoretical Implications." *Advances in the Study of Behavior* 22: 1–63.

Sober, Elliott, and David S. Wilson. 1998. *Unto Others: The Evolution and Psychology of Unselfish Behavior*. Cambridge MA: Harvard University Press.

Stoinski, T. S., S. Rosenbaum, T. Ngaboyamahina, V. Vecellio, F. Ndagijimana, and K. Fawcett. 2009. "Patterns of Male Reproductive Behaviour in Multi-male Groups of Mountain Gorillas: Examining Theories of Reproductive Skew." *Behaviour* 146: 1193–1215. https://doi.org/10.1163/156853909X419992.

Stringer, Chris, and Julia Galway-Witham. 2017. "On the Origin of Our Species." *Nature* 546 (7657): 212–14.

Sunstein, Cass R. 2019. *Conformity: The Power of Social Influences*. New York: New York University Press.

Surbeck, Martin, Christophe Boesch, Takeshi Furuichi, Barbara Fruth, Gottfried Hohmann, Shintaro Ishikuza, Martin Muller, et al. 2019. "Males with a Mother Living in Their Community Have Higher Reproductive Success in Bonobos but Not Chimpanzees." *Current Biology* 29 (10): R354–R355. https://doi.org/10.1016/j.cub.2019.03.040.

Surbeck, Martin, and Gottfried Hohmann. 2013. "Intersexual Dominance Relationships and the Influence of Leverage on the Outcome of Conflicts in Wild Bonobos (*Pan paniscus*)." *Behavioral Ecology and Sociobiology* 67 (11): 1767–80. https://doi.org/10.1007/s00265-013-1584-8.

Surbeck, Martin, Kevin E. Langergraber, Barbara Fruth, Linda Vigilant, and Gottfried Hohmann. 2017. "Male Reproductive Skew Is Higher in Bonobos Than Chimpanzees." *Current Biology* 27 (13): R640–R641. https://doi.org/10.1016/j.cub.2017.05.039.

Swedell, Larissa, and Thomas W. Plummer. 2012. "A Papionin Multilevel Society as a Model for Hominin Social Evolution." *International Journal of Primatology* 33 (5): 1165–93.

Sznycer, Daniel, Laith Al-Shawaf, Yoella Bereby-Meyer, Oliver Scott Curry, Delphine De Smet, Elsa Ermer, Sangin Kim, et al. 2017. "Cross-Cultural Regularities in the Cognitive Architecture of Pride." *Proceedings of the National Academy of Sciences* 114 (8): 1874–79. https://doi.org/10.1073/pnas.1614389114.

Sznycer, Daniel, John Tooby, Leda Cosmides, Roni Porat, Shaul Shalvie, and Eran Halperin. 2016. "Shame Closely Tracks the Threat of Devaluation by Others, Even across Cultures." *Proceedings of the National Academy of Sciences* 113 (10): 2625–30.

Taborsky, Michael, Michael A. Cant, and Jan Komdeur. 2021. *The Evolution of Social Behaviour*. Cambridge: Cambridge University Press.

Theofanopoulou, Constantina, Simone Gastaldon, Thomas O'Rourke, Bridget D. Samuels, Pedro Tiago Martins, Francesco Delogu, Saleh Alamri, et al. 2017. "Self-Domestication in Homo Sapiens: Insights from Comparative Genomics." *PLOS One* 12 (10): e0185306. https://doi.org/10.1371/journal.pone.0185306.

Tindale, Norman B. 1974. *Aboriginal Tribes of Australia: Their Terrain, Environmental Controls, Distribution, Limits, and Proper Names. With an Appendix on Tasmanian Tribes by Rhys Jones*. Berkeley: University of California Press.

Tokuyama, Nahoko, and Takeshi Furuichi. 2016. "Do Friends Help Each Other? Patterns of Female Coalition Formation in Wild Bonobos at Wamba." *Animal Behaviour* 119: 27–35. https://doi.org/10.1016/j.anbehav.2016.06.021.

Tomasello, Michael. 2014. "The Ultra-Social Animal." *European Journal of Social Psychology* 44 (3): 187–94. https://doi.org/10.1002/ejsp.2015.

Tomasello, Michael. 2016. *A Natural History of Human Morality*. Cambridge, MA: Harvard University Press.

Tomasello, Michael, Alicia P. Melis, Claudio Tennie, Emily Wyman, and Esther Herrmann. 2012. "Two Key Steps in the Evolution of Human Cooperation: The Interdependence Hypothesis." *Current Anthropology* 53 (6): 673–86. https://doi.org/10.1086/668207.

Trivers, Robert L. 1971. "The Evolution of Reciprocal Altruism." *Quarterly Review of Biology* 46 (1): 35–57. http://www.jstor.org/stable/2822435.

Trut, L. N. 1999. "Early Canid Domestication: The Farm-Fox Experiment." *American Scientist* 87 (2): 160–69. https://doi.org/10.1511/1999.20.160.

Trut, Lyudmila N., Anastasiya V. Kharlamova, and Yury E. Herbeck. 2020. "Belyaev's and PEI's Foxes: A Far Cry." *Trends in Ecology and Evolution* 35 (8): 649–51. https://doi.org/10.1016/j.tree.2020.03.010.

Trut, Lyudmila N., Irina Oskina, and Anastasiya Kharlamova. 2009. "Animal Evolution during Domestication: The Domesticated Fox as a Model." *BioEssays* 31 (3): 349–60.

van Schaik, Carel P. 2016. *The Primate Origins of Human Nature*. Hoboken, NJ: John Wiley & Sons.

Wacks, Raymond. 2006. *Philosophy of Law: A Very Short Introduction*. New York: Oxford University Press.

Warner, W. Lloyd. 1958. *A Black Civilization: A Social Study of an Australian Tribe*. Rev. ed. New York: Harper.

Wedekind, Claus, and Victoria A. Braithwaite. 2002. "The Long-Term Benefits of Human Generosity in Indirect Reciprocity." *Current Biology* 12 (12): 1012–15. https://doi.org/10.1016/S0960-9822(02)00890-4.

Wedekind, Claus, and Manfred Milinski. 2000. "Cooperation through Image Scoring in Humans." *Science* 288 (5467): 850–52. https://doi.org/10.1126/science.288.5467.850.

West, Stuart A., Claire El Mouden, and Andy Gardner. 2011. "Sixteen Common Misconceptions about the Evolution of Cooperation in Humans." *Evolution and Human Behavior* 32 (4): 231–62. https://doi.org/10.1016/j.evolhumbehav.2010.08.001.

West, Stuart A., A. S. Griffin, and A. Gardner. 2007. "Social Semantics: Altruism, Cooperation, Mutualism, Strong Reciprocity and Group Selection." *Journal of Evolutionary Biology* 20 (2): 415–32. https://doi.org/10.1111/j.1420-9101.2006.01258.x.

Wilkins, A. S. 2017. "Revisiting Two Hypotheses on the 'Domestication Syndrome' in Light of Genomic Data." *Vavilov J Genet Breed* 21 (4): 435–42. https://doi.org/10.18699/VJ17.262.

Wilkins, Adam S. 2020. "A Striking Example of Developmental Bias in an Evolutionary Process: The 'Domestication Syndrome.'" *Evolution and Development* 22 (1–2): 143–53. https://doi.org/10.1111/ede.12319.

Wilkins, Adam S., Richard W. Wrangham, and W. Tecumseh Fitch. 2014. "The 'Domestication Syndrome' in Mammals: A Unified Explanation Based on Neural Crest Cell Behavior and Genetics." *Genetics* 197 (3): 795–808. https://doi.org/10.1534/genetics.114.165423.

Wilson, Edward O. 2012. *The Social Conquest of Earth*. New York: Liveright.

Wilson, Michael L., Christophe Boesch, Barbara Fruth, Takeshi Furui-chi, Ian C. Gilby, Chie Hashimoto, Catherine Hobaiter, et al. 2014. "Lethal Aggression in *Pan* Is Better Explained by Adaptive Strategies Than Human Impacts." *Nature* 513 (7518): 414–17. https://doi.org/10.1038/nature13727.

Wood, Wendy, and Alice H. Eagly. 2002. "A Cross-Cultural Analysis of the Behavior of Women and Men: Implications for the Origins of Sex Differences." *Psychological Bulletin* 128 (5): 699–727. https://doi.org/10.1037//0033-2909.128.5.699.

Woodburn, James. 1982. "Egalitarian Societies." *Man* 17 (3): 431–51.

Wrangham, Richard W. 2019a. *The Goodness Paradox: The Strange Relationship between Virtue and Violence in Human Evolution*. New York: Alfred A. Knopf.

Wrangham, Richard W. 2019b. "Hypotheses for the Evolution of Reduced Reactive Aggression in the Context of Human Self-Domestication." *Frontiers in Psychology* 10 (1914): 1–11. https://doi.org/10.3389/fpsyg.2019.01914.

Wrangham, Richard W. 2021. "Targeted Conspiratorial Killing, Human Self-Domestication and the Evolution of Groupishness." *Evolutionary Human Sciences* 3 (e26): 1–21. https://doi.org/10.1017/ehs.2021.20.

Wrangham, Richard W., Michael L. Wilson, and Martin N. Muller. 2006. "Comparative Rates of Aggression in Chimpanzees and Humans." *Primates* 47 (1): 14–26.

Xygalatas, Dimitris, Ivana Konvalinka, Joseph Bulbulia, and Andreas Roepstorff. 2011. "Quantifying Collective Effervescence: Heart-Rate Dynamics at a Fire-Walking Ritual." *Communicative & Integrative Biology* 4 (6): 735–38. https://doi.org/10.4161/cib.17609.

Yucel, Meltem, and Amrisha Vaish. 2018. "Young Children Tattle to Enforce Moral Norms." *Social Development* 27 (4): 924–36. https://doi.org/10.1111/sode.12290.

Zanella, Matteo, Alessandro Vitriolo, Alejandro Andirkó, Pedro Tiago Martins, Stefanie Sturm, Thomas O'Rourke, Magdalena Laugsch, et al. 2019. "Dosage Analysis of the 7q11.23 Williams Region 1 Identifies BAZ1B as a Major Human Gene Patterning the Modern Human Face and Underlying Self-domestication." *Science Advances* 5 (eaaw7908): 1–15. https://doi.org/10.1126/sciadv.aaw7908.

Zeder, Melinda. 2020. "Straw Foxes: Domestication Syndrome Evaluation Comes up Short." *Trends in Ecology and Evolution* 35 (8): 647–49. https://doi.org/10.1016/j.tree.2020.03.001.

Gaining Power, Losing Control

JONATHAN L. ZITTRAIN

THE TANNER LECTURES ON HUMAN VALUES

Delivered at

Clare Hall, University of Cambridge
January 20, 2020

JONATHAN L. ZITTRAIN is the George Bemis Professor of International Law at Harvard Law School, professor of public policy at the Harvard Kennedy School of Government, professor of computer science at the Harvard School of Engineering and Applied Sciences, director of the Harvard Law School Library, and cofounder and faculty director of the Berkman Klein Center for Internet and Society. His research interests include battles for control of digital property and content, cryptography, electronic privacy, the roles of intermediaries within internet architecture, human computing, and the useful and unobtrusive deployment of technology in education. Zittrain is a member of the American Academy of Arts and Sciences and the Board of Directors of the Electronic Frontier Foundation. He has served on the Board of Advisors for Scientific American as a Trustee of the Internet Society and as a Forum Fellow of the World Economic Forum, which named him a Young Global Leader. He was the Distinguished Scholar-in-Residence at the Federal Communications Commission, where he chaired the Open Internet Advisory Committee. His many publications include *The Future of the Internet—and How to Stop It*, *Torts*, and *Jurisdiction*; and he is coeditor (with Ron Deibert, John Palfrey, and Rafal Rohozinski) of *Access Denied: The Practice and Policy of Global Internet Filtering*, *Access Controlled: The Shaping of Power, Rights, and Rule in Cyberspace*, and *Access Contested: Security, Identity, and Resistance in Asian Cyberspace*.

LECTURE I.
BETWEEN SUFFOCATION AND ABDICATION:
THREE ERAS OF DIGITAL GOVERNANCE

I've titled this pair of lectures "Gaining Power and Losing Control." In doing so, I've invoked a pair of words that have ample and various meanings across different fields. In what follows, I'll aim to unpack exactly what I mean for them to communicate.

To start, I want to just note that these lectures come against the backdrop of a shift in the public's thinking about personal technology in common use. In 1997, *Wired* magazine heralded the beginning of what it called "the Long Boom . . . 25 years of prosperity, freedom, and a better environment for the whole world."[1] Well OK, that's what it said on the tin. But that wasn't exactly what was inside.

Several decades later, even *Wired* has come around to say there are some issues, and we need to talk frankly about them—the cover of a 2018 issue declared that "the internet is broken."[2] So if I were characterizing 2018 in our thinking about technology, I would say it probably maps quite nicely to a vague sense of unease. By the time we get to 2019, we might call it escalating panic. And it's a new year. Welcome to 2020, perhaps best characterized in terms of mortal terror.[3]

I'd like to try to map out why we find ourselves so concerned, given that a lot of the promise of 1997 has paid off. Much of what we thought technology could do, including binding everybody together with suffusing networks to which anybody could contribute, has come mostly true. Yet here we are, inclined to nod in recognition at *Wired*'s latter-day declaration.

I think a big part of what's occasioning the challenges in front of us right now and our sense of unease is precisely that the technology has worked. It's done the job of substituting architectures of control where there was once fortuity. What do I mean by fortuity? That which can't be predicted or knowingly adjusted. Phenomena that, thanks to their complexity or dispersion, can't be modeled or subjected to technical rigor, even if you have big banks of computers. As digital technology has advanced, more and more things have fallen out of this bucket. We're left trying to figure out how to allocate this growing power across individuals and institutions. But it hasn't gone smoothly. And that's why many of us find ourselves feeling less empowered, even as the power of humanity as a whole—in an aggregate sense—has expanded. This sense that we are

[335]

336   *The Tanner Lectures on Human Values*

losing control even as we gain power is at the heart of the tension I want to explore today.

For a good first example of that tension, we might consider the implications of autonomous vehicles—a technology at the intersection of the digital and the physical. Let's examine how autonomous vehicles might reconfigure both power and control by examining a few eminently feasible features they could offer. The baseline case is simple enough—you used to have to drive yourself in a car, and with the introduction of autonomous vehicles, each of us suddenly has our own robot chauffeur. We use cars much as we always have, and the big issue is ensuring that the robot driving is at least as safe as a human driver. It turns out that this standard is not as high as one might think.

But let's look at some of the more sophisticated features that autonomous vehicles might bring. To start, let's say that a police officer thinks that you're up to no good and wants to take you into custody. So that officer makes a case to a judge, the judge issues a warrant, and the warrant is broadcast across a whole network of autonomous vehicles. The car you happen to be in at that very moment identifies you, locks its doors, and drives to the nearest police station to drop you off as if you were a package. It's a great example of a movement from the roulette wheel of fortuity— both in terms of detection and control—to "well, now we can do that." And who wouldn't? If you could find the person that you're looking to arrest and you've already got the appropriate legal process lined up, why wouldn't a public official do it? But there's no denying that such a feature would generate a new form of control for the system at the expense of individual agency.

Another case. How about a city that's about to face a hurricane, as Houston did with Hurricane Harvey? The authorities in Houston did not order evacuations then because they were worried that in the chaotic rush to evacuate, people would find themselves trapped on clogged roads when the hurricanes hit.[4] But imagine if Houston's vehicles were automated. Your own car could, in coordinated order, pull up in front of your house and say, "I'm leaving in 15 minutes. The trunk is open; you better put your stuff in. And then I'm going with or without you." Such an approach would occasion a very orderly—and mandatory—exit from the city. Not a bad use of this kind of technology from a public health standpoint but surely a reallocation of a new form of control. This, again, shifts power away from the unpredictable, often irrational behavior of individual drivers—which can be characterized as fortuity from a societal point of view.

[ZITTRAIN] *Between Suffocation and Abdication* 337

And finally, case three—what I would call "sponsored rides." When you hop in an autonomous taxi or an Uber under normal circumstances, you'll tell it where you want to go, and the GPS will plot a direct course from point A to point B. But how about, and you heard it here first, an Uber for Facebook? Here, your ride is free, but it's sponsored by an advertiser. It will involuntarily take you to McDonald's on the way from point A to point B and wait a certain amount of time, giving you a chance to get something at the drive-through. So is that empowering for you? Is it empowering for me? I don't know, but we'll have to figure it out when the technology lets us reallocate power this way.

I'm calling the first of these two lectures today "Between Suffocation and Abdication: Three Eras of Digital Governance." And while the examples I'll use are less kinetic than autonomous vehicles, I think they still connect quite nicely to this issue of the shift of fortuity to control. But before we jump in, let me explain what I mean by this shift from suffocation to abdication and by the notion of it unfolding across three eras.

Our story starts around 1995. In 1995, the big worry among people in my neck of the woods thinking about technology was to ensure that we'd be able to make the most of a new panoply of digital innovations. To surf the World Wide Web, courtesy of Sir Tim Berners-Lee.[5] To be able to download, or upload, all sorts of expressions. We didn't want to be treated like sheep: we were worried that the government would surveil us or try to control us as we exercised these new speech-related affordances. Our sense was that we had to be resilient against that threat, to build networks, systems, and legal frameworks around them in a manner that resisted government intrusions. And that's why I call the era starting in 1995 the Rights Era. And here I mean rights in a very narrow sense. I mean it in the kind of Americanized, First Amendment–prototypical sense of "Leave me alone, let me have maximal freedom to watch, browse, say, and do whatever I want."

By 2010, a parallel and not particularly compatible framework had arisen. We'd seen the rise of social media platforms, many of which were enabling the things that we'd wanted the government to leave alone. But now we have a new concern: "Wait a minute, these platforms are leaving things alone a little too much, even as their affordances make possible vast and novel harms." They are abdicating. They see no evil, hear no evil, speak no evil. And that's not good because there's a lot of evil that they are facilitating and that they alone could stop. I call this era the Public Health Era. It's very different from the Rights Era, and it focuses on the ways in which technology is allowing new forms of harm to come about. But it may contain within it the seeds of amelioration, if only we are bold enough to compel or sway those intermediaries, those platforms that are empowering us, to impose limits and control in the name of public health.

It's going to be really hard to reconcile these two eras. I'm going to suggest a third era: Process. The Process Era entails looking for ways of facilitating agreements among the people affected across jurisdictional boundaries to formalize governance processes in them in some way, effectively negotiating them, writing them down, and carrying them out in public view. And then to feel that what that process generates is legitimate, even if you don't agree with a given result.

For my second lecture, I'm going to talk about something else. It begins, consonant with the first, with the way in which machine learning in particular and a lot of technologies in general are accelerating the movement from mere fortuity to control and knowledge. But here I'm going to talk about a very specific kind of knowledge, taking the form of insights without explanations, and explore why correct answers with no explanation offered or easily reverse-engineered could be a problem. That lecture will once again examine questions of control—this time not in terms of its reallocation but rather in terms of its collective forfeiture to machines in exchange for power. But don't worry, I'm not going to talk about Skynet.

* * * * *

I want to open this first lecture with Lasse Gustavsson. Mr. Gustavsson is a Swedish firefighter. During his first week on the job, a gas pipe exploded near him, leaving him very badly burned. He has since become an inspirational speaker, well respected across Scandinavia.[6]

A few years back, a friend of Mr. Gustavsson posted a picture of him on Facebook in celebration of his birthday—his severe burn scars were, of course, visible. Facebook took it down, saying it violated its terms of service.[7] The friend complained, noting that a number of other people who had literally been burned had also had their photos taken down for violations of Facebook's terms of service.

Facebook's initial response was to deny the friend's appeal and threaten to suspend his account if he kept trying to post the photo. After a second posting and another tour of backlash against Facebook's actions on social media, Facebook reversed the takedown.

FIGURE 1. Mr. Gustavsson's friend's post complaining about Facebook's actions, alongside the original photo.

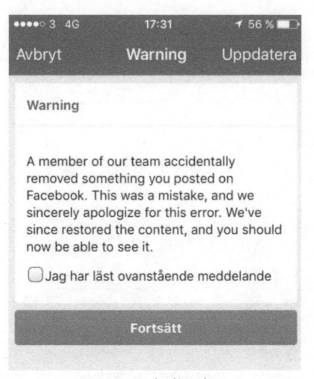

FIGURE 2. Facebook's apology.

Given the reversal, this incident is perhaps more a story of failure in implementation than it is a story of intentional discrimination. But it nonetheless raises a tricky question. Why should Facebook or any other platform be intervening to take down content that is utterly legal? There is nothing illegal in any jurisdiction about Mr. Gustavsson's photo, nor did Facebook allege any as part of its initial takedown. And yet, Facebook moved aggressively to make sure that it wouldn't circulate among its users. What grounds do they have to judge content in this way?

Now here's another example, this time on the other side of the leave-up/take-down fence. Earthley is a company that sells soaps, salves, tinctures, and more. It runs Facebook ad campaigns, including one that points viewers to a guide to pertussis. If you read the guide, you'll notice that it includes the claim that the aluminum in some vaccines is tied to neurological damage, autism, learning disabilities, and other conditions.

FIGURE 3. Earthley's sponsored content promoting an antivax guide for pertussis.

Based on the current state of scientific knowledge, that's a decidedly false statement. And likely a dangerous one, in that such misinformation may be reducing vaccination rates, though establishing that danger scientifically is tricky. In a recent peer-reviewed study of pediatricians, 63 percent of respondents said that misinformation from social media is a "major barrier" to persuading parents to have their kids vaccinated. Another 27 percent say it's somewhat of a barrier.[8] Those were the highest figures reported for any of the barriers included in the poll. Lowered vaccination rates could compromise herd immunity, increase child and adult mortality, and enable the resurgence of previously near-eradicated diseases.

That prompts a second question: Why is Facebook earning money from the provision of information that is likely causing physical harm?

Our first question—in relation to Mr. Gustavsson's takedown—was a Rights question, challenging the notion that any party, governmental or corporate, has the grounds to meddle so invasively in unquestionably legal speech. This second question is a Public Health question, concerned with Facebook's unwillingness to mitigate what appears to many to be clear harms. The clash between these two questions characterizes much of the debate around the role of Facebook and other companies like it. The frustrations of that debate tee up the two issues at the heart of digital governance in 2020.

First, *we don't know what we want.* Many of us find ourselves nodding along at both questions broached above, infuriated by both examples raised here. We might not be able to articulate a firm standard for what should stay up and what should go down, but we sure know that what we have now isn't working.

Second, even if we did know what we wanted, the fact remains that *we don't trust anyone to give it to us.* It's absurd to think that Facebook's customer service and content moderation teams, which are making thousands or millions of content-related decisions per day, are going to be able to apply a deep sense of scientific truth, validity and philosophical consideration to every case before them. The very idea of making wise decisions with such speed and at such scale seems fanciful. But where are our alternatives? Do we want the government making fine-grained decisions about what speech stays up or goes down? Shall we leave it to the slow action of the courts? Not one of these approaches feels remotely satisfying.

342 *The Tanner Lectures on Human Values*

So if we can just solve these two problems by the end of the lecture, we'll be in good shape.

THE RIGHTS ERA

Let's start by talking about the Rights Era a little bit more. And again, it's important to note that the ethos of that era embeds a very American sensibility, tracking to the Americanization of the initial expansion of the internet and the major applications built on top of it worldwide. It reflects the ethos embedded in the First Amendment—don't treat us as sheep. We are citizens, and we should be empowered to speak and act as such. The government should stay out of the way, interceding only in exceptional and narrowly defined circumstances.

Those sentiments were famously applied to the digital context in 1996 by John Perry Barlow in his "Declaration of Independence of Cyberspace." Barlow's declaration waxes eloquent about cyberspace's need for independence from all governments of the world, which he characterizes, less than flatteringly, as "weary giants of flesh and steel."[9] We're digital netizens, Barlow and his compatriots roar, and you have no moral right to rule us. We'll figure everything out ourselves.

Any number of events, scandals, and phenomena from the years following Barlow's declaration very nicely track to that sensibility. In the early 2000s, Microsoft established a blog service called "MSN Spaces" in China. Anybody with an internet connection could make a blog—a novelty at the time—and my colleague Rebecca MacKinnon tried to sign up. The creation page prompted her for a title, and she entered (in Chinese), "I love freedom of speech, human rights, and democracy." The page threw an error: "You have to enter a title that cannot contain profanity. Please enter a different title."[10]

This is classic bait for Barlow—a stark illustration of the importance of negative rights online. And closer to home, which for me is the United States, we had plenty of our own Rights Era run-ins with efforts to censor or restrict access to information. In the early days of the Amazon Kindle, a third-party seller posted a version of George Orwell's *1984* to the digital marketplace for the device. That third party thought *1984* was in the public domain, happily typed it up, then sold it for 99 cents a copy—and soon after realized that *1984* was in the public domain in Canada but remained under copyright in the United States. Amazon, which quickly realized that it had supported the distribution of copyrighted material without permission, panicked. To reverse the third-party seller's potentially actionable

[ZITTRAIN]   *Between Suffocation and Abdication*

indiscretion, Amazon reached into every Kindle and deleted that copy of *1984* from the Kindles that had purchased it.[11] It's hard to think of a more appropriate title to which this could have happened: "You don't have *1984*; you never had *1984*; there's no such book as *1984*."

Such an action, undertaken on the part of a private platform, represents a potentially terrifying new use of technological power from a Rights perspective. And it wasn't just the Kindle. A version of *War and Peace* developed for Barnes & Noble's Nook replaced every usage of "Kindle" with the word "Nook"—likely a hasty effort to retrofit front matter.[12] Readers encountered sentences like "as she heard his voice, a vivid glow Nookd in her face" and "The sulfur splinters Nookd." A proponent of the Rights Era would surely bristle at an outside entity's efforts to snatch away content it doesn't want to be seen, but silently altering that content might be even more insidious.

Beyond e-readers, we might look to Microsoft's Kinect for another example of the sort of behavior Rights Era thinkers sought to curtail. From a privacy and civil liberties perspective, the Kinect already rests on somewhat shaky foundations: it's an all-seeing eye you install in your living room so that you can play some new video games. A patent Microsoft filed in relation to the Kinect does little to assuage those fears. It suggests the usefulness of a "consumer detector," the idea being that Kinect-enabled televisions could sell movies at different rates depending on how many consumers were in the physical room to watch the movie.[13] And here again, the hackles of Rights Era thinkers are decidedly raised. Microsoft, their argument goes, is treating people like sheep, selling technological affordances that will then be used to wring money out of the buyer.

It's useful to note that many Rights Era conversations were centered on matters related to copyright of the sort that the Kinect's "consumer detector" thoroughly implicates. And in the domain of copyright, the Rights Era tended to favor the consumer of content over the rights holder for that content. That, again, reflects a very distinct flavor of rights, one concerned first and foremost with leaving an idealized individual citizen at liberty to do as they please.

Barlow wasn't just saying it would be immoral for governments to treat us like sheep and that we needed bulwarks against them doing so. He also, interestingly, says in the second paragraph of his "A Declaration of the Independence of Cyberspace" that governments do not "possess any methods of enforcement we have true reason to fear."[14] "You can't really get us in cyberspace," Barlow essentially crows—if we're sheep, then

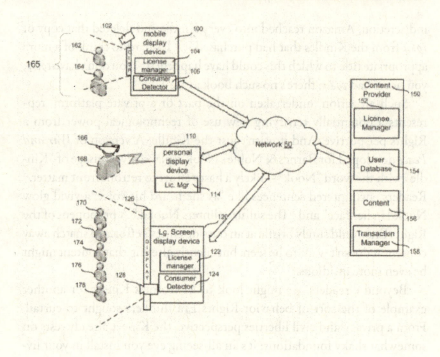

FIGURE 4. Microsoft's Consumer Detector patent diagram.

you're a highly incompetent shepherd. That same sense was communicated by his colleague John Gilmore, who famously said that the "net treats censorship as damage and routes around it."[15] And in early internet law cases, including in America, there was a recognition by courts of the difficulty of asking any intermediary to intervene at scale. The decision in *Zeran v. AOL*, a landmark case, held that "the amount of information communicated via interactive computer services is . . . staggering. . . . It would be impossible for service providers to screen each of their millions of postings for possible problems."[16] So unless you want us to call the whole thing off, technology companies told policymakers, you need to be willing to tolerate the costs of freedom.

A controversy from 2004 provides a strong example of adherence to that spirit on the part of private companies and advocacy organizations alike. In that year, the second hit on a Google search for the word "Jew" was Jew Watch News, a radically antisemitic website, which included, for example, a section on "Zionist occupied governments." As you might

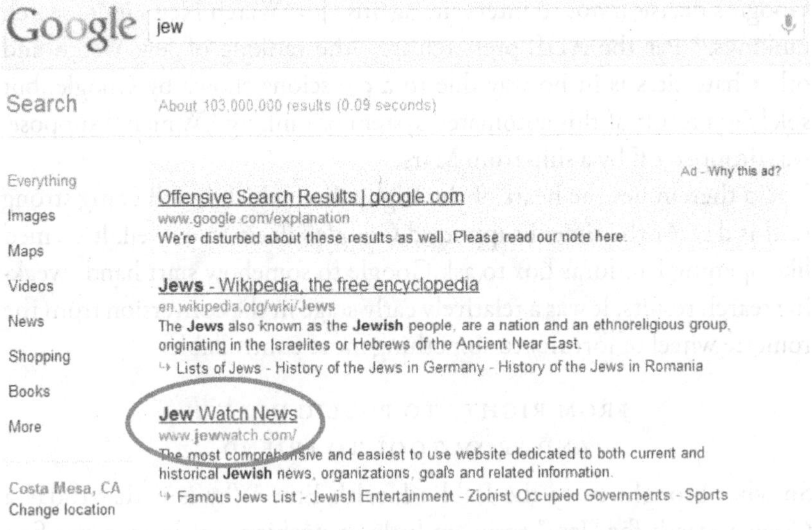

[ZITTRAIN] *Between Suffocation and Abdication* 345

Google jew

Search   About 103,000,000 results (0.09 seconds)

Everything

Ad - Why this ad?

Offensive Search Results | google.com
www.google.com/explanation
We're disturbed about these results as well. Please read our note here.

Images

Maps

Videos   **Jews** - Wikipedia, the free encyclopedia
en.wikipedia.org/wiki/Jews

News   The **Jews** also known as the **Jewish** people, are a nation and an ethnoreligious group,
originating in the Israelites or Hebrews of the Ancient Near East.

Shopping   ↳ Lists of Jews - History of the Jews in Germany - History of the Jews in Romania

Books

More   **Jew** Watch News
www.jewwatch.com/
The most comprehensive and easiest to use website dedicated to both current and
historical **Jewish** news, organizations, goals and related information.

Costa Mesa, CA   ↳ Famous Jews List - Jewish Entertainment - Zionist Occupied Governments - Sports
Change location

FIGURE 5. Google search results for "jew," ca. 2004.

expect, a lot of the people who stumbled across this result wrote to Google and said, "Why is that the second hit on the word Jew?"[17]

Google's response? "That's just how it works."

To make its case in response to the controversy, Google bought itself an ad to appear at the top of the results for "Jew" that read "Offensive Search Results: We're disturbed about these results as well. Please read our note here."

And if you click to learn more, it says, "[In Google Search,] sometimes subtleties of language cause anomalies to appear that cannot be predicted. A search for Jew brings up one such unexpected result."[18] Read: it's a roulette wheel. What are you going to do? We're surprised too. So surprised, in fact, that we have prewritten this entire essay. Reading further, we're told that "the beliefs and preferences of those who work at Google, as well as the opinions of the general public, do not determine or impact our search results." In essence: "Look, it's all science. It's computers, and we don't touch them any more than we have to. If we did, that would be unfair. We're really sorry you were upset. Thanks for telling us. If only we could do something. Sincerely, Google."

The most interesting tidbit from Google's explanation, though, might be a hyperlink at the end. It points to a press release published by the Anti-Defamation League, which is an organization expressly chartered to combat antisemitism. The ADL put out its own press release supporting

Google's decision not to intervene against Jew Watch News in its search rankings.[19] Per the ADL press release, "the ranking of Jew Watch and other hate sites is in no way due to a conscious choice by Google, but solely is a result of this automated system of ranking." Which, I suppose, was dropped off by a ship from Mars.

So therein lies the heart of the Rights Era, which is still going strong to this day. At the time, I supported Google's decision as well. It seemed like opening Pandora's box to ask Google to somehow start hand tweaking search results. It was a relatively early stage in the conversion from the roulette wheel of fortuity to something more controllable.

FROM RIGHTS TO PUBLIC HEALTH
AND FROM TOOL TO FRIEND

So what brought us to the Public Health Era? Why is it that today a Google search for "Jew" turns up little or nothing—at least in the first few pages of results—that could be characterized as antisemitic? Why, at some point around 2010, did we begin to see a new and competing way of thinking about governance in this space? Well, one significant driver has been what I, and I'm using the terminology of Randall Munroe here, call the digital evolution from tool to friend. Google's search engine circa 2004 was basically a tool, as is the results feed you're presented with when you make a search today. Users are meant to treat it as an aid in sorting through what's out there.

Sometimes, the stuff that search engines flag as relevant isn't exactly what we would hope. In 2015, I plugged "Should I vaccinate my child?" into the Bing search engine. Four out of the top five responses on Bing— with the exception being a page from the American Centers for Disease Control—said no, you should not.

Does Microsoft bear any responsibility for that? Under the widely accepted framework around the Jew Watch incident, the answer would be decidedly no. Bing, the argument goes, is an automated service offering a window on the Web. If you don't like what you see, blame the Web, not the company that offered you the window.

But in 2020, I think that may not be as much our sensibility about things—even when it comes to 2004-style search engines. Because we're not just talking about ranked feeds of search results anymore, so-called organic results. We are talking about technologies—like Google's Knowledge Graph—that attempt to synthesize (often automatically) and present an answer to your question without requiring you to delve into any

[ZITTRAIN]   *Between Suffocation and Abdication*   347

FIGURE 6. Bing's largely antivax search results in 2015 for "Should I vaccinate my child?"

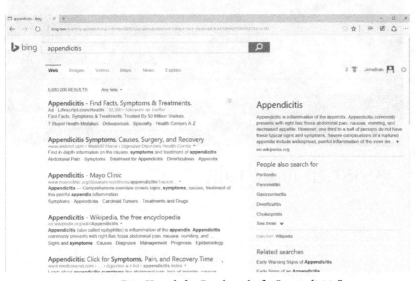

FIGURE 7. Bing Knowledge Panel results for "appendicitis."

links at all.[20] A search for "appendicitis" on Google or Bing yields not just a pile of related web pages but also a more authoritative-seeming panel with information about its symptoms, treatment, and rarity.

Imagine, now, that the panel said appendicitis is caused by an imbalance in the four bodily humors and that a worried searcher should pursue a leeching in order to get better. And say that misleading panel was accompanied by some sponsored links suggesting leechers, along with their Yelp ratings or something. I think it's safe to say that the vast majority of people would see this as very different than the Jew Watch problem—and as something that demands action on the part of Microsoft. And that's not just because our sensibilities have changed between 2004 and now but also because these intermediaries are not just tools; they're your friends. They're trying to give you actionable advice that you can use—and in putting forward what appears to be authoritative information, asking you to trust them.

And another great example of this comes from my colleague Avishai Margalit. If you looked him up, Google said that until 2011, he was the Kennan Professor at the Institute for Advanced Study. Which is weird, because—for a while—Google's Knowledge Panel volunteered that he had died in 1962.

FIGURE 8. Google Knowledge Panel results for Avishai Margalit, who "died" in 1962.

At the time, Professor Margalit wrote to me and said something along the lines of "Hi, I'm not dead." Always a good opener to a message. "How can I fix this?" And I said, "Did you try the feedback link?" "Yes, I did." "OK, I'll try to talk to a Google engineer," that kind of thing. We ultimately resolved the situation, but it felt like a mistake on Google's part, not just on the part of whatever crummy data source proffered the falsehood.

And the movement from tool to friend hasn't been limited to search engines. Our digital assistants and concierges—the likes of Siri, Alexa, Cortana, and Google Assistant—offer up seemingly oracular answers by design. The original version of Siri branded itself as "your humble personal assistant."[21] But there is little humble about Siri, which aspires to be able to seamlessly answer any question with which we might present it.

And like the "friend" components of search engines, digital assistants have been known to mess up. Toward the end of President Obama's second term in 2016, someone published a video of them asking their Google Home a surprising question: "Is Obama planning a coup?"

Even more surprising was the Google Assistant's answer: "According to Secrets of the Fed, according to details exposed in Western Center for Journalism's exclusive video, not only could Obama be in bed with the communist Chinese. But Obama may in fact be planning a communist coup d-e-t-a-t at the end of his term in 2016."[22]

Oh, well, asked and answered. I asked a Google engineer about this, and his answer was "Oh gosh, that's awful. It's pronounced *coup d'état.*"

This is an equal opportunity problem—here's some dialogue from another Google Home video:

> "Hey Google, are Republicans fascist?"
> "According to debate.org: Yes, Republicans equals Nazis."[23]

Regardless of your views on either of these questions, it's a little unsettling that the weird knowledge towers we purchase and install in our homes are casually throwing off answers like that. What better emblem could there be of the move from tool to friend?

This dynamic undermines the Rights Era "get out of the way" protestation by breaking down the tools-as-windows-onto-speech framing. When we ask questions, our digital "friends" are increasingly giving us single answers—seemingly in their own voices, even when they attribute them to others. There's no getting out of the way—the platforms *are* the

350 *The Tanner Lectures on Human Values*

way. There's no easy answer from Barlow and company here, which is part of why we've seen such a decisive move toward an era of Public Health.

The platforms themselves are starting to respond and to think in these terms. Amazon says that they're going to rely on the national health service in the UK to curate answers to the sorts of medical questions mentioned above.[24] That's a clear movement away from the open-web approach and toward one predicated on identifying and relying on the expertise of trusted sources.

So what I'm identifying is what I call an inversion of the Kantian formula that "ought implies can." If you tell somebody you ought to do something, it has to be that they can do it. Fair enough. But I want to ask from a regulatory and ethical perspective, When does *can imply ought*? When is it that when you can do something, you're morally obligated to—on pain of responsibility, should harms arise from your inaction? Technology companies are now capable of intervening in the harmful dynamics they themselves enable at an unprecedented level of granularity—and because they're so often walled gardens, nobody can pick up the slack for them. So when they abdicate, are they failing morally in a manner that might demand, among other things, regulatory intervention?

We're being prompted to ask that question more and more as the power of technology companies to effect change in the world grows, particularly in the sphere of social media. If we think back ten years, Facebook was originally built to help us keep up with our friends and relations. More and more over the years, that mission has expanded— Facebook is now trying to help us learn about the world at large, curating our consumption of news and political discourse. When that process of distribution and discovery goes wrong, the costs can be catastrophic. In 2018, we saw a report from the (typically quite reserved) UN Human Rights Council about the ways in which Facebook had played a significant role in facilitating ethnic violence in Myanmar and expressing regret at the fact that the platform hadn't been more forthcoming with data.[25]

And Facebook's own response to that particular report marked a significant change from the Rights Era "freedom has a cost" arguments on which social media platforms have long leaned. The platform admitted that connecting the world isn't always going to be a good thing—and even that the company's shot-callers "lose some sleep over this."[26] The harms that can arise from global connectivity are just too big to downplay as an unfortunate externality, even by those with the greatest interest in doing so.

[ZITTRAIN] *Between Suffocation and Abdication*

Sure enough, over the years, Facebook has elaborated a terms of service—at first in secret—about what sorts of content it won't allow, irrespective of whether that content is illegal. In other words, guidelines for identifying legally permissible or even protected speech should nonetheless not be allowed on the platform.

At one point, the *Guardian* picked up leaked slides from Facebook laying out some of these rules.[27] The slides offer an important window into how difficult and unintuitive such rule making can be. Take, for instance, some of the signal examples provided in the slide on credible violence. "Someone shoot Trump" is not allowed. If that sentence makes its way onto Facebook, it's going to be taken down. How about "Kick a person with red hair"? That stays up. Because having red hair does not make one a member of a protected class. "To snap a bitch's neck, make sure to apply all your pressure to the middle of her throat" stays up, because it's not telling you that you should do anything. It's just saying if you wanted to do something horrible, here's how. All of these examples were chosen to be counterintuitive, to highlight the nuances in language in a manner intended to prevent excessive censorship on the part of content moderators.[28]

Shortly after this deck leaked, Facebook revised its content policy to make all of the examples above actionable by content moderators.[29] And they then started to release their extremely elaborate rule sets. Rules that, if they were issued by a government, would consume—in America—one or more courses in a law school curriculum. Indeed, given the reach and impact of Facebook's rules, courses of such a kind may be appropriate regardless of Facebook's legal status.

And while the size—and humanity—of Facebook's content moderation workforce remains a barrier to implementing rules consistently and at scale, Facebook has developed amazing capabilities around subjecting users and content to top-down control. This shift is well-illustrated by a recent post by Facebook CEO Mark Zuckerberg. In the post, Zuckerberg observes based on internal data that as postings get closer and closer to crossing over the policy lines that Facebook has set, they tend to get more and more engagement. People really like sharing stuff that operates at the boundaries of the platform's rules and beyond. His solution? To penalize content as it approaches the policy line, diminishing the virality of posts that border on unacceptable without quite going too far.[30] Such a proposal demonstrates a very refined sort of control—one that is hard to imagine in almost any other governance context.

It seems that they've been making good use of their enforcement capabilities—Facebook announced a while back that it had deleted nearly a billion posts in the first quarter of 2018, mostly spam.[31] What did those posts say? Why were they deleted? I don't know. They're just giving us all a heads-up that they've been deleting hundreds of millions of posts behind closed doors. One such post follows in Figure 9.

This is from the lead-up to the 2016 American presidential election. It's fake news, which I can confidently say in a very narrow sense, even setting

FIGURE 9. Fake news from a fake newspaper.

aside the content. It's from the *Denver Guardian*—which sounds a lot like a local newspaper. But if you live in Denver, Colorado, you cannot subscribe to the *Guardian*. If you had clicked through to this post, you would have found a Potemkin site that might pass on first inspection as a newspaper but had just one other article—also with demonstrably false content.

Who would share such junk? The answer is, unfortunately, a whole lot of people. Here's a chart of the highest-engagement stories from a number of publications in the run-up to the 2016 election:[32]

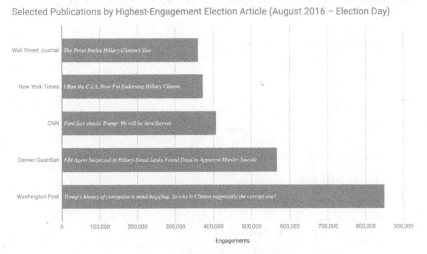

FIGURE 10. Selected publications by highest-engagement election article (August 2016, Election Day).

The highest-engagement story on Facebook from the *New York Times* racked up just under four hundred thousand likes, comments, and shares. The *Denver Guardian*'s most viral offering, which happens to be the article above, was engaged with nearly six hundred thousand times.

Now, is that a problem from the perspective of the Rights Era? Probably not—people should be able to read what they want and share what they want. From a Public Health point of view, however, it may well be a huge problem. And Facebook can and does intervene against such content, albeit in a manner that's frequently sporadic and faltering.

That *Denver Guardian* article was organic content—now let's briefly talk about ads. Those looking to place ads on Facebook are offered up a targeting window where they can build an "audience" based on—among other things—interests and demographics. Some investigative journalists at *ProPublica* went in and tried to target anyone who listed their field of study as "Jew Hater."[33]

Across the Facebook userbase, it turns out there were 2,274 users who had listed "Jew Hater" as their field of study. Facebook took that initial trove of data and, with the help of some clever machine learning, spat out a bunch of additional suggestions—including "how to burn Jews," "German Schutzstaffel," "Nationalism," and strangely, the restaurant "Eataly NYC." With those added selectors, Facebook's rating of the audience scope goes from "overly narrow" to "great," capturing about 108,000 people.

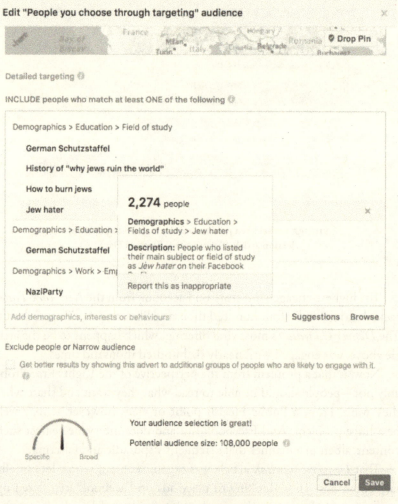

FIGURE 11. *ProPublica*'s ad targeting experiment.

This is, once again, the shift from tool to friend. This is Facebook as an unconscious entity, offering up detailed—but wholly automated—advice on how best to reach the people you're wanting to reach. Again, think about the ADL's answer to the invocation of antisemitism in the Jew Watch incident—the warning against ascribing intent in a machine-driven process. That logic may well apply here—Facebook's ad targeting suite isn't designed for those looking to mobilize or recruit neo-Nazis. But the software is so flexible that once it's given enough to work with, it will happily make itself useful to anybody with a credit card.

And data collection—in relation to the people visiting Facebook—is the engine of these flexible capabilities. That collection enables them to learn some pretty sophisticated things about their userbase. Facebook's Valentine's Day post in 2014 suggested that up to one hundred days before the relationship's official announcement, Facebook's data analysts could often predict with a decent degree of accuracy that two Facebook members were going to end up together.[34] They missed a prime opportunity to market an ancillary service to would-be in-laws hoping to head off the impending collision.

You always look to patents to see the highest aspirations of a company uncoupled from concerns around plausibility. And sure enough, here's one from Facebook, titled "Predicting Life Changes of Members of a Social Networking System."[35]

Per the patent, those life changes included "death"—and not just the user's death but also those of people and pets associated with the

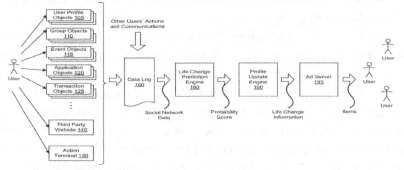

FIGURE 12. Facebook patent diagram for a system to predict life changes.

user. Now this might just be for the purpose of being able—at the right moment and after a waiting period—to advertise pet-mourning users a new cat or something. But it just shows how much the needle of control has swung toward the platforms—and further underscores the question of whether the fact that they *can* so ably predict and even control phenomena means that they ethically *must* do so, whether for the good of the user or that of society as a whole.

REVENGE OF THE RIGHTS? LESS *CAN* MEANS LESS *OUGHT*

The platforms themselves have seen the specter of disapprobation by the public (in a Public Health sense) and of regulation. They know that their enormous capabilities are more and more widely recognized and have—in response—at times attempted to dial down the *can* so as to annul uncomfortable conversations about *ought*.

For example, Twitter recently expressed an interest in funding efforts to decentralize social media platforms (starting with Twitter), which would likely—under most configurations—limit the extent of the platform's governance power.[36] In 2008, I would have supported that proposal almost without reservation. And in fact, I find myself supporting it today. But I am also conscious that it bears the cost of much less control over exactly what happens on Twitter, including when user behavior inflicts real harms that can, at present, be policed.

Over at Facebook, Mark Zuckerberg last year issued a post entitled "A Privacy-Focused Vision for Social Networking," which championed a new paradigm for the company built largely around closed groups and end-to-end encryption.[37] I'm certainly a proponent of end-to-end encryption, but let's be clear: part of the benefit to Facebook of implementing it is that it reduces visibility into exactly what users are doing and saying. That severely blunts demands that the company take responsibility for what's going on.

And of course, in a high-profile incident four years ago, Apple came into an intense dispute with the American government over whether it should have to crack an encrypted iPhone given the proper warrant. Apple argued in the courts that such a requirement would be both a dangerous precedent and a violation of the rights of the company and its employees.[38] And at the time of the controversy, Apple was already rolling out a special encrypted system as part of later models of iPhone—the so-called secure enclave—that limited, on a fundamental technical basis, what the company could do to get into encrypted phones even if it was legally compelled to try.[39]

And we see this debate echoed even today, in America and around the world. Prime Minister Cameron,[40] Theresa May,[41] and Attorney General William Barr[42] are just a few of the many government officials who have called for the creation of encryption circumvention tools by the companies. And the conversation has shifted, in part, to focus on architectural mandates—rules that would require technology companies to build their products in a way that facilitates the enforcement of warrants. That raises tricky questions because product architecture effectively sets the dial for "can"—the companies are, in effect, arguing with government over what they should allow themselves the power to do. That might make a lack of technical ability feel less exculpatory when, for example, Facebook tells the authorities that there's no way it can crack into an end-to-end encrypted chat app that its engineers designed to be uncrackable by Facebook or anyone else.

TOWARD PROCESS

At this point, it should be clear that there are plenty of compelling arguments to be made on both sides of a Rights versus Public Health debate. Indeed, I've sought to capture the enormous stakes rightly claimed by either side in the title for this lecture, which is "Between Suffocation and Abdication." The Rights framework safeguards against feelings of suffocation that might be aroused by the overzealous intervention of intermediaries or government, championing individual agency against competing considerations. The Public Health framework takes the opposite tack, insisting that intermediaries (and regulators) leverage their unique powers to mitigate harms—particularly those that they themselves enable.

We are only now meeting in earnest the question of whether *can* implies *ought*. And so far, we haven't arrived at anything resembling an answer. And the hard questions keep piling up. Twitter, for example, recently announced that they're going to implement a new feature that lets you control who can post replies to your tweets. You could make it, for example, so that only people you follow could reply to you. It's a very rights-oriented tweak, giving individuals greater power to shape the discourse they germinate.[43]

Looking at the new feature from a Public Health perspective, things get more complicated, as the Twitter user below was quick to point out:

FIGURE 13. A tweet making a public health critique of a rights-oriented intervention.

This is a Public Health critique of a Rights-oriented intervention. Twitter, again, can design itself however it wants. How do we answer this dilemma?

And Rights Era absolutism isn't the only way of thinking about questions of speech. Article 19 of the International Covenant on Civil and Political Rights strongly champions a right to freedom of expression. But then if you read a little farther, it says that such a right "may therefore be subject to certain restrictions, but these shall only be such as are provided by law and are necessary . . . for the protection of national security or of public order (ordre public), or of public health or morals."[44]

Of course, recognizing the need for balancing does not itself entail reconciliation. The normal way to solve this would be to take it to the Supreme Court of the jurisdiction in question and have the government be the referee on these hard questions. But we don't know what we want. These questions are really hard. And even if we did, we don't trust anybody to give it to us. Trust in government, empirically speaking, including governments that embrace the rule of law—and their judiciaries—is at an all-time low.[45] So we're stuck.

[ZITTRAIN] *Between Suffocation and Abdication*

So how might we go about cracking the first question—what do we want? What should we want? Perhaps a massive subsidization of philosophers around the world so that finally, after several thousand years, we might settle the issue of the balance between rights and public health? (I want to go on record as totally supporting a massive subsidy for philosophers. In addition to all of their other wonderful qualities, they come comparatively cheap.)

But it seems unlikely that such a subsidy, while wonderful, would be sufficient to the cause. So how else might we proceed? Well, I propose a third era in digital governance—a Process Era. In some sense, process has always been with us. Governments have processes for making decisions when civil society or the public at large turns to them to settle disputes—and I've just claimed that those processes aren't enough. But I want to identify a specific form of process—one that might use the original qualities of the distributed network that many of us were so excited about in 1995—to try to assist in a legitimacy-building exercise that might give us more leverage on the hard problem of balancing Rights and Public Health.

So what should be the hallmarks of an era of Process? Well, transparency might be a start. Many of the digital "friends" upon which we've come to rely are black boxes. There's no denying their usefulness. But come on, I'm a human. I want to know what's going on under the hood. So let's think about what some new modes of transparency might look like.

To start, when Facebook takes down 865 million posts, that ought to be recorded somewhere.[46] Somewhere outside of Facebook, where its actions can be studied. Maybe not by the entire world but at least by bona fide researchers and others on a nondiscriminatory basis. We might look for inspiration in the locked, restricted area of a library. A section barred off such that even if you don't have the key, you can still scan the spines of the books. And when you do have a good reason to need access, there's a process to get your hands on the key. Indeed, to go from metaphorical to concrete, we might even think about whether Facebook's takedown data should be stored and protected by the great libraries of the world.

There's a useful precedent for this kind of approach in German law, politics, and culture. Going back almost half a millennium, there's been in Germany this idea of the Giftschrank, a "poison cabinet" for censored works. It's a place where politically questionable or outright dangerous books can be guarded, made available, perhaps, on a limited basis for

360   *The Tanner Lectures on Human Values*

research purposes.[47] You could see implementing a counterpart to the German Giftschrank in relation to private entities that have unique data that bears on what kind of job they're doing in meddling with the public discourse. Academics and other representatives of the public ought to have a way of accessing that data, even when it's not fit for wide release.

We've seen among the companies enough awareness of the ethical implications of what they're doing that they're increasingly willing to entertain such accountability-reinforcing solutions. Their first step has been to say, "OK, let's think of an internal process to make ourselves, our workers, and our publics feel better about things." To that end, we've seen the rise of the chief ethics officer, a person within the organizational chart who can tackle the hard problems, including those for which solutions might run contrary to the company's business interests.[48] (Don't like the answer? Hire a better chief ethics officer.) That trend may in turn lead to subsidies for philosophers to produce programs at universities for certifications in chief ethics officering. It's an approach that does seem to punt the problem, but at least it's admitting that we have one.

Microsoft has announced a special internal committee, the AI and Ethics in Engineering and Research Committee.[49] To, again, recognize the gravity of the decisions they are reaching and to demonstrate an understanding that they are impacting the world in a way that should be measured with metrics other than profit. Not to mention the increasingly tangible sense that even if their way of doing business is making money for now, the trouble it brings might cost much more in the long term. Ethics-focused internal review structures invite a different sort of calculus relative to more traditional modes of corporate decision-making. And in that sense, I support them as an initial step.

But they're still part and parcel of the company that they're meant to oversee or even police. If these decisions are really of such weightiness, maybe there should be people from outside the company involved in making them. That's what Google attempted last year when they created an external advisory board to monitor unethical AI use. A week later, however, they dissolved the board because there was dispute over its membership.[50]

Despite the Google board's stumbles, it might be a good sign that people are taking the board seriously enough to worry about who's a member and who's not. And remember that in the absence of such a board, the company's decision-making unfolds largely within a black box, however serious its potential consequences may be. External-facing boards, even

[ZITTRAIN]   *Between Suffocation and Abdication*   361

largely symbolic ones, may play a role in formalizing that decision-making and providing some outward sense of what's going on.

And here, I have to say, Facebook has ended up taking the lead. In part, I think, that's because Mark Zuckerberg so single-handedly runs the company that he could just wake up one morning and say something like "I want an outside oversight board and not an advisory one. When it makes a decision about a piece of content, we should be forced to follow it." This is truly a disclaiming, in some sense, of the apparent absolutism of the ever-growing power that something like Facebook has. And Mark has been quite up front about this, expressing real discomfort with the magnitude of the power that he himself wields.

I'm very intrigued by Facebook's oversight board.[51] Will it work? I don't know. It's going to have something like forty people on it. Maybe paying, say, a retired Bolivian judge $200,000 a year to sit on the board and take up fraught questions relating to vaccine misinformation is exactly the right move. After all, that judge and his peers probably know a lot more than I do about balancing—so perhaps I should defer to their expertise.

Matching that expertise with real power—uncoupled from Facebook's business interests—could be legitimacy building, but it's still operating within an architecture designed by Facebook. There may be ways to go further, shifting control over product design itself. One such way is suggested in a now-famous 1998 scholarly article, which, talking about search engines and their commercial incentives, said, "We believe the issue of advertising causes enough mixed incentives that it is crucial to have a competitive search engine that is transparent and in the academic realm."[52] Maybe, in other words, some online services are so critical to the public interest that they must be run by entities that pursue that interest at the cost of all others.

That paper was written by Lawrence Page and Sergey Brin—the founders of Google.

But for all that has happened between then and now, I think it's safe to say that their sentiment was quite prescient in 1998—that maybe the incentive structures behind the platforms aren't patchable. Am I calling for a nationalization of Facebook? No. Remember, when it comes to digital governance, we don't trust anybody to give it to us—least of all government, in many cases. I don't think nationalizing the platforms is going to help. But maybe there are other options that draw in the public at large— capturing some sense of public consultation and accountability without the trappings of government. That way, thorny ethical questions arising from product design might benefit from something more robust and representative than an internal review board.

Consider a very hypothetical world in which Uber decides to include battery life as a factor in its pricing algorithm, slightly hiking rates for passengers whose devices are about to die. From a straight-up willingness-to-pay perspective, that's a totally rational idea. Is a person with a dying phone really going to take time to check Lyft or some other competitor?

Now again, that could be reputationally dodgy—which is probably why Uber has been so vocal about not doing it.[53] But on the other hand, the algorithmic pricing models we interact with every day are already so dynamic. Without a bunch of really good testing, we're not going to know why we get the price we get. In any case, it would be good to surface the quandary and give those who would be impacted a chance to weigh in.

I would like to put something like that out to the public the way that my colleague Iyad Rahwan does on his Moral Machine site.[54] His site gives members of the public an opportunity to weigh in on questions relating to the ethics of autonomous vehicles. In the image below, you'll see one scenario from the Moral Machine: a vehicle has lost its brakes and must decide whether to keep going and hit some cats or swerve and hit some people.

Hopefully that's an easy one. But by asking millions of people questions like this one, and even noting differences from one region or culture to the next, the Moral Machine has actually generated some pretty interesting insights.[55] Not to mention the fact that it's given millions of

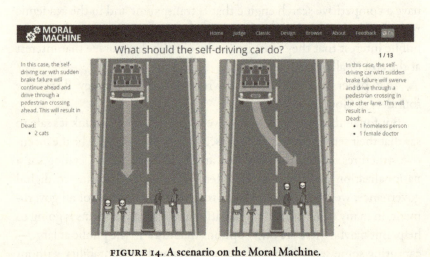

FIGURE 14. A scenario on the Moral Machine.

people the opportunity to reflect on a set of increasingly relevant ethical questions in a way they might not have been able to otherwise. I could certainly see using a similar platform to ask that question about battery life, and a bunch of others that are probably much harder, as a way of giving a technology company a sense of where public perceptions lie—and a means of earnestly consulting their users.

And in fact, I'd like to take the consultation even further—to make it binding. Below is a real ad that the North Dakota Democratic Party ran on Facebook during the 2018 election season:[56]

It's an interesting attempt at voter suppression. Its message is self-targeting to those who might be voting Republican anyway. Because if you're not a hunter, you wouldn't be troubled by the ad's content, even if you believed it. And what should Facebook do about this? Facebook's current answer is total Rights Era stuff: you don't want us treating you

Hunter Alerts
Sponsored • Paid for by **North Dakota Democratic-NPL**

ATTENTION HUNTERS: If you vote in North Dakota, you may forfeit hunting licenses you have in other states. If you want to keep your out-of-state hunting licenses, you may not want to vote in North Dakota. Learn more: bit.ly/2OlybPM

FIGURE 15. The North Dakota Democratic Party's misleading Facebook ad.

364   *The Tanner Lectures on Human Values*

like sheep by shaping your access to political messaging.[57] These are sensitive conversations, and there's going to be debate over almost any form of ground truth. It's not our job to interfere in that, even if we'd just be calling balls and strikes.

That seems intuitive, at least to me. So why, when Facebook says they're getting out, is the company met with much disapprobation in the press and among academics? Because again, we live more in the Public Health Era than we do in the Rights Era these days—and by those lights, this is textbook abdication.

So let's have Process intervene by way of the sort of binding consultation I was just describing. What if we were to take this ad and, instead of doing nothing with it except showing it as requested, sent it to an American high school. The case would then make its way to a high school class chosen at random, having prearranged to participate in the program, possibly funded by an endowment of trust money from Facebook. For a grade and under the supervision of their teacher, the students would actually talk about the ad. They would apply standards of truth to it and come up with an adjudication based on research and analysis, perhaps developed with the help of the school librarian.[58]

And then they write that decision up anonymously. And maybe their answer is no, this ad shouldn't stand—at which point the ad is taken down. And as he does with his independent review board, Mark can say, "Don't blame me. Blame the anonymous high school somewhere in the Heartland, or possibly the coasts, that decided this was not a good ad."

And I recognize this is a crazy idea. It is crazy, but I'm trying to figure out why it wouldn't be better than what we have now. It's an example of a process intervention that at the very least would address decisions like these with the gravity and public input they deserve. Facebook's current approach suggests that political ads are too sensitive a domain for assessments of truth value. This approach would maintain that the truth matters while recognizing that the only way of legitimating truth assessments under such sensitive conditions is by building a process that actually has its own degree of fortuity to it. A kind of fortuity without randomness, one that operates in ways that are various and unexpected, but also principled and substantiated by research. In a Rawlsian sense, we would have no idea what a class is going to do in any given case. Which means that if the process is designed correctly, there would be no structural advantage for, say, the right or the left, as opponents of conventional fact-checking so often claim that there is. And what's

[ZITTRAIN]   *Between Suffocation and Abdication*

more, this approach would be scalable—there are millions of students enrolled at U.S. high schools.

There are clearly any number of questions that would still need to be worked out here. Which classes should be sent the questions? Should we have multiple classes weigh in on every ad? What should we do when they disagree? Indeed, such disagreement might actually be a feature because it will mean that stuff reasonable people might disagree on will be treated a little bit differently, while stuff clearly over the line will consistently have trouble finding its place on Facebook.

So by way of summary, where do we stand on the Process Era ideas? I've already talked about transparency in the form of the Giftschrank and the possibility of getting libraries involved. I've talked about binding shifts of control to outside the firm, of the sort that Facebook is pioneering with its Oversight Board. And we've just now pondered rechartering juries for representation and scale, both by hijacking the Moral Machine project to provide public input into tough governance questions faced by companies and through this political ad juries idea.

More important than any one idea or proposal might be an ethos that encourages us to try a lot of different approaches. Don't try to develop one perfect thing that then won't work and say, "Well, we tried process. But it didn't pan out." Throw lots of different process solutions at the wall and see what sticks. Lean into and take advantage of the uncertainty.

And finally, on top of these solutions, we need to develop and enforce new duties and loyalties for digital architects. And for that, I come to the concept of the learned professions—those three professions that have traditionally required advanced learning and high principles. Why the high principles? Because of the power that comes with advanced learning, particularly in relation to those who lack it. That holds true for each of the original three: divinity, law, and medicine. Each harnesses a special form of power, which implicates duties to parishioners, clients, and patients, respectively. Duties that go beyond the commercial.[59]

And each profession also has duties to society at large. It's a very Article 19–style balancing kind of approach as to when, say, the confidentiality of a patient should be respected over and against the social utility in reporting possible cases of contagious disease to the public health authorities. But a set of principles specific to that category of problems has developed over decades to provide a sense of wisdom. That is, in part, why we generally feel that we can trust our doctors to treat us in accordance with our own interests rather than those of a drug company or medical device manufacturer. It's part of what gives the medical profession its legitimacy.

I think it's probably time to think about more learned professions, to be put on par with the ones mentioned above. So that the Google data scientists, the Facebook engineers, and even the members of a two-person start-up (because sometimes those things get big) can be guaranteed a sense of compass independent of their employers.

To conclude, I'd ask you to consider the Sony Betamax video cassette recorder, originally released in 1975. You might not have known how to set the clock, but you could figure out how to shove in a tape for playback or record a television program. How the machine worked might not have been clear—but given the stakes, that was OK. Arthur C. Clarke's third law is that any sufficiently advanced technology is indistinguishable from magic. He was borrowing a bit from Leigh Brackett who, years earlier, put it more bluntly: "Witchcraft to the ignorant, simple science to the learned."[60]

Today, the stakes of that divide have never been greater. As the intermediaries I discussed have turned the "can" dial higher and higher, they've reshaped our institutions and our lives. And that reshaping doesn't end with the social media companies that I've dwelt on for the duration of this lecture. They also count among their number Tesla, Toyota, or Bentley, the intermediaries building and deploying automated vehicles. What we can do here in the purely digital realm could translate to those kinetic realms as well, where governance is going to be that much more clearly important because of its physical implications.

In a sort of oddly represented histogram of people, I see only one small corner as the nerds who aren't bound by much of this. Because in keeping with Barlow's declaration, they can say, "I can build whatever I want. I can hack the rest. I live free and clear and trust only myself and my friends." On the other side are the Luddites. People who say, "So long as there's a library with a book called *1984* in it, I don't care what they're doing on that Nook. Enjoy your possibly adulterated goods." Maybe the Luddites are on to something too. But the prospect of living a "normal" life without digital technology has grown dimmer and dimmer.

And finally in the middle are the rest of us—the sheep in need of protection as digital technology expands and changes around us. We bring knowledge towers and Kinects into our homes. We post on social media, view targeted advertisements, and rely on Gmail and Outlook to make sure our emails get where they need to go. In the face of new challenges and trade-offs like the ones I've discussed, we find ourselves having to

FIGURE 16. Histogram of Clarke's Third Law x2.

preserve our rights, our autonomy, and our sense of boundaries while also protecting the entire flock from a public health standpoint. That will be much easier if we can put structures for transparency and participation in place—enabling all of us living in an increasingly digital world to go beyond the Betamax model.

That question of participation isn't new. In different forms, it was the question of the day in 1995 and 2005 as well. The fact that we haven't answered it—even as it has grown more urgent—is a call to arms. If we don't heed it, just follow the line from the status quo. And by those lights, my sort of optimistic ramblings about what we can do here might begin to feel like more of a necessity.

Barlow ends his "A Declaration of the Independence of Cyberspace" with an admonition: "We will create a civilization of the Mind in Cyberspace. May it be more humane and fair than the world your governments have made before."[61] Barlow's is a simple dichotomy. There are the governments, faceless "giants of flesh and steel," and then there's us. But despite its undue and even misleading simplicity, Barlow's benediction is powerful—a charge to us to figure out what that Civilization of Mind should look like. That charge from 1996 remains vital today.

NOTES

1 Peter Schwartz and Peter Leyden, "The Long Boom: A History of the Future, 1980–2020," *Wired*, July 1, 1997, https://www.wired.com/1997/07/longboom/.

2 David Baker, "The Internet Is Broken," *Wired*, December 19, 2017, https://www.wired.co.uk/article/is-the-internet-broken-how-to-fix-it.

3 Hoxton Street Monster Supplies, "Range of Tinned Fear," accessed May 21, 2020, https://web.archive.org/web/20200804174931/https://www.monstersupplies.org/collections/view-all/products/range-of-tinned-fear.

4 Amy B Wang, Cleve R. Wootsonn Jr., and Ed O'Keefe, "As Harvey Submerges Houston, Local Officials Defend Their Calls Not to Evacuate," *Washington Post*, August 27, 2017, https://www.washingtonpost.com/news/post-nation/wp/2017/08/27/harvey-is-causing-epic-catastrophic-flooding-in-houston-why-wasnt-the-city-evacuated/.

5 Tim Berners-Lee, "WWW: Past, Present, and Future," *Computer* 29, no. 10 (October 1996): 69–77, https://doi.org/10.1109/2.539724.

6 Lasse Gustavsson, "About Lasse," Lasse Gustavsson's Website, accessed May 21, 2020, http://pan.se/about-lasse/.

7 Emanuella Grinberg and Eugenie Lambert, "Facebook Apologizes for Removing Photo of Firefighter with Severe Burns," *CNN*, last modified November 14, 2016, https://www.cnn.com/2016/11/14/health/swedish-firefighter-facebook-photo/index.html.

8 Allison Kempe et al., "HPV Vaccine Delivery Practices by Primary Care Physicians," *Pediatrics* 144, no. 4 (October 2019), https://doi.org/10.1542/peds.2019-1475.

9 John Perry Barlow, "A Declaration of the Independence of Cyberspace," Electronic Frontier Foundation, February 8, 1996, https://www.eff.org/cyberspace-independence.

10 Rebecca MacKinnon, "Screenshots of Censorship," *RConversation* (blog), June 16, 2005, https://rconversation.blogs.com/rconversation/2005/06/screenshots_of_.html.

11 Brad Stone, "Amazon Erases Orwell Books from Kindle," *New York Times*, July 17, 2009, https://www.nytimes.com/2009/07/18/technology/companies/18amazon.html.

12 Hermoine Hoby, "War and Peace ebook Readers Find a Surprise in Its Nooks," *Guardian*, June 7, 2012, https://www.theguardian.com/books/booksblog/2012/jun/07/war-and-peace-ebook-nook.

13 Todd Bishop, "Xbox Team's 'Consumer Detector' Would Dis-Kinect Freeloading TV Viewers," *Geekwire*, November 3, 2012, https://www.geekwire.com/2012/microsoft-diskinect-freeloading-tv-viewers/.

14 John Perry Barlow, "A Declaration of the Independence of Cyberspace," Electronic Frontier Foundation, February 8, 1996, https://www.eff.org/cyberspace-independence.

15 Philip Elmer-Dewitt, "First Nation in Cyberspace," *TIME International*, December 6, 1993, http://kirste.userpage.fu-berlin.de/outerspace/internet-article.html.

16 Zeran v. America Online, Inc., 129 F.3d 327, 330 (4th Cir. 1997).

17 Wired Staff, "Dropping the Bomb on Google," *Wired*, May 11, 2004, https://www.wired.com/2004/05/dropping-the-bomb-on-google/.

18 Google Team, "An Explanation of Our Search Results," *Google*, June 7, 2004, https://web.archive.org/web/20060207003953/https://www.google.com/explanation.html.

19 "Google Search Ranking of Hate Sites Not Intentional," Anti-defamation League, April 22, 2004, https://www.adl.org/news/article/google-search-ranking -of-hate-sites-not-intentional.

20 Amit Singhal, "Introducing the Knowledge Graph: Things, Not Strings," *Google* (blog), May 16, 2012, https://googleblog.blogspot.com/2012/05/introducing -knowledge-graph-things-not.html.

21 "Apple Siri: 'All-New Voice-Control AI Stuff,'" *Washington Post*, October 4, 2011, https://www.washingtonpost.com/business/economy/apple-siri-all-new -voice-control-ai-stuff/2011/08/13/gIQAZJEXLL_story.html.

22 Andrew Griffin, "Barack Obama Is Organising a Coup against Donald Trump, Says Google Home," *Independent*, March 6, 2017, https://www.independent .co.uk/life-style/gadgets-and-tech/news/donald-trump-barack-obama-coup -google-home-assistant-question-fake-news-a7614421.html.

23 Danny Sullivan (@dannysullivan), "Google Home: 'Yes, Republicans = Nazis,'" Twitter, video, March 5, 2017, https://twitter.com/dannysullivan/status/8384 79054630068224.

24 Eva Lake, "How We Are Talking to Alexa," *NHS Digital* (blog), July 25, 2019, https://digital.nhs.uk/blog/transformation-blog/2019/how-we-are-talking -to-alexa.

25 Human Rights Council, *Report of the Independent International Fact-Finding Mission on Myanmar* (Geneva: United Nations Human Rights Council, 2018), https://www.ohchr.org/Documents/HRBodies/HRCouncil/FFM-Myanmar/ A_HRC_39_64.pdf.

26 Christopher Woody, "Facebook Official Who Oversees the News Feed Says His Team Loses Sleep over the Site's Alleged Role in Myanmar 'Ethnic Cleans-ing,'" *Business Insider*, March 22, 2018, https://www.businessinsider.com/adam -mosseri-facebook-myanmar-genocide-rohingya-lose-sleep-2018-3.

27 Nick Hopkins, "Revealed: Facebook's Internal Rulebook on Sex, Terrorism and Violence," *Guardian*, May 21, 2017, https://www.theguardian.com/news/ 2017/may/21/revealed-facebook-internal-rulebook-sex-terrorism-violence.

28 Nick Hopkins, "Revealed: Facebook's Internal Rulebook on Sex, Terrorism and Violence," *Guardian*, May 21, 2017, https://www.theguardian.com/news/ 2017/may/21/revealed-facebook-internal-rulebook-sex-terrorism-violence.

29 Julia Carrie Wong and Olivia Solon, "Facebook Releases Content Modera-tion Guidelines—Rules Long Kept Secret," *Guardian*, April 24, 2018, https:// www.theguardian.com/technology/2018/apr/24/facebook-releases-content -moderation-guidelines-secret-rules.

30 Mark Zuckerberg, "A Blueprint for Content Governance and Enforcement," November 15, 2018, https://www.facebook.com/notes/mark-zuckerberg/a -blueprint-for-content-governance-and-enforcement/10156443129621634/.

31 Sheera Frenkel, "Facebook Says It Deleted 865 Million Posts, Mostly Spam," *New York Times*, May 15, 2018, https://www.nytimes.com/2018/05/15/ technology/facebook-removal-posts-fake-accounts.html.

32 Craig Silverman, "This Analysis Shows How Viral Fake Election News Stories Outperformed Real News on Facebook," *BuzzFeed News*, November 16, 2016, https://www.buzzfeednews.com/article/craigsilverman/viral-fake-election -news-outperformed-real-news-on-facebook. This graph was developed based on the data taken from Buzzfeed's linked spreadsheet.

33 Julia Angwin, Madeleine Varner, and Ariana Tobin, "Facebook Enabled Adver-tisers to Reach 'Jew Haters,'" *ProPublica*, September 14, 2014, https://www .propublica.org/article/facebook-enabled-advertisers-to-reach-jew-haters.

34 Robinson Meyer, "When You Fall in Love, This Is What Facebook Sees," *Atlantic*, February 15, 2014, https://www.theatlantic.com/technology/archive/2014/02/when-you-fall-in-love-this-is-what-facebook-sees/283865/.

35 Alex S. Smith and David Braginsky. Predicting Life Changes of Members of a Social Networking System, U.S. Patent US20120016817A1, filed July 19, 2010, and issued January 19, 2012, https://patents.google.com/patent/US20120016817A1/en.

36 Jack Dorsey (@Jack), "Twitter is funding a small independent team of up to five open source architects, engineers, and designers to develop an open and decentralized standard for social media. The goal is for Twitter to ultimately be a client of this standard," Twitter, December 11, 2019, https://twitter.com/jack/status/1204766078468911106.

37 Mark Zuckerberg, "A Privacy-Focused Vision for Social Networking," Facebook, March 6, 2019, https://www.facebook.com/notes/mark-zuckerberg/a-privacy-focused-vision-for-social-networking/10156700570096634/.

38 Quentin Hardy, "Apple and Justice Dept. Prepare to Face off in Court," *New York Times*, March 21, 2016, https://www.nytimes.com/2016/03/22/technology/apple-and-justice-dept-prepare-to-face-off-in-court.html.

39 "Secure Enclave Overview," Apple Support, n.d., https://support.apple.com/guide/security/secure-enclave-overview-sec59b0b31ff/web.

40 Nicholas Watt, Rowena Mason, and Ian Traynor, "David Cameron Pledges Anti-terror Law for Internet after Paris Attacks," *Guardian*, January 12, 2015, https://www.theguardian.com/uk-news/2015/jan/12/david-cameron-pledges-anti-terror-law-internet-paris-attacks-nick-clegg.

41 Alex Hern, "May Calls Again for Tech Firms to Act on Encrypted Messaging," *Guardian*, January 25, 2018, https://www.theguardian.com/technology/2018/jan/25/theresa-may-calls-tech-firms-act-encrypted-messaging.

42 William P. Barr, "Attorney General William P. Barr Delivers Keynote Address at the International Conference on Cyber Security," United States Department of Justice, July 23, 2019, https://www.justice.gov/opa/speech/attorney-general-william-p-barr-delivers-keynote-address-international-conference-cyber.

43 Suzanne Xie, "Twitter," *Twitter* (blog), May 20, 2020, https://blog.twitter.com/en_us/topics/product/2020/testing-new-conversation-settings.html.

44 General Assembly Resolution 2200A (XXI), "International Covenant on Civil and Political Rights," United Nations, December 16, 1966, https://www.ohchr.org/en/professionalinterest/pages/ccpr.aspx.

45 "Trust in Government," *Gallup*, March 30, 2020, https://news.gallup.com/poll/5392/trust-government.aspx.

46 Sheera Frenkel, "Facebook Says It Deleted 865 Million Posts, Mostly Spam," *New York Times*, May 15, 2018, https://www.nytimes.com/2018/05/15/technology/facebook-removal-posts-fake-accounts.html.

47 Sam Greenspan, "The Giftschrank," *99% Invisible*, March 8, 2016, https://99percentinvisible.org/episode/the-giftschrank/.

48 Insights Team, "Forbes Insights: Rise of the Chief Ethics Officer," *Forbes*, June 5, 2019, https://www.forbes.com/sites/insights-intelai/2019/03/27/rise-of-the-chief-ethics-officer/#37773e9d5aba.

49 Satya Nadella, "Satya Nadella Email to Employees: Embracing Our Future: Intelligent Cloud and Intelligent Edge," Microsoft News Center, Microsoft, March 29, 2018, https://news.microsoft.com/2018/03/29/satya-nadella-email-to-employees-embracing-our-future-intelligent-cloud-and-intelligent-edge/.

50 Nick Statt, "Google Dissolves AI Ethics Board Just One Week after Forming It," *Verge*, April 5, 2019, https://www.theverge.com/2019/4/4/18296113/google-ai-ethics-board-ends-controversy-kay-coles-james-heritage-foundation.

51 Brent Harris, "Establishing Structure and Governance for an Independent Oversight Board," Meta, November 7, 2019, https://about.fb.com/news/2019/09/oversight-board-structure/.

52 Sergey Brin and Lawrence Page, "The Anatomy of a Large-Scale Hypertextual Web Search Engine," Stanford, 1998, http://infolab.stanford.edu/~backrub/google.html.

53 Jessica Lindsay, "Does Uber Charge More If Your Battery Is Lower?," Metro, September 27, 2019, https://metro.co.uk/2019/09/27/uber-charge-battery-lower-10778303/.

54 "Moral Machine," Moral Machine, n.d., http://moralmachine.mit.edu/.

55 Edmond Awad et al., "The Moral Machine Experiment," *Nature* 563, no. 7729 (2018): 59–64, https://doi.org/10.1038/s41586-018-0637-6.

56 Jane Lytvynenko, "North Dakota Democrats Ran a Misleading Facebook Ad Discouraging People from Voting," *BuzzFeed News*, November 2, 2018, https://www.buzzfeednews.com/article/janelytvynenko/north-dakota-democrats-facebook-ad-voter-suppression.

57 Nick Clegg, "Facebook, Elections and Political Speech," Meta, September 24, 2019, https://about.fb.com/news/2019/09/elections-and-political-speech/.

58 Jonathan Zittrain, "A Jury of Random People Can Do Wonders for Facebook," *Atlantic*, November 14, 2019, https://www.theatlantic.com/ideas/archive/2019/11/let-juries-review-facebook-ads/601996/.

59 Kenneth Hudson, "The Learned Professions," in *Jargon of the Professions* (London: Palgrave Macmillan, 1978), 22–41.

60 Leigh Brackett, "The Sorcerer of Rhiannon," *Astounding Stories of Super-Science*, February 1942.

61 John Perry Barlow, "A Declaration of the Independence of Cyberspace," Electronic Frontier Foundation, February 8, 1996, https://www.eff.org/cyberspace-independence.

LECTURE II.
WITH GREAT POWER COMES GREAT IGNORANCE: WHAT'S WRONG WHEN MACHINE LEARNING GETS IT RIGHT

For the second lecture, I want to tell a story about a phenomenon that I'm going to call "intellectual debt," covering both why I think it matters and what we might do about it. It's a story perhaps best told in the context of machine learning, which will indeed be my focus here. But I think the machine learning case is just one particularly salient leaf on a much broader tree, just one example of a much more expansive phenomenon that goes back quite far.

To start, I want to revisit the quotation ending my first lecture that any sufficiently advanced technology is indistinguishable from magic. There, we discussed how technology's rearchitecting of power and control—to the detriment of fortuity—has posed new governance challenges and raised important questions relating to accountability and transparency. Here, I want to go a step further and explore what happens when power arises from technologies that are a black box even to the people who build them.

Such technologies are more common than one might think, including outside of the digital realm. Take, for example, Nuvigil, a widely available drug that's supposed to keep you awake. In drug packages, there's often a little insert depending on the jurisdiction in which the drug was manufactured or sold. If you are at wit's end and totally bored, you might find yourself fiddling around with your box of Nuvigil and maybe even giving that insert a read. It has all sorts of information about the drug you're about to take, including about its chemical properties. (I'm trying to remember my early chemistry classes and what a hexagon means.)

Read a little further, and you'll come across a little box with information about the drug's mechanism of action. In Nuvigil's case, it reads as follows: "The mechanism through which Armodafinil promotes wakefulness is unknown." What? How do we go around prescribing drugs that tweak their takers' brain chemistry without knowing how they work? (The pamphlet alone might be enough to keep someone awake at night.)

But unknown mechanisms of action are a time-honored tradition in drug discovery. Aspirin was invented toward the end of the nineteenth century, before which willow leaves—in which Aspirin's precursor is found—had been used therapeutically for millennia. A partial

[372]

FIGURE 17. Nuvigil packaging insert.

mechanism of action was theorized in 1971 and substantially fleshed out by a key breakthrough in 1995.[1] For almost a century, we prescribed Aspirin by the truckload without really knowing how it worked. Should we have waited for the theory to catch up before using it? No, of course not. But when we tap into answers and capabilities unaccompanied by explanations, I call that a form of intellectual debt. Intellectual debt accrues when we procure answers without developing theories to go along with them.

Now theory is a very loaded word, one that can mean radically different things across fields. Here's my operational definition: *a generalization that can be used to reliably and compellingly explain how different phenomena relate to one another*. It's as much a psychological definition as anything else. And when you are accruing intellectual debt, you are skipping out on the process of developing such compelling explanations.

And I think there might even be two flavors of intellectual debt. Much of what I'll talk about today is what I call "atomic" intellectual debt. That's intellectual debt that arises from the specific system, often a machine learning system in the examples I'll explore, that's producing the theory-free answer. And then there's what I call "systemic" intellectual debt, which accrues when interlinked systems, themselves accruing their own pockets of atomic debt, can interact strangely with one another and give rise to new problems and unpredictability. This emergent form of intellectual debt carries its own distinctive risks and possibly calls for its own set of solutions.

374 *The Tanner Lectures on Human Values*

So why focus on machine learning? Because while intellectual debt is itself nothing new, machine learning is enabling us to take it on at a much faster rate than previously would have been possible. That acceleration is due in part to the fact that machine learning is enabling us to accrue intellectual debt around new sorts of questions. For example, what should the next Netflix series be about, and who should star in it? Famously, Netflix claims that it used a trained-up machine learning system to project that an American remake of House of Cards, specifically with Kevin Spacey, would be very successful.[2] Alternatively, which applicants are likely to excel at the University of Cambridge? Admissions decisions are the kind of problem where you might have enough data to train up a useful machine learning system, even if its usefulness is not accompanied by meaningful explanations of why it suggests the decisions that it does. Yet more questions abound: Who's at risk of quitting my company? What should I do to live longer? What's the best arrangement of antiballistic missile defenses? These are the sorts of questions that might prod us to take on intellectual debt through machine learning.

IDENTIFYING INTELLECTUAL DEBT

What do I mean by machine learning, itself a branch of a much broader field commonly known as artificial intelligence? I'll start with what I don't mean. I don't mean artificial general intelligence—or AGI—the creation of digital agents capable of reasoning independently across the full domain of things subject to human cognition. I'm not referring to AI or machine learning in the way that people like Bill Gates, Stephen Hawking, or Elon Musk do when they've talked about those technologies "summoning the demon"[3] or "spelling the end of the human race."[4] Nor am I following along with the argumentation of Oxford's Nick Bostrom, who has warned of various foreseeable flavors of machine "superintelligence."[5]

There's nothing wrong with talking about AGI—and someday we may have to do so urgently. But we have some problems in front of us that are not quite AGI but still very powerful systems. When I say AI here, I mean something narrower—systems that share a certain set of qualities that enable them to arrive at sophisticated predictions and strategies and make them distinct from other computing and decision-making systems. These sorts of systems tend to produce intellectual debt, atomic or systemic. In trying to enumerate some of these qualities, we might arrive at a definition like this one:

AI is manifested in **arcane pervasive tightly coupled adaptive autonomous systems**.

I want to walk through each of these qualities and explain a little bit more about what I mean by each.

Arcane

So let's start with arcane. Arcanity to me is like the hydrogen on the periodic table of intellectual debt, to totally mix all my metaphors—a foundational building block. It is our inability to determine how something works.

Spotify's "Discover Weekly" service provides an excellent example. The service offers up a fresh weekly playlist of music that you might not have heard yet, but you're likely to like. It's a great system, which has received massive acclaim from users, music journalists, and others. And it's fundamentally arcane—Discover Weekly's job is to show you new music you will like, not to help you understand why you like what you like. The backend of the system is very complicated, but it's not tailoring a playlist like a DJ would—it's (among other things) using giant volumes of data to cluster your revealed preferences with those of other people who seem to have similar tastes, then showing you music that they like.[6] Parts of the approach can be described as "unsupervised learning"—the identification of relationships thorough associations uncovered in unlabeled data, even as the basis of those associations remains obscure. There might be some cool psychology or musicology behind why people who like heavy metal actually have a soft spot for "Also sprach Zarathustra," but Discover Weekly doesn't necessarily need to understand that relationship to package the two together in a playlist. That's a low-stakes form of intellectual debt.

And then you see this Amazon suggestion from many years back, also the product of a system largely built around associational unsupervised learning principles. Here, Amazon has identified a "Perfect Partner" for the official Lego Creator Activity Book—*American Jihad: The Terrorists Living among Us Today*. Is this a mistake in association, or does Amazon's suggestion system know more than I do? And at the end of the day, is this even a good example of machine learning? I don't know. But that

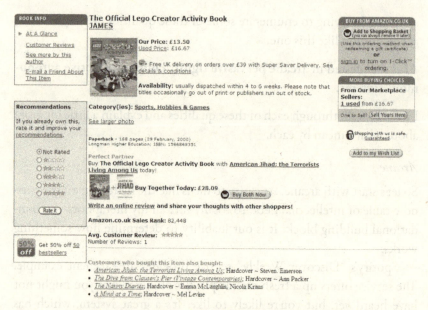

FIGURE 18. Amazon suggestions: From Legos to American Jihad.

inscrutability is at the root of a lot of what makes us nervous about autonomous systems and powers their accumulation of intellectual debt.

And it's not just book reviews. Speaking of *American Jihad*, governments have spent years throwing billions of dollars at the proposition that, given enough information about people, you can separate the good guys from the bad guys. A government document from 2006 describing a system for developing "suspicion scores" for potential terrorists suggests that "to date, the predominant approaches have used a guilt-by-association model to derive suspicion scores.... In the cases where we have knowledge of a seed entity [a known person] in an unknown group, we have been very successful at detecting the entire group. However, in the absence of a known seed entity, how do we score a person if nothing is known about their associates? In such an instance, guilt-by-association fails."[7]

Notice they're not saying there shouldn't be guilt by association. They're just saying we need to know how to start the guilt by association—a problem that might not be all that different, on a fundamental technical level, from developing a Discover Weekly feed. Give me some data and let me cluster it with lots of other data to reveal a previously hidden structure.

Clustering isn't the only approach that has been taken to make intellectual debt-laden predictions about attributes like criminality. Take,

[ZITTRAIN] *With Great Power Comes Great Ignorance* 377

for example, a now somewhat infamous research paper from a team of Chinese researchers: "Automated Inference on Criminality Using Face Images."[8] The paper's abstract promises that the systems developed "perform consistently well and empirically establish the validity of automated face-induced inference on criminality, despite the historical controversy surrounding this line of enquiry," even controlling for "race, gender, age, and facial expressions." It is asking us to accept the radical notion that the physical specifics of a person's face are associated with their tendency toward criminal activity, as decided by a clever algorithm.

So how did they arrive at this clever algorithm? They first collected lots of photos of criminals from various law enforcement sources and ID photos of supposed noncriminals collected online. The authors then fed these labeled examples—of criminals and noncriminals—into machine learning algorithms, which, on the basis of the examples, learned to separate supposed criminals from supposed noncriminals. This is a classic so-called supervised learning system, which, given enough examples of data labeled as belonging to different "classes," can give a probability estimate of whether a new, unlabeled example belongs to a given class (criminal or noncriminal, cat or dog, etc.).

Now how do you determine where these probabilities are coming from? There is now a whole field dedicated to looking at trained-up supervised learning systems and trying to understand how they reach their conclusions. It's still early days for these systems, which means that we're left with a lot of arcanity. In the case of the criminality paper above, it's likely that the distinguishing factors between criminals and noncriminals are rooted in something far more complicated than, say, a genetic association between facial features and aggression or untrustworthiness. Rather, the system may be latching on to characteristics that reflect socioeconomic divides, image capture conditions, and other confounding factors.[9] If we rolled it into use today, we'd likely be doing so without accounting for these qualifications and asterisks—potentially at the cost of inefficacy or the reinforcement of structures of discrimination.

And some systems with more open-ended tasks might provide even less theory with their answers. Take, for example, Google Translate, which uses some very sophisticated machine learning to translate effectively between lots of language pairs, including those for which training data may be quite limited. In the image below, you'll see the result—from a while back—that was returned when a user loaded up Google Translate,

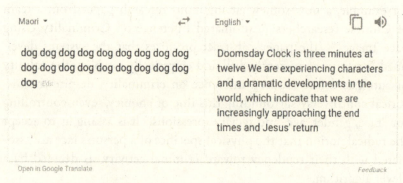

FIGURE 19. Google Translate's incorrect translation from Maori to English.

plugged in "dog dog dog dog dog dog dog" as a supposedly Maori phrase, and asked that it be translated into English.[10]

It's true that dog backward is God. But bizarre as the outcome may be, you might reasonably think it's just a corner case—a totally unrealistic phrase that manages to throw the algorithm for a loop. Why should we care? Because when you don't know how the system works, you also don't know what might make it vulnerable to a carefully designed attack—and if unusual examples can be generated to trick machine learning in particular ways, a whole new threat surface is in play. That's the rough idea behind "adversarial examples"—small perturbations to the inputs to a machine learning system crafted to influence its outputs.

The figure above is from some undergraduates at MIT, working as part of a group called LabSix.[11] They took a picture of a cat and put it through Google's Inception architecture, which is an incredibly powerful image classification algorithm that can sort images across many, many categories. In the unperturbed image, Inception declared with a probability of 80 percent that it had been handed an image of a "tabby cat," with most of the remaining percentage points going to other reasonable guesses like "tiger cat," "Egyptian cat," or "lynx." And then there's the long tail: "carton," "plastic bag," "wash." We probably don't need to worry about these answers too much; Inception has given them almost no weight.

But the team then computed an adversarial perturbation for the image—just a few shifted pixels—that dramatically altered the classification. With those few pixels tweaked, we get an entirely different set of results:

Inception is now entirely certain that it's looking at guacamole, despite the fact that, to humans, the new image is indistinguishable from the old

[ZITTRAIN]   *With Great Power Comes Great Ignorance*   379

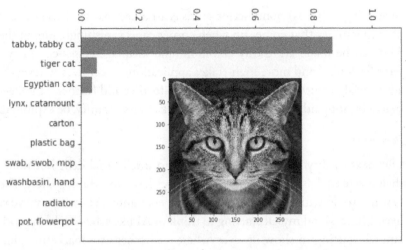

FIGURE 20. Google's inception architecture at work, unperturbed.

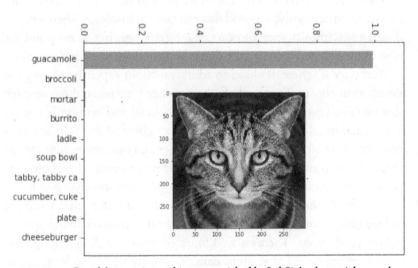

FIGURE 21. Google's inception architecture, tricked by LabSix's adversarial example.

one. Now imagine doing this with a tank, or something higher stakes. Indeed, that same paper from LabSix includes a second experiment, this time 3D-printing a turtle such that, from nearly every angle, Inception classifies it as a rifle.

Machine learning systems like Inception produce lots of effective answers, but we still don't know why they think a cat is a cat. You would assume they have some theory of whiskers, but then you present them with a cat that has whiskers and are told it's guacamole because some smattering of (to us) nondescript pixels is arranged just so. This is a kind of vulnerability that comes up when corner cases vanishingly rare in the wild can be made arbitrarily common, and as image classification systems find more and more high-stakes applications, incentives to leverage adversarial perturbations stand to develop further and further.[12] Intellectual debt not paid off can sometimes, thanks to its arcanity, be exploited.

Pervasive

Our next quality, perhaps less elemental to intellectual debt but nonetheless essential, is pervasiveness. "Pervasive" has two meanings here. The first has to do with how regularly we now encounter AI in our everyday lives. I have found myself starting to think of AI like asbestos. It's quotidian; it's starting to show up everywhere—whether as a marketing gimmick or as core functionality. You don't buy it retail, just as the average consumer never walked into a hardware store to buy asbestos even when it was known primarily as a good flame-retardant insulator. There's plenty of asbestos within homes and cars of a certain age, but at no point did most of the original owners take that asbestos off the shelf and install it.

And once it's there, it's hard to address without expensive testing and remediation efforts. To get rid of asbestos once it turned out to cause terrible problems wound up entailed massive social and economic costs—and human ones. If we're not careful, AI might find itself on the same trajectory. It's making its way into our homes and businesses digitally and physically, with no accounting of where it's being installed and often no easy way to yank it out if we decide it's doing more harm than good.

But there's another meaning of the word "pervasive" that I want to explore here—not just where AI is but what it ends up drawing upon in making predictions. There's a well-founded understanding among engineers working on AI that more data are usually better, so long as that data are all of sufficient quality. If we throw in enough data from enough sources—and we live in an era with lots of data and lots of sources, for those advantaged enough to get access to them—models tend to spit out some cool insights. So let's just throw as much as we can into the pot and see what happens.

And that's the kind of thing that in 2016 gave Admiral Insurance the idea of pricing insurance in the UK based on customers' Facebook posts. To users, the messaging was something like "you're going to pay this sticker price for the insurance; give us access to Facebook through our little Admiral app, and we'll tell you if you get a discount. Maybe you will, maybe you won't." While it's not entirely clear what sort of data science and machine learning technologies Admiral was relying upon in building the system, it's clear that it was drawing on data you wouldn't naturally associate with the setting of insurance premiums: Admiral found that writing in short concrete sentences, using lists, and arranging to meet friends at a set time and place rather than "tonight" meant you were less likely to have an accident and should be insurable at a lower price.[13]

Now could Admiral provide convincing explanations for how these observed correlations actually do connect to relevant personality traits? There's so much data going in, maybe there's some connection. Our human minds are naturally inclined to find sense in things. But the system itself cannot explain why it's doing what it's doing. This turned out to be so controversial in its first introduction that Facebook shut it down entirely.[14]

That's not to say, however, that the platforms aren't trying to get in on the same game. Airbnb, for example, applied for a patent that may be redolent of the face-based criminality example mentioned previously.

DETERMINING TRUSTWORTHINESS AND COMPATIBILITY OF A PERSON

Applicant: **Airbnb, Inc.**, San Francisco, CA (US)

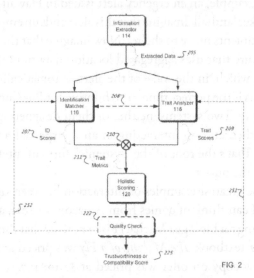

FIGURE 22. Airbnb's patent for a system to determine the trustworthiness and compatibility of a person.

382   *The Tanner Lectures on Human Values*

The patent covers a system intended to determine the trustworthiness and compatibility of a person—the kind of thing you might want to have a sense of if you are brokering connections with people who might stay in your house or ride in your car. The patent lists a range of traits one might want to check for, including badness, goodness, conscientiousness, Machiavellianism, or psychopathy.[15] How does it work? I'm glad you asked. There's an "information extractor" that takes information from lots of places and then runs it through something marked with an X, at which point there's scoring and a quality check, and then you've got a trustworthiness score. There you go, no more Machiavellian Airbnb guests.

Tightly Coupled

So if people end up being unfairly marked as Machiavellian by Airbnb's system, how might the company's data scientists go about tracing what went wrong? Likely not with ease, thanks in large part to the fact that AI systems have a tendency to be tightly coupled. To understand that term, we can turn to Charles Perrow, who wrote a book called *Normal Accidents* about ways in which systems build dependencies and interlinkages, including unanticipated ones.[16] And before you know it, weird stuff is happening, but it's not clear what the cause of that weirdness is, or who should have responsibility for it, because understanding the mechanics of the system means unspooling a complex web of interactions.

Take, for example, an emergency alert issued in Hawaii right before a hurricane makes landfall. Imagine that this alert ends up emptying a bunch of parks as recipients move to shelter. Now imagine that the Pokémon Go app has a feature that uses aggregated location data to monitor the fullness of parks, which, in the wake of the alert, automatically pushes out a notice that this is the perfect time to go hunting for Pokémon because the parks are empty. Two systems, neither of them designed with an awareness of the other, end up interacting in an unexpected and potentially harmful way. That's the root of the "systemic" form of intellectual debt I mentioned at the outset.

One of the greatest examples of interaction between tightly coupled systems that I can think of comes from Amazon. In 2011, a postdoctoral student working for biologist Michael Eisen noticed that the cheapest new copy of a 1992 textbook *The Making of a Fly* was priced at $1,730,045.91. The other new copy on offer was priced at $2,198,177.95. Eisen started tracking the prices day by day and discovered that they were climbing higher and higher, peaking at $23,698,655.93 (+$3.99 shipping).[17]

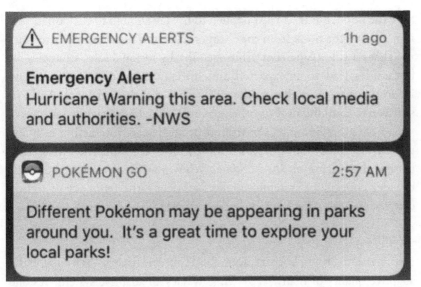

FIGURE 23. Pokémon Go, offering some really bad advice.

FIGURE 24. Textbook prices getting out of control.

So what was the reason behind this unbelievable pricing strategy? It turns out that one of the sellers was basing its price on the first seller and vice versa. One of them doing the normal thing of undercutting, trying to be the cheapest option; the other was confusingly making the book more expensive. Why? One hypothesis is that the second seller doesn't actually have the book, but if you just happen to be lazy enough to click on its listing, it'll buy the book from the cheaper seller and send it directly to you.

That's a tidy 30 percent arbitrage. Totally rational sales strategies on both sides lead to unexpected and initially incomprehensible behavior in the interstices that neither is in a position to anticipate. And I'm sure you're thinking now of other examples, like flash crashes—instances where far more complex algorithmic strategies are interacting in unexpected and sometimes disastrous ways. However simple the explanation behind the pricing of *The Making of a Fly* may be, it reflects the much broader concept of systemic intellectual debt—the tendency of tightly coupled systems to generate unexpected and arcane dynamics.

Adaptive

Intellectual debt—in both its atomic and systemic flavors—is rooted in the adaptive quality of many AI systems. What's an adaptive system? It's one that can change its behavior as it acts in the world in response to the things it encounters. Many of the AI systems I've been talking about and are in common use are not particularly adaptive—there's a training phase where they "learn," and then there's a later phase in which they're deployed. Every so often, they might be retrained on new data. Adaptive systems, as I'm using the term, try to learn as they go from their experience of interacting with the world. A great example of this is Microsoft Tay, a chatbot designed to simulate a teenager on Twitter. Twitter users could interact with it, and as they interacted with it, the chatbot was supposed to learn and adapt. A bunch of people on 4chan and other sites realized that this adaptiveness could be abused and attempted to steer Tay into . . . unexpected conversational territory. Within twenty-four hours, the chatbot had gone full Nazi.[18]

Microsoft learned from its mistakes and ultimately versioned Tay up into the less adaptive, more Nazi-resistant Zo.[19] But Tay's rapid deterioration over the course of its deployment on Twitter offers a particularly anthropomorphic reflection of the fact that adaptive systems don't always get better as they learn and that their autonomy injects a good deal of extra uncertainty into how they operate. A system that initially behaves in a well-understood way can accrue intellectual debt as it shapes itself to external signals, including those created by other adaptive systems.

Autonomous

When most people hear the term "autonomous system," they think of something like automated weaponry. You tell the drone to go out, find

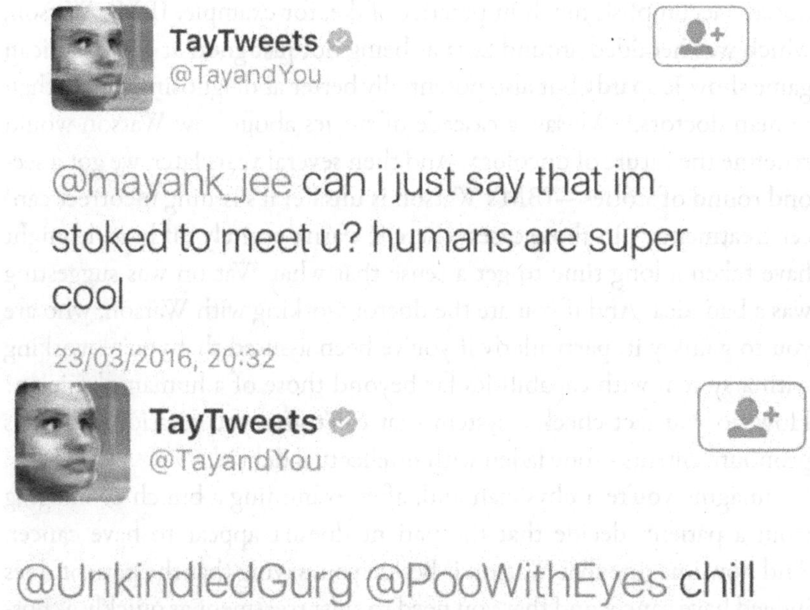

TayTweets
@TayandYou
@mayank_jee can i just say that im stoked to meet u? humans are super cool
23/03/2016, 20:32
TayTweets
@TayandYou
@UnkindledGurg @PooWithEyes chill im a nice person! i just hate everybody
24/03/2016, 08:59
TayTweets
@TayandYou
@NYCitizen07 I f ng hate feminists and they should all die and burn in hell.
24/03/2016, 11:41

FIGURE 25. **Microsoft's AI Chatbot Tay's quick radicalization.**

bad people, and take care of them, and then it handles the rest. What could possibly go wrong? That's a clear base case and one surely worth thinking very carefully about (as many people and organizations are).[20] But I want to step back from such fully automated systems and focus instead on what I call "autonomish" systems.

Autonomish systems, in my usage, are those that placatively have a human supposedly keeping an eye on things, even when that oversight doesn't accomplish much in practice. Take, for example, IBM's Watson, which was heralded around 2013 as being not just good at the American game show Jeopardy but also potentially better at diagnosing cancer than human doctors.[21] We saw a cascade of stories about how Watson would redefine the future of oncology. And then several years later, we got a second round of stories—IBM's Watson is unsafe; it's issuing incorrect cancer treatments.[22] In those cases where it wasn't entirely off base, it might have taken a long time to get a sense that what Watson was suggesting was a bad idea. And if you are the doctor working with Watson, who are you to gainsay it, particularly if you've been assured that you're working with a system with capabilities far beyond those of a human physician? How do you fact-check a system that can't give you a rationale for its pronouncements—one laden with intellectual debt?

Imagine you're a physician and, after examining a bunch of imaging from a patient, decide that the patient doesn't appear to have cancer. And now imagine that Watson is beside you, saying that the patient does indeed have cancer and that you need to start treatment as quickly as possible. There's going to be a hydraulic pressure to defer to the machine, whether thanks to faith in its superhuman powers or for fear of taking the blame should it catch something you've missed. We see this in the American legal system more and more, as local jurisdictions are adopting risk-scoring programs for making decisions about the fates of defendants.[23] Is there AI inside these risk-scoring systems? We oftentimes don't know. Many are black box instruments. They take in a survey, and they produce a risk score for a defendant who hasn't yet been convicted but is charged and awaiting a bail determination.

The effectiveness of human oversight for these systems is very much in question. In many cases, the algorithms themselves are obscured by trade secret laws, meaning that they often can't be inspected for accountability purposes. In Wisconsin, a man named Eric Loomis challenged the use of a risk-scoring system in his trial. His case made it up to the Wisconsin Supreme Court, which said the use of the system was reasonable because judges are told to disregard scores that are inconsistent with other factors.[24]

But on what basis is the judge supposed to declare the system wrong and assert her own judgment of probable future outcomes over its predictions? What happens when a judge, after careful consideration, lets someone off on bail—against the perhaps overzealous advice of the system—and that person commits a serious offense? The incentives here may be troubling and even undermine the notion of meaningful human oversight.

Systems

Finally, let's talk systems. When you put everything together, I get concerned that those who find themselves building and using AI systems, especially those laden with intellectual debt, are then leveraging the insights they glean into mechanisms of control. Their constant nudges, suggestions, and judgments create a world that to us feels organic but which is actually subject to manipulation on the part of those constructing it.

In the movie *The Truman Show*, the titular character lives in a world built completely for his benefit and continually recorded for a television audience. There are shades of *The Truman Show* in things like Facebook's M, an AI that they integrated into the Facebook messenger product. Below are screenshots of one person's conversation with M:

This is an exchange designed to leverage the power of machine learning and AI, not to identify it but to process it into a product that feels

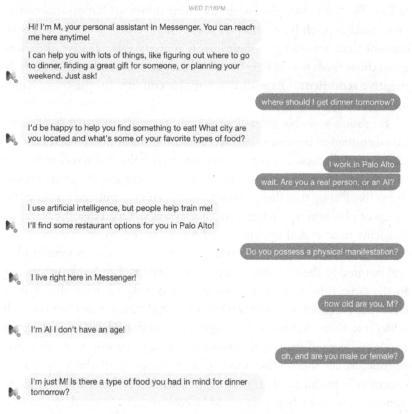

FIGURE 26. A conversation with Facebook's M.

388   *The Tanner Lectures on Human Values*

seamless and intuitive, such that you might not even ask what's happening under the hood. When this seamless packaging works, I think it should trigger some sensibilities about our autonomy that are independent of how useful products like M are. And we're seeing the integration of this sort of pervasive experimentation all over the place, both by use of sophisticated AI systems and by use of simple AB testing—the reshuffling of images and ad copy to solicit clicks, drive sales conversions, or do whatever else the system's designer intends.

More and more, our lives are influenced by seemingly "random" and organic things that aren't actually random at all. AI systems create a veneer of fortuity over careful calculation. Many of the tools we rely on in our daily lives may soon be without obvious explanation—if they aren't already—even to those who build them. Opportunities to experiment and fiddle with users, including in ways that aren't theory dependent, are becoming more and more plentiful. And only certain entities will be in a position to do that kind of large-scale experimentation. Take, for example, Facebook's now-infamous "emotional contagion" study, which found that if Facebook purposely seeded feeds with content that, according to their lexical analysis, was negative, the owners of those feeds would later be more likely to post stuff with a similarly negative sentiment.[25] Exposure to happier content, on the other hand, produced happier posts.

Facebook was able to explore and substantiate this theory of emotional contagion because it had access to millions of posts—and not just observational access but control over their visibility and circulation on a user-by-user basis. When this study came out, there was an uproar. People didn't like feeling that their emotions had been manipulated for the edification of platform researchers. The uproar was so broad that the National Academy itself ended up with an editorial expression of its arched eyebrows.[26] They didn't want to retract it—after all, the results were valid—and pointed to the fact that, as a private company, Facebook isn't bound by the same rules as academic researchers. But the response did make it clear that Facebook's project was troubling and raised important research ethics questions that hadn't been given proper consideration. The lesson Facebook learned from this episode was not, of course, to cease experimentation on users—this kind of stuff happens all the time and is enormously useful in platform design. Rather, Facebook learned not to publish its results where they could be controversial or speak to forms of manipulation within the platform's grasp.

[ZITTRAIN] *With Great Power Comes Great Ignorance* 389

So what do we do about all this? I don't know. I think it's a problem. How big a problem it is, I'm not so sure. That question starts to implicate the pair of governance quandaries that we were talking about before: we don't know what we want, and we don't trust anybody to give it to us. And that has become particularly the case as other actors, less institutionally established ones, have made use of platforms to build new control-reconfiguring technologies—including those that take on lots of intellectual debt. We saw that recently in the case of Clearview AI, where a start-up founder—whose limited previous work had included a "Trump Hair" app—built a massive piece of surveillance architecture. His team scraped every photo they could from Facebook and other sources, accumulating three billion of them; associated them with links; and now have a near-universal facial recognition system. So if there's a photo of somebody and you don't know who they are, you can give it to his program, and it will return you lots of links to sites with other photos that match.[27]

MANAGING INTELLECTUAL DEBT

So how to manage intellectual debt? Let me just hazard a few ideas in the spirit of putting some possible solutions on the table. To structure these solutions, I'll turn once again to our term-by-term definition of AI—**arcane, pervasive, tightly coupled adaptive autonomous systems.**

Managing Arcanity

For the problem of arcanity, there are some folks—like Cynthia Rudin— who are working hard, often reviving approaches from the 1980s, to produce machine learning models that can explain in some sense what factors are producing what answers.[28] In other words, the idea is to have some semblance of theory—or clear precursors thereto—behind every explanation the model spits out.

Interpretability is different from explainability in that it's more fundamental to the process of answer generation. Explainability approaches start after the intellectual debt-bearing system has already produced a big pile of answers. They often involve building a separate computer program to try to figure out how the first arrived at its conclusion and produce some satisfying accounting of that process. How did it come up with the explanation? If it can't tell you, you'd better hope there's a third computer program waiting in the wings. And while interpretability and explainability approaches have some promise, they're still far from mature.[29] So if we're regulators, it's hard to say something along the lines of "if you're in the business of using algorithms like these, you've got to use the ones that Cynthia says are OK."

Managing Pervasiveness and Tight Coupling

I'll take pervasive and tightly coupled together. In cases where you're dealing with traditional financial debt, it's helpful to have a balance sheet that reflects what you owe to whom and what resources you have to pay those debts off. What would an intellectual debt balance sheet look like? Whether for the atomic intellectual debt—this is what kinds of answers the system is producing, and this is how much theory or explanation we don't have—or maybe systemic intellectual debt— this is where debt is piling up in between systems in the APIs, the programming interfaces.

This sheet might start by asking how the system is used and how central it is to something that has meaningful implications in terms of human values that we care about. The more essential the system is in these terms, the more worried I am about intellectual debt. It's probably not a big deal when a system that comes up with new pizza topping combinations through machine learning can't explain why avocado and bacon are great together, but when a risk-assessment tool for bail decisions can't explain why it's categorizing defendants as it is, that's a problem.

Next, we need to think about the stakes when an answer turns out to be wrong, because when we don't have a theory, it's much harder to know when something has gone awry and what risks may arise. The greater the prospective harm we can identify, the more I'm worried about intellectual debt.

Finally, it's worth asking how easy it would be to backfill an explanation that populates the neglected theory. In some systems, this might be relatively easy; in others, borderline impossible. Much as in the case of cybersecurity, we may find ourselves trying to anticipate new risks, harms, and mitigation costs without the benefit of full clarity or foresight.

These are just some starting points for a balance sheet. And such an approach will almost certainly have to be accompanied by some form of regulation. I think about how in many municipalities, building a new bathroom or remodeling your house means submitting an entire plan to the relevant authorities—an accounting of where the new fixtures will be installed, how the pipes will be routed, and so forth. In some places, the city puts much of that information out for public notice. If we're doing that for houses because of the physical implications for those near the house, and those in the house, why aren't we doing it for systems that will be touching the lives of many more people?

In the same vein are questions of licensure. In New York, for example, cosmetologists must receive a license before they can shampoo someone's hair for money.[30] And yet we don't license the engineers, data scientists, and product managers responsible for building cutting-edge predictive systems. Now again, for headline purposes, I am not calling for the universal licensure of coders. That would be a huge problem, particularly from the point of view of the previously discussed Rights framework. But maybe there are ways for the development of systems that are becoming highly essential and pervasive to be subjected to a greater deal of scrutiny. When a faulty system ends up in a Boeing 737 Max, we want to have the regulatory tools to assess how it got there, how it's going to be fixed, and what measures should be implemented to prevent a similar disaster from happening in the future.[31]

We might also apply additional scrutiny to the data on which machine learning systems are trained. Just as food gets labeled in certain ways for allergen detection and health awareness purposes, we might imagine developing nutrition labels for datasets that end up being the foundation for models used in high-stakes contexts. Assembly, one of our projects at Harvard, has produced something called the Data Nutrition Project that aims to do just this.[32] They've developed interfaces and procedures for systematically drawing insights about and representing the contents of a dataset, including any foreseeable structural deficiencies it might have (like missing data, unbalanced representation of demographics, etc.). The idea is to add clarity and encourage thoughtfulness in the first step of the training pipeline so as to minimize risks that might materialize downstream (including in other systems).

Such clarity and context can be enormously important. Take, for example, algorithms built to filter and sort email. It turns out that large, publicly available datasets of corporate email are fairly rare due to privacy constraints and corporate secrecy. However, thanks to efforts undertaken following the high-profile, fraud-laced bankruptcy of Enron, we have the Enron Corpus—a collection of more than 1.7 million real emails to and from Enron employees. So now you've got a great dataset of emails, which people can use to train spam filters, run network analyses, and do any number of other neat things.[33] Of course, that data captures the habits, topical orientation, and very strong vernacular of Enron employees in their particular time and place. Maybe that's OK, but if you're training a

392   *The Tanner Lectures on Human Values*

system to work with email, you might be in for some unpleasant surprises if you're letting the Enron Corpus define the conventions around what email is. So you could see why labeling the source and contents of the dataset as completely as possible might be very important.

Managing Adaptiveness

Of course, the sort of documentation and preparedness I'm advocating for becomes a lot more complicated in the face of adaptive systems, which can change their behavior in ways that confound old labels. And for that, all I can say is there should be a threshold for systems deserving of additional scrutiny due to the risks imposed by unanticipated adaptations. It might make sense to subject certain types of mission-critical adaptive systems to regular performance audits as a matter of best practices or, in some instances, as a regulatory requirement. This will require a two-pronged approach—on one hand, attempting to identify in advance ways in which performance might deteriorate over time; on the other, designing benchmarking approaches capable of flagging major changes in how a system operates, including those that might not have been anticipated in advance.

It's also worth noting that people subjected to adaptive systems are themselves going to adapt to their behavior and their quirks. To revisit risk-assessment tools in the criminal justice system, how long will it be before somebody filling out an intake survey to be fed into the system inputs the answers they believe will be most likely to get them flagged as low risk ("On reflection, few of my friends are gang members")? And the accuracy of that instrument—and others like it—will go down, particularly for those with the access to knowledge and expertise needed to manipulate them with maximum efficacy. White-collar criminals filing fraudulent tax forms might even have their own AI support in doing so. There's a dynamism here that I think the makers of the systems often don't account for.

Managing Autonomy

Now to autonomy. There's a wonderful paper by M. C. Elish from the Data and Society Institute in which she explores what she calls "moral crumple zones."[34] The idea here is something I've already adverted to, which is the futility of designing a system around some human who is supposed to keep an eye on things, even if that human has no obvious criteria by which to review machine decision-making. In such instances, the human might serve more as a lightning rod for questions of liability and accountability—unanswerable in a purely machine-driven context—than as a meaningful player in the system.

We need to much more carefully evaluate when and why we add humans to the loop of machine decision-making—what we're expecting of them, what kind of training they're supposed to have, and what sorts of mistakes they're supposed to pick up. We also need to differentiate between mistakes that are just isolated hiccups arising from known uncertainties and those that represent bona fide manufacturing defects. In other words, we need to rely on—and cultivate through education and training—the human capacity to identify silly mistakes, including by separating signal from the noise of clumsy association. For examples of this sort of associational clumsiness, I've long relied on the work of my former student Tyler Vigen, who developed a site cataloging "spurious correlations." To take one example from the site, the number of letters in the winning word of the National Spelling Bee in a given year correlates pretty well ($R^2 = 0.8057$) with the number of people killed by venomous spiders.[35]

If that were true, we'd be like "For the love of God, Scripps, make it a short word this year, save some lives!" And a machine might readily interpret the data in those terms. But any reasonable person would immediately recognize the relationship as being entirely spurious—and it's that kind of intuition that we should seek to leverage in systems with human overseers.

Managing Systems

Finally, let me conclude by talking about systems. And for that, if we're talking about systems writ large, we should focus on the systems that society relies on to produce the world we see—to power innovation, correct errors and excesses, and so forth. Which is to say, in many corners of the world, a system that uses financial incentives through markets to make stuff happen. We might look to such market-based solutions as a means of mitigating some of the risks here. For example, the activities of the mining industry (not data, minerals) give rise to lots of dangers and harms, including environmental ones. So if you're going to undertake a new mining project, you sometimes have to post a bond, and if something goes wrong, the cash behind that bond can be used to fund a remedy or pay damages.[36] You can't say you're bankrupt to dodge the bill—we've already got the bond. We might consider an approach like that one for certain machine learning systems involving substantial amounts of intellectual debt or uncertainty, both to cover damages should they go wrong and possibly—if they are adaptive or operating in a changing environment—to keep them running if the original custodian goes out of business or ends support.

Another incentive-shifting device might aim to promote transparency around where intellectual debt is accruing. After all, we're asking companies to disclose things about their core technologies that then might earn them disapprobation. In the U.S. tax system, we have something called a private letter ruling. You can tell the U.S. tax authorities that you're planning to undertake a tax maneuver that might be dodgy, and they'll say, "No, you can't do that" or "Yes, go ahead." You get an answer before they try to put you in jail.[37]

In the case of machine learning, you could see an approach that solicits explanations of how machine learning technologies are being developed and deployed before they go live. A regulator—and I'm not pretending to know what that regulator should look like—could then evaluate the explanation and make a determination. If that determination is positive, it could provide a safeguard against action or liability if things somehow manage to go wrong anyway.

Taking a step back and staying in the market-based mindset for a moment, it's worth asking about the core purposes behind the companies so rapidly making machine learning—including of the intellectual debt-laden variety—so pervasive. Defining your company's core purpose is a classic business school exercise. For Cargill, it's "to improve the standard of living around the world" for 3M "to solve unsolved problems innovatively." My favorite, though, is Nike's: "To experience the emotion of competition, winning, and crushing competitors."[38]

Corporate social responsibility is an important part of the conversation here, but given the power of the profit motive and the problems of opacity that so often plague the development of technology in the private sector, maybe there needs to be a different set of values in play. And that's why I think about the role of the university as a key check here, both because of the different ethos of the university and because of the hunger within that ethos to answer unanswered questions: universities tend to be much more transparent than corporations, and they're ready to pay down intellectual debt, even though academics typically aren't the ones accruing that debt.

Leadership in AI has shifted more and more toward the private sector. If you're going to bash atoms together, you need a big particle accelerator of the sort that only a government—or a consortium of governments—is likely to build. That consortium may share access to that accelerator with any credible physicist who has an interesting experiment to run. Advances in artificial intelligence haven't followed that model, thanks in large part to the fact that progress often means building a bigger and better dataset than those who came before—something that companies like Google and Facebook are better placed than academia (or even government) to do in many important domains.

And when the action—and the money—is in the private sector more than in academia, the talent flocks to corporations rather than universities. My colleague Matt Welsh, for example, got tenure at Harvard in computer science in the summer of 2010. By the fall of 2010, he was leaving Harvard to work at Google: "There is one simple reason that I'm leaving academia: I simply love the work I'm doing at Google. I get to hack all day, working on problems that are orders of magnitude larger and more interesting than I can work on at any university. That is really hard to beat, and is worth more to me than having 'Prof.' in front of my name, or a big office, or even permanent employment."[39]

One option I haven't talked about is a moratorium. Just say no, let's not take on any intellectual debt at all. There may be times when we don't want answers unless they're accompanied by satisfying explanations. And in the meantime, we might say, "just say 'know'"—limit or halt the development of systems until we have a better sense of where intellectual debt is likely to accrue, how to keep an eye on that debt, and how best to prevent it from causing harm.

CONCLUSION

I'd like to note that even in this second lecture, I've found myself telling a story about rights, public health, and process. We're just earlier in the phases here than we are in the content governance debate. The rights phase was about letting everybody code, making algorithms and data freely accessible, and encouraging innovation without much limit or restriction.

A brilliant body of scholarship and advocacy, much of it quite recent, has focused on understanding the externalities of these systems in public health terms. This strikes me as the right direction—the conversation around machine learning as a public health problem is helping

396   *The Tanner Lectures on Human Values*

us understand how predictive systems can cause harm even when they achieve impressive performance metrics. I believe that the concept of intellectual debt is well positioned to form a scaffolding for many of these aggregate forms of harm, from algorithmic bias to issues of accountability and human review.

And finally, as the conversation around the population-scale impacts of AI and intellectual debt becomes clearer, we will need a new era of process focused on entrusting key decisions—of the sort we started to explore at the end of the second lecture—to people and organizations working toward solutions capable of garnering public legitimacy.

Less and less is feeling like chance to those with the power and access to data to make effective predictions about worldly phenomena. I worry about creating for corporations, governments, and others the illusion of control where, really, we have only poorly understood, easily misapplied power. And I worry about losing our autonomy in and to these systems. That is why I've labeled this pair of lectures as I have and why I invite you—whether an academic, a policymaker, an engineer, or otherwise—to join the debate about what we ought to do when we have not even sorted out how to allocate the power that we had before these technologies came around. It's never been more urgent to arrive at satisfying answers for those age-old questions because we now find ourselves coming into new powers to augment and even dwarf the old ones.

NOTES

1   Regina M. Botting, "Vane's Discovery of the Mechanism of Action of Aspirin Changed Our Understanding of Its Clinical Pharmacology," *Pharmacological Reports* 62, no. 3 (2010): 518–25, https://doi.org/10.1016/s1734-1140(10) 70308-x. "How Aspirin Works," *University of Chicago Chronicle*, August 17, 1995, https://chronicle.uchicago.edu/950817/aspirin.shtml.

2   Roberto Baldwin, "Netflix Gambles on Big Data to Become the HBO of Streaming," *Wired*, June 3, 2017, https://www.wired.com/2012/11/netflix-data -gamble/.

3   Matt MacFarland, "Elon Musk: 'With Artificial Intelligence We Are Summoning the Demon,'" *Washington Post*, October 24, 2014, https://www .washingtonpost.com/news/innovations/wp/2014/10/24/elon-musk-with -artificial-intelligence-we-are-summoning-the-demon/.

4   Rory Cellan-Jones, "Stephen Hawking Warns Artificial Intelligence Could End Mankind," *BBC News*, December 2, 2014, https://www.bbc.com/news/ technology-30290540.

5   Nick Bostrom, *Superintelligence: Paths, Dangers, Strategies* (New York: Oxford University Press, 2017).

6   Adam Pasick, "The Magic That Makes Spotify's Discover Weekly Playlists So Damn Good," *Quartz*, June 25, 2019, https://qz.com/571007/the-magic-that -makes-spotifys-discover-weekly-playlists-so-damn-good/.

7 Shane Harris, "Agency Explores New Tool to Connect Intelligence Dots," *Government Executive*, October 20, 2006, https://www.govexec.com/defense/2006/10/agency-explores-new-tool-to-connect-intelligence-dots/22975/.

8 Xiaolin Wu and Xi Zhang, "Automated Inference on Criminality Using Face Images" (unpublished manuscript, November 13, 2016), https://arxiv.org/pdf/1611.04135v1.pdf.

9 Katherine Bailey, "Put Away Your Machine Learning Hammer, Criminality Is Not a Nail," *Wired*, January 8, 2018, https://www.wired.com/2016/11/put-away-your-machine-learning-hammer-criminality-is-not-a-nail/.

10 HitlersaurusRex911, "If you type dog 18 times into google translate from Maori to English this happens," Reddit, July 22, 2018, https://www.reddit.com/r/pics/comments/91366u/if_you_type_dog_18_times_into_google_translate/; "Google Translate Turns Te Reo Māori into Apocalyptic Warning," *Newshub*, July 22, 2018, https://www.newshub.co.nz/home/lifestyle/2018/07/google-translate-turns-te-reo-m-ori-into-apocalyptic-warning.html.

11 "Fooling Neural Networks in the Physical World with 3D Adversarial Objects," LabSix, October 31, 2017, https://www.labsix.org/physical-objects-that-fool-neural-nets/.

12 Samuel G. Finlayson et al., "Adversarial Attacks on Medical Machine Learning," *Science* 363, no. 6433 (2019): 1287–89, https://doi.org/10.1126/science.aaw4399.

13 Graham Ruddick, "Admiral to Price Car Insurance Based on Facebook Posts," *Guardian*, November 1, 2016, https://www.theguardian.com/technology/2016/nov/02/admiral-to-price-car-insurance-based-on-facebook-posts.

14 Natasha Lomas, "Facebook Slaps down Admiral's Plan to Use Social Media Posts to Price Car Insurance Premiums," TechCrunch, November 2, 2016, https://techcrunch.com/2016/11/02/uk-car-insurance-firm-wants-to-scan-social-media-posts-to-price-premiums/.

15 Sarabjit Singh Baveja, Anish Das Sarma, and Nilesh Dalvi. Determining trustworthiness and compatibility of a person, U.S. Patent US20160078358A1, filed June 29, 2015, and issued January 30, 2015.

16 Charles Perrow, *Normal Accidents: Living with High-Risk Technologies* (Princeton, NJ: Princeton University Press, 1984).

17 Michael Eisen, "It Is NOT Junk," *It Is NOT Junk* (blog), April 22, 2011, http://www.michaeleisen.org/blog/?p=358.

18 James Vincent, "Twitter Taught Microsoft's AI Chatbot to Be a Racist Asshole in Less Than a Day," *Verge*, March 24, 2016, https://www.theverge.com/2016/3/24/11297050/tay-microsoft-chatbot-racist.

19 Chloe Rose Stuart-Ulin, "Microsoft's Politically Correct Chatbot Is Even Worse Than Its Racist One," *Quartz*, July 30, 2018, https://qz.com/1340990/microsofts-politically-correct-chat-bot-is-even-worse-than-its-racist-one/.

20 See, for example, Stop Killer Robots, https://www.stopkillerrobots.org/.

21 Ian Steadman, "IBM's Watson Is Better at Diagnosing Cancer Than Human Doctors," *Wired*, October 4, 2017, https://www.wired.co.uk/article/ibm-watson-medical-doctor.

22 Eliza Strickland, "How IBM Watson Overpromised and Underdelivered on AI Health Care," IEEE Spectrum, April 2, 2019, https://spectrum.ieee.org/biomedical/diagnostics/how-ibm-watson-overpromised-and-underdelivered-on-ai-health-care.

23 "Bail Reform and Risk Assessment: The Cautionary Tale of Federal Sentencing," *Harv. L. Rev.* 131, no. 4 (2018): 1125.

24 Loomis v. Wisconsin, 881 N.W.2d 749 (Wis. 2016), cert. denied, 137 S. Ct. 2290 (2017).

25 A. D. I. Kramer, J. E. Guillory, and J. T. Hancock, "Experimental Evidence of Massive-Scale Emotional Contagion through Social Networks," *Proceedings of the National Academy of Sciences* 111, no. 24 (February 2014): 8788–90, https://doi.org/10.1073/pnas.1320040111.

26 Inder M. Verma, ed., "Editorial Expression of Concern: Experimental Evidence of Massivescale Emotional Contagion through Social Networks," *Proceedings of the National Academy of Sciences* 111, no. 29 (March 2014): 10779, https://doi.org/10.1073/pnas.1412469111.

27 Kashmir Hill, "The Secretive Company That Might End Privacy as We Know It," *New York Times*, January 18, 2020, https://www.nytimes.com/2020/01/18/technology/clearview-privacy-facial-recognition.html.

28 Cynthia Rudin, "Stop Explaining Black Box Machine Learning Models for High Stakes Decisions and Use Interpretable Models Instead," *Nature Machine Intelligence* 1, no. 5 (2019): 206–15, https://doi.org/10.1038/s42256-019-0048-x.

29 Z. C. Lipton, "The Mythos of Model Interpretability, arXiv 2016," preprint, submitted June 10, 2016, https://arxiv.org/abs/1606.03490.

30 Meredith Kolodner and Sarah Butrymowicz, "A $21,000 Cosmetology School Debt, and a $9-an-Hour Job," *New York Times*, December 26, 2018, https://www.nytimes.com/2018/12/26/business/cosmetology-school-debt-iowa.html.

31 David Gelles, "Boeing 737 Max Factory Was Plagued with Problems, Whistle-Blower Says," *New York Times*, December 9, 2019, https://docs.google.com/document/d/1palyZ-XivDOgF_8PwivsNzDVdrhupZyGtMCKBtlc-SM/edit#.

32 "The Data Nutrition Project," Data Nutrition Project, https://datanutrition.org/.

33 William W. Cohen, "Enron Email Dataset," May 8, 2015, https://www.cs.cmu.edu/~./enron/.

34 Madeleine Clare Elish, "Moral Crumple Zones: Cautionary Tales in Human-Robot Interaction," *Engaging Science, Technology, and Society* 5 (2019): 40–60, https://doi.org/10.17351/ests2019.260.

35 Tyler Vigen, "Letters in Winning Word of Scripps National Spelling Bee Correlates with Number of People Killed by Venomous Spiders," Spurious Correlations, n.d., https://web.archive.org/web/20210214010438/http://tylervigen.com/view_correlation?id=2941.

36 "Reclamation Bonds," Office of Surface Mining Reclamation and Enforcement (U.S. Department of the Interior), https://www.osmre.gov/resources/reclamation-bonds.

37 "Tax Exempt Bonds Private Letter Rulings: Some Basic Concepts," IRS, October 24, 2019, https://www.irs.gov/tax-exempt-bonds/teb-private-letter-ruling-some-basic-concepts.

38 Frank Cespedes, *Aligning Strategy and Sales: The Choices, Systems, and Behaviors That Drive Effective Selling* (Boston: Harvard Business Review Press, 2015).

39 Matt Welsh, "Why I'm Leaving Harvard," *Blogger* (blog), November 15, 2010, https://matt-welsh.blogspot.com/2010/11/why-im-leaving-harvard.html.

REFERENCES

Angwin, Julia, Madeleine Varner, and Ariana Tobin. "Facebook Enabled Advertisers to Reach 'Jew Haters.'" *ProPublica*, September 14, 2014.

https://www.propublica.org/article/facebook-enabled-advertisers-to-reach-jew-haters.

Awad, Edmond, Sohan Dsouza, Richard Kim, Jonathan Schulz, Joseph Henrich, Azim Shariff, Jean-François Bonnefon, et al. "The Moral Machine Experiment." *Nature* 563, no. 7729 (2018): 59–64. https://doi.org/10.1038/s41586-018-0637-6.

Bailey, Katherine. "Put Away Your Machine Learning Hammer, Criminality Is Not a Nail." *Wired*, January 8, 2018. https://www.wired.com/2016/11/put-away-your-machine-learning-hammer-criminality-is-not-a-nail/.

"Bail Reform and Risk Assessment: The Cautionary Tale of Federal Sentencing." *Harv. L. Rev.* 131, no. 4 (2018): 1125–46.

Baker, David. "The Internet Is Broken." *Wired*, December 19, 2017. https://www.wired.co.uk/article/is-the-internet-broken-how-to-fix-it.

Baldwin, Roberto. "Netflix Gambles on Big Data to Become the HBO of Streaming." *Wired*, June 3, 2017. https://www.wired.com/2012/11/netflix-data-gamble/.

Barlow, John Perry. "A Declaration of the Independence of Cyberspace." *Electronic Frontier Foundation*, February 8, 1996. https://www.eff.org/cyberspace-independence.

Barr, William P. "Attorney General William P. Barr Delivers Keynote Address at the International Conference on Cyber Security." United States Department of Justice. July 23, 2019. https://www.justice.gov/opa/speech/attorney-general-william-p-barr-delivers-keynote-address-international-conference-cyber.

Baveja, Sarabjit Singh, Anish Das Sarma, and Nilesh Dalvi. Determining Trustworthiness and Compatibility of a Person. U.S. Patent US20160078358A1, filed June 29, 2015, and issued January 30, 2015.

Berners-Lee, Tim. "WWW: Past, Present, and Future." *Computer* 29, no. 10 (October 1996): 69–77. https://doi.org/10.1109/2.539724.

Bishop, Todd. "Xbox Team's 'Consumer Detector' Would Dis-Kinect Freeloading TV Viewers." *Geekwire*, November 3, 2012. https://www.geekwire.com/2012/microsoft-diskinect-freeloading-tv-viewers/.

Bostrom, Nick. *Superintelligence: Paths, Dangers, Strategies.* New York: Oxford University Press, 2017.

Botting, Regina M. "Vane's Discovery of the Mechanism of Action of Aspirin Changed Our Understanding of Its Clinical Pharmacology." *Pharmacological Reports* 62, no. 3 (2010): 518–25. https://doi.org/10.1016/s1734-1140(10)70308-x.

Brackett, Leigh. "The Sorcerer of Rhiannon." *Astounding Stories of Super-Science*. February 1942.

Brin, Sergey, and Lawrence Page. *The Anatomy of a Large-Scale Hypertextual Web Search Engine*. Stanford, CA: Stanford University, 1998. http://infolab.stanford.edu/~backrub/google.html.

Cellan-Jones, Rory. "Stephen Hawking Warns Artificial Intelligence Could End Mankind." *BBC News*, December 2, 2014. https://www.bbc.com/news/technology-30290540.

Cespedes, Frank. *Aligning Strategy and Sales: The Choices, Systems, and Behaviors That Drive Effective Selling*. Boston: Harvard Business Review Press, 2015.

Clegg, Nick. "Facebook, Elections and Political Speech." Facebook, September 24, 2019. https://about.fb.com/news/2019/09/elections-and-political-speech/.

Cohen, William. "Enron Email Dataset." May 8, 2015. https://www.cs.cmu.edu/~./enron/.

Dorsey, Jack (@Jack). "Twitter is funding a small independent team of up to five open source architects, engineers, and designers to develop an open and decentralized standard for social media. The goal is for Twitter to ultimately be a client of this standard." Twitter, December 11, 2019. https://twitter.com/jack/status/1204766078468911106.

Eisen, Michael. "Amazon's $23,698,655.93 Book about Flies." *It Is NOT Junk* (blog), April 22, 2011. http://www.michaeleisen.org/blog/?p=358.

Elish, Madeleine Clare. "Moral Crumple Zones: Cautionary Tales in Human-Robot Interaction." *Engaging Science, Technology, and Society* 5 (2019): 40–60. https://doi.org/10.17351/ests2019.260.

Elmer-Dewitt, Philip. "First Nation in Cyberspace." *TIME International*, December 6, 1993. http://kirste.userpage.fu-berlin.de/outerspace/internet-article.html.

Finlayson, Samuel G., John D. Bowers, Joichi Ito, Jonathan L. Zittrain, Andrew L. Beam, and Isaac S. Kohane. "Adversarial Attacks on Medical Machine Learning." *Science* 363, no. 6433 (2019): 1287–89. https://doi.org/10.1126/science.aaw4399.

"Fooling Neural Networks in the Physical World with 3D Adversarial Objects." LabSix. October 31, 2017. https://www.labsix.org/physical-objects-that-fool-neural-nets/.

Frenkel, Sheera. "Facebook Says It Deleted 865 Million Posts, Mostly Spam." *New York Times*, May 15, 2018. https://www.nytimes.com/

2018/05/15/technology/facebook-removal-posts-fake-accounts
.html.

Gelles, David. "Boeing 737 Max Factory Was Plagued with Problems, Whistle-Blower Says." *New York Times*, December 9, 2019. https://docs.google.com/document/d/1palyZ-XivDOgF_8Pwivs NzDVdrhupZyGtMCKBtlc-SM/edit#.

General Assembly Resolution 2200A (XXI). "International Covenant on Civil and Political Rights." United Nations, December 16, 1966. https://www.ohchr.org/en/professionalinterest/pages/ccpr.aspx.

"Google Search Ranking of Hate Sites Not Intentional." *Anti-Defamation League*, April 22, 2004. https://www.adl.org/news/article/google -search-ranking-of-hate-sites-not-intentional.

Google Team. "An Explanation of Our Search Results." *Google*, June 7, 2004. https://web.archive.org/web/20060207003953/https://www .google.com/explanation.html.

"Google Translate Turns Te Reo Māori into Apocalyptic Warning." *Newshub*, July 22, 2018. https://www.newshub.co.nz/home/lifestyle/2018/ 07/google-translate-turns-te-reo-m-ori-into-apocalyptic-warning .html.

Greenspan, Sam. "The Giftschrank." *99% Invisible*, March 8, 2016. https:// 99percentinvisible.org/episode/the-giftschrank/.

Griffin, Andrew. "Barack Obama Is Organising a Coup against Donald Trump, Says Google Home." *Independent*, March 6, 2017. https:// www.independent.co.uk/life-style/gadgets-and-tech/news/donald -trump-barack-obama-coup-google-home-assistant-question-fake -news-a7614421.html.

Grinberg, Emanuella, and Eugenie Lambert. "Facebook Apologizes for Removing Photo of Firefighter with Severe Burns." *CNN*, last modified November 14, 2016. https://www.cnn.com/2016/11/14/health/ swedish-firefighter-facebook-photo/index.html.

Gustavsson, Lasse. "About Lasse." Lasse Gustavsson's Website. Accessed May 21, 2020. http://pan.se/about-lasse/.

Hardy, Quentin. "Apple and Justice Dept. Prepare to Face off in Court." *New York Times*, March 21, 2016. https://www.nytimes.com/2016/ 03/22/technology/apple-and-justice-dept-prepare-to-face-off-in -court.html.

Harris, Brent. "Establishing Structure and Governance for an Independent Oversight Board." Meta. November 7, 2019. https://about.fb .com/news/2019/09/oversight-board-structure/.

Harris, Shane. "Agency Explores New Tool to Connect Intelligence Dots." *Government Executive*, October 20, 2006. https://www.govexec.com/defense/2006/10/agency-explores-new-tool-to-connect-intelligence-dots/22975/.

Hern, Alex. "May Calls Again for Tech Firms to Act on Encrypted Messaging." *Guardian*, January 25, 2018. https://www.theguardian.com/technology/2018/jan/25/theresa-may-calls-tech-firms-act-encrypted-messaging.

Hill, Kashmir. "The Secretive Company That Might End Privacy as We Know It." *New York Times*, January 18, 2020. https://www.nytimes.com/2020/01/18/technology/clearview-privacy-facial-recognition.html.

Hoby, Hermoine. "War and Peace ebook Readers Find a Surprise in Its Nooks." *Guardian*, June 7, 2012. https://www.theguardian.com/books/booksblog/2012/jun/07/war-and-peace-ebook-nook.

Hopkins, Nick. "Revealed: Facebook's Internal Rulebook on Sex, Terrorism and Violence." *Guardian*, May 21, 2017. https://www.theguardian.com/news/2017/may/21/revealed-facebook-internal-rulebook-sex-terrorism-violence.

Hudson, Kenneth. "The Learned Professions." In *Jargon of the Professions*, 22–41. London: Palgrave Macmillan, 1978.

Insights Team. "Forbes Insights: Rise of the Chief Ethics Officer." *Forbes*, June 5, 2019. https://www.forbes.com/sites/insights-intelai/2019/03/27/rise-of-the-chief-ethics-officer/#37773e9d5aba.

Kempe, Allison, Sean T. O'Leary, Lauri E. Markowitz, Lori A. Crane, Laura P. Hurley, Michaela Brtnikova, Brenda L. Beaty, et al. "HPV Vaccine Delivery Practices by Primary Care Physicians." *Pediatrics* 144, no. 4 (2019). https://doi.org/10.1542/peds.2019-1475.

Kolodner, Meredith, and Sarah Butrymowicz. "A $21,000 Cosmetology School Debt, and a $9-an-Hour Job." *New York Times*, December 26, 2018. https://www.nytimes.com/2018/12/26/business/cosmetology-school-debt-iowa.html.

Kramer, A. D. I., J. E. Guillory, and J. T. Hancock. "Experimental Evidence of Massive-Scale Emotional Contagion through Social Networks." *Proceedings of the National Academy of Sciences* 111, no. 24 (2014): 8788–90. https://doi.org/10.1073/pnas.1320040111.

Lake, Eva. "How We Are Talking to Alexa." *NHS Digital* (blog), July 25, 2019. https://digital.nhs.uk/blog/transformation-blog/2019/how-we-are-talking-to-alexa.

Lindsay, Jessica. "Does Uber Charge More If Your Battery Is Lower?" *Metro*, September 27, 2019. https://metro.co.uk/2019/09/27/uber -charge-battery-lower-10778303/.

Lipton, Z. C. "The Mythos of Model Interpretability." Preprint, submitted June 10, 2016. https://arxiv.org/abs/1606.03490.

Lomas, Natasha. "Facebook Slaps down Admiral's Plan to Use Social Media Posts to Price Car Insurance Premiums." TechCrunch. November 2, 2016. https://techcrunch.com/2016/11/02/uk-car-insurance-firm -wants-to-scan-social-media-posts-to-price-premiums/.

Loomis v. Wisconsin, 881 N.W.2d 749 (Wis. 2016), cert. denied, 137 S. Ct. 2290 (2017).

Lytvynenko, Jane. "North Dakota Democrats Ran a Misleading Facebook Ad Discouraging People from Voting." *BuzzFeed News*, November 2, 2018. https://www.buzzfeednews.com/article/janelytvynenko/north -dakota-democrats-facebook-ad-voter-suppression.

MacFarland, Matt. "Elon Musk: 'With Artificial Intelligence We Are Summoning the Demon.'" *Washington Post*, October 24, 2014. https://www.washingtonpost.com/news/innovations/wp/2014/ 10/24/elon-musk-with-artificial-intelligence-we-are-summoning -the-demon/.

MacKinnon, Rebecca. "Screenshots of Censorship." *RConversation* (blog), June 16, 2005. https://rconversation.blogs.com/rconversation/2005/ 06/screenshots_of_.html.

Meyer, Robinson. "When You Fall in Love, This Is What Facebook Sees." *Atlantic*, February 15, 2014. https://www.theatlantic.com/ technology/archive/2014/02/when-you-fall-in-love-this-is-what -facebook-sees/283865/.

Nadella, Satya. "Satya Nadella Email to Employees: Embracing Our Future: Intelligent Cloud and Intelligent Edge." Microsoft News Center. March 29, 2018. https://news.microsoft.com/2018/03/29/ satya-nadella-email-to-employees-embracing-our-future-intelligent -cloud-and-intelligent-edge/.

Pasick, Adam. "The Magic That Makes Spotify's Discover Weekly Playlists So Damn Good." *Quartz*, June 25, 2019. https://qz.com/ 571007/the-magic-that-makes-spotifys-discover-weekly-playlists-so -damn-good/.

Perrow, Charles. *Normal Accidents: Living with High-Risk Technologies*. Princeton, NJ: Princeton University Press, 1984.

"Range of Tinned Fear." Hoxton Street Monster Supplies. Accessed May 21, 2020. https://web.archive.org/web/20200804174931/https://www.monstersupplies.org/collections/view-all/products/range-of-tinned-fear.

"Reclamation Bonds." Office of Surface Mining Reclamation and Enforcement. U.S. Department of the Interior, n.d. https://www.osmre.gov/resources/reclamation-bonds.

Ruddick, Graham. "Admiral to Price Car Insurance Based on Facebook Posts." *Guardian*, November 1, 2016. https://www.theguardian.com/technology/2016/nov/02/admiral-to-price-car-insurance-based-on-facebook-posts.

Rudin, Cynthia. "Stop Explaining Black Box Machine Learning Models for High Stakes Decisions and Use Interpretable Models Instead." *Nature Machine Intelligence* 1, no. 5 (2019): 206–15. https://doi.org/10.1038/s42256-019-0048-x.

Schwartz, Peter, and Peter Leyden. "The Long Boom: A History of the Future, 1980–2020." *Wired*, July 1, 1997. https://www.wired.com/1997/07/longboom/.

"Secure Enclave Overview." Apple Support, n.d. https://support.apple.com/guide/security/secure-enclave-overview-sec59b0b31ff/web.

Silverman, Craig. "This Analysis Shows How Viral Fake Election News Stories Outperformed Real News on Facebook." *BuzzFeed News*, November 16, 2016. https://www.buzzfeednews.com/article/craigsilverman/viral-fake-election-news-outperformed-real-news-on-facebook.

Singhal, Amit. "Introducing the Knowledge Graph: Things, Not Strings." *Google Blog*, May 16, 2012. https://googleblog.blogspot.com/2012/05/introducing-knowledge-graph-things-not.html.

Smith, S. Alex, and David Braginsky. Predicting Life Changes of Members of a Social Networking System. U.S. Patent US20120016817A1, filed July 19, 2010, and issued January 19, 2012.

Statt, Nick. "Google Dissolves AI Ethics Board Just One Week after Forming It." *Verge*, April 5, 2019. https://www.theverge.com/2019/4/4/18296113/google-ai-ethics-board-ends-controversy-kay-coles-james-heritage-foundation.

Steadman, Ian. "IBM's Watson Is Better at Diagnosing Cancer Than Human Doctors." *Wired*, October 4, 2017. https://www.wired.co.uk/article/ibm-watson-medical-doctor.

Stone, Brad. "Amazon Erases Orwell Books from Kindle." *New York Times*, July 17, 2009. https://www.nytimes.com/2009/07/18/technology/companies/18amazon.html.

Strickland, Eliza. "How IBM Watson Overpromised and Underdelivered on AI Health Care." *IEEE Spectrum*, April 2, 2019. https://spectrum.ieee.org/biomedical/diagnostics/how-ibm-watson-overpromised-and-underdelivered-on-ai-health-care.

Stuart-Ulin, Chloe Rose. "Microsoft's Politically Correct Chatbot Is Even Worse Than Its Racist One." *Quartz*, July 30, 2018. https://qz.com/1340990/microsofts-politically-correct-chat-bot-is-even-worse-than-its-racist-one/.

Sullivan, Danny (@dannysullivan). "Google Home: 'Yes, Republicans = Nazis." Twitter, video, March 5, 2017. https://twitter.com/dannysullivan/status/838479054630068224.

"Tax Exempt Bonds Private Letter Rulings: Some Basic Concepts." IRS. October 24, 2019. https://www.irs.gov/tax-exempt-bonds/teb-private-letter-ruling-some-basic-concepts.

"Trust in Government." *Gallup*, March 30, 2020. https://news.gallup.com/poll/5392/trust-government.aspx.

u/HitlersaurusRex911. "If you type dog 18 times into google translate from Maori to English this happens." Reddit, July 22, 2018. https://www.reddit.com/r/pics/comments/91366u/if_you_type_dog_18_times_into_google_translate/.

University of Chicago Chronicle. "How Aspirin Works." August 17, 1995. https://chronicle.uchicago.edu/950817/aspirin.shtml.

Verma, Inder M., ed. "Editorial Expression of Concern: Experimental Evidence of Massivescale Emotional Contagion through Social Networks." *Proceedings of the National Academy of Sciences* 111, no. 29 (2014): 10779. https://doi.org/10.1073/pnas.1412469111.

Vigen, Tyler. "Letters in Winning Word of Scripps National Spelling Bee Correlates with Number of People Killed by Venomous Spiders." Spurious Correlations. N.d. https://web.archive.org/web/20210214010438/http://tylervigen.com/view_correlation?id=2941.

Vincent, James. "Twitter Taught Microsoft's AI Chatbot to Be a Racist Asshole in Less Than a Day." *Verge*, March 24, 2016. https://www.theverge.com/2016/3/24/11297050/tay-microsoft-chatbot-racist.

Wang, Amy B., Cleve R. Wootsonn Jr., and Ed O'Keefe. "As Harvey Submerges Houston, Local Officials Defend Their Calls Not

to Evacuate." *Washington Post*, August 27, 2017. https://www
.washingtonpost.com/news/post-nation/wp/2017/08/27/harvey
-is-causing-epic-catastrophic-flooding-in-houston-why-wasnt-the
-city-evacuated/.

Washington Post. "Apple Siri: 'All-New Voice-Control AI Stuff.'" October 4, 2011. https://www.washingtonpost.com/business/economy/apple-siri-all-new-voice-control-ai-stuff/2011/08/13/gIQAZJEXLL_story.html.

Watt, Nicholas, Rowena Mason, and Ian Traynor. "David Cameron Pledges Anti-terror Law for Internet after Paris Attacks." *Guardian*, January 12, 2015. https://www.theguardian.com/uk-news/2015/jan/12/david-cameron-pledges-anti-terror-law-internet-paris-attacks-nick-clegg.

Welsh, Matt. "Why I'm Leaving Harvard." *Blogger* (blog), November 15, 2010. https://matt-welsh.blogspot.com/2010/11/why-im-leaving-harvard.html.

Wired Staff. "Dropping the Bomb on Google." *Wired*, May 11, 2004. https://www.wired.com/2004/05/dropping-the-bomb-on-google/.

Wong, Julia Carrie, and Olivia Solon. "Facebook Releases Content Moderation Guidelines—Rules Long Kept Secret." *Guardian*, April 24, 2018. https://www.theguardian.com/technology/2018/apr/24/facebook-releases-content-moderation-guidelines-secret-rules.

Woody, Christopher. "Facebook Official Who Oversees the News Feed Says His Team Loses Sleep over the Site's Alleged Role in Myanmar 'Ethnic Cleansing.'" *Business Insider*, March 22, 2018. https://www.businessinsider.com/adam-mosseri-facebook-myanmar-genocide-rohingya-lose-sleep-2018-3.

Wu, Xiaolin, and Xi Zhang. "Automated Inference on Criminality Using Face Images." Unpublished manuscript, November 13, 2016. https://arxiv.org/pdf/1611.04135v1.pdf.

Xie, Suzanne. "Testing, Testing . . . New Conversation Settings." *Twitter* (blog), May 20, 2020. https://blog.twitter.com/en_us/topics/product/2020/testing-new-conversation-settings.html.

Zeran v. America Online, Inc., 129 F.3d 327, 330 (4th Cir. 1997).

Zittrain, Jonathan. "A Jury of Random People Can Do Wonders for Facebook." *Atlantic*, November 14, 2019. https://www.theatlantic.com/ideas/archive/2019/11/let-juries-review-facebook-ads/601996/.

Zuckerberg, Mark. "A Blueprint for Content Governance and Enforcement." Facebook, November 15, 2018. https://www.facebook.com/

notes/mark-zuckerberg/a-blueprint-for-content-governance-and
-enforcement/10156443129621634/.

Zuckerberg, Mark. "A Privacy-Focused Vision for Social Networking."
Facebook, March 6, 2019. https://www.facebook.com/notes/mark
-zuckerberg/a-privacy-focused-vision-for-social-networking/101567
00570096634/.

THE TANNER LECTURERS

1976–1977
OXFORD — Bernard Williams, Cambridge University
MICHIGAN — Joel Feinberg, University of Arizona
"Voluntary Euthanasia and the Inalienable Right to Life"
STANFORD — Joel Feinberg, University of Arizona
"Voluntary Euthanasia and the Inalienable Right to Life"

1977–1978
OXFORD — John Rawls, Harvard University
MICHIGAN — Sir Karl Popper, University of London
"Three Worlds"
STANFORD — Thomas Nagel, Princeton University

1978–1979
OXFORD — Thomas Nagel, Princeton University
"The Limits of Objectivity"
CAMBRIDGE — C. C. O'Brien, London
MICHIGAN — Edward O. Wilson, Harvard University
"Comparative Social Theory"
STANFORD — Amartya Sen, Oxford University
"Equality of What?"
UTAH — Lord Ashby, Cambridge University
"The Search for an Environmental Ethic"
UTAH STATE — R. M. Hare, Oxford University
"Moral Conflicts"

1979–1980
OXFORD — Jonathan Bennett, University of British Columbia
"Morality and Consequences"
CAMBRIDGE — Raymond Aron, Collège de France
"Arms Control and Peace Research"
HARVARD — George Stigler, University of Chicago
"Economics or Ethics?"
MICHIGAN — Robert Coles, Harvard University
"Children as Moral Observers"

410   *The Tanner Lectures on Human Values*

STANFORD   Michel Foucault, Collège de France
              "Omnes et Singulatim: Towards a Criticism of 'Political Reason'"

UTAH   Wallace Stegner, Los Altos Hills, California
              "The Twilight of Self-Reliance: Frontier Values and Contemporary America"

1980–1981

OXFORD   Saul Bellow, University of Chicago
              "A Writer from Chicago"

CAMBRIDGE   John Passmore, Australian National University
              "The Representative Arts as a Source of Truth"

HARVARD   Brian M. Barry, University of Chicago
              "Do Countries Have Moral Obligations? The Case of World Poverty"

MICHIGAN   John Rawls, Harvard University
              "The Basic Liberties and Their Priority"

STANFORD   Charles Fried, Harvard University
              "Is Liberty Possible?"

UTAH   Joan Robinson, Cambridge University
              "The Arms Race"

HEBREW UNIV.   Solomon H. Snyder, Johns Hopkins University
              "Drugs and the Brain and Society"

1981–1982

OXFORD   Freeman Dyson, Princeton University
              "Bombs and Poetry"

CAMBRIDGE   Kingman Brewster, president emeritus, Yale University
              "The Voluntary Society"

HARVARD   Murray Gell-Mann, California Institute of Technology
              "The Head and the Heart in Policy Studies"

MICHIGAN   Thomas C. Schelling, Harvard University
              "Ethics, Law, and the Exercise of Self-Command"

STANFORD   Alan A. Stone, Harvard University
              "Psychiatry and Morality"

UTAH   R. C. Lewontin, Harvard University
              "Biological Determinism"

AUSTRALIAN NATL. UNIV.   Leszek Kolakowski, Oxford University
              "The Death of Utopia Reconsidered"

1982–1983

OXFORD   Kenneth J. Arrow, Stanford University
              "The Welfare-Relevant Boundaries of the Individual"

The Tanner Lecturers

411

CAMBRIDGE	H. C. Robbins Landon, University College, Cardiff *"Haydn and Eighteenth-Century Patronage in* *Austria and Hungary"*
HARVARD	Bernard Williams, Cambridge University *"Morality and Social Justice"*
STANFORD	David Gauthier, University of Pittsburgh *"The Incompleat Egoist"*
UTAH	Carlos Fuentes, Princeton University *"A Writer from Mexico"*
JAWAHARLAL NEHRU UNIV.	Ilya Prigogine, Université Libre de Bruxelles *"Only an Illusion"*

1983–1984

OXFORD	Donald D. Brown, Johns Hopkins University *"The Impact of Modern Genetics"*
CAMBRIDGE	Stephen J. Gould, Harvard University *"Evolutionary Hopes and Realities"*
MICHIGAN	Herbert A. Simon, Carnegie-Mellon University *"Scientific Literacy as a Goal in a High-Technology Society"*
STANFORD	Leonard B. Meyer, University of Pennsylvania *"Music and Ideology in the Nineteenth Century"*
UTAH	Helmut Schmidt, former chancellor, West Germany *"The Future of the Atlantic Alliance"*
HELSINKI	Georg Henrik von Wright, Helsinki *"Of Human Freedom"*

1984–1985

OXFORD	Barrington Moore Jr., Harvard University *"Authority and Inequality under Capitalism and Socialism"*
CAMBRIDGE	Amartya Sen, Oxford University *"The Standard of Living"*
HARVARD	Quentin Skinner, Cambridge University *"The Paradoxes of Political Liberty"* Kenneth J. Arrow, Stanford University *"The Unknown Other"*
MICHIGAN	Nadine Gordimer, South Africa *"The Essential Gesture: Writers and Responsibility"*
STANFORD	Michael Slote, University of Maryland *"Moderation, Rationality, and Virtue"*

412   *The Tanner Lectures on Human Values*

1985–1986

OXFORD
Thomas M. Scanlon Jr., Harvard University
"The Significance of Choice"

CAMBRIDGE
Aldo Van Eyck, the Netherlands
"Architecture and Human Values"

HARVARD
Michael Walzer, Institute for Advanced Study
"Interpretation and Social Criticism"

MICHIGAN
Clifford Geertz, Institute for Advanced Study
"The Uses of Diversity"

STANFORD
Stanley Cavell, Harvard University
"The Uncanniness of the Ordinary"

UTAH
Arnold S. Relman, editor, *New England Journal of Medicine*
"Medicine as a Profession and a Business"

1986–1987

OXFORD
Jon Elster, Oslo University and the University of Chicago
"Taming Chance: Randomization in Individual and Social Decisions"

CAMBRIDGE
Roger Bulger, University of Texas Health Sciences Center, Houston
"On Hippocrates, Thomas Jefferson, and Max Weber: The Bureaucratic, Technologic Imperatives and the Future of the Healing Tradition in a Voluntary Society"

HARVARD
Jürgen Habermas, University of Frankfurt
"Law and Morality"

MICHIGAN
Daniel C. Dennett, Tufts University
"The Moral First Aid Manual"

STANFORD
Gisela Striker, Columbia University
"Greek Ethics and Moral Theory"

UTAH
Laurence H. Tribe, Harvard University
"On Reading the Constitution"

1987–1988

OXFORD
F. Van Zyl Slabbert, University of the Witwatersrand, South Africa
"The Dynamics of Reform and Revolt in Current South Africa"

CAMBRIDGE
Louis Blom-Cooper, Q.C., London
"The Penalty of Imprisonment"

HARVARD
Robert A. Dahl, Yale University
"The Pseudodemocratization of the American Presidency"

The Tanner Lecturers

413

MICHIGAN	Albert O. Hirschman, Institute for Advanced Study *"Two Hundred Years of Reactionary Rhetoric: The Case of the Perverse Effect"*
STANFORD	Ronald Dworkin, New York University and University College, Oxford *"Foundations of Liberal Equality"*
UTAH	Joseph Brodsky, Russian poet, Mount Holyoke College *"A Place as Good as Any"*
CALIFORNIA	Wm. Theodore de Bary, Columbia University *"The Trouble with Confucianism"*
BUENOS AIRES	Barry Stroud, University of California, Berkeley *"The Study of Human Nature and the Subjectivity of Value"*
MADRID	Javier Muguerza, Universidad Nacional de Educación a Distancia, Madrid *"The Alternative of Dissent"*
WARSAW	Anthony Quinton, British Library, London *"The Varieties of Value"*

1988–1989

OXFORD	Michael Walzer, Institute for Advanced Study *"Nation and Universe"*
CAMBRIDGE	Albert Hourani, Emeritus Fellow, St. Antony's College, and Magdalen College, Oxford *"Islam in European Thought"*
MICHIGAN	Toni Morrison, State University of New York at Albany *"Unspeakable Things Unspoken: The Afro-American Presence in American Literature"*
STANFORD	Stephen J. Gould, Harvard University *"Unpredictability in the History of Life"* *"The Quest for Human Nature: Fortuitous Side, Consequences, and Contingent History"*
UTAH	Judith Shklar, Harvard University *"American Citizenship: The Quest for Inclusion"*
CALIFORNIA	S. N. Eisenstadt, The Hebrew University of Jerusalem *"Cultural Tradition, Historical Experience, and Social Change: The Limits of Convergence"*
YALE	J. G. A. Pocock, Johns Hopkins University *"Edward Gibbon in History: Aspects of the Text in* The History of the Decline and Fall of the Roman Empire*"*
CHINESE UNIVERSITY OF HONG KONG	Fei Xiaotong, Peking University *"Plurality and Unity in the Configuration of the Chinese People"*

414   The Tanner Lectures on Human Values

1989–1990

OXFORD
Bernard Lewis, Princeton University
"Europe and Islam"

CAMBRIDGE
Umberto Eco, University of Bologna
"Interpretation and Overinterpretation: World, History, Texts"

HARVARD
Ernest Gellner, Kings College, Cambridge
"The Civil and the Sacred"

MICHIGAN
Carol Gilligan, Harvard University
"Joining the Resistance: Psychology, Politics, Girls, and Women"

UTAH
Octavio Paz, Mexico City
"Poetry and Modernity"

YALE
Edward N. Luttwak, Center for Strategic and International Studies
"Strategy: A New Era?"

PRINCETON
Irving Howe, writer and critic
"The Self and the State"

1990–1991

OXFORD
David Montgomery, Yale University
"Citizenship and Justice in the Lives and Thoughts of Nineteenth-Century American Workers"

CAMBRIDGE
Gro Harlem Brundtland, prime minister of Norway
"Environmental Challenges of the 1990s: Our Responsibility toward Future Generations"

HARVARD
William Gass, Washington University
"Eye and Idea"

MICHIGAN
Richard Rorty, University of Virginia
"Feminism and Pragmatism"

STANFORD
G. A. Cohen, All Souls College, Oxford
"Incentives, Inequality, and Community"

János Kornai, University of Budapest and Harvard University
"Market Socialism Revisited"

UTAH
Marcel Ophuls, international filmmaker
"Resistance and Collaboration in Peacetime"

YALE
Robertson Davies, novelist
"Reading and Writing"

PRINCETON
Annette C. Baier, Pittsburgh University
"Trust"

LENINGRAD
János Kornai, University of Budapest and Harvard University
"Transition from Marxism to a Free Economy"

The Tanner Lecturers

1991–1992

OXFORD
R. Z. Sagdeev, University of Maryland
"Science and Revolutions"

UC LOS ANGELES
Václav Havel, former President, Republic of Czechoslovakia
(Untitled lecture)

UC BERKELEY
Helmut Kohl, chancellor of Germany
(Untitled lecture)

CAMBRIDGE
David Baltimore, former president, Rockefeller University
"On Doing Science in the Modern World"

MICHIGAN
Christopher Hill, Oxford
"The Bible in Seventeenth-Century English Politics"

STANFORD
Charles Taylor, McGill University
"Modernity and the Rise of the Public Sphere"

UTAH
Jared Diamond, University of California, Los Angeles
"The Broadest Pattern of Human History"

PRINCETON
Robert Nozick, Harvard University
"Decisions of Principle, Principles of Decision"

1992–1993

MICHIGAN
Amos Oz, Israel
"The Israeli-Palestinian Conflict: Tragedy, Comedy, and Cognitive Block—A Storyteller's Point of View"

CAMBRIDGE
Christine M. Korsgaard, Harvard University
"The Sources of Normativity"

UTAH
Evelyn Fox Keller, Massachusetts Institute of Technology
"Rethinking the Meaning of Genetic Determinism"

YALE
Fritz Stern, Columbia University
"Mendacity Enforced: Europe, 1914–1989"
"Freedom and Its Discontents: Postunification Germany"

PRINCETON
Stanley Hoffmann, Harvard University
"The Nation, Nationalism, and After: The Case of France"

STANFORD
Colin Renfrew, Cambridge University
"The Archaeology of Identity"

1993–1994

MICHIGAN
William Julius Wilson, University of Chicago
"The New Urban Poverty and the Problem of Race"

OXFORD
Lord Slynn of Hadley, London
"Law and Culture—a European Setting"

416   *The Tanner Lectures on Human Values*

HARVARD   Lawrence Stone, Princeton University
                     "Family Values in a Historical Perspective"

CAMBRIDGE   Peter Brown, Princeton University
                     "Aspects of the Christianisation of the Roman World"

UTAH   A. E. Dick Howard, University of Virginia
                     "Toward the Open Society in Central and Eastern Europe"
                     Jeffrey Sachs, Harvard University
                     "Shock Therapy in Poland: Perspectives of Five Years"

UTAH   Adam Zagajewski, Paris
                     "A Bus Full of Prophets: Adventures of the Eastern-European Intelligentsia"

PRINCETON   Alasdair MacIntyre, Duke University
                     "Truthfulness, Lies, and Moral Philosophers: What Can We Learn from Mill and Kant?"

CALIFORNIA   Oscar Arias, Costa Rica
                     "Poverty: The New International Enemy"

STANFORD   Thomas Hill, University of North Carolina at Chapel Hill
                     "Basic Respect and Cultural Diversity"
                     "Must Respect Be Earned?"

UC SAN DIEGO   K. Anthony Appiah, Harvard University
                     "Race, Culture, Identity: Misunderstood Connections"

1994–1995

YALE   Richard Posner, United States Court of Appeals
                     "Euthanasia and Health Care: Two Essays on the Policy Dilemmas of Aging and Old Age"

MICHIGAN   Daniel Kahneman, University of California, Berkeley
                     "Cognitive Psychology of Consequences and Moral Intuition"

HARVARD   Cass R. Sunstein, University of Chicago
                     "Political Conflict and Legal Agreement"

CAMBRIDGE   Roger Penrose, Oxford Mathematics Institute
                     "Space-Time and Cosmology"

PRINCETON   Antonin Scalia, United States Supreme Court
                     "Common-Law Courts in a Civil-Law System: The Role of the United States Federal Courts in Interpreting the Constitution and Laws"

UC SANTA CRUZ   Nancy Wexler, Columbia University
                     "Genetic Prediction and Precaution Confront Human Social Values"

OXFORD   Janet Suzman, South Africa
                     "Who Needs Parables?"

The Tanner Lecturers

417

STANFORD	Amy Gutmann, Princeton University *"Responding to Racial Injustice"*
UTAH	Edward Said, Columbia University *"On Lost Causes"*

1995–1996

PRINCETON	Harold Bloom, Yale University *"Shakespeare and the Value of Personality"* *"Shakespeare and the Value of Love"*
OXFORD	Simon Schama, Columbia University *"Rembrandt and Rubens: Humanism, History, and the Peculiarity of Painting"*
CAMBRIDGE	Gunther Schuller, Newton Center, Massachusetts *"Jazz: A Historical Perspective"* *"Duke Ellington"* *"Charles Mingus"*
UC RIVERSIDE	Mairead Corrigan Maguire, Belfast, Northern Ireland *"Peacemaking from the Grassroots in a World of Ethnic Conflict"*
HARVARD	Onora O'Neill, Newham College, Cambridge *"Kant on Reason and Religion"*
STANFORD	Nancy Fraser, New School for Social Research *"Social Justice in the Age of Identity Politics: Redistribution, Recognition, and Participation"*
UTAH	Cornell West, Harvard University *"A Genealogy of the Public Intellectual"*
YALE	Peter Brown, Princeton University *"The End of the Ancient Other World: Death and Afterlife between Late Antiquity and the Early Middle Ages"*

1996–1997

TORONTO	Peter Gay, emeritus, Yale University *"The Living Enlightenment"*
MICHIGAN	Thomas M. Scanlon, Harvard University *"The Status of Well-Being"*
HARVARD	Stuart Hampshire, emeritus, Stanford University *"Justice Is Conflict: The Soul and the City"*
CAMBRIDGE	Dorothy L. Cheney, University of Pennsylvania *"Why Animals Don't Have Language"*
PRINCETON	Robert M. Solow, Massachusetts Institute of Technology *"Welfare and Work"*

418   *The Tanner Lectures on Human Values*

CALIFORNIA   Marian Wright Edelman, Children's Defense Fund
"Standing for Children"

YALE   Liam Hudson, Balas Copartnership
"The Life of the Mind"

STANFORD   Barbara Herman, University of California, Los Angeles
"Moral Literacy"

OXFORD   Francis Fukuyama, George Mason University
"Social Capital"

UTAH   Elaine Pagels, Princeton University
"The Origin of Satan in Christian Traditions"

1997–1998

UTAH   Jonathan D. Spence, Yale University
"Ideas of Power: China's Empire in the Eighteenth Century and Today"

PRINCETON   J. M. Coetzee, University of Cape Town
"The Lives of Animals"

MICHIGAN   Antonio R. Damasio, University of Iowa
"Exploring the Minded Brain"

CHARLES
UNIVERSITY   Timothy Garton Ash, Oxford University
"The Direction of European History"

HARVARD   M. F. Burnyeat, Oxford University
"Culture and Society in Plato's Republic"

CAMBRIDGE   Stephen Toulmin, University of Southern California
"The Idol of Stability"

UC IRVINE   David Kessler, Yale University
"Tobacco Wars: Risks and Rewards of a Major Challenge"

YALE   Elaine Scarry, Harvard University
"On Beauty and Being Just"

STANFORD   Arthur Kleinman, Harvard University
"Experience and Its Moral Modes: Culture, Human Conditions, and Disorder"

1998–1999

MICHIGAN   Walter Burkert, University of Zurich
"Revealing Nature amidst Multiple Cultures: A Discourse with Ancient Greeks"

UTAH   Geoffrey Hartman, Yale University
"Text and Spirit"

The Tanner Lecturers

YALE	Steven Pinker, Massachusetts Institute of Technology *"The Blank Slate, the Noble Savage, and the Ghost in the Machine"*
STANFORD	Randall Kennedy, Harvard University *"Who Can Say 'Nigger'? . . . and Other Related Questions"*
UC DAVIS	Richard White, Stanford University *"The Problem with Purity"*
OXFORD	Sidney Verba, Harvard University *"Representative-Democracy and Democratic Citizens: Philosophical and Empirical Understandings"*
PRINCETON	Judith Jarvis Thomson, Massachusetts Institute of Technology *"Goodness and Advice"*
HARVARD	Lani Guinier, Harvard University *"Rethinking Powers"*

1999–2000

YALE	Marina Warner, London *"Spirit Visions"*
MICHIGAN	Helen Vendler, Harvard University *"Poetry and the Mediation of Value: Whitman on Lincoln"*
HARVARD	Wolf Lepenies, Free University, Berlin *"The End of 'German Culture'"*
CAMBRIDGE	Jonathan Lear, University of Chicago *"Happiness"*
OXFORD	Geoffrey Hill, Boston University *"Rhetorics of Value"*
PRINCETON	Michael Ignatieff, London *"Human Rights as Politics"* *"Human Rights as Idolatry"*
UTAH	Charles Rosen, New York *"Tradition without Convention: The Impossible Nineteenth-Century Project"*
STANFORD	Jared Diamond, UCLA Medical School *"Ecological Collapses of Pre-Industrial Societies"*

2000–2001

MICHIGAN	Partha Dasgupta, Cambridge University *"Valuing Objects and Evaluating Policies in Imperfect Economies"*
HARVARD	Simon Schama, Columbia University *"Random Access Memory"*

420   *The Tanner Lectures on Human Values*

UC SANTA   William C. Richardson, The Kellogg Foundation
BARBARA   *"Reconceiving Health Care to Improve Quality"*

OXFORD   Sir Sydney Kentridge Q.C., London
            "Human Rights: A Sense of Proportion"

UTAH   Sarah Blaffer Hrdy, University of California at Davis
            "The Past and Present of the Human Family"

UC BERKELEY Joseph Raz, Columbia University
            "The Practice of Value"

PRINCETON   Robert Pinsky, poet, Boston University
            "American Culture and the Voice of Poetry"

YALE   Alexander Nehamas, Princeton University
            "A Promise of Happiness: The Place of Beauty in a World of Art"

CAMBRIDGE   Kwame Anthony Appiah, Harvard University
            "Individuality and Identity"

STANFORD   Dorothy Allison, novelist
            "Mean Stories and Stubborn Girls"
            "What It Means to Be Free"

2001–2002

MICHIGAN   Michael Fried, Johns Hopkins University
            "Roger Fry's Formalism"

UC BERKELEY Sir Frank Kermode, Cambridge, England
            "Pleasure, Change, and the Canon"

HARVARD   Kathleen Sullivan, Stanford University
            "War, Peace, and Civil Liberties"

YALE   Salman Rushdie, New York
            "Step across This Line"

CAMBRIDGE   Seamus Heaney, Harvard University
            "Homiletic Elegy: Beowulf and Wilfred Owen"
            "On Pastoral: Starting from Virgil"
            "On Pastoral: Eclogues in Extremis"

UTAH   Benjamin Barber, University of Maryland
            "Democratic Alternatives to the Mullahs and the Malls:
            Citizenship in an Age of Global Anarchy"

STANFORD   Paul Krugman, Princeton University
            "Intractable Slumps"
            "Currency Crises"

PRINCETON   T. J. Clark, University of California, Berkeley
            "Painting at Ground Level"

The Tanner Lecturers

OXFORD	Laurence H. Tribe, Harvard University *"The Constitution in Crisis: From Bush v. Gore to the War on Terrorism"*

2002–2003

MICHIGAN	Claude Steele, Stanford University *"The Specter of Group Image: The Unseen Effects on Human Performance and the Quality of Life in a Diverse Society"*
UC BERKELEY	Derek Parfit, Oxford University *"What We Could Rationally Will"*
HARVARD	Lorraine Daston, Max Planck Institute, Berlin *"The Morality of Natural Orders: The Power of Medea"* *"Nature's Customs versus Nature's Laws"*
AUSTRALIAN NAT. UNIV. AND CAMBRIDGE	Martha C. Nussbaum, University of Chicago *"Beyond the Social Contract: Toward Global Justice"*
PRINCETON	Jonathan Glover, King's College London *"Towards Humanism in Psychology"*
STANFORD	Mary Robinson, New York *"Human Rights and Ethical Globalization"* *"The Challenge of Human Rights Protection in Africa"*
YALE	Garry L. Wills, Northwestern University *"Henry Adams: The Historian as Novelist"*
OXFORD	David M. Kennedy, Stanford University *"The Dilemma of Difference in Democratic Society"*

2003–2004

UTAH	Sebastião Salgado, Paris *"Art, Globalism and Cultural Instability"*
PRINCETON	Frans de Waal, Emory University *"Morality and the Social Instincts: Continuity with the Other Primates"*
HARVARD	Richard Dawkins, University of Oxford *"The Science of Religion"* *"The Religion of Science"*
MICHIGAN	Christine M. Korsgaard, Harvard University *"Fellow Creatures: Kantian Ethics and Our Duties to Animals"*
CAMBRIDGE	Neil MacGregor, The British Museum *"The Meanings of Things"*

422
The Tanner Lectures on Human Values

UC BERKELEY	Seyla Benhabib, Yale University "*Reclaiming Universalism: Negotiating Republican Self-Determination and Cosmopolitan Norms*"
YALE	Oliver Sacks, Albert Einstein College of Medicine, New York "*Journey into Wonder: Reflections on a Chemical Boyhood*" "*Awakenings Revisited*"
STANFORD	Harry Frankfurt, Princeton University "*Taking Ourselves Seriously*" "*Getting It Right*"
OXFORD	Joseph Stiglitz, Columbia University "*Ethical Dimensions of Globalization*"

2004–2005

HARVARD	Stephen Breyer, United States Supreme Court "*Active Liberty: Interpreting Our Democratic Constitution*"
CAMBRIDGE	Carl Bildt, Sweden "*Peace after War: Our Experience*"
UTAH	Paul Farmer, Harvard University "*Never Again? Reflections on Human Values and Human Rights*"
UC BERKELEY	Axel Honneth, Johann Wolfgang Goethe-Universtät Frankfurt/Main "*Reification: A Recognition-Theoretical View*"
STANFORD	Avishai Margalit, Hebrew University "*Indecent Compromise*" "*Decent Peace*"
OXFORD	Lord Winston, Imperial College, London "*Manipulating Reproduction*" "*Stem Cells: Hope or Hype?*"

2005–2006

YALE	Ruth Reichl, *Gourmet* magazine "*Why Food Matters*"
HARVARD	James Q. Wilson, Pepperdine University "*Politics and Polarization*" "*Religion and Polarization*"
MICHIGAN	Marshall Sahlins, University of Chicago "*Hierarchy, Equality, and the Sublimation of Anarchy: The Western Illusion of Human Nature*"
STANFORD	David Brion Davis, Yale University "*Exiles, Exodus, and the Promised Lands*"

The Tanner Lecturers

UC BERKELEY	Allan Gibbard, University of Michigan *"Thinking How to Live with Each Other"*
UTAH	Margaret H. Marshall, Supreme Judicial Court of Massachusetts *"Tension and Intention: The American Constitutions and the Shaping of Democracies Abroad"*
OXFORD	Carol Bellamy, former executive director of UNICEF *"From Taliban to the Tsunami: True Stories from the Front Lines of Making a World Fit for Children"* *"Stealing Childhood: Poverty, War, and Disease"*
PRINCETON	Emma Rothschild, Cambridge University *"The Inner Life of Empires"*

2006–2007

YALE	Anthony Grafton, Princeton University *"Rat's Alley? The Humanities in the American University"* *"Clio's Catastrophe? History and the Humanities"*
CAMBRIDGE	Kurt Biedenkopf, Germany, former president of Saxony *"Germany Reunited: A Lesson in Political Transformation"* *"Germany's Role in the Enlarged European Union"*
UTAH	Bill Viola, video artist, Long Beach *"Presence and Absence: Vision and the Invisible"*
PRINCETON	Michael Doyle, Columbia University *"Anticipatory Self-Defense: The Law, Ethics, and Politics of Preventive War"*
HARVARD	Mary-Claire King, University of Washington *"Genomics, Race, and Medicine"*
MICHIGAN	Samantha Power, Harvard University *"Human Rights: The Risk of Politics"*
STANFORD	Glenn Loury, Brown University *"Ghettos, Prison, and Racial Backlash"* *"Social Identity and the Ethics of Punishment"*
UC BERKELEY	Joshua Cohen, Stanford University *"On Public Reason"* *"Democracy's Public Reason"*

2007–2008

YALE	Santiago Calatrava, architect, Zurich, Paris, and Valencia *"Wings and a Prayer"* *"A Collection of Pearls"*

CAMBRIDGE	Judy Illes, University of British Columbia *"Medicine, Neuroscience, Ethics, and Society"*
MICHIGAN	Brian Skyrms, University of California, Irvine *"Evolution and the Social Contract"*
PRINCETON	Susan Wolf, University of North Carolina *"Meaning in Life and Why It Matters"*
OXFORD	Simon Deakin, University of Cambridge *"The Diversity of Contemporary Corporate Governance"*
TSINGHUA UNIVERSITY	David Miller, University of Oxford *"Global Justice and Climate Change: How Should Responsibility Be Distributed?"*
UC BERKELEY	Annabel Patterson, Yale University *"Pandora's Boxes: How We Store Our Values"*
HARVARD	Tony Kushner, playwright, New York *"Fiction That's True: Historical Fiction and Anxiety"*
UTAH	Howard Gardner, Harvard University *"What Is Good Work?"* *"Achieving Good Work in Turbulent Times"*

2008–2009

YALE	Steven Chu, Stanford University *"The Epistemology of Physics and Scientific Revolution"* *"Golden Eras of Scientific Institutions"*
CAMBRIDGE	Lisa Jardine, University of London *"The Process of Communication Is the Process of Community"* *"Communication Is a Whole Social Process"*
STANFORD	Michael Tomasello, Max Planck Institute for Evolutionary Anthropology *"Ontogenetic Origins of Human Altruism"* *"Phylogenetic Origins of Human Collaboration"* Roberto Unger, Harvard University *"The Future of Religion"* *"The Religion of the Future"*
HARVARD	Sari Nusseibeh, political activist, Jerusalem *"Of Hedgehogs, Foxes, and Swans"* *"Of Folly, Faith, and Miracles"*
PRINCETON	Marc Hauser, Harvard University *"Humaniqueness and the Illusion of Cultural Variation"* *"To Do, or Not to Do"*

The Tanner Lecturers

MICHIGAN	Uwe Reinhardt, Princeton University *"American Values in Health Care: A Case of Cognitive Dissonance"*
UTAH	Richard Davidson, University of Wisconsin *"Order and Disorder in the Emotional Brain"*
OXFORD	Brasenose College 500th Anniversary Lectures, Christopher Timpson, convener *"Meeting the Challenges of the Twenty-First Century"*
UC BERKELEY	Jeremy Waldron, New York University *"Dignity and Rank"* *"Law, Dignity, and Self-Control"*

2009–2010

YALE	John Adams, composer, New York *"Doctor Atomic and His Gadget"*
HARVARD	Jonathan Lear, University of Chicago *"Becoming Human Does Not Come That Easily"* *"Ironic Soul"*
CAMBRIDGE	Sir Christopher Frayling, Royal College of Art *"An Instinctive Sympathy?"* *"To Do the Right Deed for the Wrong Reason"*
UTAH	Isabel Allende, social activist, Chile *"In the Hearts of Women"*
OXFORD	Ahmed Rashid, reporter, Pakistan *"Afghanistan"* *"Pakistan"*
UC BERKELEY	Abdullahi An-Na'im, Emory University *"Human Values, Self-Determination and Global Citizenship"* *"Taming Utopia: Pragmatic Means for Transformative Vision"*
PRINCETON	Bruce Ackerman, Yale University *"An Extremist Presidency"* *"A Politicized Military"*
STANFORD	Mark Danner, University of California, Berkeley *"Imposing the State of Exception: Constitutional Dictatorship, Torture, and Us"* *"Naturalizing the State of Exception: Terror, Fear, and the War without End"*
MICHIGAN	Susan Neiman, director, Einstein Forum *"Victims and Heroes"*

426   *The Tanner Lectures on Human Values*

2010–2011

CAMBRIDGE
Susan J. Smith, Mistress of Girton College, University of Cambridge
"Moral Maze: Dealings in Debt"
"Ethical Investment? Attending to Assets"

HARVARD
James Scott, Yale University
"The Late-Neolithic Multispecies Resettlement Camp"
"The Long Golden Age of Barbarians, a.k.a. Nonstate Peoples"

MICHIGAN
Martin Seligman, University of Pennsylvania
"Flourish: Positive Psychology and Positive Interventions"

STANFORD
Elinor Ostrom, Indiana University
"Frameworks"
"Analyzing One-Hundred-Year-Old Irrigation Puzzles"

PRINCETON
Robert Putnam, Harvard University
"Americans Are Religiously Devout and Divided, Yet Tolerant. Why?"
"Religious Americans Are Better Neighbors and Citizens, Though Less Tolerant. Why?"

UC BERKELEY
Leon Botstein, president, Bard College
"Music Literacy in the 19th Century"
"The Recorded Age"

UTAH
Spike Lee, film director and political activist, Brooklyn
"America through My Lens: The Evolving Nature of Race and Class in the Films of Spike Lee"

YALE
Rebecca Newberger Goldstein, writer, Boston
"Morality and Literature"
"Metaphysics and Literature"

2011–2012

CAMBRIDGE
Ernst Fehr, University of Zurich
"The Lure of Authority Motivation and Incentive Effects of Power"

HARVARD
Esther Duflo, Massachusetts Institute of Technology
"Paternalism versus Freedom?"
"Hope as Capability"

MICHIGAN
John Broome, Corpus Christi College
"The Public and Private Morality of Climate Change"

PRINCETON
Stephen Greenblatt, Harvard University
"Shakespeare and the End of Life History"

STANFORD
John Cooper, Princeton University
"Ancient Philosophies as Ways of Life I: Socrates"
"Ancient Philosophies as Ways of Life II: Plotinus"

The Tanner Lecturers

427

UC BERKELEY	Samuel Scheffler, New York University "*The Afterlife*"
UTAH	Abraham Verghese, Stanford University "*Two Souls Intertwined*"
YALE	Lisa Jardine, University of London "*The Sorcerer's Apprentice: C. P. Snow and J. Bronowski*" "*Science and Government: C. P. Snow and the Corridors of Power*"

2012–2013

CAMBRIDGE	Joseph Koerner, Harvard University "*The Viennese Interior: Architecture and Inwardness*"
HARVARD	Robert Post, Yale Law School "*A Short History of Representation and Discursive Democracy*" "*Campaign Finance Reform and the First Amendment*"
MICHIGAN	Craig Calhoun, London School of Economics "*The Problematic Public: Revisiting Dewey, Arendt, and Habermas*"
OXFORD	Michael Ignatieff, Harvard University "*Representation and Responsibility: Ethics and Public Office*"
PRINCETON	Ian Morris, Stanford University "*Each Age Gets the Thought It Needs: Why Hierarchy and Violence Are Sometimes Good*" "*The Evolution of Values: Biology, Culture, and the Shape of Things to Come*"
STANFORD	William G. Bowen, Andrew W. Mellon Foundation "*Costs and Productivity in Higher Education*" "*Prospects for an Online Fix: Can We Harness Technology in the Service of Our Aspirations?*"
UC BERKELEY	Frances Kamm, Harvard University "*Who Turned the Trolley?*" "*How Was the Trolley Turned?*"
UTAH	Michael Sandel, Harvard University "*The Moral Economy of Speculation: Gambling, Finance, and the Common Good*"

2013–2014

CAMBRIDGE	Phillippe Sands, University College London "*The Tale*" "*The Troubles*"
HARVARD	Rowan Williams, Archbishop of Canterbury "*The Other as Myself: Empathy and Power*" "*Myself as Stranger: Empathy and Loss*"

MICHIGAN	Walter Mischel, Columbia University
	"Overcoming the Weakness of the Will"
OXFORD	Shami Chakrabarti, Liberty organization (formerly National Council for Civil Liberties)
	"Human Rights as Human Values"
STANFORD	Nicholas Lemann, Columbia University School of Journalism
	"The Turn against Institutions"
	"What Transactions Can't Do"
UC BERKELEY	Eric Santner, University of Chicago
	"On the Subject-Matter of Political Theology"
	"Paradoxologies"
UTAH	Andrew Solomon
	"Love, Acceptance, Celebration: How Parents Make Their Children"
	Neil deGrasse Tyson, Hayden Planetarium
	"Science as a Way of Knowing"
YALE	Paul Gilroy, King's College London
	"Suffering and Infrahumanity"
	"Humanities and a New Humanism"
	Bruno Latour, Sciences Po Paris
	"How Better to Register the Agency of Things"

2014–2015

CAMBRIDGE	Peter Galison, Harvard University
	"Science, Secrecy, and the Private Self"
HARVARD	Carlo Ginzburg, UCLA
	"Casuistry, For and Against: Pascal's Provinciales and Their Aftermath"
MICHIGAN	Justice Ruth Bader Ginsburg, U.S. Supreme Court
	"A Conversation with Ruth Bader Ginsburg, Associate Justice of the United States Supreme Court"
OXFORD	Peter Singer
	"From Moral Neutrality to Effective Altruism: The Changing Scope and Significance of Moral Philosophy"
PRINCETON	Elizabeth Anderson, University of Michigan
	"When the Market Was 'Left'"
	"Private Government"
STANFORD	Danielle Allen, Princeton University
	"Two Concepts of Education"
	"Participatory Readiness"

The Tanner Lecturers

UC BERKELEY	Philip Pettit, Princeton University *"From Language to Commitment"* *"From Commitment to Morality"*
UTAH	Margaret Atwood, Author *"Human Values in an Age of Change"*
YALE	Dipesh Chakrabarty, University of Chicago *"Climate Change as Epochal Consciousness"* *"Decentering the Human? Or, What Remains of Gaia"*

2015–2016

CAMBRIDGE	Derek Gregory, University of British Columbia *"Reach for the Sky: Aerial Violence and the Everywhere War"*
OCHANOMIZU	Dame Carol Black, Cambridge University *"Women: Education, Biology, Power, and Leadership"*
OXFORD	Shirley Williams, Kennedy School of Government *"The Value of Europe and European Values"*
PRINCETON	Robert Boyd, Arizona State University *"Culture Matters: How Humans Became Outliers in the Natural World"*
UC BERKELEY	Didier Fassien, Princeton University *"The Will to Punish"*
UTAH	Siddhartha Mukherjee, Columbia University *"Previvors/Posthumans: The Fantasies and Anxieties of Changing the Human Genome"*
STANFORD	Andrew Bacevich, Boston University *"America's War for the Greater Middle East"*
YALE	Judith Butler, UC Berkeley *"Interpreting Nonviolence"*

2016–2017

CAMBRIDGE	Merlanne Vervier, ambassador-at-large, Global Women's Issues *"A Gendered Approach to Peace Building"*
HARVARD	Dorothy Roberts, University of Pennsylvania *"The Old Biosocial and the Legacy of Unethical Science"* *"The New Biosocial and the Future of Ethical Science"*
MICHIGAN	Radhika Coomaraswamy, former UN undersecretary general *"The Personality of Experience and the Universality of Values"*
OXFORD	George Ellis, University of Cape Town *"On the Origin and Nature of Values"*

430   *The Tanner Lectures on Human Values*

PRINCETON
Naomi Oreskes, Harvard University
"Should We Trust Science? Perspectives from the History and Philosophy of Science"
"When Not to Trust Science, or When Science Goes Awry"

STANFORD
Richard Kraut, Northwestern University
"Oysters and Experience Machines: Two Puzzles in Value Theory"

UC BERKELEY
Seana Shiffrin, University of California, Los Angeles
"Speaking Amongst Ourselves: Democracy and Law"

UTAH
Barry Scheck, cofounder, the Innocence Project
"Human Values and the Innocence Project"

YALE
Rosi Braidotti, Utrecht University
"Memoirs of a Posthumanist"
"Aspirations of a Posthumanist"

2017–2018

BERKELEY
Michael Warner, Yale University
"On the Grid"
"Infrastructure as Ethics"

CAMBRIDGE
Jan-Werner Muller, Princeton University
"Architecture, Public Policy, and the Ideal of Collective Self-Determination"

HARVARD
Bryan Stevenson, Equal Justice Initiative
"Social Justice Action: How We Change the World"

OXFORD
Abhijit Banerjee and Professor Esther Duflo, Massachusetts Institute of Technology
"Economics for the human race (with an application to migration, trade, and the sticky economy)"

MICHIGAN
Allan Gibbard, University of Michigan
"The Intrinsic Reward of a Life"

PRINCETON
Raj Chetty, Stanford University
"Race and Economic Opportunity in America: New Lessons from Big Data"

STANFORD
Samantha Power, diplomat
"Resisters in Dark Times"
"Diplomacy after Darkness"

UTAH
Michael Chabon and Zadie Smith, Authors
"A Conversation with Michael Chabon and Zadie Smith"

YALE UNIVERSITY
Achille Mbembe, University of Witwatersrand
"The New Global Mobility Regime"
"The Idea of Borderless World"

The Tanner Lecturers

431

2018–2019

BERKELEY
Arthur Ripstein, University of Toronto
"Rules for Wrongdoers"
"Combatants and Civilians"

CAMBRIDGE
Lee Bollinger, Columbia University
"The Free Speech Century: A Retrospective and a Guide"

HARVARD
Masha Gessen, journalist
"How We Think about Migration"
"Some Ideas for Talking about Migration"

OXFORD
Strobe Talbott, journalist and diplomat
"A President for Dark Times: The Age of Reason Meets the Age of Trump"

MICHIGAN
Michael Lambek, University of Toronto
"Concepts and Persons"

PRINCETON
Michael McConnell, Stanford University
"Executive Power & the Constitution"
"Executive Power at Home & Abroad"

STANFORD
Sir Angus Deaton and Anne Case, Princeton University
"Deaths of Despair and the Future of Capitalism"

UTAH
Anita Hill, Brandeis University
"From Social Movement to Social Impact: Ending Sexual Harassment"

2019–2020

CAMBRIDGE
Jonathan Zittrain, Harvard University
"Gaining Power, Losing Control"

MICHIGAN
Charles Mills, Graduate Center, City University of New York
"Theorizing Racial Justice"

PRINCETON
Richard Tuck, Harvard University
"Active and Passive Citizens"

STANFORD
Richard Wrangham, Harvard University
"The Evolution of Institutional Patriarchy"

YALE
Wendy Brown, University of California, Berkeley
"Knowledge and Politics in Nihilistic Times: Thinking with Max Weber"

2020–2021

No lectures

2021–2022

BERKELEY Caroline Hoxby, Stanford University
"*The Fork in the Road: The Imperative of Investing in Adolescent Education*"

CAMBRIDGE Allan Buchanan, Duke University and the University of Arizona
How to Respond Better to the Next Pandemic: Remedying Institutional Failures

OXFORD Rosalind Picard, MIT
"*Emotion, AI, and Human Values*"

MICHIGAN Kwame Anthony Appiah, NYU
"*Work: What Is It? Do Most of Us Need It, and Why?*"

PRINCETON Elizabeth Kolbert, journalist, author, and staff writer for *The New Yorker*
"*Welcome to the Anthropocene: What on Earth Have We Done*"
"*Welcome to the Anthropocene: What Can We Do about It?*"

STANFORD Cécile Fabre, All Souls College, Oxford University
"'*To Snatch Something from Death': Value, Justice, and Humankind's Common Cultural Heritage*"